We Were the
All-American Girls

ALSO BY JIM SARGENT AND
ROBERT M. GORMAN

The South Bend Blue Sox: A History of the All-American Girls Professional Baseball League Team and Its Players, 1943–1954 (McFarland, 2012)

We Were the All-American Girls

Interviews with Players of the AAGPBL, 1943–1954

JIM SARGENT

Foreword by Merrie A. Fidler

McFarland & Company, Inc., Publishers
Jefferson, North Carolina, and London

LIBRARY OF CONGRESS CATALOGUING-IN-PUBLICATION DATA

Sargent, Jim, 1941–
We were the all-American girls : interviews with players of the AAGPBL, 1943–1954 / Jim Sargent ; foreword by Merrie A. Fidler.
    p.   cm.

Includes bibliographical references and index.

ISBN 978-0-7864-6983-3
softcover : acid free paper ∞

1. All-American Girls Professional Baseball League — History. 2. Baseball for women — United States — History — 20th century.   I. Title.
GV875.A56S37   2013   796.357082 — dc23   2013007259

BRITISH LIBRARY CATALOGUING DATA ARE AVAILABLE

© 2013 Jim Sargent. All rights reserved

No part of this book may be reproduced or transmitted in any form or by any means, electronic or mechanical, including photocopying or recording, or by any information storage and retrieval system, without permission in writing from the publisher.

On the cover: Betsy Jochum follows through on a swing at Playland Park circa 1946 (courtesy of Betsy Jochum); *top to bottom left:* Isabel "Lefty" Alvarez (courtesy of Isabel Alvarez); Betty (Petryna) Mullins (courtesy of Betty Mullins); Audrey (Haine) Daniels (courtesy of Audrey Daniels); Dottie (Wiltse) Collins (courtesy of Patricia Collins)

Manufactured in the United States of America

McFarland & Company, Inc., Publishers
Box 611, Jefferson, North Carolina 28640
www.mcfarlandpub.com

To the exceptional women of
the All-American League,
heroines all

Table of Contents

Foreword by Merrie Fidler 1
Preface 3
Introduction by David Hillman 5
A Brief History of the All-American Girls Professional Baseball League 8

PART I: THE EARLY YEARS, 1943–1945

Annastasia "Stash" Batikis 25
Dottie (Wiltse) Collins 31
Audrey (Haine) Daniels 38
Betsy Jochum 44
Vivian Kellogg 52
Sophie Kurys 58
Elizabeth "Lib" Mahon 66

Marge (Callaghan) Maxwell 74
Grace Piskula 81
Rose (Folder) Powell 85
Mary Pratt 91
Ellen (Ahrndt) Proefrock 97
Lucella (MacLean) Ross 102
Joyce (Hill) Westerman 108

PART II: THE POSTWAR YEARS, 1946–1949

Isabel "Lefty" Alvarez 116
Mary "Wimp" Baumgartner 123
Erma Bergmann 129
Wilma Briggs 134
Shirley Burkovich 145
Marge (Villa) Cryan 150
Terry Donahue 156
Lillian "Lil" Faralla 163
Jean Faut 168
Betty Francis 175
Frances "Fran" Janssen 180

Glenna Sue Kidd 187
Betty (Petryna/Allen) Mullins 197
June Peppas 203
Maxine (Kline) Randall............ 209
Eilaine Roth 214
Doris Sams 218
Lou (Erickson) Sauer 227
Pat Scott 232
Inez Voyce 239
Delores "Dolly" (Brumfield) White .. 244

PART III: THE LAST YEARS, 1950–1954

Mary Lou (Studnicka) Caden 252
Jean (Geissinger) Harding 259
Katie Horstman 263
Joan (Berger) Knebl 271

Mary Moore 277
Mary (Froning) O'Meara 283
Janet "Pee Wee" (Wiley) Sears 288

Epilogue: From the 1954 Season to the Newsletter, the Reunions, A League of
  Their Own, *and Beyond* 297
Index 299

Foreword by Merrie A. Fidler

Jean Faut, who played for the South Bend (Indiana) Blue Sox from 1946 to 1953, was considered by her teammates and opponents alike to be among the best, if not the best, overhand pitcher in the history of the All-American Girls Professional Baseball League (AAGPBL). Contributing to this reputation was the fact that she was the league's ERA leader in 1950 (1.12), 1952 (0.93), and 1953 (1.51), and her lifetime ERA was a tidy 1.23. As one of only two players to earn Player of the Year honors twice (1951 and 1953), she was instrumental in helping the Blue Sox win the World Series of Women's Baseball in 1951 and 1952. Jean missed acquiring her third Player of the Year Award in 1952 when Betty (Weaver) Foss received one more vote than she did. In addition, Jean pitched two perfect games in her career with the Blue Sox. The first occurred July 21, 1951, against the perennially tough hitting Rockford (Illinois) Peaches, and the second occurred September 3, 1953, versus the up-and-coming Kalamazoo (Michigan) Lassies.

Jean played her last game with the South Bend Blue Sox at the end of the 1953 season, and at that time, no one could have predicted that during the next sixty-plus years, she would become a stellar primary resource for the publication of a history of the AAGPBL, a history of the South Bend Blue Sox, and now, this book containing 42 AAGPBL player interviews and profiles.

In 1972, Jean graciously and magnanimously loaned an invaluable collection of league and team documents, given to her by former South Bend Blue Sox team president Dr. Harold Dailey, to an unknown University of Massachusetts, Amherst, grad student interested in researching and writing a master's thesis about the AAGPBL. The publication of the updated thesis would occur 34 years later as *The Origins and History of the All-American Girls Professional Baseball League* (McFarland, 2006).

In the summer of 1995, Jean met Jim Sargent through league mate Helen "Gig" Smith, whom he encountered at an all-sports card show at the Roanoke Civic Center in Virginia. Gig's tenure in the league lasted only through the 1947 and 1948 seasons, so she referred Jim to Jean. She knew Jean could provide him with more information about the league.

Prior to Jim's chance encounter with Gig, he had not seen *A League of Their Own* and even though his expertise is in American history of the time period, he had not previously encountered the AAGPBL. However, as both a historian and baseball enthusiast, he was intrigued to learn more about the league and its players, so he rented the film and sought an interview with Jean. She graciously consented, and as a result Jim wrote articles about Jean's baseball career which were published in baseball magazines. He also sought and obtained interviews with the team and league mates Jean referred to him.

In 2012, Jim Sargent's continued acquaintance with Jean, his growing knowledge of other AAGPBL players' accomplishments, and his friendship with Bob Gorman (reference librarian at Winthrop University's Dacus Library, where Jean and teammate Lib Mahon's AAGPBL memorabilia are held), led to the publication of *The South Bend Blue Sox: A History of the All-American Girls Professional Baseball League Team and Its Players, 1943–1954* (McFarland, 2012).

Now, in this book Jim has compiled an invaluable collection of AAGPBL player interviews and profiles which began with Jean in 1995 and emanated from her.

When Jean met Jim, she recognized that his background uniquely qualified him to write her baseball profile and she didn't hesitate to refer him to her team and league mates. She learned that as a Flint, Michigan, native, he played on school and community baseball teams through the 1950s; he collected baseball cards as a kid when Al Kaline was king to him and his buddies; and he was still a longtime Tigers fan. In addition, Jim related that he'd earned a master's and Ph.D. in U.S. history at Michigan State University in the late 1960s with particular interest in the FDR/New Deal era, and that he was teaching U.S. history at Virginia Western Community College in Roanoke.

Jean also learned that Jim's educational credentials were complemented by the prior publication of Major League Baseball player profile articles, as well as profile articles of professional basketball, football, and hockey players who competed from the 1930s through the 1970s. Thus, when Jean chaired the AAGPBL Players Association National Reunion in Myrtle Beach, South Carolina, in 1997, she invited Jim to be the keynote speaker. His presentation was "The AAGPBL in 1947: 50 Years Later."

In the process of preparing for that presentation, Jim made a research trip to the Baseball Hall of Fame in Cooperstown, New York, and to South Bend, Indiana, to visit the University of Notre Dame, where Jean had donated Dr. Harold Dailey's collection of league and team documents, and to the Northern Indiana Center for History (now the Center for History), the national repository for the AAGPBL Players Association. The Players Association was incorporated in 1987 for the purpose of providing memorabilia to the National Baseball Hall of Fame for the opening of its "Women in Baseball" display on November 5, 1988. During that trip, Jim met and interviewed some of Jean's South Bend teammates and opponents, including Dottie Collins in Fort Wayne, Indiana, and Lib Mahon, Betsy Jochum, and Fran Janssen in South Bend.

At the 1997 reunion in Myrtle Beach, Jim met and interviewed a number of other AAGPBL players who then, over time, introduced him to additional players. He was impressed with how unique the players' achievements were and continue to be because what they had the opportunity to experience and accomplish has not been replicated to date. These interviews led to Jim's publication of and posting of more than a dozen AAGPBL player profiles in baseball magazines, on the AAGPBL website, and for the Society for American Baseball Research's Biography Project.

The publication of the AAGPBL player interviews in this book is the culmination of Jim's now decades-long interest in and research of AAGPBL players' stories, which began in 1995 with Jean Faut. It contains interviews begun in the 1990s — when player memories were sharper and before collecting and publishing AAGPBL player interviews became a focus for league authors and documentarians. The questions asked come from a U.S. and baseball historian's perspective, so the responses elicited contain some otherwise unknown content.

This book, like the player stories it relates, is intriguing, enlightening, and enjoyable to read. Most importantly, it adds an invaluable dimension to the historical record of the All-American Girls Professional Baseball League.

Thank you, Jean Faut, for your largesse in sharing your experience, knowledge, and materials of the AAGPBL with those who contacted you. Thank you for enthusiastically conveying your AAGPBL story to historian Jim Sargent in 1995, and for introducing him to your team and league mates. Thank you for graciously and magnanimously sharing, for 60-plus years, what have turned out to be vital contributions to the historical record of the All-American Girls Professional Baseball League.

Retired teacher and coach Merrie A. Fidler wrote *The Origins and History of the All-American Girls Professional Baseball League* (2006). She is also the author of several articles regarding the history of women in sports.

Preface

Most baseball fans know that during the war years of the 1940s and into the early 1950s, women played professional in a league located in the upper Midwest. But few people today know more than can be gleaned from the 1992 movie *A League of Their Own*, a wildly popular, fictionalized account of the All-American Girls Professional Baseball League (AAGPBL) and its players. It is my hope that this book, which presents the women's stories in their own words, will flesh out that story for readers eager to know what really happened, and when, and to whom.

Since 1995, I have written several articles about former AAGPBL players, and in 2012 Robert M. Gorman and I published the major outgrowth of that research and writing in our book *The South Bend Blue Sox: A History of the All-American Girls Professional Baseball League Team and Its Players, 1943–1954* (McFarland). During my research for that book, I interviewed a number of former players, paying special attention to those who played for the Blue Sox. Along the way I discovered that no book-length collection of interviews had been published.* As a result, I contacted more than fifty women about interviews, and most were willing to tell their stories in print. I talked with several of them in person, spoke with many more by telephone, and exchanged letters with others. Because my earliest interviews with the players were conducted in the 1990s, I was also able to include a few conversations with women who died before work on the present collection was under way.

In almost every case, former players shared useful, interesting, and often amusing memories about their glory years. Many women identified their experiences in the league as the best time of their lives, and most consider the time a turning point that helped them grow up, learn about life as well as baseball, make friends that lasted a lifetime, and gain new opportunities, including the chance to pursue advanced education and, subsequently, careers in a wide variety of fields.

The book is organized chronologically into three sections: The Early Years, 1943–1945; The Postwar Years, 1946–1949; and The Last Years, 1950–1954. A brief history precedes the main text and explains this structure, describing the league's development from a four-team startup built around a 12-inch softball and underhand pitching to a ten-team loop that adopted overhand pitching and finally to a five-team league that adopted a regulation baseball and near-major league field dimensions. The epilogue identifies overarching themes of the interviews and brings the story of the league and its players up to date. To paraphrase Jim Bouton, we find that, just like the males who played the national pastime, the females in their own league were gripped by the baseball, not the other way around.

In addition to the players, without whose cooperation there would be no book, I owe thanks to several individuals and institutions for their help along the way. The National Baseball Hall of Fame's staff, primarily through Freddy Berowski, provided me with copies

---

*Susan E. Johnson's When Women Played Hardball *(Seattle: Seal Press, 1994) includes chapters featuring interviews,* and Patricia L. Brown's A League of My Own: Memoir of a Pitcher for the All-American Girls Professional Baseball League *(Jefferson, NC: McFarland, 2003) includes eight interviews.*

of items from the files of many players. Archivist Kristen Madden of the Center for History in South Bend likewise provided useful information. Some pictures appear courtesy of the Louise Pettus Archives and Special Collections of Winthrop University, thanks in part to the efforts of Bob Gorman, head of the Dacus Library's reference department. David Hillman, retired as the director of Virginia Western Community College's Library, not only proofread the manuscript and offered valuable suggestions but also wrote a perceptive introduction for the book. Merrie Fidler, author of the excellent book *The Origins and History of the All-American Girls Professional Baseball League* (2006), read several of the interviews and provided a thoughtful foreword; I appreciate her support for this project. Many of the players, family members, and friends of players that I spoke with lent their support as well, and while they are too numerous to mention, I appreciate all of them.

Last but not least, I thank my wife, Betty, who accompanied me during many interviews, heard me talk more about baseball, memories, and the AAGPBL than anyone else in the world, and read a great deal of what I have written.

Introduction by David Hillman

Within the limits of its Hollywood framework — the inevitable glosses and distortions and the subjugation of fact to plot and script — Penny Marshall's hit movie *A League of Their Own* did a wonderful job of making modern audiences aware that women baseball players had once had a professional league. Indeed, the ladies interviewed in this collection repeatedly assert that the movie, along with the All-American League's exhibit a few years earlier at the Baseball Hall of Fame, sparked public interest in their history, transforming what had been fond private memories of the best period of their lives (as many ex-players said it was) into sharable stories that, until then, even their children and grandchildren had not been told. Whereas the movie focuses on one fictionalized team during the opening year of the league and encapsulates this in a kind of coda based on the Cooperstown event, the present book reveals the real stories of these groundbreaking women, their hopes and dreams, their qualms and disappointments, and the nitty-gritty realities they experienced along with the thrills.

In the end these interviews are stories about young people leaving home for adventure, a type of story as old as the hills but here served with a modern spin — the heroes have been replaced by heroines. It will occur to baby boomers reading through this book that our own mothers belonged to the same generation as these women. I remember my mother wistfully telling me about a chance she had had when young to venture out into the world, but alas, she passed it up and spent all of her life in her hometown. The women in this book did not make that mistake. Their stories are vividly told in their own words, and by the end of the book you feel that you know them both individually and collectively. In fact, it is a collective profile that may linger in memory. Jim's book effectively answers the question, Who was this All-American League girl who dared to think she could play professional baseball?

She might have come from the East Coast, California, the heartland, Canada, and, later, even from Cuba. She was likely to be unmarried and she might even still be going to high school off-season. Likewise, there were teachers whose baseball season had to be adjusted to their teaching year. Others were destined to become teachers, after they left the league or after the league closed down, and not surprisingly the most popular major for those who went to college appears to have been physical education. Some chose to stay home and raise children after their adventure in the larger world, but others had long careers in business, manufacturing, or teaching. After the excitement of the road, the games, the fans, and the bonding with other women of exceptional talent, one suspects that in their post-league lives they were less likely than the average World War II factory girl to be reabsorbed into home and family.

Our girl might have grown up on a farm or in a town or even in a city, but she had traveled little and only with her family. She had probably never flown. Now she was always on the road, traveling in buses, trains, and sometimes even in cars packed with other young women. For one lucky cohort there was even a plane flight to Cuba for spring training. Early bouts of homesickness were replaced by a new maturity and sophistication. In the parlance of the time, she continued to call self and teammate "girl" but quickly passed into womanhood. The wearying cycle of travel/practice/play could not diminish the heady sense of freedom — the liberating knowledge that she had relinquished the protection of her family and was now out in the world where real success and real failure were both possible. Her salary seemed almost too much and indeed may have exceeded her father's — each paycheck a pleasant dividend to add to the delight of playing a game she loved. Now money accrued in her purse and small indulgences were affordable. She may have tasted her first cigarette, drunk her first glass of beer, played cards for the first time. We can imagine her one day catching the bus and going on a personal errand to downtown Racine or South Bend, or maybe just sitting alone in a restaurant, and with a sudden thrill it dawned on her that for the first time in her life she was truly on her own, unsheltered and anonymous, and not a single person from her life — not her parents, her chaperones, or even her teammates — knew exactly where she was at that moment on the face of the planet. But in her home team city she might not be anonymous, for on the street there would be nods of recognition and requests for autographs, especially if she were a star player. A girl who might have been slopping hogs on her daddy's farm the year before was now a local hero. She learned to endure pressure, to know that a thousand people had their eyes on her, were waiting for her next pitch, her next swing. She complained about it but was secretly proud of her impractical uniform which drew attention to her legs but also to cuts and bruises (badges of honor, as it were) from sliding on bad surfaces.

A love for all kinds of sports would have manifested itself early, along with a natural athletic ability. A baseball-minded father might have recognized her flair for the game and helped develop her skills. Very likely she would have played some form of baseball or softball with her brothers and neighborhood boys. These informal, pick-up games would accept a girl who had the right stuff, even if she was usually not allowed to play alongside boys on organized teams. The paucity of girls' sports in the high schools of that era was offset by the abundance of opportunity to play softball and other games on local teams. Reading these interviews, one gets the impression that in 1930s and 1940s America softball teams were as common as FDR's voice on the radio. Almost every organization, church, manufacturer, small business, and town had a team, or so it seems. A young woman might be hired at a plant with the understanding that the big attraction was her athletic ability and what she might contribute to the company's softball team. Opportunities to play and be discovered were out there, and Philip Wrigley (the league's founder) seems to have had scouts everywhere.

Usually home team players stayed in private homes and visiting players in hotels, ostensibly making it hard to fraternize with the enemy, but over time she got to know women from other teams. Teams sometimes dissolved, their demise scattering players among rivals. Rarely did a woman spend her whole career in the league with one team. Trades were frequent, or she might be loaned out to help a team crippled by injuries, which were bad for everyone; poorly performing teams robbed the game of excitement and pulled the whole league down. For a while she might have been with the Sallies or Colleens, two monogamous teams that traveled together and played only each other in exhibition games all over the country to promote women's baseball and attract new talent. It helped to be flexible and open to change. Without much warning she might be shifted to a new position or even to a new team. As the years progressed, she was expected to hit a smaller, livelier ball and, if a pitcher, to pitch like men in the majors. Along with constant change was the uncertainty caused by economic realities of which she had only an inkling. Would her team last the season? Would it still be around next year? For that matter, would the league still be around next year?

Later she said they were the best years of her life. She had probably felt this way all along, but it was only later in life looking back that she realized the full significance of those years for women, for sports history, and for the country.

After the league folded, there was a quiescence of several decades; then along came the Players Association, the reunions, Cooperstown, and the movie. To this lineup is added the solid scholarship of two serious historians, Jim Sargent and Merrie Fidler, who has written the foreword to this book. It is safe to say that the All-American League has now secured a permanent spot in mainstream baseball history. For example, Ken Burns devoted his two-hour video essay on baseball in the 1940s (part of his 10-disc DVD set on the history of the game) to four events that he felt highlighted the decade: Joe DiMaggio's 56-game hitting streak, Ted Williams' batting .406, the introduction of African Americans starting with Jackie Robinson, and the rise of the women's All-American League in response to male players going off to war.

Attendance figures do not distinguish repeaters from first-time visitors, so there is no way of knowing how many different people saw at least one game during the league's twelve years. Hundreds of thousands certainly and maybe even millions, especially when you factor in the many exhibition games played around the country. The lesson these people absorbed was that superior women athletes could play a man's game and make it just as exciting to watch as the best male players. Whether in men or women, talent is talent, and watching a competition between women of exceptional talent is hugely entertaining. By demonstrating this, the All-American League helped foster in the public mind a new openness to women playing ball like men and paved the way for later generations of women to engage in professional sports.

The league was thrilling in its execution, poignant in its demise, and a landmark in the history of women and sports. As their game evolved to be more and more like major league baseball, external forces were conspiring to end the twelve-year experiment. The league was dying in the front offices and in the marketplace even as the women were playing their hearts out on the field. In interviewing these ladies, whose memories are still as sharp as the crack of a bat and stretch back to the past like a long hit ball, Jim Sargent has produced another valuable book on the All-American League and a tribute to a unique group of female athletes who long ago and all too briefly graced our national pastime.

David Hillman is a lifelong baseball fan and avid reader of books about baseball history. He retired after a long career as library director at Virginia Western Community College in Virginia.

A Brief History of the All-American Girls Professional Baseball League

Ballparks are where people go to dream in public, and there was a time in America when women enjoyed baseball dreams of their own as well as the opportunity to realize them. Indeed, the ballparks and the stadiums that hosted the fast-paced games of the historic All-American Girls Professional Baseball League in the 1940s and the early 1950s were not much different than the men's ballparks of the era. Further, the women who populated the league's teams— the 1948 season featured a peak of ten ball clubs— were first-rate athletes who had succeeded against stiff athletic competition as well as the low expectations in a traditionally male-oriented culture to play baseball, not softball, in the best women's circuit in the country. The virtually universal reaction of fans, male and female, was that they came out to the ballpark for the fun of seeing girls playing ball in skirted uniforms, but they returned because they enjoyed the skill level of the players and the excitement and the competitive quality of the games.

Terry Donahue, an infielder turned catcher who grew up on a farm in Saskatchewan, spent four seasons playing for the Peoria Redwings after World War II. Terry lived all four years with the Turnbull family in Peoria, and she remembered Lloyd Turnbull's comment about her first game: "We're going out to the game, and we'll have a good laugh about women playing ball in skirts!" Years later, Terry observed, "When they came out and saw how well we played, they never missed a game."[1]* Donahue's experience was repeated by other players over and over again.

1943: The All-American Girls Professional Baseball League, or the All-American League, as it was widely known during the years it existed, was born out of fear that during World War II the United States government's manpower needs for its military forces would decimate the numbers of men playing baseball in the major leagues. However, Philip Wrigley, the gum magnate who was the owner of the Chicago Cubs, conferred with several close associates, and they devised a workable alternative for the 1943 season. Wrigley helped finance a women's league of four teams located in the hinterland of Chicago that would play a fast-paced game of modified girls' softball. Taking advantage of their sex appeal, girls would wear skirted tunic-type uniforms. Also, players would use 12-inch circumference softballs, regulation baseball bats, gloves and spikes, and the game would be played mostly at night on diamonds that featured a pitching distance of 40 feet and base paths of 65 feet. By comparison, men's and women's softball was played on diamonds with 60-foot base paths, and the pitching distance was 35 feet for women and 40 feet for men, but all softball leagues used the same 12-inch "deadball." Further, an important change for the AAGPBL was that base runners could lead off and steal, but runners were not allowed to lead off in softball.[2]

Regardless, the major difference in the All-American League beginning from day one was that the loop's creators figured to move their game toward baseball, although in incre-

---

*See Notes beginning on page 23.

ments, because girls playing hardball in the U.S. and Canada were accustomed to playing softball, not baseball. Reflecting the league's evolution, the name changed various times, for example, from the All-American Girls Soft Ball League in 1943, to the All-American Girls Professional Ball League in 1944, to the All American Girls Professional Baseball League in 1945, to the All-American Girls Baseball League in 1946. Later, when the team's owners voted to buy out the Management Corporation after the 1950 season, the official name for the last four years became American Girls Baseball League. Typically, the players had other interests than the loop's name, finances, or logistics. Fran Janssen, who pitched for four seasons starting in 1948 with Fort Wayne, later learned the name changed in 1951. "I wasn't aware of that until I started looking at the materials in the league's archives [in South Bend]," Janssen remembered. "Any contract the players had, the league crossed out the All, and it was the 'American Girls Baseball League.'"

Softball had long been popular in the U.S. and Canada. For example, during the Great Depression of the 1930s, Betsy Jochum, who grew up in Cincinnati and later was known as a standout outfielder for the South Bend Blue Sox, played softball on city streets and vacant lots as a young girl. Later, she played for two teams sponsored by businesses. Softball tournaments for girls' teams were held on state, regional, and national levels, and Betsy recalled, "We went to national softball tournaments that were held each year in Detroit or Chicago." The Canadian girls who came to the All-American League were also playing softball, but, recalled Lucella (MacLean) Ross, a native of Lloydminster, Alberta, and a catcher for the Blue Sox in 1943 and 1944, "We used the 12-inch ball, but there was nothing 'soft' about the ball, I'll tell you!"

During the league's inaugural summer, the Racine Belles won the first half of the season with a 34–20 record, the Kenosha Comets won the second half with a ledger of 33–21, and Racine won the Scholarship Series Championship, as the playoffs were called in 1943 and 1944, in three straight games. Ironically, Kenosha's ace right-hander, Helen Nicol (later Fox), beat Racine in all but the first game the two teams played during the regular season. Nicol was the circuit's top pitcher with a 31–8 ledger in 1943. "In the playoffs," remembered Sophie Kurys, Racine's star second sacker, "we beat her. I think we beat her two games, which was unusual, because Nickie Fox would knock our socks off every time she pitched. But we got our revenge in that series."

South Bend finished in second place in both halves of the All-American League's first campaign, and the other original All-American team, the Rockford Peaches, finished fourth in each half. Rockford's Terrie Davis won the first half batting title with a .332 mark, and South Bend's Betsy Jochum captured the second half hitting crown with a .295 mark. The AAGPBL was a pitcher's league, but the players didn't care. Most of them knew their diamond dreams would continue in 1944, because Wrigley's financial backing guaranteed another season.

1944: The All-American League expanded for the 1944 season, adding two new teams: the Minneapolis Millerettes and the Milwaukee Chicks. Both teams were slated to play home games at the Double-A American Association ballparks in their respective cities, Nicollet Park, the home of Minneapolis' Millers, and Borchert Field, home to Milwaukee's Brewers. League officials, however, miscalculated in choosing these two cities, because AAGPBL teams would neither receive adequate press coverage nor draw sufficient fans when competing in a large city that hosted a men's professional baseball team. Even in wartime, with factory workers and other fans looking for leisure activities, the prevailing attitudes about masculine superiority meant that in the 1940s, most fans, male and female, would pay to see the men's team play ball even though many talented players were at war, not at the ballpark.

To the players on all six girls' teams, their baseball dreams were alive and well. Dottie (Wiltse) Collins, one of the first California girls to grace the league in 1944, remembered that despite the Millerettes losing their home stadium and living out of suitcases in hotels on the road for the latter part of the season, they enjoyed a great summer. "We were young, and we were having a good time, and we had money in our pockets," Dottie recalled. "I mean, what more could you ask for? We didn't care that we were the 'Orphans,' the Minneapolis Orphans."

The league adjusted the game subtly in 1944, but those changes went almost unnoticed by the players. As Lavonne "Pepper" Paire of Minneapolis later expressed it, "We were playing a game that was a cross between softball and baseball."[3] The regular season was again divided into a first and second half, the pitching remained underhand, and the distance from the mound to home plate was still 40 feet. The ball's size was again 12 inches in circumference, but it was reduced to 11.5 inches at mid-season. The base paths started at 65 feet, but the distance was increased to 68 feet at mid-season. In fact, those changes were designed to give an advantage to the hitters.[4]

For the players, the format of the second season, the rules, and the equipment, notably baseball bats, were now familiar. In the end, the league's championship series climaxed when Milwaukee beat first-half winner Kenosha in a best-of-seven playoff, winning the finale, 3–0, on a sterling three-hitter hurled by the Chicks' Connie Wisniewski, a tall, talented rookie right-hander from Detroit.[5] Helen Nicol was again the loop's top pitcher as measured by her ERA of 0.93, and she fashioned a record of 17–11. The pitcher with the best record was Jo Kabick of Milwaukee, who compiled a 26–19 ledger, followed by Wisniewski at 23–10, Rockford's Carolyn Morris at 23–19, and Racine's Mary (Nesbitt) Crews at 23–17. Betsy Jochum led all hitters by averaging .296 for the season, but for the 102 batters who played ten or more games, 40 averaged above .200, and the remainder hit below that mark, thus indicating the league was pitcher-dominated.

To the girls, who were earning salaries between $50 and $85 per week, statistics didn't matter to them as much as did the camaraderie and the shared experiences. South Bend's Lucella Ross later observed, "We were a close bunch. We loved the game. We played at it very hard. We didn't have much social life because we were either playing ball, or practicing, or traveling."

The teams had chaperones, and many players remembered their mother and father being reassured by the presence of a chaperone who would look out for their daughter's interests. The league continued to build community relations by having the players housed in the private homes of fans, and the chaperones made those arrangements. Not every player followed all of the league's rules, including the dress code and the ban on smoking and drinking in public, but most followed the rules rather than risk being penalized or even dropped from the loop.

Rose (Folder) Powell, who played in 1944 for Kenosha, recalled that the league's charm school during spring training for the second (and final) year was useful, because most players were tomboys. "They told us how to put on lipstick, and how to walk in high heels," Rose said. "I didn't even own a pair of high heels. I had to borrow a pair. We had to learn how to lift our little finger when we drank a cup of tea, but I don't drink tea. The Helena Rubenstein people came in and did that for us, and they were looking down their noses at us tomboys, you know, but we did learn a lot. The chaperones helped, because they were always pretty much with us."

1945: Beginning with this season the league's ownership changed from the non-profit trusteeship created by Wrigley and his associates to a for-profit Management Corporation that carried out all functions of the league, including recruiting players, hiring managers and umpires, creating schedules, operating a spring training camp, and generating regional and national publicity. Arthur Meyerhoff, Wrigley's chief advertising agent, bought the Cubs owner's AAGPBL interests and created Management, although such structural changes were of little interest to ballplayers.

For what turned out to be the final year of World War II, Management did little to change the game on the diamond. First and foremost, the pitching remained underhand. Also, the ball was still 11.5 inches and the base paths were still 68 feet, but the pitching distance was lengthened from 40 to 42 feet at mid-season.

As *Life* magazine phrased it on June 4, 1945, "Girls' professional ball is something less than regulation professional baseball, something more than softball." The nationally-read story included pictures of several players, featuring a large lead photo of South Bend's Bonnie Baker smiling through her softball catcher's mask. *Life's* story and photo helped promote the league as well as make the talented and photogenic Baker a part of the circuit's desired glamour image.[6]

The same six All-American teams returned, but the Millerettes were moved from Minneapolis to Fort Wayne, Indiana, and renamed the Daisies, and the Chicks kept their moniker but were shifted from Milwaukee to Grand Rapids, Michigan. Also, the league adopted a single-season schedule and the Shaughnessy Playoff system. The playoffs would feature the loop's top four teams. In one semifinal round, the first-place team would square off against the third-place team, and the other semifinal round would match the second-place team against the fourth-place team, and in the finals, the two winners would battle for the playoff championship. Bill Allington's Rockford team won the regular season race with a 67–43 record, and the Peaches defeated third-place Grand Rapids in three straight games of the best-of-five semifinals. The Fort Wayne Daisies ranked second, and they stopped fourth-place Racine in four games. In the best-of-seven championship round, Rockford, the last-place team in 1943, defeated Fort Wayne in five games.

The league's third successful season was over, but team batting averages as well as the hurlers' earned run figures indicated the girls' game was still dominated by pitchers. By mid-season, when he ordered lengthening of the base paths, Max Carey, the new president, knew changes were needed to help the hitters as well as to appeal to the growing fan base. By the end of the final wartime season, Carey and league officials were planning to expand to eight teams for 1946.[7] The Girls' Pro League, as newspapers often called it, was thriving in the Midwest. Replying to a friend shortly after Christmas, Dottie Schroeder, who became the only player to compete in all twelve seasons, told her about the upcoming season, "Well, that's about all I've been thinking and talking about too."[8] Hope springs eternal in the diamond sport, and the experienced players were already anxious for baseball to start again.

1946: The war was over, major and minor league players were returning from military service, and the All-American League was booming. The circuit's total attendance grew from approximately 176,000 in 1943, to 260,000 in 1944, and to 450,000 in 1945. Based on eight teams in 1946, the league set a new record of nearly 755,000 paid admissions. Expansion made sense, and AAGPBL owner Arthur Meyerhoff understood the connection between growth and promotion. The league's publicity budgets for 1944, 1945, and 1946 were about $5,000, $4,000, and $4,000, respectively.[9]

Further, Meyerhoff and president Max Carey devised a spring training camp to be held in the warmer climate of Pascagoula, Mississippi, instead of the colder Midwest, where the league trained during wartime. Despite problems with the conditions of the barracks where the players lived and the quality of the ball fields in Pascagoula, spring training attracted nearly 200 qualified women, easily enough to staff the eight teams with 18-player rosters (up from a maximum of 16 players in 1945 and 15 in 1943 and 1944). The Redwings of Peoria, Illinois, and the Lassies of Muskegon, Michigan, joined the established teams. Also, the teams chartered or purchased special buses for travel to league cities, whereas during the war the ball clubs traveled mainly by railroad. "We could wear our shorts on the bus when it was hot," recollected Betsy Jochum. "No more dragging your suitcase to the next train."[10]

In the postwar world, the girls faced further adjustments to the game they played on the circuit's inadequately-lighted diamonds. In keeping with league officials' plan to evolve into baseball, as the 1992 movie *A League of Their Own* indicated was true for the 1943 season, the changes for 1946 included reducing the ball's size from 11.5 to 11 inches, moving the pitcher's mound back from 42 to 43 feet, and increasing the base paths from 68 to 70 feet,[11] despite Harold Dailey's later mistaken claim that base paths were set at 72 feet in 1946.[12] Further, to limit stolen bases, the league allowed a "half-balk" move to make it harder for runners to read a pitcher's delivery. More important, Carey wrote, the "pitching rules were relaxed sufficiently to allow for a limited side-arm pitch from an underhanded delivery with certain restrictions."[13]

Necessity, however, is the mother of invention. All teams needed pitchers, and what began to happen was managers that needed new hurlers converted hard-throwing position players into pitchers by having them drop their arm motion down and throw sidearm. Racine's Anna Hutchison, who began as a catcher, recalled being the first sidearmer in 1946.[14] Joyce (Hill) Westerman, then a catcher, confirmed Hutch "starting the sidearm pitching in 1946. She started as a catcher, but used to throw batting practice all the time, and when they saw that, they made her into a sidearm pitcher."

Sidearming caught on quickly. Jean Faut, who never played softball but grew up playing baseball and pitched in a few semipro exhibitions games, the new style. Faut, one of the top rookies in 1946, recalled that pitching sidearm meant her delivery could not be above the shoulder, an often-used motion for a third baseman, and the league's umpires, hired to officiate baseball, not softball, allowed it.[15] Also, Muskegon's Erma Bergmann recollected that manager Ralph "Buzz" Boyle converted her from a third baseman to, at first, a submarine pitcher. "But as the 1946 season moved along," Bergmann recalled, "the league gradually raised the rule until you were throwing sidearm, and that was real easy for me. I never had a sore arm throwing sidearm, and the first thing you know, the league was pitching overhand."

The league enjoyed another stellar season, attendance records were broken, and the Shaughnessy Playoffs again excited the fans. Racine paced the regular season with an excellent 74–38 ledger, and the Belles matched the Grand Rapids Chicks by having four starters picked to the league's first official All-Star team. Racine also defeated third-place South Bend in the semifinals, three games to one, and fourth-place Rockford eliminated the youthful Grand Rapids Chicks in three straight games. Finally, in perhaps the best-played game of the season, Racine won the best-of-five championship round over Rockford in the fifth game, 2–1, when the Belles' hustling Sophie Kurys, who led the league with 201 steals in 203 attempts and was voted Player of the Year, scored on Betty Trezza's single in the fourteenth inning. Even though the nation was facing political, social, and economic problems in the fall of 1946,[16] girls' baseball was thriving in the eight medium-sized Midwestern league cities that hosted All-American teams.

1947: By 1947, most of the circuit's veterans figured the league was there for good, like the major leagues. After all, professional ballplayers don't think much about team budgets or rules changes or attendance figures or logistics of how things get done. Instead, they practice baseball every day, and they play the game, day after day and week after week, for an entire season. Further, they talk baseball every day and every night, especially after finishing a game. Most of the girls hoped and dreamed 1947 would be another glorious season, and it happened.

For starters, the league planned and carried out its greatest spring camp: a two-week jaunt to Havana, Cuba, for 200 players and league personnel, followed by exhibition tours with four pairs of teams playing their way back to the Midwest. According to the *Official Girls' Baseball Rules*, the game was unchanged, featuring the same 11-inch ball, 43-foot pitching distance, and 70-foot base paths used in 1946,[17] and Fort Wayne's *1947 Year Book* reprinted a diagram from the Official Rules to illustrate those dimensions.[18] More important, sidearm hurling was authorized, moving the game a big step toward overhand pitching—baseball's trademark.[19]

For batters, adjusting to more sidearming pitchers was a big change. In 1946, led by South Bend's team mark of .220, six of the eight teams batted .200 or more, but Fort Wayne at .184 and Peoria at .181 ranked seventh and eighth, respectively. In 1947, Muskegon averaged .223 and Peoria batted .217, but the other six teams averaged below .200, and Fort Wayne's .176 was the lowest. The Howe News Bureau, the league's statistical service, kept no team records for pitching, but in 1946, Connie Wisniewski, the tireless underhander, led all hurlers with a 33–9 record and a 0.96 ERA, and eight of the loop's thirty-seven regular pitchers (those who worked more than 45 innings) posted an ERA below 2.00. In 1947, Grand Rapids' Millie Earp, who went 20–8 with a 0.68 ERA, topped the circuit, but 17 of the 40 regular hurlers compiled an ERA below 2.00.[20] Despite using the large white-seamed near-softball (a regulation baseball measures 9.0 to 9.25 inches) and the new motion, the pitchers often dominated the hitters.

Regardless, America was changing, and so was baseball. The All-American League was largely a baseball circuit, except for the larger ball and the shorter diamond distances. The women were playing a men's game and, consequently, they were continuing to buck societal norms broken by females who worked at nontraditional jobs during wartime, changes idealized by "Rosie the Riveter." Also, the league's feminine image and the reality of living in a "man's world" off the diamond were so different that the contrast seemed like a split personality. The players accepted their divided lives, or as Susan Johnson observed in her book about women playing hardball, "To them it was simple: they were tomboys who had to look like girls, and sometimes like women, so they could play baseball like men."[21]

In any event, unlike the events surrounding Jackie Robinson of the Brooklyn Dodgers breaking major league baseball's "color" barrier, the AAGPBL broke no social barriers in 1947. "Fan appeal," Merrie Fidler observed, "was more important than defying the era's social conventions."[22] In the circuit's ten-team 1948 season, eleven Latinas played,[23] but no black woman was ever signed by a league team. Sue Macy found that two African Americans worked out with the Blue Sox in May 1951, but they did not make it. After the season, the league's board of directors debated the issue. The minutes noted, "The consensus of the group seemed to be against the idea of colored players, unless they would show promise of exceptional ability."[24]

1948: Baseball, as fans understood the national pastime, arrived in the All-American League in 1948. In a history prepared for Dell's 1949 edition of *Major League Baseball*, the author, likely Max Carey, wrote, "The [1948] season saw the further opening up of the game by the adoption of full overhand pitching regulations, a 50-foot pitching distance, an increase of the distances between bases to 72 feet and the adoption of a still smaller ball, ten and three-eighths inches in circumference." He added, "The original under-hand pitch disappeared entirely from the game and the season was memorable for its development of fine overhand pitchers, with curves, drops, change of pace and other scientific wizardry."[25]

Overhand hurling dealt a death blow to most of the underhand pitchers who populated the league during the war years, because few could adjust. Sugar Koehn (pronounced *Cane*), for example, recalled her downfall occurred with the switch to sidearming: "I did have a few good years, but the unorthodox throw took its toll."[26] On the other hand, Jean Faut, who never played fast-pitch softball, later remarked, "When the league went to overhand pitching in 1948, I was home free."[27]

The adoption of the overhand delivery also meant the league needed to develop more new pitchers, because softball hurlers couldn't learn the delivery, the pitches, and the control needed for baseball in two weeks of spring camp.[28] Further, the overhand motion is harder on a pitcher's arm, due partly to throwing breaking balls — pitches that require using different grips and twisting, or snapping, the wrist during delivery. As a result, few baseball pitchers can work more often than every fourth or fifth day. Therefore, a good team needs a rotation with at least three strong hurlers as well as "spot" starters in order to win consistently.

In addition, the All-American League expanded to ten teams in 1948 — and created financial problems that plagued the teams' budgets and foreshadowed the end of the Management Corporation. The creation of the Springfield (Illinois) Sallies, and the Chicago Colleens led league officials to devise Western and Eastern Divisions, but by expanding the playoffs to include the top four teams in each division, the upshot was that all eight established teams had a virtual lock on the playoffs. On the other hand, the Sallies and Colleens, who were given weaker rosters, had little chance for a winning season. Indeed, Springfield became a traveling "Orphan" team in mid-season, much like the Millerettes in 1944, and Chicago went out of business after the season ended. The league's total attendance peaked at 910,000 in 1948, but never again would a season's paid admissions rise significantly for any All-American team. By comparison, attendance for major league and minor league baseball also peaked during the 1948 season, so the gradual decline in paid fans that began in 1949 and continued into the 1950s was not peculiar to the AAGPBL.

The 1948 season was also notable for several highlights, including another southern spring training camp, this time in Opa-Locka, Florida, just north of Miami. Also, the league added several Cuban players, but these rookies were all allocated to the expansion ball clubs, Springfield and Chicago. The Sallies drew two, Georgiana Rios, a third baseman, and Zonia Vialat, a catcher. The Colleens received five Cubans: second baseman Maria Hernandas; third baseman Migdalia "Mickey" Perez; infielder-pitcher Luisa Gallego; outfielder Gloria Ruiz; and right-hander Mirta Marrero. South Bend's Shoo-Shoo Wirth, raised by her Cuban-born mother in Tampa, grew up speaking Spanish and English at home. At Opa-Locka, Wirth acted as an interpreter for the Cubans, since she was one of the few All-Americans who could speak Spanish.[29]

Unlike the often hostile treatment received by nonwhite players in major league baseball after 1946, Cubans in the All-American League had a better experience, partly because they were welcomed by most American and Canadian players. For example, Dolly Brumfield, who was fifteen and studying Spanish in high school when she trained at Opa-Locka, received help with Spanish from more than one Cuban. Dolly recalled, "Mickey Perez was a big help and was a good friend over all those years."[30]

Still, the Cubans were separated from their families, and if Mirta Marrero's experience was typical, the language barrier caused problems. Mirta, who was seventeen in 1948, didn't know any English, and communicating with her Chicago teammates was difficult. "I cried a lot because the American girls couldn't understand me and I couldn't understand them," Marrero recollected in 2003. "I had a hard time." When it came to chatter, players learned different phrases. For example, Marrero yelled "Oye, fulana!" (Hey, you!) to her American teammates, and "Dale, chica!" (Go, girl!) to Latinas.[31] Isabel "Lefty" Alvarez, a southpaw pitcher who spent two seasons on the developmental tour and played for Fort Wayne in 1951, remembered, "When I came into the other league [AAGPBL], it was different. We were all separated. We all lived in different places. We all lived with a family. I found many outside friendships with fans."

As it developed, the AAGPBL's greatest expansion season turned out to be its costliest decision, and South Bend president Harold Dailey fought the additional expense of fielding two new teams from the beginning. Still, the larger question was whether the glamour circuit would continue to prosper. In retrospect, while the women's teams were now playing baseball, but with a larger ball and smaller diamond distances, several officials correctly feared the circuit had reached its memorable high water mark.[32]

1949: The All-American League returned with eight teams and made some critical changes in 1949, but not until mid-season. Still, girls' baseball was alive and well, even if twenty-eight managers had resigned or been fired since the circuit began in 1943. For the record, players now earned from $85 to $125 per week. On the field, they took orders from men. Off the field, reported Bill Fay in *Collier's*, they were counseled by women, "vigilant team chaperones who knew how to discourage bleacher wolves and dugout-door Johnnies." For perspective, the women *looked* like they ran and threw a baseball as well as men, but that was an "optical illusion." As Max Carey explained, "by putting our bases 72 feet apart, fixing our pitching distance at 50 feet and using a ball that's not quite as lively as that big-league jack-rabbit, our girls play baseball that looks as fast as a major-league game on a 90-foot [base path] diamond."[33] Altogether, the AAGPBL was still combining femininity with skills, good looks with talent, and grace with hustle.

The league continued to evolve, and in mid-season, further changes were made to appeal to the players and the fans. For starters, the circuit adopted a red-seamed, livelier ball that was ten inches in circumference, down from the ten and three-eighths inch baseball used in 1948. The new ball was introduced on July 16, 1949, and to balance the hoped-for harder hitting, the pitching distance was moved from 50 to 55 feet.[34] "Finally, league management, always concerned with what the public wanted," Barbara Gregorich explained in *Women at Play*, "concluded that what fans liked most of all was a live ball — one that traveled far and fast and resonated with a resounding crack when the bat met it squarely."[35]

The All-American game as played mainly in the evenings on women's diamonds in eight Midwestern cities was now quite similar to regulation baseball, but maybe that wasn't enough to survive. The circuit already found it harder to attract talented new players, and

South Bend made the only profit in 1948, just $236.16. The pioneering loop was beginning a slow decline.[36]

On the field, however, Rockford and South Bend waged a season-long battle for first place, the dream of the league's funders and the goal of circuit officials since 1943. In the end, the Peaches and the Blue Sox tied for first place with identical 75–36 records. However, Max Carey ruled the teams must play off for first place, and the winner of a best-of-seven series would claim the regular season championship. As it developed, the Peaches won the title in four straight games, and they won the Carey Cup playoffs by defeating Grand Rapids, also in four straight games.

Looking at women playing the fast-paced game on the field, observers believed the league was on the rise. In a story inspired by the league's office, Adie Suehsdorf, writing for the *Los Angeles Times*, pointed out differences in the AAGPBL game, including how a star like Dottie Collins of Fort Wayne could get pregnant and depart in mid-season of 1948, or how others could get married and leave the pro game. Regardless, the league wasn't "softball, or vaudeville, or a leg show," but rather, the girls were playing *professional baseball*. They threw overhand, used "man-sized" gloves, wore spiked shoes, hit a slightly smaller baseball with Louisville Slugger bats, and they executed drag bunts, squeeze plays, and delayed steals. To top it off, Suehsdorf wrote, these were nice girls with good athletic ability, or "sluggers in skirts."[37]

Sluggers or not, many All-Americans, notably the younger girls, could hardly wait for the next season. They loved playing the game. Further, the league's brightest innovation was to launch a two-team rookie development tour in 1949 using the equipment and uniforms of the Colleens and the Sallies. The two teams traveled around the nation, playing more than 50 games. Pitcher Sue Kidd, from Choctaw, Arkansas, who later starred for the Blue Sox, got a tryout and made the tour when the Colleens and the Sallies met in a pair of contests in Little Rock. Her entire life changed when the touring teams came to Arkansas, and she joined the Sallies. "I hated to see the season end," Kidd recalled, "and I just hoped and prayed I'd get to play the next summer."

1950: The All-American League's 1950 season started with high hopes for players and team officials, but the year ended in a financial crisis and the demise of Management. Teams in Rockford and Peoria survived the season only by conducting drives to sell team stock at $100 per share. Grand Rapids held a drive but raised only $4,000, when $20,000 was needed. The Chicks were able to complete the season partly because the players and the manager agreed to play with no guarantee of salaries. Also, the Jets, a local semipro team, allowed the Chicks to use the club's ballpark. In addition, the Muskegon franchise shifted to Kalamazoo, Michigan, because the Lassies' board ran out of funds.

Moreover, the entertainment life of consumers was changing. Most people spent less on local amusement, including baseball, and stayed home to watch programs like "sitcoms" and big league baseball on television, the technological change revolutionizing American culture in the 1950s. Regardless, no financial changes could solve the league's greatest problem: the more the game evolved toward baseball, the lesser the talent pool from which to select new players.[38]

On July 19, 1950, faced with a growing deficit, the league voted to eliminate meal money for road trips, a decision that caused no little controversy, notably among veteran players. By that time, the Korean War had just begun. Thousands of families were directly affected as United Nations troops, the majority of whom were Americans, intervened to stabilize the conflict at the thirty-eighth parallel, the boundary between North and South Korea. The Korean War was blamed on the Soviet and Chinese Communist specter, a growing concern since 1947. The fighting in Korea turned into a stalemate, and the Cold War heightened fears of Communist subversion at home.[39]

Within that cultural milieu, one major message of the media, now featuring TV, was that a "woman's place" was in the home taking care of the family, preferably in the growing white-populated suburbs.[40] At the same time, attendance for major league baseball had peaked in 1948 when close to 21 million fans entered turnstiles, but the numbers fell to 17 million in 1950. The majors were unable to reverse the decline until 1957.[41] Minor league baseball peaked with 59 circuits in 1949. One league failed in 1950, but the Korean conflict helped reduce attendance in the minors to 34 million, a drop of seven million in one year.[42]

Regardless, the All-American game on the field was stable. Indeed, the league was fed by young players who competed on the touring Colleens and Sallies, like Sue Kidd and Wimp Baumgartner in 1949 and Mary Moore and Shirley Burkovich in 1950, and the quality of hardball played in the eight-year-old All-American League was better than ever. Overall, the game as played by top female athletes, featuring the 10-inch ball, the 55-foot pitching distance, and the 72-foot base paths, helped boost batting averages and make the game more exciting.

The excitement peaked in the finals of the Shaughnessy Playoffs when Rockford, managed by Bill Allington, won the title by outlasting Fort Wayne, now managed by Max Carey, in seven games. Susan Johnson, who grew up as a proud Peaches fan, later captured the events and personalities surrounding Rockford's last championship in her book, *When Women Played Hardball*. However, the league only lasted four more seasons, and after the 1954 campaign, Johnson observed, "All that remained of girls' baseball were yellowing newspaper clippings, uniforms that no longer fit, trophies tarnishing in the attic, and scars and aching knees. And, occasionally, the sharp memory of a crucial run batted in, a perfect throw, the roar from the crowd, and that thrilling call: 'Play Ball!'"[43]

A typical story inspired by the league—although budget cuts made such stories less and less frequent—appeared in *McCall's* for September 1950. Morris Markey praised the girls' game, indicating that nearly a million spectators (he was using figures from the 1948 season) bought tickets to contests in 1949, more than half of them women. Many men were fans, but after gawking at the players' bare knees and legs for an inning, they watched in "wonderment at the skill of the fielders, the lusty swings of the batters, the assortment of 'stuff' the pitchers display." Citing Jean Faut along with Merle Keagle and Dottie Collins as mothers as well as first-rate ballplayers, and offering Lib Mahon, a teacher in the offseason, as an example of a star who was preparing for the future by using baseball earnings to pay for a master's degree, the scribe declared the game was great for players and fans, but especially for the athletes. "The opportunity to show that you are good at something," Markey observed, "to have people yell their approval of you, injects powerful ingredients into the soul."[44]

1951: Although few players realized it, the girls' circuit they had known for years changed substantially for the 1951 season. At the All-American League's board meeting in Chicago on December 18, 1950, a new organizational structure was officially adopted and, accordingly, the name was changed to the American Girls Baseball League.[45] New rules were soon completed. In addition to teams owning player contracts, the major changes included that teams were limited to a maximum of $5,400 in salary per month, not counting the pay of managers and chaperones; ball clubs could have a minimum of fourteen and a maximum of sixteen active players on the roster as of July 1, meaning teams could give rookies more time to develop; a team's list of players would be forwarded to the league office at the end of each season so those players could be reserved for that team in the future; and no team could employ a "feminine manager,"[46] which was the male backlash against Bonnie Baker managing the Lassies in 1950. Also, teams such as South Bend and Fort Wayne adopted new uniform insignias to help with local and regional promotional efforts.[47]

Also, the teams' directors voted to buy out the contract with Arthur Meyerhoff's Management Corporation for $1,000 per team, or $8,00 total,[48] and to operate each team on an independent basis, with a commissioner to supervise the league. The circuit's eight teams were community owned, but none had a wealthy backer that could supply $10,000 to $15,000 per year to offset the revenue lost from declining ticket sales.

The new structure was basic. Fred Leo, president during the 1950 season, was selected as commissioner for 1951. Leo replaced Management by functioning as the circuit's business manager. Edward J. Ruetz, judge of the Kenosha Municipal Court, became the powerless president. Previously, the league's front office consisted of the president, a secretary, and a publicity agent. In 1951, the teams switched to decentralized management and the budget was cut further, eliminating scouting expenses, touring teams, tickets, and a secretary's salary.[49]

For all practical purposes, the league supervised, without regulating, the affairs of individual teams. Also, each team now handled its own personnel problems, scouting, recruitment, contracts, and spring training, but the league created the schedule. Leo explained the necessity of making the changes, indicating the circuit attracted a total of 481,981 fans in 1950, a loss of almost 100,000 in paid attendance from 1949 and just over half of the loop's 910,000 admissions during the seemingly halcyon season of 1948.[50]

For the first time in the league's nine-year history, South Bend won the Shaughnessy Playoff Championship—thanks to excellent pitching, timely hitting, good fielding, and better camaraderie. The Blue Sox prospered against long odds, clinching a playoff spot in the split season with a remarkable sixteen-game winning streak in late August. Voted the league's Player of the Year in a postseason poll of sportswriters, right-hander Jean Faut, who pitched a no-hitter in 1948 and another in 1949, hurled the circuit's first-ever perfect game against Rockford on July 21, 1951. Further, the league, desperate to attract fans, adopted a split-season format (used in 1943 and 1944), and South Bend earned a trip to the playoffs by winning first place with a second half record of 38–14.[51]

1952: The heroic nature of the Second World War was fading into the nation's memory, and the ugly portrayal of the Korean conflict filled the newspapers and magazines. The economic, social, and political problems of the postwar atomic era affected Americans in every walk of life, including pro sports, and baseball attendance continued to decline. Taking South Bend as an example, during 1947, the year of the Havana adventure, the Blue Sox drew 104,000 fans. In 1948, the year the league introduced overhand pitching, South Bend's attendance slipped to 93,600. In 1949, the year of the smaller, livelier baseball, the team's admissions climbed a couple of thousand to nearly 96,000. When the 1950s and the Korean War arrived, the Blue Sox fell to fifth place and fan interest dropped to around 67,000. In 1951, after Management was gone, the South Benders won the championship and drew a thousand more spectators, 68,268. In 1952, the club won another championship but entertained just over 57,000 folks.⁵² The team's directors, facing a $20,000 debt by July, voted to sell the franchise to Toledo,⁵³ but the Ohio city later declined the deal. Ironically, even though the game on the diamond looked more exciting than ever, the American Girls Baseball League was in serious financial trouble.

The circuit as well as the teams, hoping for the best, made plans for the 1952 season. The league's board elected Fort Wayne hotel magnate Harold Van Orman as president and Earl McCammon, of Kalamazoo, as business manager. By December 1951, it appeared all eight teams were returning for another season, but later, Peoria and Kenosha withdrew, lacking the needed funds. In late March 1952, league officials, in order to divide equally players from the disbanded Peoria and Kenosha clubs, held a drawing with representatives from the six teams.⁵⁴

The six All-American teams continued to play an intensely competitive brand of baseball, and the players, including the younger girls, thrived on the competition. "You know," recollected Fort Wayne's youthful hurler Pat Scott, "never in my dreams did I think I could go up there to that league and do that, not having any more experience than I did. Once I made up my mind that's what I wanted to do for the team and Max [Carey], and whoever the manager was, I did my best — and I had good players behind me."

In early September 1952, Rockford, a four-time Shaughnessy champion, met defending champion South Bend in the best-of-five final round of the playoffs. The Blue Sox remained in high spirits, despite being reduced to twelve players after five team members walked out in support of Shorty Pryer, who was suspended by manager Karl Winsch the previous weekend. Five see-saw contests — one was replayed due to Winsch's successful protest — left the contenders tied at two wins, and the teams rode their respective buses to Illinois on Thursday, September 11, for the clincher.

In perhaps the greatest game of the season, the Peaches hosted the Blue Sox at Read Park in Freeport, Illinois, thirty miles west of Rockford, because Rockford's Beyer Stadium was being used for high school football. The Blue Sox, moved by enthusiasm and desire and determined to prove themselves, came through with an inspired effort worthy of Hollywood. The teams entertained 2,200 fans in a ballpark set up for men's baseball, and South Bend, led by Jean Faut, who pitched and also slammed two triples as part of the twelve-hit attack, captured a winner-take-all 6–3 triumph. Jette (Vincent) Mooney was safe on an error in the first inning, and Joyce (Hill) Westerman doubled her home. Visiting South Bend took a big lead with a three-run burst in the third, starting with Betty Wagoner's base hit, an error, and Mooney's RBI single. Jo Lenard singled, Westerman hit into a force play, and Faut, connecting for her greatest hit, boomed a two-run triple to left center for a 4–0 lead. The Peaches replied with a run in the fourth on a single, a walk, and an error, cutting the lead to 4–1.

In the sixth, Faut slammed another triple. Her blast could have been a home run, but Jean was so tired after rounding third base that she stopped, walked back, and sat down on the bag. Out of Rockford's dugout the Blue Sox could hear Rose Gacioch's comment, "My God, that girl is tired!"⁵⁵

The memorable season was all but over. Moments later, Gertie Dunn scored Faut with a grounder, and South Bend added an insurance run in the seventh for a 6–1 lead. In a fitting finish, all nine of the Blue Sox hit safely, and longtime stars Wagoner, Lenard, and Faut collected two hits each. Rockford used Mickey Jinright and Marie Mansfield on the mound, but not even two runs in the ninth could make any difference. After a photographer captured the timeless moment showing the league's Earl McCammon making the trophy presentation to Faut on behalf of her team, the twelve women headed for the locker room, the showers, and the happy trip home.[56]

1953: The AGBL and the six remaining franchises faced financial struggles throughout the 1953 season. Several officials calculated a home gate of 1,000 per night was needed, but seldom did teams reach that goal. Fewer and fewer fans were coming out to see girls' baseball. Also, the league made minor adjustments on the field. The ten-inch ball, manufactured by the DeBeer Company and adopted in mid–1949, was used again, but DeBeer's was working on making it "a little harder and a little faster."[57] As a result, the pitching distance was increased one foot to 56 feet, and base paths were lengthened from 72 to 75 feet.[58]

In other changes, McCammon was named commissioner for 1953. Ball clubs were allowed to contract with sixteen or seventeen players, but the salary limit again was $5,400 per month for sixteen players, or $5,700 for seventeen. The league continued the player draft, but thus far the draft had proven inadequate to attract enough new talent. Last but not least, the salary maximum again meant no raises for veterans, so teams were mainly signing rookies or second-year players with less skill and experience. The loop was facing a talent drain.[59] Since there were no girls' minor leagues, the biggest need for success on the diamond was the developmental tours of 1949 and 1950. Instead, the teams' boards, facing deficits, figured such innovations were too costly.

During the 1950s, the girls who left after each season told a similar story. Kalamazoo star Doris Sams, Player of the Year in 1947 and 1949, led the loop in homers with 12 in 1952, but in 1953, Sammye had to overcome an off-season illness. She returned in July and batted .312, but belted only two homers (one in the playoffs). Sams explained that she retired following the 1953 season partly because she was offered a job as a computer operator with the Knoxville Utilities Board. She added, "I had a feeling that league wouldn't go much longer. The league was going down by 1953. You could see it. It was getting to be the same old teams, over and over, and the same old players. It was time to leave." Wimp Baumgartner recollected, "In the fall of 1953, I started college, because I knew I was going to go sooner or later, so I might as well get started, because I knew the league was only going to have maybe another year."

Jean Faut was voted the league's Player of the Year in 1953. The South Bend standout was voted the same honor in 1951, and she missed by one vote of repeating in 1952. Faut was the heart of the Blue Sox, and she would have been an exceptional athlete in any era. She also helped her teammates. Explained Wimp Baumgartner, "I want to say about Jean Faut that when I was catching her, she did more to help me and the other pitchers than the manager. Jean always told you how to do it better in a nice way, but she got her point across. Jean was a terrific person."[60] In fact, Faut capped her career by hurling her second perfect game, a 4–0 victory over Kalamazoo on September 3, 1953. The ace right-hander lost the final game she hurled, but during her remarkable nine-year career, she pitched two no-hitters, two perfect games, and fashioned a 140–64 record with a sterling 1.23 ERA in 235 games.

In a development soon well-known to the players, the league suffered a life-threatening loss when Muskegon became an "Orphan" traveling team on Thursday, August 6, after the Belles beat the visiting Lassies, 6–2. The franchise reverted to the circuit because the team could no longer pay its bills or the players' salaries. The Belles performed well enough early in the season. Joe Cooper's squad of rookies and veterans entertained 800 fans on opening night at Marsh Field, but they attracted as many as 1,000 fans only twice that summer.[61] In the end, the league spent $8,600 to carry the Belles through the remainder of the team's away games, because the alternative was a five-team league for the rest of 1953.[62]

1954: After Muskegon went broke, local and circuit officials struggled through the following winter trying to find new financial resources and a sixth city in which to relocate the failed Belles. By the time the league's final season began, President Dwight Eisenhower was serving his second year in the White House, the Korean War had been followed by a troubled armistice abroad and an economic contraction at home, television was dominating the national and local market for family entertainment, and declining attendance suggested that professional baseball was slipping in popularity.[63] Fewer women showed interest in pro baseball, and players and fans wondered if the league was dying. "By this time," observed Lois Browne, "only a handful of All-American veterans remained," including longtime stars such as Rockford's Dottie Key, Grand Rapids' Gabby Ziegler, and Fort Wayne's Dottie Schroeder. "Most of their former teammates were long gone," concluded Browne, "back to factories, farms, and families."[64]

The AGBL reflected the decline of minor league baseball, but television was booming because many people enjoyed seeing programs such as *The Milton Berle Show*, *I Love Lucy*, *The Lone Ranger*, and many other shows they could watch in the comfort of their homes. Also, America's biggest social trend in the 1950s was the moving of families to the rapidly-growing suburbs, meaning the local professional ballpark was no longer a few blocks away for most fans. Further, many minor league parks—AGBL fields were no exception—had been built during the Great Depression. Most of these facilities needed improvements. However, ball clubs lacked the funds for upgrades, and local governments set aside little money for what used to be seen as civic gathering places.[65]

The biggest sign of decline for the circuit was that only five teams found the funds and the players to compete in 1954, and Rockford only survived due to financial backing by its fans' organization. The Blue Sox and the Peaches, the only two teams left from the league's inaugural season of 1943, were joined by the Fort Wayne Daisies, the Grand Rapids Chicks, and the Kalamazoo Lassies. Regardless, after no backers were found to restart the Belles, Fort Wayne's Harold Van Orman, the loop's president, proposed the five-team league as a last-ditch alternative to dropping girls' baseball. All five teams approved the concept on April 10, 1954.[66]

The league was on life support. For example, circuit personnel held another three-day "rookie school" before spring training, but only 27 candidates tried out, down from 46 in 1953.[67] Spring training, an important part of the league's glory years during the 1940s, all but disappeared in 1954. The teams conducted fielding and hitting practices, worked on bunting, hit-and-run plays, and held strategy meetings, all at their own ballparks.

By June, when the schedule was causing teams to play fewer games in a series and travel more in order to play at least two three-team double-headers each week, league officials voted for changes to go into effect on July 1. First, the circuit discarded the 10-inch ball and adopted a regulation baseball. Second, adopting the even livelier ball meant making on-field changes. The pitching distance was lengthened from the current 56 feet to 60 feet, half a foot short of the length used in major league baseball, and the base paths were increased from the current 75 feet to 85 feet, five feet short of the dimensions for baseball.[68]

Initially a start-up league based on underhand pitching, a 12-inch softball, a 40-foot mound distance, and 65-foot base paths, the pioneering All-American Girls Soft Ball League of 1943 had evolved by increments into the near-regulation American Girls Baseball League of 1954.

However, attendance had peaked in 1948, and paid admissions were declining almost yearly. By 1954, circuit and team officials, looking at growing deficits, reduced each team's salary maximum from $5,400 to $4,400 per month, with no player to earn more than $400 monthly. Lacking enough new talent, they dropped the rookie rule.[69] The circuit's leaders, overlooking the social factors working against women deciding to play pro ball, believed technical changes to the game would resurrect fan interest. Instead, the latest changes overlooked the real strength of the girls' league: the natural appeal of females playing baseball. The all-important fan sympathy was tied to the players' *sex*, as Chet Grant explained, not to their speed, strength, or power.[70]

On Thursday, July 1, after one night to practice with the new baseball and with Playland Park set up with the new diamond dimensions, South Bend, for example, entered the circuit's "home run era" by splitting a three-team twin bill. In the opener against Grand Rapids, entertaining the largest crowd since opening night, an estimated 1,200 fans, the Blue Sox produced a twelve-hit barrage and cruised behind Dolly Vanderlip's seven-hit hurling to a 5–2 victory. Betty Wagoner hit a two-run single in the first inning for a 2–0 lead, but the Chicks' Marilyn Jenkins tied the game in the second with a two-run blast, the first home run at Playland with the regulation baseball. The Blue Sox took the lead with two runs in the fifth on Wagoner's RBI double and Gertie Dunn's fly ball. In the nightcap against Fort Wayne, South Bend's Janet Rumsey failed to stop the Daisies' Betty Foss, who slugged a two-run homer in the third, or Katie Horstman, who hit a solo shot in the fifth. The Daisies' Pinky Leduc allowed only five hits, and the Blue Sox lost, 4–1. The new horsehide led to more extra-base hits, but most who saw the games agreed the hard-hit balls caused the infielders more trouble with grounders.[71]

Still, the long ball became a major feature of most games, and fortunately for South Bend, Wilma Briggs, traded from the Daisies to the Blue Sox in 1954, swung a big bat. A left-handed hitting outfielder, Wilma, who grew up playing baseball in East Greenwich, Rhode Island, broke into the league with Fort Wayne in 1948 and averaged .258 over her seven-year career. Briggs led the loop in home runs in 1953, slamming the 10-inch ball for nine four-baggers. In 1954, she slugged 25 homers, third behind the league's leader, Jo Weaver, who, averaging an all-time league record .429, set another new mark with 29 home runs. Also, Briggs delivered 73 RBI, third to Fort Wayne's Jean Geissinger with 91 and Jo Weaver with 87.[72]

Most observers knew money was short and talent was thin. "The dearth of players was amply illustrated by the fact," observed Fort Wayne sports editor Bob Reed, "that pitchers and catchers were playing in the outfield and elsewhere."[73] The signs of demise were evident to most players. "I suppose, even though I didn't want to believe the league would end," observed Sue Kidd, "I could see it coming. "Most of the players suspected that the 1954 season would be our last one," recounted Mary (Froning) O'Meara. "Some said, 'I guess I'll go back to college and get some education,' and a lot of them did. Others, like me, had to look for a job." Katie Horstman observed, "My baseball dream came true, and that's all I wanted. But the league ended after the 1954 season, and I was devastated." Every season ends, and sooner or later for all ballplayers, the cheering stops. But after the glory fades, players still retell their favorite tales of yesteryear.

In the end, Kalamazoo won the league's last crown, starting with the defeat of South Bend in the best-of-three semifinal round. In the other semifinals, Fort Wayne defeated third place Grand Rapids, but in unusual fashion. On Saturday night, the Chicks played the game under protest but beat the Daisies, 8–7. After that, Grand Rapids forfeited, at the insistence of manager Woody English, both on Sunday night and again on Monday. After winning on Saturday, English refused to let his team play again, because he objected to the league permitting the Daisies to replace their injured catcher with Rockford's star receiver, Ruth Richard.[74] In any event, Kalamazoo outlasted Fort Wayne in five games, and June Peppas helped pitch and hit the Lassies to the circuit's final Shaughnessy Championship.[75]

Notes

1. Subsequent quotes taken from interviews published in this book are not cited in the following notes.
2. Merrie Fidler, *The Origins and History of the All-American Girls Professional Baseball League* (Jefferson, NC: McFarland, 2006), p. 71.
3. Pepper Paire Davis, *Dirt in the Skirt* (Bloomington, IN: AuthorHouse, 2009), p. 105.
4. The AAGPBL web site has a section summarizing the various changes in the game on the field and the rules as the league evolved from modified fast-pitch softball to baseball. See: http://www.aagpbl.org/league/rules.cfm.
5. "Chicks Capture Pro Girls' Title," *South Bend Tribune* (hereafter cited as SBT), September 18, 1944.
6. "Girls' Baseball: A Feminine Midwest League Opens Its Third Professional Season," *Life*, June 4, 1945, pp. 63–66.
7. "Belles Drew 70,357 ... Muskegon and Peoria May Join to Make 8-Team Loop in 1946," *Racine Journal-Times*, September 13, 1945.
8. Dottie Schroeder to Carolyn Odell, January 6, 1946, Odell Letters, AAGPBL Files, Center for History (hereafter cited as CFH), South Bend, IN.
9. Fidler, *Origins and History of the AAGPBL*, p. 137.
10. Letter from Betsy Jochum, October 6, 2009.
11. The diamond dimensions were listed in *Official Girls' Baseball Rules/Adopted by the All-American Girls Baseball League*, pp. 1–3, copy in AAGPBL Files, CFH, and noted in "Jim Costin Says," SBT, August 2, 1946. The men's softball distances were 60-foot base paths and the women's base paths were 70 feet. Both used the same 43 mound distance, but the women's baseball was now 11 inches in circumference and the men's softball was 12 inches.
12. "Evolution of the Ball Size Used in All American Girls Base Ball League from 1943 to 1949, and Diamond Changes," Dailey Notebooks, volume 1, p. 32v, AAGPBL Files, Joyce Sports Collection, Hesburgh Libraries of the University of Notre Dame.
13. See Carey, "All American Girls Baseball League" [n.p.]. Also, Carey confirmed the distances and ball size explained by Costin in note 11 (above), including the 70-foot base paths.
14. Anna May Hutchison, Information Sheet, n.d., copy in AAGPBL Files, CFH.
15. Interview with Jean Faut, October 17, 2009.
16. Pauline Maier, et al. *Inventing America: A History of the United States* (New York: W.W. Norton, 2nd ed., 2006), pp. pp. 791–804.
17. See *Official Girls' Baseball Rules/Adopted by AAGPBL*, pp. 1–3, copy in AAGPBL Files, CFH.
18. See *Fort Wayne Daisies: 1947 Year Book* (Fort Wayne, IN: Wayne Paper Box & Printing Corp., 1947), p. 5, copy in Faut Collection at Winthrop University's Dacus Library.
19. "All-American Girls Baseball League" in *Major League Baseball: 1948* (New York: Dell, 1948), pp. 128 ff.
20. Batting and pitching records are taken from official figures provided by the Howe News Bureau, copy in AAGPBL Files, CFH.
21. Susan E. Johnson, *When Women Played Hardball* (Seattle: Seal Press, 1994), p. 96.
22. Fidler, *Origins and History of the AAGPBL*, pp. 71–72.
23. Dan Cobian, "Women in Baseball: Latinas in the All-American Girls Professional Baseball League," http://www.chicla.wisc.edu/publications/workingpapers/DanCobian.html.
24. Sue Macy, *A Whole New Ball Game: The Story of the All-American Girls Professional Baseball League* (New York: Henry Holt, 1993), pp. 52–54; and interview with Jean Faut, October 17, 2009.
25. *Major League Baseball: 1949*, pp. 2–3.
26. "Phyllis Koehn — Kenosha Comets," in AAGPBL Newsletter, *Touching Bases*, May 2001, p. 35, copy in Koehn File, AAGPBL Files, National Baseball Hall of Fame Library (hereafter cited as BB HOF), Cooperstown, NY.
27. Interview with Jean Faut, October 31, 2009.
28. Fidler, *Origins and History of the AAGPBL*, pp. 71–73; and Lois Browne, *Girls of Summer* (New York: HarperCollins, 1993), pp. 152–153.

29. "Cuban Girls Bid for Jobs in Pro Loop," SBT, April 8, 1948.
30. Message from Dolly (Brumfield) White, January 7, 2010.
31. Mirta Marrero was interviewed for a story with the title, "Language Barrier Made Playing Difficult at First," in *Palm Beach Post*, September 12, 2003.
32. Dailey to Meyerhoff, November 18, 1947, typescript in Dailey Notebooks, volume 2, p. 20.
33. Bill Fay, "Belles of the Ball Game," *Collier's*, August 13, 1949, p. 44.
34. Fidler, *Origins and History of the AAGPBL*, p. 71.
35. Barbara Gregorich, *Women at Play: The Story of Women in Baseball* (New York: Harcourt Brace, 1993), pp. 84–85.
36. Browne, *Girls of Summer*, pp. 177–182; and Fidler, *Origins and History of the AAGPBL*, pp. 77–79.
37. Adie Suehsdorf, "Sluggers in Skirts," *Los Angeles Times*, July 31, 1949.
38. Fidler, *Origins and History of the AAGPBL*, pp. 83–85.
39. David Halberstam, *The Fifties* (New York: Fawcett, 1993), pp. 59–77.
40. For a discussion of changes in postwar America, see Maier, et al., *Inventing America*, pp. 790–816, and Eugenia Kaledin, *Daily Life in the United States, 1940–1959: Shifting Worlds* (Westport, CT: Greenwood, 2000), pp. 20–22.
41. John Thorn, et al., *Total Baseball* (Wilmington, DE: Sports Media Publishing, 8th ed., 2004), pp. 2417–2422.
42. Lloyd Johnson and Miles Wolff, eds., *The Encyclopedia of Minor League Baseball* (Durham, NC: Baseball America, Inc., 2nd ed., 1997), p. 347.
43. Johnson, *When Women Played Hardball*, p. xxiv.
44. Morris Markey, "Hey Ma, You're Out," *McCall's*, September 1950, pp. 40, 41, 68, 74, 77, 80.
45. Journal entry, Dailey Notebooks, volume 5, p. 14.
46. "American Girls Baseball League Rules," February 22, 1951, Dailey Notebooks, volume 5, pp. 2–2v.
47. South Bend's insignia was a white circle representing a baseball with the blue letters saying "So. Bend" on the top half of the ball and "Blue Sox" on the bottom part, and a pair of red baseball seams to complete the design.
48. "Brief Historical Summary of the South Bend Blue Sox," Dailey Notebooks, volume 4, pp. 2–3.
49. See Fidler, *Origins and History of the AAGPBL*, pp. 83–85, 125–129.
50. "Immediate Release," November 21, 1950, Dailey Notebooks, volume 3, pp. 136v–137.
51. Sox Manager Karl Winsch Credits Team Spirit in "On the Level," SBT, September 18, 1951.
52. "Attendance of the South Bend Club for Entire Nine Years: 1943 to & Including 1951," Dailey Notebooks, volume 7, pp. 3, 6, 11–11v.
53. Journal entry, July 18, 1952, Dailey Notebooks, volume 7, p. 140v.
54. "According to Doyle," SBT, May 14, 1952.
55. Interview with Jean Faut, August 9, 1995.
56. "Blue Sox Defeat Peaches, 6 to 3, for Title," *Freeport Journal-Standard*, September 12, 1952.
57. AGBL Minutes, February 8, 1953, Dailey Notebooks, volume 9, pp. 139–140.
58. AGBL Minutes, January 20, 1953, Dailey Notebooks, volume 9, pp. 133–138.
59. Fidler, *Origins and History of the AAGPBL*, pp. 125–131.
60. Ibid.
61. "Muskegon Belles Franchise Turned Back to Girls League," *Muskegon Chronicle*, August 8, 1953.
62. "Report on League Status," AGBL Minutes, September 12, 1953, Dailey Notebooks, volume 9, p. 164.
63. John Thorn, Phil Birnbaum, and Bill Deane, eds., *Total Baseball: The Ultimate Baseball Encyclopedia* (Wilmington, DE: Sports Media Publishing, 8th ed., 2004), pp. 2417–2422.
64. Browne, *Girls of Summer*, pp. 189–190.
65. Johnson and Wolff, *Encyclopedia of Minor League Baseball*, p. 411.
66. AGBL Minutes, April 10, 1954, Dailey Notebooks, volume 9, pp. 172–173.
67. "Tryout School Report — Drawing of Rookies," AGBL Minutes, May 16, 1954, Dailey Notebooks, volume 9, pp. 175–175v.
68. "Girls' League Votes to Use Regulation 9-Inch Ball," SBT, June 11, 1954.
69. AGBL Minutes, April 10, 1954, Dailey Notebooks, volume 9, pp. 172–173.
70. Chet Grant, "Girls' Baseball," SBT's *Sunday Magazine*, August 15, 1954, pp. 8–10.
71. "Blue Sox Split Pair as Home Run Era Dawns," SBT, July 2, 1954.
72. Interview with Wilma Briggs, January 28, 2011.
73. The Girls League Situation in Bob Reed's "Sports Roundup," *Fort Wayne Journal-Gazette*, September 1, 1954.
74. "Ft. Wayne 'Wins' Again on Forfeit," SBT, August 31, 1954.
75. "Lassies Whip Ft. Wayne in Playoff Series," SBT, September 7, 1954.

Part I: The Early Years, 1943–1945

Annastasia "Stash" Batikis
Racine, 1945
Interviewed at the home of Joyce (Hill) Westerman in Kenosha, Wisconsin, on July 26, 2011.

Born: 1927
Height: 4'11"
Weight: 125
Positions: Utility, OF
Batted: L
Threw: L
Career Batting Average: .000 for 11 at-bats in 5 games (league statistics were incomplete for players who appeared in less than ten games)

Annastasia, or Ann, or "Stash," Batikis, was the only daughter of Steve and Mary Batikis, who were Greek immigrants. Along with brothers John and Alex, she was raised in Racine, Wisconsin. She spent the rest of her life in the Belle City of the Lakes, located 30 miles south of Milwaukee. Stash went through the Racine school system from kindergarten until she graduated from Washington Park High in 1945. She was always the shortest girl in the neighborhood, but that never bothered her. She grew up playing ball with boys, and she finally settled on throwing and batting left-handed. By the time the teenager reached Park High, she was playing fast-pitch softball in a local recreation league with women. In 1943, when the Belles of the All-American League came to town, Stash often went with friends to see their games at Horlick Field. In the spring of 1945, one year after her mother passed away, the league held tryouts in Racine. The 4'11" Stash and Joyce Hill, from Kenosha, were the only two out of fifty girls who made the cut. A few days later, they were invited to the league's spring camp on the north side of Chicago.

Stash, an energetic, enthusiastic, and determined young woman, needed baseball shoes and a glove. Her father took her to a shoe repair shop, and the owner attached spikes to an old pair of bowling shoes. A buddy from high school gave Stash an old right-handed glove, and she took some padding out of the middle three fingers so it would fit on her right hand, since she threw left-handed. Now she had the spikes and glove needed to make the league, and she still owns them. When the spring camp ended, she found her name on Racine's 16-person roster. Unlike the other players who roomed with families, Stash lived at home, where she was keeping house for her widowed father, and her brothers were in the service. The rookie signed for $50 a week, more than her father earned at Racine's Case Company.

Batikis didn't play much in her only AAGPBL season, because Racine had a set lineup. She did play a few games in center field before Clara Schillace, a teacher, arrived after the school year ended in Chicago. For the rest of the season, Stash practiced every day, cheered

Annastasia "Ann" Batikis — A utility player for Racine in 1945, Batikis appears in an informal team picture taken during spring training in 1945. After showering and changing, the players were asked to put on their uniform again, but most wore comfortable shoes. Pictured in the front row (left to right) are Batikis, Irene "Tuffy" Hickson, and Betty Emry. Second row: Joanne Winter, Lou Stone, manager Charles Stis, Anna May Hutchison, and Ellie Dapkus. Back row: Chaperone Ruth Peterson, Mary Nesbitt, Agnes Zurkowski, Jane Jacobs, Marnie Danhauser, and Sophie Kurys (courtesy Ann Batikis).

on her team, and traveled with the Belles, waiting for the opportunity that never came. While official statistics are incomplete for those who played less than ten games, available records indicate she stepped to the plate 11 times, but didn't hit safely. Also, Lou (Stone) Richards, a shortstop, roomed for a few weeks at the Batikis home, and Betty Emry, an infielder, lived there later in the season. Because of Racine's strong team (Racine won the league's playoff championship in 1946), Stash was not asked to return for another season. However, the Belles told her she could be called up in case of an injury, the girls treated her like a teammate, and she saw many of the home games at Horlick.

Batikis went on to earn bachelor's and master's degrees at La Crosse State College, now the University of Wisconsin at La Crosse, and she taught health and physical education for 35 years in the Racine Public Schools. Later, Stash enjoyed the AAGPBL reunions, and she and other players frequently spoke to audiences ranging from school children to adults about their participation in the historic All-American League. Ann Batikis' professional career was short, but the baseball dream never really dies, so in her mind, she will always be a Belle.

JS: How do you say your name?
 Batikis: Annastasia "Stash" Batikis [Ba-teek-us].

Tell me about your background and how you got interested in playing ball and in the league.

I started playing ball on the playground when I was in the third grade in Racine. Our playground wasn't real big, so the only ball that we were allowed to use at that time was a 14-inch softball. There wasn't enough activity playing with the girls, so I played with the boys.

I went through the Racine school system from kindergarten through high school, and I graduated from Washington Park High School in 1945. The boys taught me how to play, and some of them were right-handed and some were left-handed. I didn't know which hand to use, but finally I felt comfortable batting and throwing left-handed, even though I write and eat right-handed. There wasn't any other sport for girls to play at that time. I really liked playing ball, and I followed the boys' team at elementary school. They let me play for one game, and having a girl on a boys' team was unheard of at that time.

When I got into junior high school, we started playing with the 12-inch ball. By the ninth grade, I was playing well enough for some of the girls that played on a city team to ask me to play for them. Racine was an industrial town and several of the factories had fast-pitch teams, and I ended up playing with several different teams. The city recreation department sponsored the games, and they used the 12-inch softball.

When I was in high school from 1943 through 1945, the All-American League started, and those of us playing in the recreation league would go out to the games to watch those girls play. In 1944, I was out to Horlick Field watching the Belles, and I was just in awe of how well those girls played ball. I thought, "It would be wonderful if I could get on a team like that." I suppose it's the same feeling boys had when they dreamed of being major leaguers.

In 1945, the spring of my senior year, the league held tryouts at Horlick Field. There were about fifty of us who tried out that day. I didn't know Joyce Hill at that time, but she was at the tryout. She and I were the only two that made the cut. Afterward, I got a letter saying they wanted me to go to spring training, which was held at Waveland Park on the north side of Chicago.

I was told that I needed to have a glove and spikes. My dad took me to a shoe repair store in downtown Racine. The man there found an old pair of bowling shoes, and he put an extra-hard sole and spikes on them, so that I had a pair of spikes. A boy in my high school class gave me one of his old gloves, but he was right-handed. So he helped me take some of the padding out of the middle three fingers, and also the outside two fingers. He oiled it, and we played catch for quite a while, so I could learn to wear a glove on the "wrong" hand. I still have that glove, and I still have those shoes, and they worked for me! *[She laughs.]*

Even though I was making money when I played for the Belles, I got so used to playing with those shoes and that glove that I didn't buy new ones.

What about your parents?

My father's name was Steve Batikis, and my mother's name was Mary. She passed away in 1944 when I was a junior in high school. Dad came over to this country from Greece during the First World War. He joined the U.S. Army here to get away from the Turks, who had invaded Constantinople, which is now Istanbul. After the war, he went home and brought my mother here. I had two brothers, John and Alex.

My brothers didn't know that I was playing ball until they saw my picture in a 1945 issue of *Life Magazine.* They took pictures during spring training. John was serving in the Army Air Force in the China-Burma-India Theater, and one of the guys got a "care" package from home, and his mom sent him the magazine. He was reading it, and he said to my brother, "Here's a girl in this magazine that's got the same last name that you have." John looked at it and said, "That's my sister!" That's how he found out I was playing pro ball. Alex was serving in the Navy at Pearl Harbor, and I was able to write to him more.

At spring training, we weren't assigned to any particular team. But at the end, just like in the movie, *A League of Their Own*, I was reading the roster and found I was assigned to my home town team, Racine. I watched those gals for two years, and now I was going to be able to play with them. That was so neat, because I really thought a lot of the Belles.

Most of those girls were on Racine's team in 1943 when they won the league's first playoff championship. I got to play with Hutch [Anna May Hutchison], Choo-Choo [Irene Hickson], Mary Nesbitt Crews Wisham, and Maddy English, who played third base. Sophie Kurys, who played second base, was the one who taught me how to hook slide. Marnie Danhauser played first base, Edie Perlick played left field, and Eleanor Dapkus was in right field.

I played in center field early in the season, until Claire Schillace joined us. She was still teaching school when the season began, but she was the center fielder. I got to play in the games during spring training, and I got to play when we were on the road early in the season.

It seems like they were looking for a shortstop. Lou (Stone) Richards played shortstop, and she lived for a while at our house. Betty Emry stayed at our house for a little while, but I think they wanted to be in a house where there were more girls, so Lou and Betty didn't live with us for the whole season.

I lived at home and took care of the house for my dad. The boys were in service in the Pacific, and my mom had passed away. Like I said, that was my senior year in school. The school let me take my final exams early. After I made the Belles, they let me come back and graduate with my class in June of 1945.

I always thought that playing for Racine was like a dream come true. In the city league, I played center field and deep short, and I even pitched a little. But I knew my pitching wasn't good enough to try out at that position for the Belles. I just played that one season. Charlie Stis was our manager, and our chaperone was Ruth Peterson. By mid-season, the team had Leo Murphy for the manager and Mildred "Willie" Wilson for chaperone.

The team was looking for a shortstop. Later, after Lou Stone got traded, Racine had people like Pepper Paire and Betty Trezza playing shortstop. The outfield remained the same for a long time, and so did the infield, except at shortstop. I think that's one reason I didn't get to go back in 1946. The teams could only have fifteen or sixteen players, and Racine had a set lineup everywhere but at shortstop and pitcher, and I couldn't play either position.

They told me it would be easier to let me go than any of the others because I lived in Racine, and they could call me back if they needed me. But they let me into the games for free. I don't know what to call it. I was there, and people treated me like I was a player, but I wasn't in uniform after 1945. I got to know people like Audrey Wagner in Kenosha, and Shirley Jameson, also in Kenosha. Shirley was short, like me, so I wanted to know her. Connie Wisniewski became a friend, and she was quite a player. Dottie Collins was another friend, and Anna Hutchison was really very nice to me. Hutch was a catcher in 1945, and she became a pitcher later — and a real good one, too.

In early 1945, I took the first empty locker I could find in the locker room. Somebody came in (I don't remember who) and said, "Who's in my locker?"

I said, "I took it because it was empty." She said, "Well, get out of there!" I was too shocked to know who said it to me, but I didn't go back to that locker again. *[She laughs.]*

I remember playing Kenosha in the fog. The ballpark was down by Lake Michigan, and when the fog came in, you couldn't see the players. When a ball was hit, they'd come running through the fog!

Can you talk about playing at Horlick Field in Racine?

At the time the whole field was a ball diamond. It remained a ball field all of the time the league existed. But now, even though it's still Horlick Field, they divided it into two fields. At one end, they play softball and baseball. The other end is a football field.

The same score board is still out there at Horlick Field, and the big flag pole in center field is still there. The locker rooms have been changed to fit both football and softball teams. We used to have Junior Belles, but that team didn't last long. Now they have a girls' softball team called the Racine Belles, and they travel all over the place.

We played at some of the Army and Navy bases in 1945, before the regular season started. I remember we played at the Great Lakes Naval Station and at Fort Sheridan. I have a team picture of the Belles at Savanna Ordnance, and all three bases are in northern Illinois. Soldiers and sailors would take leave and ride the local train to Chicago, or Racine, or Kenosha, or Milwaukee.

When I played, we also traveled by train, the North Shore Elevated, or El. It ran from Milwaukee to Racine to Kenosha and to Chicago, and we took another train in Chicago to South Bend or to Rockford. We had another little train system called the Interurban, and it was more like a streetcar, but it ran from Milwaukee to Racine and to Kenosha.

So the whole time you played, you lived at home, and girls like Lou Stone and Betty Emry stayed with you for a few weeks?

Yes, that's right. Sophie Kurys and Maddy English lived about four blocks away from our house, close to the Johnson Wax Building. About two more blocks away, there was an elementary school with a house next to it, several girls lived there, and Edie Perlick was one of them. There were also some girls who lived on the north side of town, closer to Horlick Field. But they all lived in private homes. That's how we lived when I played in 1945. You became part of the family.

You called Irene Hickson "Choo-Choo."

Irene came from Chattanooga, like the "Chattanooga Choo Choo." You didn't call her "Tuffy" to her face. You may not know this, but she was a boxer. She did some boxing, and that's why they called her Tuffy.

I believe you played mainly night games in 1945. What do you remember about the games?

We had several games that went many, many innings, and they were called off because of the 11:30 P.M. curfew. But another reason for ending games at 11:30 was the buses ran until midnight. You had to get the people home, and with gas rationing, most people rode buses to the ball games. Also, we had a railroad track that ran outside center field, and you'd see people sitting on box cars outside the field and watching our games. *[She laughs.]*

Do you have favorite memories? I know you talk to school and other groups.

We talk to school kids about the movie, *A League of Their Own*, because they can relate to that. You can't talk to little kids about the World War, because they don't know about that. Joyce Westerman and I also talk to retired teachers, Kiwanis groups, Rotary groups, church groups, college students — they can relate to the World War years.

To the older groups, I talk about being a rookie making $50 a week in 1945, and that was more than my dad made working at Case Company. They made tractors and also war equipment. You have to talk about things they can relate to in their lives.

It sounds like the league made an impact on your life.

The league did make an impact on my life. I didn't think my dad would let me play, being from a Greek family and my mom not being alive and me taking care of him. In a typical Greek home of our era, a girl almost had to have a chaperone there. The teams had chaperones, so my dad said, "I'll let you go." But I took care of the house and I took care of my dad.

People always ask, "Could you hear the crowd? Could you hear the people in the stands when you were up to bat?"

I really couldn't, except for one man, and he was the father of one of my girl friends in high school. Every time I came up to bat, he would yell out, "Get off of your knees," or, "Are you standing in a hole?" He was referring to me being 4'11" tall. He'd say, "Hit that ball!" That was the only thing I could hear clearly. His voice really stuck out!

A lot of the girls that I played ball with before I got into the league, and a lot of the girls in my high school class would come out to the games. So we had a nice following.

The people in Racine really backed their team. Those gals who lived in the private homes really became part of the families. I was able to save almost all of my money, because I was living at home. That $50 a week was a lot of money to me.

In later years, I've really enjoyed going to the AAGPBL Reunions and renewing acquaintances, but it's kind of hard when you keep reading about more of the girls passing away.

One of the other things that happened since we were put into the Hall of Fame at Cooperstown is that others have noticed us. One Greek man was writing a book about Greek men in baseball. He did research at Cooperstown, and he found out about me. He contacted me, and he included me in his book about Greek men in baseball because I played pro ball. That was nice.

Later, I taught junior high health and physical education for thirty-five years. I earned my bachelor's degree at La Crosse State College in Wisconsin, and I also got the master's there. Now it's called University of Wisconsin at La Crosse.

Later, when I taught junior high, I also substituted in Science, Home Economics, and Wood Working. I started in Manitowoc, and the rest of the time I taught in Racine at Franklin Junior High — where I went to elementary and junior high — and at Mitchell Junior High.

But when I taught the softball unit, the kids would say, "You throw so hard." I would say, "I played pro ball." They would look at me, and especially the boys wouldn't believe me. After the movie was made, and by that time I was retired, some of those young people — who weren't kids any more — would say, "We believe you now, coach!"

One of the other things I think is neat is so many of the former players have schools and streets named after them, and so many of us are in halls or walls of fame at colleges and ballparks. We have such varied backgrounds. There were teachers and farm girls and secretaries and models and nuns, and we sure did open the doors for the gals of today.

DOTTIE (WILTSE) COLLINS
Minneapolis, 1944; Fort Wayne, 1945–1948, 1950
Interviewed on May 31, 1997.

Born: 1923
Deceased: 2008
Height: 5'7"
Weight: 125
Positions: P
Batted: R
Threw: R
Career Batting Average: .099 in six seasons
Lifetime Pitching Record: 117–76 with 1.83 ERA
Won 20 or More Games: 1944, 1945, 1946, 1947
Career Strikeouts: 1,205

Dottie (Wiltse) Collins — The standout pitcher with Minneapolis in 1944 and, after the franchise moved, with Fort Wayne from 1945 to 1948 and again in 1950. Married in 1946, Collins, known as the "Strikeout Queen," totaled 1,205 strikeouts over her stellar six-year career (courtesy Patricia Collins).

Dottie (Wiltse) Collins (1923–2008), one of the first California girls to grace the All-American League in 1944, not only enjoyed a stellar six-year pitching career but also became one of the circuit's enduring stars and role models. Born and raised in Inglewood, California, Dottie, thanks to the influence of her father, Dan Wiltse, thrived on fast-pitch softball. During an important game in 1936, when the starting pitcher of the Mark C. Bloome team didn't have her stuff, the manager called on Dottie, the bat girl, to pitch. Backed by good hitting, the twelve-year-old won her first-ever game and Bloome's team took the *Los Angeles Examiner* Championship. Wiltse, who continued to pitch softball, graduated from Inglewood High in 1941. She worked for the Payne Furnace Company, and when World War II erupted, she moved to Payne's factory and made airplane parts. The war introduced blackouts and ended night games in California, but in the Midwest by 1943, Philip Wrigley and his associates had launched the All-American League. In 1944, Bill Allington, once Dottie's manager in California, was contacted by the league, and he persuaded five

California girls to try out. Wiltse and several of her friends were allocated to the expansion Minneapolis Millerettes, and while she excelled at pitching, the Millerettes drew too few fans, lost the use of Nicollet Park by mid-season, and became an "Orphan" traveling team.

In 1945, the franchise moved to Fort Wayne, and Wiltse, with her Hollywood attractiveness, warm personality, and nice assortment of pitches, still led the Daisies' staff. After winning 20 of her last-place team's 45 victories in 1944, Wiltse produced three stellar seasons, winning 29, 22, and 20 times while striking out 293, 294, and 244, respectively, in 1945, 1946, and 1947. Known as the "Strikeout Queen," the right-hander relied on a wicked curveball. She long remembered pitching and winning both ends of a double-header against the Rockford Peaches on August 19, 1945, because, she observed, it was always tough to beat Bill Allington's team, and because she met her future husband, Harvey Collins, after the twin bill. They were married on March 10, 1946. Dottie continued her stellar pitching, and Harvey often took a carload of friends to see the Daisies play away games. Three seasons later, Dottie left the team on August 1, 1948, because she was five months pregnant. Patricia was born that fall, and Daniel was born in 1954. Dottie sat out the 1949 season, and she retired from the game after posting a 13–8 mark in 1950.

Dottie and Harvey Collins were an exceptional baseball couple. Dottie loved the game and excelled at it, and she loved her husband and her family. Harvey, who spent four years in the Navy during World War II, loved his wife, the game, and his family. Years later, when June Peppas spearheaded the All-American newsletter and the reunions began at Chicago in 1982 and continued at Fort Wayne in 1986, Dottie became deeply involved, first, with organizing the Players Association in 1987, then working on *Touching Bases*, starting in 1987, and later, serving as the newsletter's editor from 1994 through 2000. A fine ballplayer who epitomized the league's ideal of athletic skills combined with femininity, Dottie's star shone on and off the diamond during her playing years. Later, when the AAGPBL was working for recognition, she worked to help the players association as well as the players. "Whether you played one game or for every year the league existed," Dottie said in 1997, "we want to find you. The memories of some of those who hardly played at all are sometimes the most gratifying."

JS: Harvey Collins, your future husband, came back to Fort Wayne from the Navy a few days after World War II ended in the Pacific, and the day you met him, you pitched and won both games of a double-header. That evening, Harvey was taking beer to an upstairs apartment near where you lived on Anderson Avenue in Fort Wayne.

Collins: There were five of us living together in an apartment in Fort Wayne, and Vivian Kellogg and Tex Lessing were two of them.

You pitched and won the double-header on August 19, 1945, at Northside High Field in Fort Wayne. Later, on August 27 in Grand Rapids, you pitched and won both games of another double-header.

I beat the Rockford Peaches twice that night in Fort Wayne, and that was the night I met Harvey. A friend of his, Jimmy Haskins, was helping Harvey carry the beer.

Harvey and several of his high school buddies enlisted in the Navy on the Monday after Pearl Harbor was bombed, and he spent four years in the Navy. Harvey was a senior, and he would have graduated in 1942. Faye Dancer made what the newspaper called a "circus catch" in one of those games, but Faye made all of her catches into circus catches! She was really good.

I remember winning both of the double-headers, but I always remember the two wins in Fort Wayne against Rockford for two reasons. One, I met Harvey, and number two, it was great to beat Rockford. Rockford, you know, was the number-one team. It was just great to beat 'em.

Also, Bill Allington, who managed Rockford, was my old manager in California, and I always enjoyed beating his team. He was the best manager in our league. You had to be able to take him, because he was rough on you, but he was good.

You grew up in Inglewood, California. What were your parents' names?

My father and mother were Dan and Eleanor Wiltse, and I was an only child.

You started pitching fast-pitch softball around 1936 when you weren't quite thirteen.

I pitched my first game in 1936 at the old Wrigley Field in Los Angeles, and we won the championship of southern California. That was the first league game I ever appeared in. In those days, you played maybe one or two games a week, and I was the bat girl on the Mark C. Bloome team. Our pitcher was great, but she couldn't find the plate that week.

The manager came up to me and said, "Go warm up. You're going in the game." I was twelve. He took her out and put me in, and we were down by four or five runs, and some way or other, the girls just relaxed, and we came back and won the ball game. That was the first time I pitched a league game, and we won the *Los Angeles Examiner* Championship.

Did you later work for Payne Furnace?

Yes, and everyone in the office was a ballplayer.

Where and when did you graduate from high school?

I graduated from Inglewood High School in 1941, and that was the same high school where my mother graduated. As soon as I got out of school, I went to work for the Payne Furnace Company. When the war started, I went to work in Payne's factory making airplane parts, and I did some bowling on Payne's team. *[Editor's note: Night ball games in California ended with the blackout in 1942.]*

Why didn't any of these California girls get involved with the All-American League in 1943?

I'm not sure, because I never really asked, but somehow Bill Allington got involved, and he's the one that made all the preparations for us to go back [to Illinois] and try out in 1944.

Our league in California was not in operation in 1944 and for most of 1945. We had blackouts in southern California, so you couldn't play at night. The league organization out there tried to have us play on Saturdays and Sundays, but it didn't go over at all. People had gas rationing and stuff like that.

Once Bill Allington got involved, he got several girls to try out.

He [Allington] chose myself, Pepper Paire, Faye Dancer, Tiby Eisen, and Alma Ziegler. Those were the five he picked to try out with the All-American League in 1944. We came back on the train, and we're the ones that got Bill into the league. We pushed for him to be a manager.

Where did you try out in 1944?

Peru, Illinois, that's where everyone tried out.

You were allocated to the Minneapolis Millerettes.

Tiby and Faye went with me to the Millerettes, and Alma Ziegler went to Minneapolis. We only lasted half a season, at least at home! *[She laughs.]*

I believe it was 600 miles from Minneapolis to Rockford, the closest team.

The team wasn't making any money at Nicollet Park in Minneapolis. It was a minor league baseball diamond, and we were just too far away from the fans. That's one thing the fans liked — they liked to be close to the girls. They liked the closeness, and the league just did not go [in Minneapolis].

The first year was a real struggle for you, playing on the road and living in hotels all the time.

Oh, yeah, but you have to consider how young we were. We didn't care! *[She laughs.]*

I can't remember being upset about that. We were young, and we were having a good time, and we had money in our pockets. I mean, what more could you ask for? We didn't care that we were the "Orphans," the Minneapolis Orphans.

That's what I keep telling young people. Geez, this was the greatest thing that ever happened to us. We didn't have TV, we didn't have swimming pools, we didn't have tennis courts, we didn't have any recreational place. They just look at me with their mouths open! They can't believe it, you know, that we didn't have all those things.

This league was the greatest thing that could happen. We didn't care how many hardships we had. Most of the girls had never been away from home before.

Including you.

Really, I hadn't. I made a trip to Oregon once with my mom and dad, but a lot of people had never done any of that.

What was your mother and dad's attitude about you playing in the All-American League?

Dad was thrilled to death. Mother cried a lot — she didn't want me to leave home. They came out and saw some games one year. I talking to some of the girls, and you'll find that a lot of the parents came either once or twice to see some games.

Betsy Jochum told me her brother Nick saw her play amateur ball in Cincinnati, but he never saw her play in the All-American League.

That's an exception, but I think the parents backed the players. When we were at Cooperstown in 1988, so many of the kids, they didn't even know their mother had even played ball. It was amazing! It was a case that most of them went home, and most of their stuff went to the attic. They didn't even talk about it. I've had more than one young person talk to me and say, "I knew my mother played softball, and stuff like that, but I never knew she did all of this."

It wasn't a big issue at my house. I had scrapbooks down in the basement, and the kids knew they were there, but I didn't have a bunch of trophies and stuff sitting out, you know. In our league there weren't many trophies, but I had twenty million from the California leagues! The only one I really keep is the Examiner Championship Trophy that I won in 1936.

We just didn't talk about the league, you know. Everybody went their own way, and they had other things to do in their own lives. I didn't hardly go to ball games after I quit the league. I was ready to change my life.

I have one article saying "Dot Wiltse Hurls No-Hit Game." That must have been in 1945. The story says you beat the Rockford Peaches, 2–0.

That story had to be before March 10, 1946, because from then on, I went with my married name. If they wrote an article, it would say like, "The former Dottie Wiltse...."

Your dad, Dan Wiltse, was a semipro ballplayer, right?

Dad played semipro ball in Inglewood with Lou Novikoff, who later played with the Chicago Cubs. In fact, he "found" Louie Novikoff. Louie lived down in Russiantown in

LA, and he was a kid, fifteen, sixteen years old. He was a fast-pitch softball pitcher when they found him. I have seen him pitch a softball game and actually throw three balls to half the guys on the team, and then laugh and strike 'em out! Louie was the cockiest little guy you'd ever want to meet in your life. He got into baseball. We had a park in Inglewood called Centinela Park, and it was down in a gully. There were statues up on top, because it was right across the street from a cemetery, and I don't know many statues he ruined by hitting balls up on top of that hill. I remember we'd go down to Russiantown and pick him up and take him to the ball game with dad, and he taught me a lot. Dad and Louie would travel to Bakersfield and places like that to play semipro ball.

What pitches did you throw in the All-American League?
I had a fastball, and my curve ball was my best one — overhand and underhand either way. I had a terrific curve. I called my curve a "rise" ball. I wasn't too good with a slow ball, the change-of-pace, but I had a ball that went in and dropped, so I had four pitches. But my curve was my best pitch.

You had a real good season for Fort Wayne in 1945. You won a double-header twice, you pitched a no-hitter, you won your most games in a single season, 29, and you met Harvey.
Yes.

Most of the players lived with families and some in apartments, right?
I'm talking about living in the years prior to 1950. All the people who rented contacted the league and told them they had a room or an apartment to rent to the girls who were playing ball. In 1945 we lived in the upstairs of a house made into an apartment, and the lady lived downstairs. Her husband had died.

I remember in Minneapolis in 1944, Pepper [Paire] and I lived in a house with two old maids, until our team became the Orphans. The ladies didn't know one thing about baseball, and they didn't go to our games, but they always listened to the games on the radio. If Pepper got hurt, or something, we'd find everything sitting on the table, like Ace bandages, or whatever they thought she needed. Sometimes they'd have cookies and milk sitting on the table for us. *[She laughs.]*

I didn't know your games were on the radio.
They were on the radio in Minneapolis.

That's strange, because the city of Minneapolis never supported the team.
No, they didn't, because the city was too big. I think you have to go to smaller cities, at least in that day and age. People couldn't go anywhere during the war.

Did you travel by train?
Yes. The Pennsy [Pennsylvania Railroad] came from Chicago through Fort Wayne. We'd take the Pennsy into Chicago, and walk a couple of blocks, and take the North Shore [Elevated] to Kenosha, or Racine, or whatever. The North Shore was like a commuter train. I remember that Pennsy train was so dirty. We'd be black by the time we got into Chicago.

You got married in March 1946. What was the difference in playing between being married and being single?
It wasn't too bad. Harvey was interested in me playing ball, and he went to all the games. He'd take the car and some friends, and he'd follow us to games out of town. Harvey is still interested. We didn't have any kids yet. I didn't have my first child until 1948.

I remember Helen Callaghan, and she married Bobby Candaele, her first husband, in 1948. Bobby used to come in from Canada, and he'd travel with us. He used to ride our bus. We used to sing all night long when we were traveling.

I can remember a few other girls who were married, and their husbands usually came to the games. But being married made no practical difference in playing ball.

My daughter Patricia was born in 1948 and my son Daniel was born in 1954. Harvey worked at a lot of different jobs, and he began running an auto dealership in 1954 or 1955.

What did Harvey do before that?

He sold insurance, he worked at the steel mill, and he worked for Essex Wire. I think he only worked one day at Essex Wire. He also worked at Dana Corporation making auto parts. He was working there when they closed down in the latter part of 1954. We got in the car and took off for California to see my mom and dad, which was the best move we ever made, because my dad didn't live much longer after that. When we came back, Harvey's brother was selling automobiles at a Ford dealership here in town, and Harvey didn't have a job, and we had two kids. His brother said, "Come on down to Bob Barry Ford and work." Harvey got a job, and that started his automobile work. He became manager at Heffner Chevrolet, and then he went into business for himself, and then he worked for DeHaven Chevrolet.

Now [1997] he's working part-time, because he had about ten years of bad health. Harvey had a heart attack in 1978, and he had a major stroke in 1980. He had another stroke in 1982, and then he had an aneurysm, and he had gall bladder surgery. He wasn't able to work for ten years. Then he began working part-time to do something. This all started in 1978.

In 1948 you played a little more than half the season.

We were out in California after the 1947 season, and Harvey was selling encyclopedias out there. We decided to come back to Fort Wayne, because Harvey missed his friends here. He had really close friends in Fort Wayne, you know, the guys were very close. We came back to Fort Wayne for the 1948 season, and I told Dick Bass, the manager, that I was pregnant.

You pitched 24 games in 1948, after pitching 40 games in 1947.

I remember pitching the first game of a double-header against Peoria in early August. Going up to the clubhouse after the game, I told Dick Bass, "I think I've had enough." The doctor had told me to play. He said it was better for me to play than quit all of a sudden. I said, "Well, when should I quit?" The doctor say, "You'll know," and he was right. I knew it was time. I was four months pregnant, and Patty was born in December.

[Editor's note: Dottie pitched her last game in 1948 in the first game of a double-header at Memorial Field in Fort Wayne on August 1. She allowed just four hits but lost, 1–0, to Peoria and Dottie Mueller, who spaced six hits.]

You stayed out in 1949 and you came back in 1950 and you pitched 26 games.

I decided to start playing again in 1950. My mother-in-law was great on taking care of Patty, and we could use the money. They let me train in Fort Wayne, so I didn't have to go to spring training. There was a place here in town called Turners, and I used to go down there and work out all the time. I joined the team after they finished spring training and started their tour back up towards Fort Wayne.

Do you know where Fort Wayne trained in 1950?

I don't remember. Actually, since 1948 I hadn't made many trips. I didn't even go to Cuba in 1947. That didn't interest me. I was married, and that made a difference. In 1950, I played the whole season. But afterward, I decided, "Hey, I played enough baseball. It's time to quit."

Fort Wayne had good pitching that year. They had Maxine Kline, who was a great overhand pitcher, and they had Kay Blumetta and Millie Deegan. Max Carey was our manager. I don't know, but I never got along with Max too well. *[She laughs.]*

Oddly enough, your records were 13–8 in both 1948 and 1950.

I noticed that the other day. Somebody was asking me about it, and I was looking at my baseball card. I didn't realize that.

Were you mainly raising your children after baseball?

No, I worked. The first job I had in Fort Wayne was at the old Vim store, which was a sporting good store. I worked there, and the Zollner Pistons basketball team used to hang out there. We knew all those guys.

I worked for General Electric for a while. That's so we could get furniture for the house! *[She laughs.]* Then I went to work for Baseball Blue Book, and I worked for Earl Moss. That was in the early 1960s, when Daniel started school.

The first AAGPBL Reunion was held in 1982 in Chicago, and the newsletter started around 1980. Is that right?

Yes, and June Peppas started the newsletter.

When did you get involved with the organization?

I got involved when we [the AAGPBL Players Association] became a nonprofit organization in 1987. We formed the nonprofit organization in South Bend, Indiana, at Fran Janssen's house. I started out as the treasurer, and things kept piling up, and I got involved with the newsletter.

Even though the 1992 movie A League of Their Own *is out there, lots of people still don't know that women played baseball.*

I know, but every place I go, people are more aware of the league. I went to a wedding shower today. My nephew's son is getting married, and I knew no one in the whole room. I hadn't even met the bride. Yet I hadn't sat down for more than five minutes when this woman came over and said, "I'd like to meet you and shake your hand!" She knew who I was, because I played in the league, and it just went from there. So when I got ready to leave, she came over and told me how excited she was to meet me. She said, "I can't wait to get home. The kids are going to be so excited!" *[She laughs.]*

That's pretty neat. It must make you feel good.

Yeah, it really does, but that happens constantly, constantly. That's what's so great for all of the girls, because they're constantly being treated like this.

You get fan mail, right?

All of the girls are getting fan mail now, because I'm releasing their names and addresses. This has to benefit us to have people ask for our autographs. I'm going to ask the board at the Myrtle Beach Reunion [October 1997] to release names and addresses of former players, so long as they want to be on the list.

Do you know how many girls altogether that played in the league?

It's close to 600 girls. We have statistics for about 575 girls who have confirmed they played in a league game. Jean Harding found an article that said at one point 700 women were playing in the All-American Girls Professional Baseball League. I think that many showed up for spring training, but they didn't sign a contract.

I just heard from a former player who made a team, but she never got in a game. She said, "I never had so much fun in my life, and I never met so many great people." Those are the women we really want to find. Whether you played one game or for every year the league existed, we want to find you. The memories of some of those who hardly played at all are sometimes the most gratifying.

AUDREY (HAINE) DANIELS
Minneapolis, 1944; Fort Wayne, 1945–1946;
Grand Rapids, 1946–1947; Peoria, 1947–1948;
Rockford, 1951 (home games only)
Interviewed on June 24, 2011.

Born: 1927
Height: 5'9"
Weight: 150
Positions: P
Batted: R
Threw: R
Three No-Hitters: Haine, working the seven-inning first game of a double-header at Kenosha on August 27, 1944, pitched a no-hitter to help the Minneapolis Millerettes beat Helen Nicol and the Comets, 1-0, and Haine got her team's only single. Haine, pitching for Fort Wayne (the franchise moved from Minneapolis in 1945), faced Kenosha's Helen Nicol, and they hurled a double no-hit, no-run game at Kenosha that lasted six innings on June 15, 1945, but the 0–0 game was halted due to rain. Haine, traded to Peoria in mid–1947, hurled a nine-inning no-hitter on August 4, 1948, but she gave up two runs while helping the Redwings win, 4–2, over the visiting Muskegon Lassies.
Career Batting Average: .174 for six seasons.
Lifetime Pitching Record: 72–70 record with 3.48 ERA for 167 games.

Audrey Haine, one of more than sixty Canadians that came to the United States to play in the All-American League, was born in Winnipeg, Manitoba. Growing up with her mother and older sister Dorothy (three older brothers lived on their own), Audrey learned

One of the more than 60 Canadians who played in the league during the 1940s, Audrey Haine, from Winnipeg, pitched for five teams. Audrey is pictured with Grand Rapids circa 1947 (courtesy Audrey Daniels).

to play softball in the streets with the boys. In 1942, at age fifteen, she began working. She also pitched for the St. Vital Tigerettes, and her team won the city championship. In late 1943, she was visited by Dottie Hunter, another Winnipeg girl who played with the Kenosha Comets in the AAGPBL's inaugural season. Dottie recruited Audrey, and when she had second thoughts, Dorothy insisted that her sister grab the opportunity. Audrey agreed, and the big adventure of her life began with the league's 1944 spring training camp in Peru-LaSalle, Illinois. The right-hander made the six-team circuit, and she was sent to one of two new teams, the Minneapolis Millerettes. The shy brunette earned $65 a week at a time when men in Winnipeg were earning $35–45.

Audrey recalled not doing well that first year (her record was 8–20), but she was a rookie and everything about the league and the faster-paced blend of baseball and softball was new. However, the Millerettes, who became a traveling team in mid-season because they couldn't attract enough fans in a minor league city, had several Canadians. In the league's early years, Audrey remembered that girls from north of the border usually stayed together, enjoying a close camaraderie. Also, the Millerettes had several California girls, including star pitcher Dottie Wiltse and catcher "Pepper" Paire, and the players from the West Coast often showed the ropes to the Canadians. Audrey, a figure-eight hurler like most of the Canadians (most Americans were windmillers), had no trouble with the loop's underhand style of pitching. She also adjusted easily to the decreased size of the ball and the increased pitching distances and base paths as the years progressed. Indeed, the attractive brunette with the curly hair and the winning smile hurled a seven-inning no-hitter to defeat the Kenosha Comets on August 27, 1944, and her team won partly because of her single, the game's only hit. In 1945, the franchise moved to Fort Wayne, where the city welcomed the girls' pro team with open arms.

Haine, who was tall and strong at 5'9" and 150 pounds, showed plenty of natural talent, and she couldn't remember receiving any pitching instructions in Winnipeg or later in the U.S. She kept gaining confidence and winning games by firing mainly fastballs, whether in Fort Wayne, Grand Rapids, Peoria, or Rockford in 1951. When her control was good, she was tough. Audrey proved her skills by tossing two more no-hitters, one for Fort Wayne in 1945 and another for Peoria in 1948, the year she won a personal-best 17 games. After the 1948 season, she married Winnipeg native Austin Daniels and left the game. When Austin moved to Rockford for an engineering job, she pitched home games for the Peaches in 1951. Remembering the changes that occurred as the league evolved toward sidearm pitching in 1946 and 1947 and to overhand pitching in 1948, she observed, "We had our own game with our own rules, and we wore skirts. That's appealing." Later a stay-at-home mom, Audrey credited her self-confidence and her success to what she learned in the AAGPBL. "I've had a wonderful life. I've been blessed. I have a wonderful family, three boys and three girls." For a young woman from Winnipeg who was at first reluctant to try her excellent pitching skills in the U.S., she later called the league a "fabulous experience."

JS: How did you get started playing softball?

Daniels: I started out playing baseball on the street with boys in Winnipeg, where I was born and grew up. We all played on the streets because there wasn't any other place to play. At that time [mid–1930s], there weren't too many cars going by to stop our game. That's what we did, and later, I played at intermediate school. I went to Isaac Newton High School, but there wasn't any softball for girls. What they had at that time was volleyball, so I did join the volleyball team. We won the city championship in grade ten, which was my last year of high school, because I had to go to work. There was just my mother Katherine and my sister Dorothy and I, and my father wasn't present. Things were tough.

I found a job, and I was making $8 a week. The next year [1943], I joined a senior softball league and played for the St. Vital Tigerettes. That was my first organized softball team, and we played in the stadium in Winnipeg, which was quite a thrill — and also pretty scary. We won every game that I pitched, and we won the city championship that year. I had a good year for the Tigerettes, and that was the year I received an offer from the All-American Girls League explaining the league and asking me if I wanted to try out.

I also got a call from Dottie Hunter, who played in the league in 1943, the first year, and she was also from Winnipeg. Dottie got in touch with me and said one of the scouts had seen me play. She came to my home to see if I was interested. I'd never heard of the league, so she told us what was going on. Dottie said the league was operated on very high standards. The girls lived in private homes with good families when we were in the league cities, and they stayed in the best hotels on the road, and they got meal money. I was only sixteen, and I'd never been more than one hundred miles from home, and I'd never ordered or eaten a meal out.

But I was quite interested, and I wanted to try. I received a contract from the league offering me $65 a week to play ball. Since men were only bringing home $35 to $45 a week, it sounded great to us, particularly since it was only my mother, my sister, and I, and life was very difficult. Signing the contract was a big event for me, and at the last moment, I had second thoughts. But Dorothy, who was three years older, insisted that I go. She said, "Yes, you are going!" When I got on the train, I had just turned seventeen that day. I don't even know what clothes I took with me. I didn't take clothes for summer because I didn't have very much.

I remember sweltering in my woolen skirt, because it was warmer in Illinois in May than it was in Manitoba! It seemed like all those players from California had the right thing to wear. We headed to Chicago and took another train to the training camp in Peru, Illinois, outside Chicago. We met the officials of the league, and we worked out, and we all went on to our teams. I was listed to play for the Minneapolis Millerettes, one of the two new teams in the league that year! That was my first year in the league.

Many of the players on our team came from California, and they were much wiser about playing ball than those of us from Winnipeg or from the Canadian provinces. *[She laughs.]*

There were several of us from Canada on the Millerettes, so we felt good about that. I played for Minneapolis, and I didn't do very well that first year [her record in 1944 was 8–20], because I was very nervous when I pitched, everything being new to me. But I won a few games. In 1945, we moved to Fort Wayne.

You probably remember that the expansion Millerettes didn't draw enough fans, and you became a road team half way through the 1944 season.

The Millerettes were a new team, and they didn't draw very well. The field where we played, Nicollet Park, was much too large for the type of game we played. So in the middle of the season, the Millerettes became an "orphan" team — we just traveled around. We had no name, really, and they called us the Orphans.

You were a pitcher. Did you use the figure-eight delivery?

I was a figure-eight pitcher. Actually, all of the pitchers that came from Canada threw figure-eight style. Windmill pitching was done in the States. I can't remember any girl that came from the Canadian leagues that threw windmill.

Do you remember your roommate with the Millerettes?

I roomed with Audrey Kissel. Our manager was Bubber Jonnard, and I didn't do so well in 1944 — I was probably scared to death!

When Bubber Jonnard saw the baseball mitt I brought with me, he strongly suggested that I get a new one. I think he said mine looked like something the streetcar drivers used when they were turning the wheels, or whatever! *[She laughs.]*

I did go out and buy myself a new baseball mitt, and it cost me $35. At the time, that was a lot of money. But I had one great mitt, and I still have it. When I go around giving talks about the league, I take my "Great Mitt." Really, it's not too good looking. *[She laughs.]*

In 1945, I played for Fort Wayne, which was the Millerettes in a new city and renamed the Daisies. There were a lot of Canadians on that team, so we all felt quite at home. I did fairly well with Fort Wayne. Our manager was Bill Wamby [Wambsganss], who, of course, once made an unassisted triple play in a World Series game, I believe in 1920. Bill Wamby was a great manager. He was very well liked. From Fort Wayne, I moved on to Grand Rapids in 1946.

What were your favorite pitches, or the pitches you threw most of the time?

I threw mostly fast balls. *[She laughs.]*

Nobody ever gave me any instructions or ideas on how to pitch. When you went to the All-American League, you pitched the way you pitched when you first started playing. I'm sure there were corrections made, but I don't remember receiving any.

Do you remember where you lived in Fort Wayne?

I can't remember the address, but I can remember who I lived with — Penny O'Brian, a Canadian. We shared a room, and also in that home were Marge and Helen Callaghan. We always felt at home when we had Canadians along with us. We pretty well stuck together, and we had a couple of other Canadians on the team as well. In the first couple of years, you pretty well stayed with the people from your own country, but after that, it was one big happy family.

You had a couple of good seasons there. You had a 16–10 record in 1945 and a 14–11 record in 1946, and during that time you moved to Grand Rapids.

I was sent to Grand Rapids early in the 1946 season, and the manager there was John Rawlings. In 1947, I was sent to Peoria, and I pitched for them in 1948 too. I enjoyed playing with all my teams. Later, in 1951, I played for Rockford.

Was there a big difference in playing for Fort Wayne or Grand Rapids or Peoria, either in the team or the city?

I don't think so. It depended more on how many Canadians were on the team. There were always four or five Canadians, so you never felt like you were by yourself, because, as I said, they pretty well hung together.

You pitched for Peoria in 1948, but in 1949 and 1950 you were out of the league.

Yes, because I got married to Austin Daniels in 1948, and we had our first little girl, Marilyn, in 1950. When I played for Rockford in 1951, we had all moved to Rockford. We moved partly because of playing ball, but my husband felt he had a better chance to get a job in Rockford. He's an engineer now, but at the time he worked in the metal industry, and Rockford had a lot of work in that line.

Since we were living in Rockford, I agreed to play home games for the Peaches, and that was the end of my baseball career after the 1951 season.

In 1946 the league started allowing sidearm pitching, and in 1948 they started overhand pitching. What difference did that make to you?

I continued to pitch sidearm, which was acceptable. During the winter, when the league decided to make those changes, they sent all the pitchers the new baseballs. Almost each year the ball became smaller, so in the winter they sent us the balls that were gradually becoming smaller, so we could get used to them. One of the other players, Doris Barr, who lived close to where I lived in Winnipeg, was able to get into the armory so we could practice with the smaller ball.

How hard is it for an underhand figure-eight pitcher to go sidearm?

It wasn't very difficult at all. I liked sidearm a lot. They also lengthened the bases and made the baseballs smaller and changed the pitching to sidearm to make the game more appealing.

It was more like baseball, but not quite. If it had been baseball, I don't think we'd have had the crowds that we drew in the 1940s. We were something different. We had our own game with our own rules, and we wore skirts. That's appealing.

So pitching overhand wasn't really a problem for you?

I never pitched overhand. I only pitched sidearm, and that was acceptable. You could pitch either overhand or sidearm starting in 1948.

I pitched home games for Rockford in 1951, but that was the end of my career. We moved back to Winnipeg once, and I played on a team here, but then we moved back to the States. We just picked up and moved whenever we felt like it.

Do you have favorite memories?

Oh, yes, I have a lot of great memories. I guess my favorite memory was when they inducted us into the Baseball Hall of Fame in 1988, and remembering each other, and talking old times. That was wonderful, and the stories were endless. It was, "Remember when...?"

I had one unusual game in 1945. I was pitching for the Daisies, and we were playing at Lakefront Stadium in Kenosha. The stadium was right near Lake Michigan, and the weather was often affected by the lake. I was pitching against Helen Nicol, also a Canadian, and she was playing for the Comets. It was rainy and misty, and they wanted to get the game in, and as the game went on, the weather got worse, but we played six innings before they called the game. But it was good for Nicky and myself, because we both pitched no-hitters. The fact is nobody could see the ball by the time it got up to home plate, because it was so misty. Helen Nicol Fox was an excellent pitcher, but the weather helped us. Nobody got any runs or any hits because of the mist and fog. It's in the record book. That was my second no-hitter.

I do have a funny story. It was the first year in the league, and I was playing for Minneapolis, and I was kind of shy. There were California girls and girls from the Midwest on the team. I was rooming on that trip with Vivian Kellogg. Viv is a little older than I am, and she had friends on the team, and they were going out to get something to eat after the game. They asked me to go with them, and I was kind of bashful, and I stayed in the hotel room.

I was all by myself in the room, and I'd never been in a hotel by myself, and I got kind of scared. I couldn't go to sleep, and I thought, "Someone is going to come in this room." So I got the dresser and pushed it up against the door. I thought, "Now I'm safe," and I got back into bed.

A short while after that, I got a phone call. She said, "Audrey, this is Viv. I can't get in the room. The key works all right, but the door won't open."

I said, "Oh, I think I know why!" So I got up and quickly pulled the dresser away from the door, and I jumped back in bed. Of course, I never heard the end of that! Viv made sure everyone heard about that the next morning. *[She laughs.]*

I'd never stayed away from home, and I certainly never stayed in a hotel room. That's one of my stories that people usually enjoy when I go around talking about the league.

There must have been lots of girls who were shy and bashful, and many of them were away from home for the first time.

I think those of us who were like that tended to get together. We needed friendship, and the girls from California and the Midwest had already played lots of organized ball.

Eventually you got a little crowd together, and the lonely ones finally got in your group. When we get together at reunions, we just laugh and laugh!

What kind of impact did the league make on your life?

It taught me a lot. The league taught me independence and self confidence, and it gave me strength to do things that I may have been able but not brave enough to do. I got a lot of confidence playing in the league. It was a great time in my life and it made a great difference. When I went to spring training in 1944, it was really my first time away from home.

Later, after five seasons in the league, I married Austin. He's from Winnipeg. We never dated anyone else. He never finished high school either, because he also had to work. He took an apprenticeship for 29 cents an hour, but those were the war years, and that worked out well. Later, he became an engineer, and life has been fabulous for us.

I've had a wonderful life. I've been blessed. I have a wonderful family, three boys and three girls. Marilyn was the oldest, and then Craig, and Cheryl, and Katherine, and the twins, Scott and Douglas, are the youngest. Playing in the All-American League was a fabulous experience.

BETSY JOCHUM
South Bend, 1943–1948

Interviewed on April 16, 2012, November 24, 2007, November 2, 2008, March 20, 2012; letter of December 30, 2007.

Born: 1921
Height: 5'7"
Weight: 140
Positions: OF, 1B, P
Batted: R
Threw: R
All-Star Team: 1943
Career Batting Average: .246 for six seasons
Lifetime Pitching Record: 14–13 in 1948

Betsy Jochum, who was born and raised in Cincinnati, was one of the All-American League's sixty original players in 1943. Tall, agile, and fast at 5'7" and 140 pounds, she grew up playing a variety of sports on the vacant lots and streets of her hometown. Her favorite game was softball, and her natural ability and skills carried her to a six-year career in the AAGPBL. In 1939 she graduated from Hughes High at age eighteen, and afterward, she attended a business school and learned to use a then high-tech office machine, the comptometer. She worked in the offices at the H.H. Meyer packing house and later the French Bauer Dairy. In 1943, with World War II impacting American lives for the second full year, Jochum read about Chicago scout Jack Sheehan holding tryouts in Cincinnati for a new women's professional league sponsored by Philip K. Wrigley, owner of the Cubs. The talented brunette and five others made the grade, and later, she succeeded in tryouts held at Wrigley Field, thus joining the "glamour league," as magazines and newspapers dubbed the AAGPBL in the 1940s. Allocated to South Bend, Betsy became a stellar performer for six seasons, playing mainly left and center field. During the war years, the league played a speeded-up version of fast-pitch softball, but in 1946 and 1947, sidearm pitching was adopted, despite the illusion created by the film *A League of Their Own* that overhand pitching was used in the first season. In 1948, when overhand hurling was adopted, the right-hander pitched, fashioning a 14–13 record, and she played 72 games in the outfield.

During Jochum's illustrious All-American career, she enjoyed a long string of highlight games and plays, including once catching a fly ball bare-handed and, in 1944, hitting the longest home run by a woman in Nicollet Park in Minneapolis. A right-handed hitter who averaged .246 lifetime, she could spray singles and doubles all around the ballpark. Betsy could

Shown in a glamour picture taken in 1943, Betty Jochum, an outfielder from Cincinnati, also began pitching in 1948, winning 14 games (courtesy Betsy Jochum).

hit with power, and she could run with grace and speed. An excellent outfielder, she was the ultimate team player, happy to play any position, including pitcher, where she was asked to perform. A timely hitter with a quick bat, she was usually listed as one of the top five batters in the lineup. In fact, Jochum won the league's hitting title in 1944 with a .296 mark during the second of the league's "deadball" years when good pitchers usually dominated. Often at the plate with runners aboard, Betsy was one of the top run-producers for the Blue Sox, starting with 35 RBIs in 1943, peaking with 63 in 1946, and finishing with 33 in 1948, her final AAGPBL season.

Pleasant, friendly, and modest, Jochum provided the kind of dependable performances and exhibited the positive, friendly behavior that made her a longtime fan favorite in South Bend. However, when she asked for a raise following 1948 season (after being encouraged to do so by the manager), the team's president responded by arranging to trade her to the Peoria Redwings. Instead, Jochum left the game she loved, moved to South Bend year around, and worked in the offices for Bendix. In the 1950s, she earned bachelor's and master's degrees, and starting in 1957, she taught physical education in middle and elementary schools for 26 years. Jochum enjoyed seeing part of *A League of Their Own* filmed in Evansville in 1991. Later, she was picked to help represent the Smithsonian's exhibit on "Sports, Breaking Records, Breaking Barriers." Proud of her opportunity to compete in the AAGPBL as well as her accomplishments on and off the diamond, Betsy Jochum will always be one of the pioneers for women's baseball.

Interview on April 16, 2012

JS: Can you tell me about your background in Cincinnati?

Jochum: My parents immigrated to the America from what used to be Hungary, but the area in which they lived is now Romania. My grandmother, on my mother's side, came to America first, eventually bringing their children through Ellis Island to settle in Cincinnati. My father came to America all by himself. He was a carpenter and cabinet maker. My parents spoke German and later learned to read and write English. For a while, they would speak to us in German and we would reply in English. Later, we all spoke, read, and wrote in English. My parents became bonafide citizens of the USA.

My older brother was Nicholas, or Nick, and my younger sister was Frances. Nick played baseball at Hughes High School, and he played soccer on my dad's team, but he hurt his knee, and that was the end of soccer. I used to practice soccer with them at an athletic club, but I never played on a team.

You graduated from Hughes High School in 1939. Was it a big school?

I graduated from Hughes High in 1939. It was one of the largest high schools in Cincinnati with more than 2,000 students from grade nine to twelve. They didn't have much in sports for girls. Sometimes they had a few intramural sports, but they lasted for a short span of time, and there were no away games.

When did you start playing fast-pitch softball?

I started playing ball on teams when I was in my early teens. Before that, the kids in the neighborhood would meet at an empty corner lot and play ball. We played with any old ball that one of us would bring. Someone else would bring an old bat. This was during the Great Depression in the early 1930s. We'd play until the cover fell off the ball, and then we would tape it up with friction tape and roll it in the dirt to get the stickiness off the ball. If the old bat cracked, we used the good old friction tape again to hold it together! There was no duct tape at that time!

In the evening, the kids in the neighborhood would meet on a side street. There weren't many cars around in those years. I remember one game we played was "Red Rover, Red Rover, I Dare You Come Over." We always had fun things to do in our neighborhood. There was no TV, computers, or cell phones. We just had radios.

When we were a little older, we used to go to nearby U.C., the University of Cincinnati, and play on their tennis courts, which were bright enough from the band practicing in the nearby stadium at night. It was called Nippert Stadium at that time.

During the Depression, when it was hard to find jobs, my brother and I worked at the H.H. Meyer packing company. I played on their softball team. Dottie Kamenshek and Marian Wohlwender also played on that team. We went to national softball tournaments that were held each year in Detroit or Chicago.

One year we went to the finals and lost to a team from Arizona. On another trip to the nationals, we played a team from Richmond, Virginia, and won. Later, much later, I found out that Helen "Gig" Smith played on that Richmond team, and she played on the Grand Rapids team in the AAGPBL in 1947.

Before playing on the H.H. Meyer team, I played softball for Vic Brown's Rosebuds, a flower shop in Covington, Kentucky, across the river from Cincinnati.

How did you first hear about the All-American League?

There was a story in the Cincinnati paper about a new girls' league. Jack Sheehan, a

Chicago Cubs scout, came to Cincinnati in the spring of 1943 to hold tryouts. I was selected along with Dottie Kamenshek, Marian Wohlwender, and some others to go to Chicago for the final tryouts.

When did you go to work with comptometers?

After I graduated from high school, I went to a business school for comptometers. It was hard to find jobs at that time, so I worked at H.H. Meyer for a while, and then I found a job at French Bauer Dairy in their office. I did comptometer work, and I also learned to run the key punch machine. I was working at French Bauer when I started to play in the All-American League. I was lucky to always have a job there during the offseason.

I moved to South Bend after I retired from our league in 1948. I worked in an office as a comptometer operator at Bendix Home Appliances, and then at Bendix Brake Corporation. Later on I decided that I wanted to go to college. While I was working, I took night classes for a while and saved some money. I went to college fulltime at Illinois State in 1953. I earned my bachelor's degree in physical education, and I earned my master's degree at Indiana University in 1961. I spent two summers on campus at IU to earn my MS. I was already teaching in South Bend at that time.

Do you know why you were traded to Peoria after the 1948 season?

Marty McManus, our manager in 1948, said I deserved more money. When I wasn't pitching, I played in the outfield most of the time. Marty encouraged me to see Dr. [Harold] Dailey, who was president of the Blue Sox at that time, and ask for a raise, which I did. Dr. Dailey told me no. After the 1948 season was over, Dr. Dailey told one of the players, Lib Mahon, about me being traded to Peoria. He didn't tell me, and Lib was told not to say anything. I found out much later that Dr. Dailey and Marty McManus didn't get along too well. So that probably had a lot to do with the trade, especially since I told Dailey that Marty said I deserved more money. I heard that Peoria needed someone who could pitch and play the outfield. I really don't think that was the main reason, since I played in 107 games in 1948, went up to bat 339 times, pitched 29 games, and produced 33 RBIs! When I won the batting title in 1944, I had 23 RBIs. It was a sleazy deal all around. No way was I going to Peoria, so I quit. I got a job in South Bend, and later I went to college and earned my degrees, and I taught in the South Bend schools.

When did you begin teaching?

I got my bachelor's degree in June 1957, and I started teaching in September 1957 in the South Bend Community School Corporation. I taught physical education.

Do you remember a time when you caught a long fly ball bare-handed?

It was at Bendix Field, and I was playing left field. I went to my right, and the ball went over my head, so I reached up right-handed and caught it! That's the only time I did that.

How about the long home run you hit off Dottie Collins in Minneapolis at Nicollet Park in 1944?

I don't remember hitting that home run, but the Millerettes had a humongous baseball field. If someone hit the ball over your head, you would run forever trying to track it down. I must have gotten a good roll on that ball, because I only hit two home runs in 1944. I hit more doubles than anything else. One of the fans in South Bend, Arnold Bauer, used to give us silver dollars for hitting home runs.

Do you have favorite baseball memories?

One of my baseball memories came the day World War II ended in August of 1945, when we were playing a game in Racine. We were staying at the Hotel Racine, which was located on the town square. People started jumping into this fountain and just having a party! I remember looking out of the hotel window at this party going on in the town square. People were so happy the war finally ended.

Interview on November 24, 2007

I'd like to ask some questions about the league in 1943. What about the spring training in Chicago?

When they had tryouts at Wrigley Field, they would run the outfielders to the left, to the right, then forward and backward, hitting the ball where you really had to move to catch it. It was quite a workout. We also had to one-hop a throw to home plate.

We stayed at a very nice hotel, the Belmont. You could see all the fancy yachts in the harbor from our rooms. We had excellent meals, until one day they served us kippered herring! They made the cuts at the end of the tryouts by posting the names on the hotel's bulletin board the next morning.

The league had the Helena Rubinstein charm school in 1943 and the Tiffany's charm school in 1944, but did you go to the charm school at the hotel?

We had our sessions at the hotel in the evenings. They usually ran for a couple of hours each. They demonstrated how to put on makeup, and how to go down stairs, gracefully, one step at a time, and how to sit down and cross your legs properly, all things like that, and we were given makeup kits. Of course, we had a good time discussing all of the above later!

The South Bend Tribune *reported the girls arrived in South Bend from Chicago on Wednesday, May 26, 1943, at 11:30 in the morning on the South Shore El, or Elevated, and local officials had a luncheon for the players at the city hall.*

I remember we lived with a Scottish lady that first year. I roomed with two or three other girls, and we walked to Bendix Field from where we lived. In my scrapbook, there is a nice series of stories about the girls living in private homes in 1943. The stories were written by Mina Costin, who must have been the daughter of Jim Costin, the sports editor of the *South Bend Tribune*.

[Editor's note: When, along with Robert M. Gorman, I was researching and co-authoring our book, The South Bend Blue Sox, *published in November 2011, Betsy read over the early chapters and sent me detailed letters that helped with our understanding of the Blue Sox and life in South Bend. What follows is one such letter.]*

Jochum's Letter of December 30, 2007, Explaining Life in South Bend During the War Years

What I do remember — everyone treated us royally. Wherever we went, we were always welcome. I don't remember anyone ever booing us in South Bend or any other town. When we played at Bendix Field [1943–1945] on the west side of South Bend — the home of the former Bendix Brakes men's softball team — I lived in the upstairs part of a house owned by a Scottish lady named McAdams with Dottie Schroeder, "Jo" Hageman, and Lucella "Frenchy" MacLean. You have a newspaper clipping of us doing our laundry there. We used to eat breakfast and lunch, always the best hamburgers, at a restaurant down the street called the Black Cat.

We walked to and from the ballpark for our games and practices. When we were in South Bend on a Sunday, we would walk down Lincoln Way West to eat around noon downtown at the Philadelphia, a restaurant and candy store. We walked all the way back, around forty-five minutes one way.

Dan Clark, one of the best Blue Sox presidents, owned Clark's Lunch Room downtown. The visiting teams would sometimes eat there. Al McGann, the first Blue Sox president, was the president of a bank downtown. On the street corner by the bank was a huge square clock, and that clock was kind of a landmark.

A local downtown jeweler gave me a gold watch for winning the 1944 batting championship. Several years ago, a few former All-Americans were introduced before a Notre Dame women's softball game, and afterward, we signed autographs. A lady came by and spoke to me, saying she worked at the jewelry store and remembered giving me the watch. She also said they enjoyed our games. Small world! It's nice to be remembered.

Another memory — you would see a lot of Studebaker cars in South Bend, since they were manufactured here. They used to make ambulances during World War II, but that plant is not in existence any more. I liked Studebaker's "Starlite Coupe," which came out later, with the round bullet nose and the wrap-around rear window. The Studebaker Car Museum is now part of the Center for History [in South Bend], where our AAGPBL archives is kept.

Dressed appropriately to travel in this 1944 picture, the Blue Sox players standing outside Rockford's Beyer Stadium are (left to right): Lucella MacLean, Betsy Jochum, Dottie Schroeder, chaperone Helen Moore, Lee Surkowski, and Rose Gacioch (courtesy Betsy Jochum).

In 1943, our chaperone wore a player's uniform. In 1944, Helen Moore, a high school English teacher from West Allis, Wisconsin (near Milwaukee), was our chaperone. That was the year they started wearing a chaperone's uniform, which changed over the years. Lucille Moore, a local person, was our chaperone in 1945 and for several years.

In the early years, the visiting teams stayed at the Oliver Hotel with its very ornate old-time lobby. They remodeled it and changed it into a Holiday Inn. Later, the teams stayed at the Hoffman Hotel.

Most of us stayed at the homes of our fans near the ballpark. Starting in 1946 at Playland Park, at the corner of Lincoln Way West and Ironwood, the Blue Sox directors used to sit in the box seats behind home plate in the lower part of the concrete grandstand. All of them were prominent people in South Bend. The people were always good to us. Sometimes they had us over for dinner or to an outing at the South Bend Country Club. Our games were a welcome form of entertainment, especially for people who worked in the large industrial "war" factories here. Bendix, Studebaker, Singer, and Ball Band were in South Bend, and Honeywell aircraft and landing systems, controls, and accessories used to be Bendix.

At Playland Park, we had a loyal Blue Sox Ushers Club that helped out at our games. Come the fall, some of them worked at the Notre Dame football games. Many of the loyal Notre Dame fans became Blue Sox fans in the summer.

Playland Park was part of Pete Redden's amusement park. Pete used to stand outside the gate to the ballpark wearing his white spats and one of those old, stiff straw hats. He would greet people before the games.

The "Sockum Jochum" rooting started at Playland Park by people who used to sit behind our dugout. By the way, the home team's dugout at Playland was on the third base side of the field, and the visitors' dugout on the first base side. In order to get up to bat, players had to walk across the cinder racetrack to get to home plate.

Later on I had my own car in South Bend. I had a black Pontiac coupe with a rumble seat (remember those?) and the silver streak on the hood with the Indian head for the hood ornament. You don't see those any more. At gas stations, I remember the attendant pumped the gas, washed the windshield, and checked the air in our tries — all for free! The "good old days," as Tom Brokaw said in his book, *The Greatest Generation*.

When we had time in South Bend, we sometimes drove to Lake Michigan or to a small nearby lake, Pleasant Lake, for some sun and relaxation.

When part of "our" movie was made in Evansville, Indiana, people, men and women, wore dress clothes to our games. "Pee Wee" Wiley, Lou Arnold, and myself drove to Evansville to watch Penny Marshall direct the movie, *A League of Their Own*. That was when I realized people wore hats to our games. They had "extras" in the stands with hats on. Men used to wear those wide-brimmed felt hats that you often associate with the old-time gangsters, and you also saw some men wearing the old straw hats.

Interview on November 2, 2008

In 1943 and 1944, you had Bert Niehoff for manager in South Bend, and you finished in second place. But in 1945, you came in fifth out of six teams and you missed the playoffs under manager Marty McManus. In 1946 and 1947, you had Chet Grant for manager. What was the difference between the way McManus and Grant managed the team?

I think Marty McManus had a lot more baseball knowledge than Chet Grant. Chet was more of a football man. Marty showed us more about fundamentals like bunting, hit-

and-run, and that kind of stuff. Chet always had his typewriter with him, and he was always typing. I think he was in charge of Notre Dame's history archives for a while.

Was the relationship with players better with McManus, or was it that McManus knew more about teaching baseball?

I would say both.

Do you know why McManus didn't return in 1946? The team hired him again in 1948.

Marty didn't get along with Doctor Dailey very well. Dailey later put a document in the Notre Dame archives saying Marty was "drunk" 90 percent of the time, and several of the players, including myself, signed it saying the statement by Dailey wasn't true. We never saw Marty drunk when he came to the ballpark or at any other time.

When Marty McManus was the manager for Kenosha in 1944, the Comets got into the playoffs, but Racine beat them. When Marty was hired by South Bend in 1945, he traded for some of the Kenosha players, Lib Mahon, Phyllis "Sugar" Koehn, and "Pinky" Pirok.

What was the difference between playing at Playland Park in 1946 compared to Bendix Field the previous three seasons?

At Playland Park it was a big, huge area with a cinder racetrack around the ball field and a concrete grandstand on the hill behind home plate. At Bendix Field they had bleachers all around, and it had a small clubhouse. Playland seated a lot more people than Bendix, and it was more centrally located for people, where Bendix was out on the west side of South Bend.

In the middle of 1946, the league began to allow sidearm pitching. Did that make much difference in terms of batting?

I don't think sidearm pitching made much difference, really.

In 1947, it was sidearm all year long, so you're saying it didn't make much difference to the batters. Did pitchers like Jean Faut sort of lean over to pitch sidearm?

Jean never pitched underhand, so it didn't seem to matter to her. Dottie Collins threw that curveball most of the time, and it was kind of sidearm.

You started pitching in 1948 when the league went overhand. How hard was it for you to learn how to pitch?

It wasn't hard for to learn how to pitch at all. A lot of the outfielders became pitchers because they had strong arms. We had underhand pitchers like Connie Wisniewski, and she was a good hitter, so she switched to right field.

Was it harder to hit the overhand pitching than the sidearm pitching?

I think it was harder to hit overhand pitching, because pitchers could put more "stuff" on the ball.

Interview on March 20, 2012

What kind of impact did the league make on your life?

When I tried out for the new All-American League in 1943, I was working in the office for a large dairy in Cincinnati, French Bauer, as a comptometer and key punch operator. Playing in our league changed my entire life, as it did with so many other players. I had the opportunity to travel by bus and train, and I made my first airplane flight in 1947 to Cuba.

Traveling and playing with the Blue Sox opened up many avenues to meet all kinds of people on and off the playing field as well as to visit places I probably never would have seen.

In 1948, I moved to South Bend and became an avid fan of Notre Dame sports with the never-ending spirit that prevails here.

All the AAGPBL players' names are on a roster with a display of our league in the National Baseball Hall of Fame at Cooperstown, New York. Also, at the Center for History in South Bend, they have pictures of the Blue Sox players and other memorabilia from our league in a special All-American League display.

In 1983, I donated my uniform and other items to the Smithsonian Institution in Washington, DC. In October 2004, I was invited to the grand opening of the exhibition "Sports, Breaking Records, Breaking Barriers." What a great experience that was! My uniform traveled to many places, all thanks to the Smithsonian.

Penny Marshall's 1992 movie, *A League of Their Own*, focused attention on our league. After all those years, we were virtually forgotten. Now we hear from fans old and new again. I had the opportunity to watch part of the filming of the movie in Evansville, Indiana. It was so interesting to meet the stars and see a movie being produced about our unique league.

My career as a professional ballplayer helped me save money so that later I could attend college. I earned my college degree and became a physical education teacher in South Bend. Later, I received the master's degree at Indiana University.

Now we have reunions to spend time with players and with associate members, who keep everything rolling and share our memories of the "Golden Years." Our very first reunion was held in Chicago in 1982. That was something else! Most of us had not seen each other for forty years and several pounds later!

It was a wonderful experience to get paid to play a professional game and share it all with so many people. How often did that happen to women in the 1940s? It was like having ice cream on cake when we tried out at Wrigley Field! There have been books written about our league, but only one about a team, *The South Bend Blue Sox* (published last year), and I'm part of it.

None of these experiences would have happened to me if I didn't play in the All-American Girls League. The league made a huge impact on my life when I was one of the fortunate few who were chosen to play in our league beginning in the inaugural season of 1943. I am very proud to have been a member of the AAGPBL.

All this is thanks to P.K. Wrigley's insight of a new venture back in 1943. We really did have a "league of our own." What a huge adventure it was for everyone!

Vivian Kellogg
Minneapolis, 1944; Fort Wayne, 1945–1950
Interviewed on October 24, 1997, and February 7, 1998.

Born: 1922
Height: 5'7"
Weight: 149
Positions: 1B, C

Batted: R
Threw: R
Career Batting Average: .221 for seven seasons

Vivian Kellogg, who grew up in Jackson, Michigan, with six older sisters and brothers, tagged along with her next oldest sibling, John, who was seven years her senior, when he went with buddies to play ball. By the time she reached elementary school, Vivian, who had exceptional hand-eye coordination, was playing sandlot baseball and softball with the boys. She never played on all-girls teams until she reached Jackson High, where she competed in basketball, volleyball, tennis, softball, and field hockey. By 1943, the spring of her senior year, she was playing for a fast-pitch softball team, Regent Café. Her team lost in the first round of the state tournament. The Lansing Vans, who beat them, could take two players from Regent's team, and they picked Kellogg. Indeed, a scout who saw her playing for Regent's already had signed her to a contract with the All-American League, but she chose to finish the year with the Vans. As a result, Viv reported to spring training with the AAGPBL in 1944, the last year the league sponsored charm school, and the Jackson teenager liked learning about the proper dress and social behavior.

The Daisies' popular Vivian Kellogg, from Jackson, Michigan, is pictured before a night game in 1945 at Fort Wayne with her niece, Diane Vanalsburg (courtesy Vivian Kellogg).

Kellogg, a blue-eyed brunette who stood 5'7" and weighed nearly 150 pounds, was big, strong, and hard-hitting. Allocated to the expansion Minneapolis Millerettes, she and her teammates, many of them also rookies, embarked on the biggest adventure of their young lives, playing professional ball, traveling around the Midwest, and, after mid-season, living on the road out of suitcases, because the Millerettes didn't draw enough fans at Minneapolis' Nicollet Park. In 1945, the franchise moved to Fort Wayne, and, after a contest for fans, the team was renamed the Daisies. Hitting in the middle of the lineup and playing first base, Kellogg, or "Kelly" continued her stellar career, batting .214 and producing 38 RBIs, after hitting .202 and driving in 46 runs in 1944. Always a team leader in RBIs, she was a timely hitter, the ultimate team player, and a fun person when she and other girls went out to eat or got together after a Daisies' night game. Talented, modest, and friendly, the Jackson star was a dedicated athlete who not only enjoyed playing baseball but she also became one of the most popular ballplayers in Fort Wayne.

Kellogg suffered an injury to her right knee during the 1946 season. She had surgery later, and during her last four years in the league, she was slowed by a heavy knee brace. Never known for her speed, she used to joke that she once received a standing ovation for stealing second base! A standout first sacker who batted .221 lifetime but drove 264 runs, she enjoyed her teammates, the fans, and life in Fort Wayne. The Daisies finally made it to the final round of the Shaughnessy Playoffs in 1950, Viv's final season. Rockford won the title, and with her knee problematic, Kelly decided it was time to work for a living. After two years with Lincoln Life, she returned to Jackson. In the daytime, she worked for a dentist until retiring in 1983, and at night, she supervised programs for the Jackson Recreation Department, including the softball program in the summer. Reflecting on her career, Viv observed that after the league ended, most people, when told about the AAGPBL, figured it must have been softball, not baseball. Later, Kelly enjoyed the reunions as well as the speaking engagements and public appearances that came once *A League of Their Own* appeared. Always gracious and a good spokesperson for the league and her life's greatest opportunity, she would thank people who wanted her autograph, smiling and chatting with everyone who finally came to like the league that she had loved since 1944.

Interview on October 24, 1997

JS: I want to write an article about your baseball career for a magazine called Autograph Times, **and I'd like to ask you some questions about your years in the All-American League. You were the youngest of seven children?**

Kellogg: My mother, Amelia Kellogg, died when I was seven months old, and my three older sisters and three brothers raised me. My father, Klien Kelcher Kellogg, was working, and my oldest sister was twenty years older than me, and my next brother, John, was seven years older. My brothers all played baseball, but my sisters didn't play ball. I tagged along with my brother when he played baseball, and that's how I got started.

Did you go to school in Jackson?

I went to three different elementary schools, and that's when I started playing ball. I used to play sandlot softball and baseball with the boys. I graduated from Jackson High in 1943, and in high school is when I first played on all-girls teams. We had basketball, volleyball, tennis, softball, and field hockey.

How did you find out about the All-American League?

When I was in high school, I made it with a fast-pitch softball team in Jackson, the Regent Café team.

We lost out in the local tournament to represent Michigan in the state tournament in 1943. The winning team, the Lansing Vans, could pick up two players, and they took me. I was already signed by a scout from the All-American League, but I wanted to finish the season for the Vans. So I didn't start playing All-American ball until 1944.

At the time [1943], I was working for the phone company, Michigan Bell. I was getting $37.50 a week, and I signed a contract for $75 a week. I was a millionaire!

What did you think about all the traveling with Minneapolis in 1944, after they lost their home base and became the "Orphans"?

We didn't mind it, because we were having the time of our lives. Whenever we got to a town, there would be a Laundromat and we would do the laundry. Actually, we just lived out of a suitcase. But it was fun! *[She laughs.]*

What do you remember about the 1944 season?

I played first base and I caught. I caught a few times when our catcher was injured, but mainly I played first. I played one year for Minneapolis and six years for Fort Wayne, but it was the same team.

Minneapolis, along with the Milwaukee Chicks, was one of the league's two expansion franchises in 1944, but Minneapolis lost the use of Nicollet Park midway through the season and became a road team. Pictured with the Millerettes in the front row are (left to right): Ruth Lessing, Annabelle Lee, Helen Callaghan, and Betty Trezza. Middle row: Faye Dancer, Elizabeth Farrow, Marge Callaghan, Audrey Kissel, and Margaret Wigiser. Standing in the back row: Manager Bubber Jonnard, Dottie Wiltse, Vivian Kellogg, Audrey Haine, Lavonne "Pepper" Paire (who had recently suffered a broken collarbone and had her arm in a sling), Kay Blumetta, Lillian Jackson, and chaperone Ada Ryan (courtesy Vivian Kellogg).

I believe you injured your right knee after a couple of seasons.

I injured my right knee back in 1946. I had cartilage torn. After the season ended I had surgery, and I wore a knee brace most of the time. In 1950 I got to where the knee brace wasn't really helping much. And I thought, "I'm not getting any younger. I've got to think about my future." So that's when I quit.

In 1945, the team moved to Fort Wayne. Where did you play home games in Fort Wayne?

When we first went to Fort Wayne, we played on the Northside High School baseball diamond, and that was gravel. After that, they fixed up Memorial Field for the Daisies.

Were the fans pretty good to you?

The fans were very good to us. But for all the recognition we have received, the sad part is the people who supported us were no longer around to see the recognition.

For years nobody would believe that we played women's baseball, so I quit talking about it. Then when the Hall of Fame and the recognition came along, they would say, "Why didn't you tell us?" Well, they didn't believe us after it [the league] ended in 1954. I would say, "Well, you weren't interested!"

One spring coming back to Fort Wayne [1945], we played exhibitions at some Army camps, and some of the fellows had seen the women's game. But after the league was over, they forgot about it.

Do some of the people who used to be fans come to reunions like this one at Myrtle Beach?

Yes, we see quite a few fans. One umpire used to come to the reunions, Barney Zoss, but he passed away. We were at a reunion in Fort Wayne in 1986, and we got to talking about the managers, and they said, "Where are the managers?" We outlived them all! *[She laughs.]*

Who were your managers in Fort Wayne?

Well, I had Bubber Jonnard, Bill Wambsganss, Dick Bass, Harold Greiner, and Max Carey. Jimmy Foxx came later, but 1950 was my last season.

It seems like Fort Wayne had a pretty strong team, but you didn't make it to the championship playoffs until 1950.

We did have a good team, but we had different managers about every year. We seemed like we were always changing ballplayers. You notice that most of our managers were former ballplayers. The league recruited the managers for their "names," and they were a drawing card.

Do you have favorite memories?

I've got a little comedy. In Fort Wayne, they had a home for elderly men. The women's service clubs would go out to the home and pick these gentlemen up, so they could come to the ballpark. There were two gentlemen who always hanging around behind first base. I was playing first base, so I always spoke to them and asked them how they were doing. When the game was over, we went out the same gates as the fans on our way to the clubhouse. If we lost, I'd say, "Gee, fellas, I'm sorry we couldn't win that game for you tonight." They'd say, "That's all right, Kelly. We want to be here when you split those shorts!" I thought, "Well, I was here to entertain, so I guess I was doing my part!" *[She laughs.]*

Who were some of the favorite people you played with in the league?

I'll start with South Bend, and they had Bonnie Baker and Jean Faut. Grand Rapids, there was Connie Wisniewski and Alma Ziegler. Muskegon had Doris Sams. There were always a couple of players on each team that everyone liked. Kenosha had Lee Harney. I can't remember all of them, but I can see them in my mind.

You used to be a pretty good hitter.
 I might have been able to hit the ball, but I wasn't known for my speed! *[She laughs.]* I got a standing ovation once for stealing second base! *[She laughs.]*

You had your knee in a brace, so that didn't help.
 Well thank you, Jim! *[We both laugh.]*
 I just had my right knee replaced in 1993, and I plan to have the other one replaced when I get back from this reunion [1997]. I'm fortunate, because I healed fast, and it only took about a month, but it's not like having your old knee. You say your prayers at night sitting down, not kneeling down! *[She laughs.]*
 It does bother me to walk any place where it's not level, but otherwise it doesn't bother me. Some people have problems, and I know Dottie Collins has problems with her knee.

What are some of the questions that children ask when you speak at a school?
 One question always is, "Why did you play in skirts?" The answer is that Mr. Wrigley designed the uniforms, and they wanted us to look and act like ladies. That's why we had charm school for personal grooming and social behavior. *[Editor's note: The league included charm schools during the spring training camps for the 1943 and 1944 seasons.]*

So you went to charm school in your first season in 1944.
 Did you see the movie, *A League of their Own*? They didn't show us how to sip tea, but they did show us how to apply make-up and how to sit and how to come down stairs.
 I thought it was a neat thing, because most of the girls came from farms, and not having the opportunity to learn about the style of the day and make-up, they didn't know those things.

I think Wrigley was on the right track in the 1940s in having women who looked like women but played ball like men.
 The league was supposed to take the place of the men who were away in the service in the war, so we were entertaining the home front, but by 1946, the war was over. We took a lot of ribbing and criticism at first, but when we got the fans out, we had them.
 Do you know how they advertised the Fort Wayne Daisies in 1945? They flew an airplane and dropped pamphlets over Fort Wayne to advertise that women's baseball was coming to Fort Wayne. They had a contest to pick the name, and the person who won the contest got a season pass. I used to know the girl's name who picked the name. They had several names to choose from, and that's how they got the name Daisies.

Interview on February 7, 1998

The franchise moved to Fort Wayne in 1945, and became the Daisies. I know you and Dottie Collins and Tex Lessing and a couple of others lived together in an apartment in Fort Wayne that season. Did you live in Fort Wayne over the winter?
 The first two years I played for Fort Wayne, I returned home to Jackson, Michigan, over the winter. I worked at two different places, and when I quit, I didn't tell them I would be quitting to play ball. After that, I lived in Fort Wayne in the offseason the rest of the time I played ball. I lived with a family in Fort Wayne.

Is that when you worked for Michigan Bell?
 No, I worked for the phone company in Jackson before I joined the league in 1944. I worked for Lincoln Life in Fort Wayne.

When did you move back to Jackson?

I lived in Fort Wayne, and after baseball, I worked for Lincoln Life. In 1953, I came home and worked for a dentist in Jackson. I worked for Doctor William Schriner for thirty years, and when he retired, I retired, and that was around 1983.

You also bowled, right?

I bowled and golfed all the years I worked in Jackson, and I worked night programs for the Jackson Recreation Department. I started working for Jackson Recreation before I went away to play ball, when I was still in high school. When I came home, I supervised night programs, and in the summertime, I worked the softball program. I supervised the summer programs. I quit working for the recreation department people when I retired from the dentist's office.

When I first came home, I was coaching Little League baseball for one summer. I was the only woman working with Little League. The problem was they still couldn't get the idea that women played baseball and that women were capable of coaching boys and teaching them baseball. But I became involved with the Recreation Department, so I didn't have time for the coaching.

We had the same problem when we broke the barrier playing baseball in the 1940s, and it took us a while to convince the public that women could play baseball.

Do you still go to schools and groups and speak to kids and adults about the All-American League?

Next month [March 1998], I'm going to speak to girl scouts at four different little cities in my area. I'm also going to appear at one of the local malls for Women's History Month. I have also spoken to Kiwanis and other men's organizations. They're really interested, and they ask a lot of questions. Years ago, they didn't believe women played baseball.

SOPHIE KURYS
Racine, 1943–1950; Battle Creek, 1952
Interviewed on July 25, 1996, and June 19, 2011.

Born: 1925
Height: 5'5"
Weight: 120
Positions: OF, 2B
Batted: R
Threw: R
Honors: Player of the Year, 1946; set league single-season stolen baseball record of 201 in 1946; set league career record in stolen bases with 1,114
All-Star Team: 1946, 1947, 1948, 1949
Career Batting Average: .260 in nine seasons

Sophie Kurys grew up in a Ukrainian-Polish family in Flint, which, along with Detroit, was one of Michigan's two great auto manufacturing centers. She came of age during the

Great Depression. A talented athlete who loved softball, basketball, volleyball, and track, she won Flint's Mott Decathlon at age fourteen in 1939. Because of hard times, Sophie left school in the eleventh grade to work and help her family. She also played ball, for example, starring for the CIO Autos fast-pitch softball team in 1942. In April 1943, Sophie attended a tryout at Berston Field House. With snow flurries outside, she and two other Flint girls impressed the scout and were invited to final tryouts for the new All-American League based in Chicago. After the circuit's tryouts at Wrigley Field, Kurys was one of fifteen women allocated each of the wartime league's four teams. Sent to the Belles of Racine, Wisconsin, she spent the next eight years of her life starring on the venerable diamond at limestone-walled Horlick Field.

Kurys wrote her own rags-to-riches story in the AAGPBL. In 1943, after Racine's regular second sacker was hurt, Sophie, a right-handed batter who had played shortstop and third base in Flint, took over at second base for the rest of her career. Racine finished first in the first half of the 1943 season, the Kenosha Comets won the second half title, and the Belles won the best-of-five Scholarship Championship in three straight games, twice beating their nemesis, Helen "Nickie" Nicol. In 1944, playing in the expanded six-team league, the Belles finished in fourth place in both halves of the season. Playing a single-season format in 1945, Racine captured fourth place, but lost in the semifinal round of the Shaughnessy Playoffs to the Fort Wayne Daisies.

The league boomed early in the postwar era, expanding to eight teams in 1946 and, midway through the season, the circuit permitted sidearm as well as underhand pitching. Adjusting, Sophie and her close-knit Racine teammates won the title again. After beating the South Bend Blue Sox in the semifinal playoff, the Belles topped the Rockford Peaches for the championship in the sixth game of the finals, a 1–0 thriller that lasted fourteen innings and finally saw Sophie single, steal second, and score with her signature hook slide on Betty Trezza's base hit. Kurys enjoyed a sterling season, batting .286, second in the league, stealing—her forté—a remarkable 201 bases in 203 tries, and being voted Player of the Year by the loop's managers.

Racine never again won first place, but the speedy Kurys, a 5'5" 120-pound brunette who was smart, spirited, and serious, made fielding plays and produced runs with the league's greatest stars. She loved her years in Racine, became like a sister to the other Belles, and won recognition on the league's All-Star team from 1946 through 1949. Bright, focused, and down-to-earth, she was widely respected and a fan favorite—thanks to the excitement she generated—wherever Racine played. When the city lost the Belles' franchise after the 1950 season, Sophie switched to the National Girls Baseball League in Chicago, a softball circuit. She spent the first 17 games of the 1952 season with the Battle Creek Belles, but returned to the Chicago's Admiral Music Maids for three more seasons. An intense competitor who later turned to golf, she set the AAGPBL record for career stolen bases with 1,114 and the single-season mark of 201 in 1946. Sophie Kurys, dubbed the "Flint Flash," proved that women could excel in the national pastime.

Interview on July 25, 1996

JS: Can you tell me about getting started playing baseball in the All-American League?
Kurys: I played fast-pitch softball in Flint, Michigan, and I understand you're from Flint. I went to All-Saints Catholic School through the eighth grade, and that was the top grade at

Dubbed the "Flint Flash" because of her hometown in Michigan and her speed on the base paths, Sophie Kurys stole an AAGPBL record 1,114 bases, topped by a record 201 steals in 1946 (courtesy Sophie Kurys).

All-Saints. From there I went to Emerson Junior High, and then I went to Northern High School. Later, I went to college here in Scottsdale, Arizona, where I had a golf scholarship.

When you played softball in Flint, what position did you usually play?
I played shortstop and third base.

Did you play sports in high school?
I played basketball and softball and volleyball, and those were the three sports girls could play at that time. In 1939, when I was fourteen, I participated in the Mott Decathlon,

and I won the city championship by getting 4,693 points out of a possible 5,000. I didn't graduate from Northern, because that was the Great Depression, and my family was pretty poor, so I left school to work and help out. Later, I earned the GED and got a diploma here in Scottsdale.

In the middle of the 1930s, the federal government under President Roosevelt started the National Youth Administration, and later I worked in the NYA in Flint. After that, I worked in an office and in a dry cleaning establishment.

When I was in the eleventh grade, I was going to get a job, and a guidance counselor came to talk to my mother. Sure, she would have loved to have me finish school, but I didn't have any transportation or enough clothes to continue my education. He said he would get me a job. Since I didn't have transportation, I got up at five in the morning, and I would walk about three miles to this woman's house, and I would help her clean house from six to twelve o'clock. I had school starting at noon, so by one o'clock, I was practically asleep. I couldn't handle that schedule for too long, so I said, "I'm going to get a job and help out with the family."

The league came along in 1943 and you were playing softball in Flint. You played for the CIO Autos team in 1942, and in 1943 you were going to play for the Merchants and Mechanics Bank team.

Johnny Gottselig was a scout, and there were going to be tryouts. I hadn't read the paper that day, and a couple of the girls that I played ball with tracked me down and asked me if I was going to the tryouts. I said, "What tryouts?"

They said, "Well, there's a guy here from Chicago. They are going to start a women's league, and he's here to scout some of the girls."

I said, "Scout?" I looked outside, and I said, "It's snowing out there. We got snow flurries." It was April. I found out they were holding the tryouts at Bertson Field House, which was close to my home. I said, "O.K." They said, "Well, we'll pick you up." I had a skirt and sweater on, and I got my glove. We went to the field house, and we played catch and batted, and we fielded some grounders on that hard floor.

In the movie, *A League of Their Own*, the windows in the gymnasium were not protected, but at Berston Field House, they had bars on the windows. Berston had two gyms, one where the girls played and one where the boys played. So I didn't break any windows, because the windows were protected! *[She laughs.]*

The scout picked three of us, and he sent me a contract. My brother was in the Army, and I asked my sister, "Well, what do you think? Do you think I should go?" She said, "If they paid me money to go play ball, I certainly would!" Then my brother sent a letter and said, "Go ahead and go. You love to play. Why don't you go?"

My father, Antoni Kurys, wasn't too keen on the idea. My mother, Antonina, was a strong supporter, "For heaven's sake, go." She knew how much I loved to play. When she backed me, of course I went.

Can you talk about the tryouts in Chicago?

We all tried out at Wrigley Field. They had big league managers, and they said at "allocation day" they would pick the group that they thought would be good enough ballplayers to make the league. We stayed at the Belmont Hotel, which was just about three blocks from Wrigley Field. We walked to Wrigley Field, and we walked back. We didn't have our uniforms yet, so we were all wearing slacks and sweatshirts, or whatever. We had to be dressed in skirts and sweaters and walk to Wrigley, and we'd change clothes there and practice.

At the Belmont Hotel, we never rode the elevators. We had to walk up and down the stairs — it was all part of our training. *[She laughs.]* On a certain day, they said when we came downstairs, our names would be on this chalkboard. We came down the stairs that morning, and I looked to see if my name was there. I saw my name under Racine. I thought, "Racine? God, where's Racine?" *[She laughs.]* I never heard of Racine.

So we left a little bit early, because it had been raining in Chicago. They decided that we would go to our respective hometowns and continue our training, and get familiar with the field. We went to Racine on the trains, these "els." There was a North Shore and a South Shore [train]. The South Shore went to South Bend, and the North Shore went to Racine and Kenosha and Milwaukee. We took the train, and we were met by the people from the town, and the mayor. They had a rabbi from the Kiwanis Club meet us. Then we had lunch the next day at the Kiwanis to meet the town's people.

They really treated us royally. We were a family, because we stayed in their homes. They had allocated two girls to a home. As it was, along with my roommate and I, these people had three boys. They would go to all the ball games. Of course, the boys would always give us tips on playing ball. "Maddy" English and I stayed with the Thielens. They would go to the ball games. I think the tickets were about 75 cents. We were part of their entertainment, because I don't think TV had come into being yet.

We really drew. First, they came out because they were curious, to see whether we could play ball. When they saw that we could, we drew very well, until the waning years. My last year in Racine was 1950. By then there was everything else to do, so I guess we weren't entertainment any more, or maybe not as much, anyhow.

Racine had pretty good teams for most of the years.

We won the playoff championship in 1943. It was called the Scholarship Championship. We defeated Kenosha that first year, and we won the championship again in 1946.

Did you play second base all the time?

Claire Schillace was a schoolteacher, and she didn't get out of school until early June, so I played a few games in the outfield when Claire was gone. Our second baseman, Charlotte Smith, got hurt, and I moved to second base, and I played second base all the rest of 1943. Second base was new to me, because I played short and third when I was playing softball in Flint. Johnny Gottselig was a hockey player, and he didn't know that much about softball. He didn't really know that much about talent either. He only lasted two years with Racine. The league sent him to Peoria in 1947, and the girls there got pretty angry with him. They didn't care for his tactics or his knowledge, and he only lasted one season there.

What happened was that when Charlotte Smith got hurt, I took over at second base, and after the season, the newspaper said I was the "most improved" ballplayer. I thought, "How could I be most improved when I wasn't even playing there before?" *[She laughs.]*

What about that championship in the first year?

We played Kenosha, Wisconsin, and won the best-of-five playoff in three straight games. The league had divided the season in two halves. We played 59 games in the first half and 59 games in the second half. Racine won the first half, and Kenosha won the second half. So it was like our World Series, Racine against Kenosha.

The strange part of it was that Kenosha's star pitcher was "Nicky" Nicol Fox. *[Editor's note: Nicol was married after the 1943 season.]* We beat her the first game that she pitched in 1943 [against Racine], and then we never beat her again all year. And they would say,

Racine's 1946 team won the Shaughnessy Championship by defeating Rockford in six games. The Belles won the final game, 2–1, when Betty Trezza singled and Sophie Kurys scored from second base in the fourteenth inning. Pictured at Racine's Horlick Field, the Belles in the first row are (left to right): Maddy English, bat girl Heather Black, and Claire Schillace. Seated in middle row: Irene "Tuffy" Hickson, Pepper Paire, Betty Trezza, Sophie Kurys, Edie Perlick, Betty Emry, and Ruby Stephens. Back row: chaperone Mildred Wilson, Doris Barr, Anna May Hutchison, Marnie Danhauser, Joanne Winter, Betty Russell, Eleanor Dapkus, Thelma Walmsley, and manager Leo Murphy (courtesy Sophie Kurys).

"Well, Nicol is pitching tonight. All she has to do is put her glove down on the mound and the Belles are beaten."

In the playoffs, we beat her. I think we beat her two games, which was unusual, because Nickie Fox would knock our socks off every time she pitched. But we got our revenge in that series.

Helen (Nicol) Fox must have been one of the better pitchers in the league.

Yes, she was. Nicky was a Canadian, and she pitched a "figure-eight" delivery. She had a great rise ball, and she was quite fast. Most of the pitchers were windmill pitchers, but most of the Canadian girls pitched the figure-eight, which was where your arm goes in and out and around.

You're pretty well known for stealing bases. The first year you stole 44 bases.

When Johnny Gottselig managed Racine, he would tell us when to steal. The other managers let me steal on my own. In the playoffs in 1946, I told our shortstop, Betty Trezza, who was batting next, "When I tip my cap, take a pitch for me." That was in our playoff series, but otherwise, they would only take one pitch for me. Sometimes some of the players would fake a bunt to help me out. You put your bat up to bunt so it would be in the catcher's vision.

In 1946, we went fourteen innings to win the final playoff game against the Rockford Peaches, 1–0. I singled, and when Joanne Winter struck out, I stole second. Betty [Trezza] hit to right field, through the infield. It was sharply hit, and Rosie Gacioch was playing shallow. I had started to steal third, and Leo Murphy, our manager, just kept waving me to go, winding his arm up, and "Go! Go!" When I slid into home, I slid away from the tag. The throw was coming from right field. That was a close play, but I was safe, and we won the game.

Max Carey, the league president, was there, and there was so much hitting—I think they got 13 hits off our pitcher, Joanne Winter. Bill Allington, of Rockford, was classified as one of the smartest managers in our league. I think they had about four squeeze plays. But he tried them with the bases loaded, and they just kept bunting the ball right at Joanne, and she'd just flip it to the catcher, because she [catcher] didn't have to tag the runner. It was a force at home. I think he tried that four times, and it didn't work. Credit Joanne for that.

There were so many sensational catches in that game. I have seen Willie Mays make his "basket" catches, but I have never seen a catch like Edie Perlick made. We had a brick wall that was about 400 feet away from home plate, and people were sitting up against that brick wall, and naturally we couldn't hit that ball that far, but if the ball got to the people, it was a home run. Rosie Gacioch was a fairly good hitter. She really nailed the ball, and I don't know, Edie, whatever sense she had, sixth sense, or whatever, she just seemed to take off at the crack of the bat. Right at the last second, she turned around and leaped and caught the ball! I can still see it, to this day. It was the most tremendous catch I've ever seen in my life, and it saved a home run.

Did Perlick's catch come at a critical time in the game?

It came in the last inning, and it would have been a home run, if it rolled in with the fans, but of course, we still had our last at-bat. Carolyn Morris had pitched a no-hitter for nine innings. As I was saying, Max Carey was in the stands, and he said that was one of the best games he'd ever seen, bar none. He's in the Baseball Hall of Fame, and for Max Carey to say that was quite a compliment. I wish in all my heart that game had been televised, because it would have really done something for women's baseball.

How did the shift of the ball getting smaller and the pitching going from underhand to sidearm in 1946 and 1947 to overhand in 1948 affect you?

It didn't really affect me. In baseball, you have more time to see the ball coming from the pitcher, but in softball, the pitcher is closer, and you don't have as much time to see the ball. You're really got to be ready to hit it, or forget it—the ball's past you before you can get the bat off your shoulder. I liked baseball better, because I could see the ball better, because in softball the ball comes at you too fast.

I was talking to one of my friends the other day, and she said, "We were born too soon. Today [1996] we could be in the Olympics with basketball or softball or track." But those are the breaks, right? *[She laughs.]*

I notice that in 1945, your stolen bases fell off, from 166 in 1944 to 115 in 1945. Were you hurt in 1945?

I had a couple of sprained ankles in 1945. You know, those league fields weren't the greatest ball fields in the world, especially in Fort Wayne. In Fort Wayne, it was like sliding on rock! *[She laughs.]*

If we had a good crowd, the teams were going to play that game, no matter what. If they had to wait, or if they had to burn the field. You'd go out there and the smell and the smoke would be there, but the team officials could care less. They got the money from the people, and that was big stuff at the time. Players couldn't refuse to play, you know.

It just looks like after a while, your legs would get torn up so much from sliding that you just couldn't stand it.

Now I'm feeling the effects of sliding when I sit too long or when I first wake up in the morning, especially in the hip. What I call my "sliding leg," the right leg, is worse than the other leg. I did mostly hook sliding, and I'd slide on my right leg.

It looks like it was harder on the pitchers than the batters when the league shifted from softball to baseball.

Some girls left the league. Carolyn Morris came back here and played here in Phoenix and played with the softball league. There were a few girls that did go overhand. Joanne Winter went overhand. Connie Wisniewski, a great pitcher, was a good hitter, so she became an outfielder playing for Grand Rapids. Most of the other girls who were underhand pitchers just quit the league and went home, and played in softball leagues.

When you were Player of the Year in 1946, that must have been a great honor.

Being Player of the Year really was an honor. I didn't have a clue that I was going to be picked. Don Black, who was our PR man in Racine, wrote me a letter and asked me to give some kind of history of my playing days in Flint. I thought it was just for the Yearbook. He worked for Western Printing, and Western Printing wrote the Dell Books [called *Major League Baseball*]. He wrote the "Flint Flash" stuff.

That would have been a clue that I was being considered, but I never thought about it. Then when I was picked, well, I have a little bit of pride about that, because it was the managers that did the picking, and most of them were major league managers.

When you set the all-time stolen base record of 201 in 1946, you also had one of the league's best batting averages. You hit .286, and the only regular higher was Dottie Kamenshek at .316.

Dottie was a left-handed batter. I wish I could have learned how to hit both ways, because a left-hander has a couple of steps advantage going to first base.

Your last full season was 1950. What happened to cause you not to play in 1951?

Racine didn't resume the franchise in 1951, and a man came from Chicago to recruit us to play in the Chicago League [the National Girls Baseball League]. We went back to softball again, and played in Chicago. We won the championship with the Admiral Music Maids, you know, sponsored by Admiral Radio.

In 1952, you went back to the Belles?

The league came after me and offered me quite a bit of money as a bonus to play for the Battle Creek Belles. I put it to this guy in Chicago, Frank Darling, and he said, "No, I won't meet that offer." I went to Battle Creek in spring training down south for two weeks. Then we came to Battle Creek, and they had a dinner for us. Guy Bush was our manager, and I couldn't play for that guy. But I stayed. The Music Maids weren't doing too well in Chicago, and Frank Darling got word to me that he would meet the league's offer. He asked me to come back to Chicago, and I did. I played seventeen days into Battle Creek's season, and I moved back to Chicago.

Interview on June 19, 2011

What about your Racine teammates? Many of you were together from 1943 to 1950.

We were a very closely knit team, like a family. When we were on the road, we didn't stay with the teammates that we stayed with in Racine. Our chaperones had us stay with every teammate that we played with through the year. My closest teammates were Joanne Winter and Maddy English. We were like sisters. We got along really well, and all of us were pretty close. We had a lot of fun together. Those were some of the best times of my life.

What are some of your favorite memories from the league years?

Some of my best memories were playing in the league and for the Belles, and winning the first championship in our league in 1943. That was awesome. The next great thing was winning the championship against Rockford in 1946, and scoring the winning run after 14 innings. Being chosen Most Valuable Player in 1946 was very special to me, because I was chosen by ex-major leaguers who were the managers.

What kind of impact did the league make on your life?

I don't where I would be if I hadn't played in the AAGPBL. It had a huge impact on my life, as I went into business in Racine. I loved Racine. It was a great little town, and the fans were terrific.

ELIZABETH "LIB" MAHON
Kenosha, 1944; South Bend, 1945–1952
Interviewed on June 23, 1997, and August 30, 1997.

Born: 1919
Deceased: 2001
Height: 5'7"
Weight: 136
Positions: OF, 2B
Batted: R
Threw: R
All-Star Team: 1946, 1949
Season: Led league in RBIs twice: 1946 (72), 1949 (60)
Career: Tied for fourth in lifetime RBIs with Lavonne "Pepper" Paire, 400
Career: Batting average for nine seasons, .248

Elizabeth "Lib" Mahon (1919–2001), born the year after the Great War ended, grew up in Greenville when it was the biggest mill town in South Carolina. For many young girls in similar circumstances who came of age during the Great Depression, life's prospects often included going a few years to high school, working at home or at a mill, playing neighborhood sports, and getting married and raising a family in a small town or on a farm. However, Lib, slender, strong, and well-coordinated, was blessed by two great opportunities. First, a maiden aunt offered to help send the athletic-minded girl to college. One year after graduating from Greenville's Parker High, Lib rode the train upstate to Rock Hill and enrolled in Winthrop College, today a university. She completed the bachelor's degree in Physical Education in 1942, the first full year of the United States participation in World War II. She taught seventh grade in a small town for one year, spent another year working in the U.S. Post Office in Greenville, and received her second great opportunity in 1944 — the chance to play ball in the All-American League.

Mahon's life was never the same. Like most of her contemporaries who had the talent, determination, and good fortune to make the league, Lib worked hard, improved with experience, endured baseball's grinding summers, and lived the kind of dream ordinarily experienced by young male players. Regardless, she displayed one critical ability that every ballplayer yearns for: the ability to drive home base runners in clutch situations.

From Greenville, South Carolina, Lib Mahon, pictured in 1951, was a two-time All-Star outfielder for the Blue Sox. Lib finished her nine-year career with 400 RBIs, tying her for fourth place on the league's all-time list (courtesy Susan Wilson Odasz).

Baseball was usually a man's world, and dusty diamonds were hardly the places that women might be expected to excel, but excel Mahon did. Although she hurt her arm during spring training of 1944 and could no longer play shortstop or third base, she always swung a potent bat, and she wielded a dependable glove in the outfield. The 5'7" Greenville native spent her first season with Kenosha, one of the league's four original teams. Her manager, Marty McManus, left Kenosha in 1945 and signed with South Bend, and he soon engineered a trade that brought Mahon from the Comets to the Blue Sox in return for a little-known rookie.

Mahon proved her worth time and time again, batting .248 lifetime and leading the league in RBIs with 72 in 1946 and 60 in 1949, the first season the circuit adopted a smaller 10-inch ball in order to help boost batting averages. Witty, friendly, dependable, and also outspoken on behalf of teammates, the brunette flychaser made her mark in South Bend, developing a strong presence on the field, in the dugout, and away from the ballpark. She often counseled rookies. Later, after baseball, she worked as a physical education instructor and a school counselor in South Bend.

Mahon enjoyed many highlights during her nine league years, but the greatest was helping South Bend win the franchise's first Shaughnessy Playoff title in 1951, a season when she batted .269, her second highest average, and drove in 68 runs, tops for the Blue Sox and the second highest total for her career. However, the bottom fell out at the end of August 1952, when she joined a player walkout over what she considered the unfair treatment of a teammate, "Shorty" Pryer, by South Bend's manager, Karl Winsch. Thus, Mahon wrapped up her final two seasons by living the best high followed by the worst low of her nine-year AAGPBL career. Still, as family members recall, Lib inspired them and set standards for other women to strive for in their lives.

Interview on June 23, 1997

JS: You were born and raised in Greenville, South Carolina. What were your mother and father's names?

Mahon: My mother's name was Pearl, and her maiden name was Massey. Dad's name was David Mahon. I had two brothers and three sisters. I'm one of six children, and I was next to the youngest.

Were your brothers playing ball when you grew up?

Not really. My younger brother was a pretty good athlete, but my older brother was never a participant. He was a good sports fan, but he never participated in sports himself.

How about your father?

Dad was a great baseball fan, but not a player.

How did you get going in sports?

My younger brother Fred and I used to play together a lot. I had three older sisters who would be given duties by my mother inside the house, and I was the youngest girl, so I would participate in games, including shooting marbles with my brother. We started playing baseball, and I would play with his friends. Girls usually weren't good enough, but I was always pretty well coordinated and a good enough athlete, even early on.

Do you remember when you played on your first team?

I was a junior in Parker High School.

Schools never had any sports for girls, right?

Schools only had intramural sports for girls. When I was twelve years old, my dad worked for the Brandon Mill in Greenville, and I was playing for an organized basketball team representing that cotton mill. In my family, three girls played on that same team, two older sisters and me, when I was twelve. Kathryn was four years older than I was, and Nancy was two years older. The mill sponsored a men's baseball team, and they sponsored these men and women's basketball teams.

In basketball, my sister Kathryn and I played forward, and my sister Nancy played guard. In those days, there were six players on a [girls] basketball team, two-court basketball, you know. There were three forwards and three guards, and you couldn't cross the center line in those early years.

When I was a kid, my dad drove a truck for this company, and he dragged the baseball field on Saturday mornings when they were going to play a game at home that afternoon.

I would go with him, and if we were there long enough, I'd shag flies in the outfield when the men came out to warm up for their baseball game.

What about your first softball team?

The mill where my dad worked did not sponsor what they called interscholastic teams that would go play teams from other plants. But another more progressive industrial concern did, the Dunean Mills. Their coach and athletic director had seen me play basketball. So he would send a guy on a 6–8 mile drive to pick me up to play on their team. The Dunean Mills team was the first organized softball team I played on, and we would travel to cities 25 or 30 miles away to play other teams. I used to play shortstop or third base.

On one of those jaunts, I met Viola Thompson, a southpaw pitcher. She was the pitcher for the Anderson team, and her dad worked for a mill, too. I remember I hit a home run over the center fielder's head off her, and she said, "Lib, did you have to do that to me?"

We traveled to Anderson, which was 30 miles, and to Spartanburg, which was another 30 miles, and sometimes we'd play teams right in Greenville.

So the softball games started in the summer of your junior year of high school?

Yes, the *organized* softball games. We'd go pick up little games in a cow pasture, but we played with a hard baseball, you know. We were very poor, "Poor but proud." Someone would have a baseball and someone would have a bat, and we'd find something for bases. So we were playing baseball in a cow pasture when I was much younger than when I was a junior in high school, just recreation play.

I also played field hockey, basketball, and softball as part of the high school intramural teams, but we did not have interscholastic sports at all. We never had any tennis clubs or anything like that until I got to Winthrop College.

You graduated from Parker in 1937?

That's the year.

But you didn't go right to Winthrop?

I was out of school a year, and one of my dad's sisters, who never married, had a little money. She came to me one day and said, "Elizabeth how would you like to go to Winthrop?" She had the college picked out for me. *[She laughs.]*

I had done well academically in high school, not because anybody was pushing me, but just because I wanted to. I had made probably a B average in high school. She just came and said, "How would I like to go to Winthrop?"

I said, "Go to Winthrop on what? I don't have any money." "Well, I'm going to send you."

"Well, I'll have to talk this over with my parents." I talked to my mother and dad about it, and I had three older sisters. It was agreed that I could go. I even asked my aunt, "What am I going to do for spending money? I have to have money for personal supplies." My dad always gave me enough to get by on for things like that.

Things were cheap back then. My dad would buy me a ticket from Greenville to Winthrop College in Rock Hill with a five dollar bill. The ticket was a dollar and 20 cents, I remember, and he'd give me the change from the five dollars, and that would last me until the next time, maybe a month or two. The next time I saw him, I could have more money. Parents would send food back to their kids in college, every now and then.

I went to school on a shoestring, and my aunt paid the tuition. My sisters, who were working, helped me out some, you know, financially. They'd give me a few bucks here and there. My aunt who sent me to college could sew well, so she would make me some clothes. We had to wear uniforms at Winthrop College, it was called then, South Carolina College for Women. It had to be navy blue or white, or some combination thereof. It was a tough row to hoe, but I made it! *[She chuckles.]*

I finished college in 1942 with a BS degree in physical education. I had minors in Finance and English, because I always liked English-type subjects.

You must have worked somewhere after you graduated and before you joined the league.

I worked for one year at Brandon Mills when I was a senior in high school. I worked from four in the afternoon until twelve at night, because I only had to take four subjects, and I got out of school at noon my senior year, and I worked for another year after I got out of high school. That's what I might have ended up doing, working in the cotton mill, had I not got to go to college.

Thank God for a college education, and getting the opportunity to play ball, too. That changed my life completely when I came up north and saw how other people lived, instead of that Southern Baptist upbringing. Nothing wrong with that, but I don't follow that strict strategy any more, like my sister, who is here visiting in Roanoke. *[Editor's note: Mahon's niece Susan Wilson Odasz was living just outside Roanoke in Fincastle, Virginia.]*

My oldest sister Kathryn and I are the only two living out of a family of six children, and my sister is here with me right now in my niece's house.

You graduated in 1942, so did you teach right away?

I taught one year in Whitmire, South Carolina, self-contained seventh grade, which I hated every minute of it. There were very few full-time physical education jobs in the entire state of South Carolina when I finished college. You'd have to be in a big city like Greenville or Spartanburg, or some of the bigger towns were the only places you could get a physical education job. So I taught seventh grade in 1942–43 in Whitmire. I had to teach all the subjects for $90 a month. I got by, barely.

In that little town, all the teachers lived in two houses. We lived in two houses, all the teachers in town, high school and elementary. It cost us $30 a month, and our food was wonderful. I had a room in this house, and our meals were served there, breakfast and dinner. I'm not sure if we went home for lunch. I can't remember what we did for lunch. At the end of that school year, I had $33 between me and starvation. I paid my board, had to buy a few clothes, and I had $33 left.

Five of us from that little town in South Carolina went to Myrtle Beach for a week. When I was getting ready to go, my dad said, "Well, honey, are you going to have enough money to go?" I said, "I'll get by." He gave me a $10 bill and said, "Take this, in case you need it." At that time, you could get a room at Myrtle Beach for $5 a week per person.

I only taught at Whitmire that one year, and the next year I got a job in the U.S. Post Office making 65 cents an hour, which is more money than $90 a month, and I lived in Greenville with my parents.

That's when the president of the Greenville Spinners came up to my window [at Post Office]. He knew me. I was playing amateur softball again in Greenville on the same team with Viola Thompson. She had moved to Greenville, and we were playing on the same organized softball team. Jimmy Gaston, president of the Greenville Spinners, who came up here to watch us play ball, knew I'd go to ball games with my dad and watch the Spinners play.

Jimmy Gaston came to my window one day and he said, "Lib, how would you like go to up north and play ball for money?" That's the way I got the opportunity to go up with the All-American Girls League. He had scouted both me and Viola Thompson on this amateur softball team, and Viola and I came up to Peru-LaSalle, Illinois, to spring training in 1944. We came up together. Thank God for the Army. Those guys kept us headed in the right direction.

Do you know how many were at those tryouts?

That was the spring training site. The players from the original four teams were all there, and they were going to have six teams in 1944. They had to bring in all these new players because they had to have enough to fill rosters of two additional teams. But the players for the original four teams were there also. They looked at what we were able to do, you know, throw and pitch and hit and field the ball. So Viola and I got assigned to a team.

How long did the spring training last?

About ten days, I believe.

You ended up with Minneapolis, right?

I was with Minneapolis for three weeks. I came in as an infielder, and I was on third base, and Marty McManus was hitting me ground balls. He was watching me throw to first base, and all that stuff. Incidentally, I had not properly warmed up, and I kind of hurt my arm. I never did throw as well after that. I did some damage to my shoulder, I guess.

Marty was watching me. He was the manager of the Kenosha Comets, and he had watched me try out. So he had the opportunity to make a trade for a fifteen-year-old girl, Anna Meyer [from Aurora, Indiana]. He sent her to Minneapolis and he brought me to Kenosha to become a member of the Kenosha Comets. I was only in Minneapolis for three weeks.

I spent the remainder of the year in Kenosha playing second base, because I hurt my arm and didn't throw as well. I was either a shortstop or a third baseman most of the time, but at second base I had a shorter throw.

You must have had a pretty decent year with Kenosha.

I don't remember exactly what my batting average was, but I do remember in every year I was either fourth or fifth, or sometimes sixth batter. I was third, fourth, fifth, or sixth batter, and usually I was either clean-up or fifth. In my own mind, I didn't think I was that good a hitter.

You got traded to South Bend in 1945, right?

Marty McManus managed Kenosha in 1944, and he came to South Bend as manager in 1945, and he traded somebody to get me in South Bend in 1945, around the time the season started. In addition to that, after the season started, he traded two other South Bend players to get two other Kenosha players. He got "Pinky" Pirok, Pauline Pirok, shortstop, and he traded Dottie Schroeder for Pinky. I couldn't believe that kind of trade. And he also traded Lois Florreich to Kenosha for Phyllis Koehn. She played in Kenosha in 1943 and 1944, and the announcer at the Kenosha Comets' games gave her the nickname "Sugar" Koehn. Dottie Schroeder was one of the most graceful and one of the most beautiful shortstops you ever saw.

So you came to South Bend from 1945 on through 1952.

The story I told you in South Bend about when I quit is the honest-to-God truth about what happened. I don't care what you read or heard other people say, that is the way that thing happened, when I quit, because of this girl [Charlene "Shorty" Pryer] being suspended without pay for a week — for doing nothing, really.

I believe you said she had her spikes off on the bench and sat down to put them on.

We were in the last inning of the ball game and she [Pryer] had her moccasins on to get back on the bus. You know, we had to change shoes and not wear our spikes onto the bus. She had changed into her moccasins to get back on the bus, when Karl [Winsch] called on her to pinch run. And she had to take a minute to get her spikes back on, and he suspended her for it.

But what you said was the same thing happened to you earlier in the same game.

The same game. Karl called on me to pinch hit. Maybe I still had my shoes on sitting there, but I had to take time to tie my shoes. He didn't do anything to me. He knew better. I'd have told him off. Karl didn't like Shorty in the first place. I told you that. She was not one of my favorite people either, but what he did to her was completely unfair. It was wrong. Karl was a bull-headed man. It was his way, or it was wrong.

You made the All-Star team in 1946, right?

I made the All-Star team in 1946, period. My [baseball] card said I made the All-Star team '46 through '49, and that is not true.

What you're remembering is usually you batted third or fourth or fifth.

More often I batted fourth or fifth all the years I played.

What do you remember about going to Cuba in 1947?

It was absolutely beautiful spring training weather, because it was hot in the daytime. We stayed at the Seville-Biltmore Hotel, and it was cool at night. You had the sea breeze at night. It was hot. You had to be extremely careful not to get too much sun, because some of the gals stayed out in the sun too long when we weren't on the ball field, and they got severe sunburns. You know, it was ideal training conditions. The weather was beautiful, and we trained at two different stadiums. They broke the league up into two groups, you know, to have two different retraining sites. One of the places was the Havana Stadium, and I can't think of the name of the other. They took the entire league down there. I remember all of us flying out of Miami. I think we were there ten days. I know it had to be very, very expensive for the league.

We flew back to Miami, and we had by then been assigned a team. We played our way north with pre-arranged exhibition games at various cities on the way between Miami and where we were going to end up playing ball for that summer.

So you did the allocation in Havana that year.

Yes.

Looks like the system was each team kept the top nine or ten players, and the only allocating the league did was either new people or the other four or five players.

I think they did that in those original years. They did the allocating to try to even up the competition in the various teams. It didn't make you feel too good to be traded, but sometimes those trades were made to equalize the competition, so one team wouldn't dominate.

South Bend must have played one team all the way up to the Midwest.

They would assign two teams to play against each other in four or five different cities on the way back to where we're going to play for that year. I can't remember the team we played against, so help me. I don't remember playing in Roanoke.

We did play in some city in Ohio near Cincinnati, and Betsy's brother came over, brought us back to Cincinnati, and Phyllis Koehn and I — we had permission to do this, of course — stayed a day or two at Betsy's house, and we drove Betsy's car on to South Bend. Phyllis Koehn and Betsy Jochum and I were really close friends. Sometimes more close than we are now! *[She laughs.]* I live next door to Betsy, and sometimes we don't see eye-to-eye on things.

In 1948, is that the year they held spring training in Opa-Locka?

In the fall of 1947, I didn't ask for a job in South Bend, but they asked me, because they were so short of physical education teachers. After that, I did not get to go to spring training. I had to work myself into condition, and from then until school was out, I would only go to cities like Fort Wayne that were close by so that I could drive back to go to school the next day.

I retired from the South Bend School system in June of 1981.

I guess baseball did a whole lot for your career.

It surely did. Baseball changed my life completely. My family is still living in South Carolina, and I did not intend to stay in South Bend. I was treated so beautifully by my principal at my first school. They included me in everything they did. It was so pleasant that I never left. I used to spend ever Christmas and every spring vacation going to see my family.

How were the fans in South Bend?

We had enough fan support for most of the years, but the very best year we had attendance-wise was 1946. I know we had 10,000 people, the largest crowd ever to watch one of the girls' baseball games in 1946 in South Bend. I believe it was the Fourth of July game in 1946.

I have some of my baseball cards with me, and I led the league in 1946 with 72 RBIs, and in 1949 I had 60 RBIs. I guess it means I led the league those two years.

When you filled out that questionnaire for the Baseball Hall of Fame, are there favorite memories you think about, like winning the championship in 1951?

That was the epitome when we won the league championship in 1951. But I intended to quit after that year, but I thought, "If I do, what am I going to do during the summer?" I didn't make that much money that I could save enough money to live on all summer. I was going to have to get a job. "Well, I'll try one more year," I thought.

I'd already told Karl, the manager, I was going to quit, so he brought in another outfielder, Jo Lenard, when I decided to play another year. I did not get to play regularly my last year. I got to play, I don't remember how many games, but that was my own fault. I played maybe half the games.

In 1951, what team did you beat for the championship?

We beat Rockford. They always had a good team. Bill Allington was a good teacher. He really helped those people that played for him. Everybody didn't always like him, but sometimes the best teachers are not the most well liked. Bill Allington was a real teacher of baseball.

Jean [Faut] and I both had said this: We learned more baseball from Marty McManus than any other manager we had. Jeannie played from '46 through '53, I believe. She played for Karl from 1951 until she quit. We learned more baseball from Marty McManus.

Rockford always had a good team when Bill Allington was there, because he knew how to get the most out of the girls who played for him.

Marty McManus must have been quite a manager too.

Marty was. He managed me in Kenosha in 1944, and in 1945, he traded for me. I played for him again in 1948. Jeannie started in 1946 and she played for Marty in 1948.

Interview on August 30, 1997

I wanted to follow up on the situation when you left South Bend in 1952.

There is a book called *The Dutiful Dozen* by W.C. Madden, about the Blue Sox in 1952, but it's not a good book. No matter what the author said about me, Shorty Pryer was not a close friend, but she was treated unfair, and that's why I left the team.

Madden made a comment about me which is insulting, and I even considered suing. He portrayed me as being a "mean-spirited" person. Madden said I had a "mean streak which she got from her Indiana-born mother and her Scots-Irish father." I'm very upset about that book.

What was your comment about Karl Winsch?

Anybody who played ball won't have kind words for him. It was Winsch's way, or it was wrong.

MARGE (CALLAGHAN) MAXWELL
Minneapolis, 1944; Fort Wayne, 1945–1948;
South Bend, 1949; Peoria, 1950–1951; Battle Creek, 1951
Interviewed on October 3, 2011.

Born: 1921
Height: 5' 3"
Weight: 120
Positions: 3B, 2B
Batted: R
Threw: R
Best Fielding Average at 3B: 1944 and 1945
Career Batting Average: .190 for eight seasons

Marge Callaghan, born in Vancouver, British Columbia, was the fourth of six children of Albert and Hazel Callaghan. Their mother died early, Albert remarried, and he and his wife Anne had three children. Marge and her sister Helen, a year and a half younger, played softball in the streets with neighborhood kids. The Irish Catholic sisters went to the same elementary and junior high schools, and both attended King Edward High, and they played on the same teams, including basketball in the winter and track and field in the chilly spring. Marge graduated in 1939, and the sisters were teammates on the same softball teams, the

Pictured on the right, Marge Callagham, one of two Callaghan sisters from Vancouver, British Columbia, who joined the league in 1944, runs toward home plate after hitting one of her few career home runs at the Gran Stadium in Havana during spring training in 1947. Bonnie Baker, from Regina, Saskatchewan, is South Bend's catcher on the left, and Faye Dancer (#15) waits to congratulate her teammate (courtesy Marge Maxwell).

Young Liberals and, later, the Western Mutuals. During World War II, Marge worked for Boeing Aircraft. In 1944, Helen was invited to the All-American League's spring training Peru-LaSalle, Illinois, where she made the second-year circuit and was allocated to the Minneapolis Millerettes. In mid-summer, Marge, who obtained special permission to leave her wartime job, joined the Millerettes, now a traveling team due to declining attendance in Minneapolis. Marge recalled the change between playing for the Mutuals compared to the Millerettes wasn't great, except with the American pro team, they lived out of suitcases and she needed a bigger glove. The sisters performed well as rookies, with Marge hitting .182 and Helen batting .287, the second-best mark in the league.

Marge, a 5'3" right-handed batter, and the flamboyant, Helen, a 5'1" outfielder who threw and batted left, moved with the franchise in 1945 to Fort Wayne, and the sisters, along with several other Canadians, played four seasons there. Marge enjoyed those years, including living in homes of local families and sporting the team's pink uniforms with burgundy trim. A graceful fielder with quick hands and good speed, she played mostly third base, where her strong arm made her a fixture. She also played second base, but seldom shortstop. The Vancouver speedster batted second, following Helen, who was the Daisies' leadoff hitter. Marge loved to bunt, and though her average was well below Helen's, they worked well together. Marge often bunted to advance her sister to the next base, or if Helen stole second and maybe third base, Marge sacrificed to score the run. Besides other Canadians, the sisters' best friend with the Daisies was Dottie Collins, the circuit's great underhand pitcher who was called the "Strikeout Queen."

Marge, bright, spirited, and likeable, with her long brown hair and dark brown eyes, gave the game her best effort every day. An excellent teammate, she favored her time in Fort Wayne because she spent four of her baseball years there, but she gave South Bend a good season in 1949 and Peoria almost two good seasons, before being traded to the Battle Creek Belles late in the summer of 1951. Returning home that fall, she met and later married Mervin Maxwell, and the couple had two sons, Guy and Dale. The sisters played softball together on Vancouver teams after their league years, and later, they also enjoyed the AAGPBL Reunions. Marge liked the feature movie, *A League of Their Own*, a film gem that brought the All-American League to the attention of millions of movie-goers around the world. However, the Canadian infielder explained the film was not about particular sisters like Helen and her. Instead, the characters were fictional composites, and the movie was about the *league*, not individuals. Marge still enjoys many memories from the league years, including one home run that she blasted so hard in South Bend that it caused the local sportswriter to dub her a "feminine Ted Williams."

JS: You're from Vancouver, British Columbia. Can you tell me about your family and how you got involved in playing ball when you were growing up?

Maxwell: My father's name was Albert Callaghan, and my mother's name was Hazel. I was the fourth of their six children, and our names were Kay, Pearl, Lewis, Margaret, Helen, and Patrick. My mother died very young, and my father remarried Anne, my stepmother. We have a younger half sister and two younger half brothers, Wayne, Elaine, and Dan.

Helen and I were like most kids when we started playing ball in the streets and all. We went to a Catholic school, St. Patrick's, in Vancouver, through grade 6. I went to grade 7 at St. Patrick's and to grade 8 at Florence Nightingale, and Helen went to grades 7 and 8 at Florence Nightingale. St. Patrick's didn't allow much in sports, but we both attended King Edward High School. We got started in sports, and we were playing ball in the local parks.

You and Helen grew up going to the same schools and playing ball together, right?

Yes, we did. I finished school in 1939. We played on the same teams for all our lives, except for the one year in the All-American League when she got traded from Fort Wayne to Kenosha in 1949.

What about your fast-pitch softball teams in British Columbia?

We were scouted in Detroit when we went down there in 1943 to play in the World Championship tournament. We were playing for the Western Mutuals for two or three years. They changed the names along the way, because at first it was the Young Liberals. They changed names according to the sponsors.

Western Mutual was an insurance company that sponsored the team, but none of us worked for them. Before I went down to play for the league, I was working for Boeing Aircraft. That was my last job before I left to play in the States, and I had to get special permission to leave.

Did you try out for the league at Peru-LaSalle, Illinois, in 1944?

I went to the league halfway through the season. Helen started in spring training, but I had to get special permission from the government to go down and play professional ball.

She was also working for Boeing, but I was a squad leader, and they figured I was more essential for the war effort, so I had to get special permission. Helen had to get permission too, but she got it and was able to leave and go to spring training. I still have that written permission! *[She laughs.]*

You went down in the middle of the season and joined Minneapolis.
When I joined the team, they had changed it to the Minneapolis "Orphans," because we traveled and played all road games for the second half of the season. I never even went to the city of Minneapolis, but I gather the team didn't go over too well, because they didn't get enough attendance.

What was the difference in playing for the Mutuals and in the All-American League?
At first, it wasn't too much different, because the All-American League was playing softball at the time. It was just an adjustment to how things went down there. But I didn't find it too much different than at home, except that I didn't have the type of glove they wanted me to have. I had a glove that just fit my hand. We couldn't afford to buy real good gloves when we were playing at home. After I started playing in the States, I had to go and buy a new glove.

Audrey (Haine) Daniels told me the same thing—the manager asked her to buy a new glove in 1944, because hers was too small. I believe you both played for Minneapolis.
Audrey was on our team. In 1945, after we moved to Fort Wayne, we had half a dozen Canadians on the team. Besides me and Helen, we had Penny O'Brian, and we had Yolande Teillet and Audrey Haine, and Arleene Johnson, but I don't remember all the names.

How did you travel?
The first two years we traveled by trains, because those were the war years, and then we changed over and traveled by bus.

What do you remember from that first season?
What I remember is packing clothes in and out of a suitcase every time we turned around! We were on the road all the time, so we lived out of a suitcase. We were getting money for eating out, so that helped. They allowed us $3 a day, if I remember correctly.

When the season finished, you went back home.
We came home after the season, and we played basketball. We played regular basketball with five players, a center, two forwards, and two guards. We played sports the year around. Helen and I played lacrosse for three years, and that was a rough game.

Was that before you began with the league?
Yes, we played lots of sports before the league. We did just about everything that we could do. We ran track and field in high school, and Helen won medals in track and field. We played soccer on the street with the boys, and we played roller hockey with the boys. There were no girls playing, so we did that on the side. We were busy! *[She laughs.]*

You moved with the Millerettes to Fort Wayne in 1945, when the team became the Daisies.
Yes, and I played in Fort Wayne until 1948. We went to spring training in 1945, and I think it was in Chicago.

How was it different to be in Fort Wayne?
We lived in people's homes. People rented us rooms. One year three or four of us lived with Dottie Collins, after she got married. Her husband Harvey was still in the U.S. Navy.

Did you know that Dottie couldn't throw overhand? That's what she told me, and I never saw her throw overhand. When she fielded the ball, she threw to first base either sidearm or underhand. When the league went overhand, she pitched sidearm. She didn't play much longer after the league went to overhand, because she was married and had her first baby. She sat out the 1949 season, and she returned in 1950.

Dottie was a beautiful underhand pitcher too when we were playing softball. Every time we played the team that had Carolyn Morris, I think it was Rockford, and Dottie and Carolyn pitched against each other. Boy — what games those were!

The Daisies wore those sort of pink uniforms, right?

I'd say the uniforms were pink, and the trim was a deeper color.

You and Helen were together through the 1948 season, and you played the infield.

Most of the time I played third base, and I played second base part of the time, but most of the time it was third base. A couple of times I didn't play the whole season. I got traded to South Bend in 1949, so I didn't play the whole season there. They had another third baseman, Helen Filarski. She played the most of the first half of the season, and I played the biggest part of the last half of the season. I broke my ankle another year, I believe in 1950, and I didn't play many games at all.

Did you have a favorite team?

I did favor Fort Wayne the best, because I played there the longest. You just got used to it, you know.

Did you remember anything unusual that happened?

You wouldn't believe how I got traded from Peoria to Battle Creek in the last part of the 1951 season. In one game I was playing third base, and I picked up a grounder, and I turned around to throw to second, and the runner was there, but not the second baseman. So I turned and threw the ball to first base, and I got the runner going down to first. I was always taught, "If you can't get two, get one." After the inning was over, the manager, Johnny Rawlings, came screaming out of the dugout, and he said, "What the hell do you think you're doing?"

I got my Irish temper up, and I screamed right back, "What the hell do you think I was doing?" All the people in the stands stood up and yelled, "Atta girl, Marge — You tell him!" And I guess that made him mad.

I said to Johnny Rawlings, "I was always taught if I couldn't get two outs, get one." He said, "You should have thrown to second base." I said, "It would have gone out between center field and right field, and the run would have scored." He said, "You should have thrown it anyway."

I couldn't believe it! That just doesn't make sense. I didn't say any more, and I went over and sat down on the bench. Three weeks later, I got traded to Battle Creek. After Johnny Rawlings traded me, he got fired. He made everyone mad in Peoria, and he got fired. All those years and I never talked back to the coaches. I did what they told me, but I couldn't see any sense to what the manager said on that play. He would have blasted me if I hadn't thrown it to first. And I couldn't figure out why he didn't wait until I got into the dugout to say something to me.

It didn't matter, because it was my last year anyway.

Do you have favorite memories of things that happened to you and your sister Helen?

I think mainly we remembered how nice the people were down there, and how they invited us out to dinner so much. They were so nice to us.

What position did Helen play?
  She played center field and left field.

I've read that you were both fast.
  Helen used to lead off, and I batted second, and I did an awful lot of bunting. I would wait until Helen stole second, and I would bunt her to third. If she got to third on her own, or some play didn't work, we had a squeeze play, and I did a lot of bunting on the squeeze play, too.

That's what they call "small ball" today.
  They don't do it too much today. Half the men can't bunt anyway! By the way, my sister had a son who played in the majors, Casey Candaele.

Did you ever play together after you were traded away from Fort Wayne?
  We played ball together at home here on the Western Mutuals, until Helen and her family moved down to California.

Did you go to any of the AAGPBL Reunions?
  I've been to a few of the reunions. I've been to Cooperstown twice, and I've been to South Bend and Fort Wayne, and to Milwaukee.

Were you one of the people involved when they made the movie A League of Their Own*?*
  No, I wasn't.
  It's interesting, but a lot of girls say that movie was written about them, but it wasn't. The movie was written about the *league*. When anybody asks me, I always say the movie was about the league. My nephew, Kelly Candaele, took the idea of the movie to Penny Marshall in the first place. He produced a documentary, called *A League of Their Own*, about our league. Kelly took the story to Penny Marshall, but he did not have the rights to the title, so Penny Marshall and the producers called the movie *A League of Their Own*. But as I said, the story was not about anybody in particular — it was about the league.

I understand that all the characters in the movie are composites, not based on any individual All-Americans.
  The movie featured two sisters, but not any two particular sisters. I've had people ask me, "Who played your position?" I say, "Nobody played my position. The movie was about the league." And that's all I say. I think it was a good movie, and the people who acted in the show did a marvelous job.

Do you have favorite memories that you like to talk about?
  So many things happened that it's hard to pick out just a few things. One thing that I did enjoy in Fort Wayne, and it sounds kind of silly, was that I went on the first hayride of my life on a farm outside town. We had a lot of people invite us out to their homes for dinner.
  One person I really liked was a lady in Fort Wayne we called "Mum" Guyatte, and she was a nurse. She'd invite Dottie and Helen and me out to her house quite a few times. I really enjoyed her, and she was such a nice person. We stayed with her off and on quite a bit. She favored Dottie and Helen and me and Vivian Kellogg the most.
  I want to tell you about a time when the league allowed the players that had a car to drive to the ball games. Dottie Collins had a car, and five of us — we were all first-string players — had five flat tires going from Fort Wayne to Racine, Wisconsin, and we were late getting to the ball game. The manager put all the other players in, and they were winning

the ball game. He was so mad at us. He put us all in, and we lost the game! We thought it was kind of comical, in a way. He should have left the other players in the game, because they were going fine. The ones on that car trip were Dottie and Helen and myself, but I'm not sure of the other two.

Would you say the league made a big impact on your life?

Yes, it did. Playing in the league was what I call a tremendous time in my life. There's a lot of good things to remember. I really met some wonderful people, and I made a lot of friends. Penny O'Brian, who played the 1945 season, later moved out here from Edmonton, and we kept in touch over the years, until Penny passed away last year [2010]. We kept in touch and visited back and forth a lot. I kept in touch with Colleen (Smith) McCulloch. She played the one year for Grand Rapids [in 1949], and she was from Vancouver too.

You're the best person to tell me about your sister. You grew up together and you played on so many teams together. What was Helen like as a person and a ballplayer?

Helen was a very good ballplayer. She was a left-handed batter and a good drag bunter. She almost led the league in hitting her first year, 1944, and she did win the championship in 1945.

[*Editor's note: Helen averaged .287 in 1944, placing second for the league batting championship behind South Bend's Betsy Jochum at .296. In 1945, Helen won the batting championship with a .299 mark in 111 games. Racine pitcher Mary Crews batted .319 in 66 games, but Mary's 135 at-bats did not qualify her for the batting title.*]

Your sister was pretty fast too.

Helen always beat me by one step! [*She laughs.*]

My reflexes were faster than hers, and I got started faster, but she always beat me. She finished faster by about a step. So I never went into competitive racing against her. But it never bothered me, and I never worried about it.

You were the older sister, right?

I was older by fifteen months.

How would you describe Helen? Were you similar in terms of personality?

No, we weren't alike in personality. Helen was more forward than I was. She was more of a flamboyant type of ballplayer. We had a few ballplayers on our Daisies team that were like that. I was a little more reserved. I wasn't going to go down and play in the league at first, but Dad wanted me to go because of Helen. He wanted me to keep an eye on her. That's what he told me anyway! [*She laughs.*]

Helen played a couple of years less than you. Do you know why?

Because she had a family—five boys. She had two boys first, Richard and Robert, and a set of twins, Kelly and Kerry, and then Casey.

You played through the 1951 season, when you were traded to Battle Creek, but you left the game. Did you already have in mind that you weren't going to play after 1951?

I didn't know it at that point. When I came home, I met my future husband, Mervin Maxwell, but I call him Merv. We got married six months later. I knew then I wasn't going back to the league. Later, we had two sons, Guy and Dale.

It must have been really neat for you as two sisters to play on so many teams.

I don't think we were much different from other sisters who played in the league. Because of the fact that we were close in age, I was never that far ahead that I would go up to the next bracket in softball here in British Columbia. There weren't that many teams around Vancouver when we first started playing.

Did you have the same color hair and eyes?

Helen's eyes were kind of hazel, and my eyes are dark brown. My hair was a lot darker than Helen's. At one point, my hair was black and it turned brown, and Helen's was brown. Later, she changed her hair to different colors! *[She laughs.]*

In 1947, the league went to sidearm pitching, and in 1948, they shifted to overhand. Did that make any difference to you as a batter?

I never set the world on fire with my hitting, but I did a lot of bunting. You can see that on my baseball card! I hit better here at home when I was playing softball. When I was forty-two at home, I had a .475 batting average!

So whether the league's pitching was underhand or sidearm or overhand, it didn't matter to you as a batter.

No, not really. You got used to it, just like anything else.

I did hit a few long balls. I recall one game at South Bend where they recorded a home run I hit as the longest hit ball at that point in the league. The article in the paper said, "Marge Callaghan, who is one hundred and some odd pounds soaking wet, hit the longest ball of the season, and Betsy Jochum is still chasing it!" I thought it was hilarious. I only hit two or three home runs all the time I played in the league, but I really hit that one!

[Editor's note: On July 25, 1947, Marge blasted a two-run homer in the ninth inning off Ruth Williams in Fort Wayne's 7–0 victory over South Bend at Playland Park. The ball carried over Betsy Jochum's head in left field and bounced into Playland's bleachers. Jim Costin, sports editor of the South Bend Tribune, *compared Callaghan to a "feminine Ted Williams." Costin called her home run "the longest ball ever hit in a girls' pro game here, and probably as long as any other ever hit in any other park in the league, too."]*

GRACE PISKULA
Rockford, 1944
Interviewed on February 7, 2012.

Born: 1926
Height: 5'7"
Weight: 123
Positions: OF
Batted: R
Threw: R
Career Batting Average: Less than 10 games — no statistics available

Grace Piskula, one of three children of Peter and Regina Piskula, was born and raised on the south side of Milwaukee. Active, energetic, and fun-loving, she played ball with boys in the neighborhood partly because there was only one other girl for a playmate. Grace

Pictured circa 1942, on her team in West Allis, near Milwaukee, Grace Piskula (third from right in front row) was signed by Rockford in early July 1944. She spent the rest of the season with the Peaches, but she arrived too late to appear in the team's picture (courtesy Grace Piskula).

thrived on sports, and starting in elementary school, she played softball, volleyball, and basketball at playgrounds and at social centers near her family's home on Thirteenth and Manitoba Streets. Their mother wouldn't allow Richard, her older brother, and Chester, her younger brother, to play football, but most kids played games in the streets during the Depression-era 1930s. The Piskula youngsters all attended St. John Catholic Grade School and, later, Pulaski High. Her brothers graduated during the early years of World War II, and like millions of other young men, they joined the Army. During the war, Grace went to high school, and she played softball on teams in the West Allis League coached by Fred Zirkle. Martin's Maids was one of Zirkle's winning teams. A month after Grace graduated from Pulaski High at age eighteen, she was looking for a job to earn money for college when the All-American League came calling.

Piskula, with sandy blond hair, blue eyes, and a nice smile, received a telegram from Jack Kloza, manager of the Rockford Peaches, asking her to report to the team for a game in Racine, Wisconsin, on July 2. Grace, who stood 5'7" and weighed 120 pounds, had played first base, shortstop, and left field for teams in Milwaukee and West Allis. Kloza, a former major leaguer who later managed a team on Milwaukee's north side, had seen Piskula play, and he needed help after a couple of the Peaches suffered injuries. Piskula reported, worked out, and traveled with Rockford for the rest of the season. In late July, however, the team changed managers, and Californian Bill Allington replaced Kloza. Grace was used in a handful of games as a reserve left fielder. Although she loved getting the professional experience and playing alongside Peaches teammates such as Dottie Kamenshek, Piskula decided not to return. Instead, she enrolled at La Crosse State University in September 1944, and she completed her freshman year of credits toward the bachelor's degree in Health and Physical Education. Early in 1945, she was called by Chicago's National Girls Baseball League, a fast-pitch softball circuit, and she played first base for the Chicago Chicks that summer. They played night games, and the girls held jobs in the daytime. Grace earned the rookie minimum salary of $50 a week in the AAGPBL, and the Chicks paid her $40 a week, which she saved for college expenses.

Piskula, who still enjoys duplicate bridge, the opera, and golf, completed the degree in 1948. She found a position in Racine. She taught physical education and recreation classes for two years at McKinley Junior High and almost 23 years at Park High. Later, she directed Health and Physical Education for the school district until 1986, retiring after nearly 40 years of service. Even later, thanks to former Milwaukee star and South Bend player Ellen Tronnier, the AAGPBL Players Association found Piskula. Irene Applegren talked Grace into attending the 1993 league reunion in South Bend, and league great Dottie Collins persuaded her to locate a picture and be included in the Frisch baseball cards. Grace Piskula has fond memories of the West Allis, Milwaukee, the All-American League, and Chicago leagues, and she's grateful that the movie, *A League of Their Own*, brought recognition to the hundreds of women who played hardball so many years ago.

JS: How did you begin playing ball?

Piskula: I grew up in Milwaukee, and I began playing volleyball, basketball, and softball at the social centers. In the summer, Jack Kloza and "Bunny" Brief, both former major leaguers who also used to be Milwaukee Brewers, had teams in the Milwaukee Recreational and Industrial League. I played for Bunny Brief on the south side team against Jack Kloza's north side team. I played first base, shortstop, and left field in Milwaukee and also in the West Ellis Softball League. Fred Zirkle was my manager when I played on several winning teams in West Allis. We played lots of games in West Allis, and we always drew lots of fans.

Where were you born and raised?

I was born on the south side of Milwaukee, and our parents, Peter and Regina Piskula, and our family lived at Thirteenth and Manitoba Streets. I grew up in a neighborhood where there was only one other girl, so I grew up being a tomboy, and we played all the sports with the boys in the neighborhood. I had two brothers, Richard was my older brother and Chester was my younger brother. Chester was a runner, but my mother never let the boys play football. Later, they went from college into the Army during World War II, and I had to fund my own college.

We had playgrounds and social centers nearby. You could go there for a whole year for $2. I played ball on the playgrounds and at the social centers. Later, I wound up playing in a city league and an intercity league and on all-star teams.

Where did you go to school?

I went to St. John Catholic Grade School and I went to Pulaski High School, and they are on the south side of Milwaukee. We could never miss school. Father and mother valued education since neither had completed high school. Mother was so proud to have two children with master's degrees and one with a PhD.

Later, I went to college and completed my bachelor's degree in Health and Physical

Education, and I graduated in 1948. I took a job teaching health and physical education at McKinley Junior High School in Racine. After that, I taught at Park High School in Racine. I taught for nearly 25 years. Eventually I became the director of Health and Physical Education for the district, and I retired in 1986.

In 1952 during the summer, I was at New York University during graduate work, and I went with grad students to Helsinki, Finland, for the Olympics. It was a wonderful experience. In 1955, I taught at the University of Hawaii. Both were very memorable experiences. Later, after I retired, I enjoyed trips to Greece, Italy, Portugal, Spain, England, Norway, Sweden, and Denmark.

How did you get the opportunity to play in the All-American League?

To make a long story short, I received a telegram from Jack Kloza, who was managing the Rockford Peaches, saying he had a position for me on the Peaches and I should report to the Peaches in Racine on July 2, 1944. That telegram is now framed and it will go to my family.

I knew nothing about the All-American Girls League, so I called Bunny Brief, my coach in Milwaukee. Bunny gave me the needed information. I was planning to start going to college in September of 1944, so I needed a job.

At first my mother said, "You're not going anywhere." Then Bunny Brief asked her, "Where else can Grace go to make $50 a week and $2.50 a day meal money?" She couldn't answer that question. *[She laughs.]*

I played for a short time for Rockford, from July to the end of the 1944 season. When I got into the games, I played left field. At that time, the All-American League was using underhand pitching, and they were playing with an 11½ inch ball.

When you were with Rockford, did you get to play in many games?

I can't say I played in that many games, because they had a great team. They didn't have a team doctor, if you got hurt, so the chaperone would take care of injuries. The team coach would be at third base during the games, giving you signals when you were batting. If you didn't do what the signal suggested, you were fined 50 cents! *[She laughs.]*

If you didn't obey the coach's signals, even if you hit a home run, you still had to pay the 50 cents! Nobody ever talked about that, but I remember it.

Jack Kloza was the manager when I went to Rockford, and that's why I got the job. I had played against his north side team in Milwaukee, and he knew what I could do. I think Rockford had a girl who sprained an ankle, or something, but she couldn't play, and they needed another player.

Jack left the team late in July of 1944, maybe because the wins and losses weren't so good. He was replaced by Bill Allington, and Rockford won more games with our new manager.

We had some great players, like Dottie Kamenshek at first base. The team had good support in the city, and the stands were full, as I recall, for the games. There were groups in towns that had us come in for lunch and things like that, so the Peaches had support in Rockford.

I'm not in the team picture for Rockford. The picture on my baseball card is a high school picture. I missed the pictures in Rockford. I was there only for the later part of the season, and I wasn't that big a contributor for the Peaches.

After the season ended, I went to college at La Crosse State University (now the University of Wisconsin at La Crosse). When I was at La Crosse, I got a telephone call from someone in Chicago, and they wanted me to come and try out for the Chicago Chicks in the National Girls Baseball League, which was really a softball league. I played first base for the Chicks. I earned $40 a week in the 1945 season. We played at night, so during the day we could have full-time jobs. I was saving up money to go to college, and the degree I would earn would give me the opportunity to be a teacher of Physical Education.

These days I play some duplicate Bridge, enjoy the theater and the opera, play golf, and volunteer at a street hospital.

I would like to thank some people for helping me with the opportunity to play in the AAGPBL. Ellen Tronnier, who was a super athlete, reported to someone that I had played in the league in 1944, and that's how I became part of the Players Association.

Irene (Lefty) Applegren talked me into going to the AAGPBL Reunion in South Bend in 1993. I roomed with Irene in Rockford back in 1944. For the few months that I did play for Rockford, we each had a room at the house of a local fan.

Dottie Collins kept bugging me for a picture, since I was not present for the Rockford team pictures in 1944. That's how my picture appeared on the Fritch baseball card.

It is important that many of our enthusiastic associate members in the Players Association are helping to keep the league going, because it's an interesting story.

I also thank the many fans who cite the movie, *A League of Their Own*, as their source of interest about our once-in-a-lifetime league.

ROSE (FOLDER) POWELL
Kenosha, 1944
Interviewed on July 5, 2011.

Born: 1926
Height: 5'6"
Weight: 140
Positions: P-OF
Batted: R
Threw: R
Career Batting Average: .261 for 71 games in 1944
Lifetime Pitching Record: 2–7 with 5.67 ERA in 14 games

Rose Folder, born in 1926, grew up in a working class family with five brothers and two sisters, all younger, in Springfield, Illinois. The oldest child, Rose received little of the attention given to her siblings, so she turned to playing ball in the neighborhood with boys. When she was thirteen, the pastor at the family's church taught the athletic-minded girl how to pitch softball. While attending Feitshans High School, which lacked sports for girls, she traveled to Peoria, an hour and a half trip to the north, and played for the Peoria Chicks against teams like Peoria's Caterpillarettes. In the summer of 1942, as World War II raged, Rose lived in Peoria with the Farrow family, and the father owned the Chicks. Talented,

Rose Folder is pictured with three Kenosha teammates in 1944, when she averaged .261, the seventh best average in the league. The Comets are (left to right): "Sugar" Koehn, Rose Folder, Shirley Jameson, and Audrey Wagner (courtesy Rose Powell).

considerate, and determined, the right-handed batting hurler also played for two teams in Springfield. The manager would take the girls in his car and drive to nearby towns, and sometimes they played games in a cow pasture on a makeshift diamond. In 1943, Rose moved to Chicago and worked for the Tungsten Sparkplug factory, earning $35 a week and playing for the company's team. She was seen by a scout from the All-American League, and in 1944, she was invited to spring camp at Peru-LaSalle, Illinois. Earlier she was teased as a "tomboy," but her persistence paid off when she made the league.

Folder savored spring training, including the charm school operated at night by the Helena Rubenstein Company as well as the hitting and fielding drills during the long days. Assigned to Kenosha, she and pitcher Mary Pratt, soon Rose's best friend, roomed with the Advik family, within walking distance of Lakefront Stadium. At 5'6" and 140 pounds, the independent-minded Illinois teenager, with her dark brown eyes and brown, wavy, shoulder-length hair, mainly roved the outfield, but she pitched a few games. Folder loved the league and her teammates. The Comets were close-knit, and she made many friends. Folder liked manager Marty McManus, who, she recalled, taught her more about baseball than anyone. Excelling, she batted .261, a mark that tied her for seventh in the loop, four points above Rockford's Dottie Kamenshek. At the summer's end, with Kenosha set to play in the circuit's Scholarship Series, Folder tripped on a rock and sprained her ankle chasing a fly ball in center field. McManus told her she must rest the ankle and miss the playoffs. Instead, she took the bus home, thus ending her greatest adventure.

Folder's stubbornness cost her any further chance with the AAGPBL, but when her ankle healed, she moved to Chicago and played fast-pitch softball briefly with the Blue Birds in the National Girls Baseball League. She returned to Springfield in 1945 and tried attending Normal University (now Illinois State University), but when she couldn't get her chosen classes, she worked as a spot welder in a local defense plant. In 1946, she moved to Sparta, Wisconsin, to live with an aunt and uncle. Working in a pharmacy, she met her handsome future husband, Edward Powell, who had just returned from wartime service in the Navy. Soon married, the couple lived on a farm for eleven years, before Edward took an opportunity to earn $300 by driving a new car to Washington state. They already had five of their eventual six children, and the trek caused the Powells to settle in Carnation, Washington. A stay-at-home mom, Rose raised her family and baby-sat other children for 30 years. Later, she enjoyed the AAGPBL Reunions, renewing old friendships and remembering her league days, where the girls learned morals, manners, and a better way of life. "All those things," Rose said, "go together with playing ball."

JS: Can you tell me about your background and how you got interested in playing ball?

Powell: I grew up in Springfield, Illinois, and when I was thirteen, the pastor of our church taught me how to pitch softball. I went to a Lutheran parochial school through the eighth grade. He organized a little team for recreation at recess, so in the eighth grade, I was pitching softball. Eventually I went down to the city park, which had a softball team, and I got to play with that team. Later, I played softball for teams in Chicago and Peoria.

I went to Concordia Lutheran School through the eighth grade, and it was right across the street from our house. After that, I attended Feitshans High School in Springfield. My mom was Bertha Folder, and my dad was Joseph Folder. I had five brothers and two sisters, all younger than me, and when you have so many younger brothers and sisters, you feel kind of pushed out of the way. Playing ball was my outlet. My mom and dad never argued with me at all about playing ball. They let me go wherever I wanted to play ball. I ended up going to Peoria, Illinois, and playing for the Peoria Chicks. We played against teams like the Peoria Caterpillarettes.

Mr. Farrow owned the Peoria Chicks ball team. Elizabeth Farrow was his daughter, and I got to go that summer of 1942 and live with their family in Peoria. I also played in Springfield for the Green for Governor team and the Springfield Merchants team. We played teams from small towns all around Springfield, like Peru and Carbondale. The manager would pile all of us he could into his car, and we'd go. Sometimes we'd play in a pasture that had cows, and we had to run the cows out. We usually ended up taking shovels and markers, so we could clean up, and pick up the "cowpies," and mark the field. We had loads of fun, and we were good! I can't believe how good we were.

What did you do in the summer of 1943?

I went to Chicago and played for the Tungsten Sparks, and we worked shifts at the Tungsten Sparkplug factory. We worked three hours a day, three days a week, and made $35 a week. We were put up at the Carrie McGill Memorial Residence, which was a YWCA in Chicago. We got our room and board there. I learned to put tungsten tips on the spark plugs.

You were playing what they used to call semiprofessional ball, because you had to work on for the factory in order to play ball for the Sparks.

That's right. We had some awesome players for the Tungsten Sparks. I met some great gals. Sunny Berger was one who came to Chicago to pitch for our team, and later she went to the All-American League. We played good ball. We wore metal spikes, and I sure had the marks on my feet from the slides into home plate, you know, covering the plate, to prove it! *[She laughs.]*

Did you graduate from Feitshans High School?

Yes, I did graduate. The school sent my diploma and my scholarship from the National Honor Society to Kenosha. I graduated in June 1944. After I got my letter about the All-American League from Mr. Wrigley, I took all my tests so I would have it all done, and I got my diploma by mail.

I went to Peru, Illinois, for spring training, and I never knew there were so many girls who could play ball. It was absolutely mind-boggling, because I always had to play with boys in the neighborhood, because most girls couldn't play ball.

How did you first find out about the All-American League?

Mr. Wrigley sent a letter inviting me to spring training. I rode to Peru on the bus on May 15, 1944.

What was spring training like in 1944?

It was awesome. For one thing, I had never seen so many girls who could really play ball. Growing up, I used to get teased a lot for being a "tomboy," but I loved playing ball. There was nothing else I would rather do, so I played ball.

At spring training, they had us all doing different things — throwing, catching, pitching, chasing flies, and then they'd sort us out into groups and try us at another position. At the end of it, they put the list on the locker door, and I was lucky enough to make it with the Kenosha Comets.

Do you remember about charm school?

Charm school was such a kick, but I really learned a lot that I didn't know. With five brothers in your house, you don't learn much "girlish" stuff. I was the oldest, and I was out of the house before my brothers grew up. They always said they didn't know me because I was gone before they grew up.

The charm school was at night during spring training, and we had ten days of it. The Helena Rubenstein Company did it, and they told us stuff like, "There are two eyebrows, not one," and that stuck. They told us how to put on lipstick, and how to walk in high heels. I didn't even own a pair of high heels. I had to borrow a pair. We had to learn how to lift our little finger when we drank a cup of tea, but I don't drink tea. The Helena Rubenstein people came in and did that for us, and they were looking down their noses at us tomboys, you know, but we did learn a lot. The chaperones helped, because they were always pretty much with us.

Most of us had not eaten out in a restaurant. We learned how to hold the fork and the knife, and how to cross your ankles, right over left. They told us to tip 15 percent of our meal, and we weren't allowed to wear pants in town. We had to wear our skirts. We learned, but we laughed a lot too. When I think of how I must have looked, and I've seen pictures of me, I had both eyebrows growing together, and my hair that looked like you had to get a bristle brush to get through it. *[She laughs.]*

It still was fun. Being in the league was the most fun I've ever had in my life.

What about moving to Kenosha?

When we went to Kenosha, we lived in private homes. I lived with the Conrad Advik family. They had two extra rooms, and they had agreed to let two girls stay at their home. We could walk to the ballpark. I lived there with Mary Pratt, and she's still my best friend.

We played at Lakefront Stadium. I believe it was built for the league. I understood that the city paid part of the funding for the league to come to Kenosha, and the mayor supported it. Shirley Jameson was our center fielder, and when the fog came in during the evening, she didn't have any legs! *[She laughs.]* Shirley was a short little gal anyhow, so you couldn't see her from the waist down for the fog. But it was a really nice stadium.

You must have had good friends on the team.

We were all like family in Kenosha. When I first went to the Comets, I had dark hair and dark skin. Lou Colacito was the catcher, and she said, "Good, another Italian." I said, "No, I'm not Italian. Why?" Lou said, "Well, you look like it."

Audrey Wagner, one of Kensoha's stars, was about the same coloring as I was, and they thought she was my sister.

I kept in touch with the Kenosha players over the years, and Anna Meyer and Mary Pratt are two of the few that are still with us.

Do you have favorite memories from games?

I could hit. Mary Pratt always said that. I didn't really do well as a pitcher, because they were thinking about making the overhand change, which they didn't do until 1948, but that was kind of tough on me — because that's not how we learned to play softball. I could hit, and I could run, and I could catch, so I played a lot of outfield. In softball in the Chicago League [the National Girls Baseball League], they had a roving "shortstop," a tenth player, and that was really my position, and I loved that.

Marty McManus was our manager, and he was an awesome guy. He taught us a lot. Marty was more like a dad to most of us.

What about travel?

Lex McCutchan, our chaperone, was there to help with travel. She was like an extra mom. She was there for us, if we needed to talk, sew on a button, or whatever we needed to do.

We didn't know anything. My family had an outhouse when I was growing up. Everyone in our neighborhood had outhouses, and they got dumped over every Halloween! Where we roomed in Kenosha, they had indoor plumbing — they had two bathrooms with flushing toilets. It was quite an experience for most of us.

A manager of one of the big league teams said, "I went from an outhouse to a penthouse," and I thought, "That's pretty much the way we did!" I'll never forget the first toilet that had a chain on the tank above my head. I was scared to pull the chain for fear of getting the water on my head! *[She laughs.]*

In Springfield, we lived outside of town. South Grand Boulevard was the closest main street to where we lived, and we had to walk to that boulevard, and we rode streetcars to town. That was the "good old days"! We played ball at Iles Park, which turned out to be a pretty nice softball field. They finally put lights out there when I played on the Green for Governor and the Springfield Merchants' teams. We had to go out and get sponsors for our shirts, and we wore their names on the back of our shirts.

"Jerry" [Janice] O'Hara was a pitcher, and later she played for the Kenosha Comets, and then she went to the Peoria Redwings. She and I used to share a white shirt. The girls in the games at night would wear navy blue shirts. When you'd go in to pitch, the white shirt glared against the batter's eyes. So when we changed pitchers, we'd go over behind the bushes and change shirts, so Jerry would have the right shirt, the navy blue one, to pitch. That worked out okay, because we didn't have to run to the locker room — until some little boys found out we were changing behind the bushes, and then we had to go into the locker room to switch shirts. We always laughed about that, because of the little boys sneaking a peek! *[She laughs.]*

Jerry O'Hara was a good pitcher and a good all-around player.

What else do you remember about Kenosha?

I think Kenosha was one of the sweetest little towns I've ever been in. Everybody was so friendly, and they were so nice to us. They were happy to have us there. I sure enjoyed it. Like I said, we could walk to Lakefront Stadium for practices and the games. The family was so good. If they cooked a meal and we were there, we were invited to eat with them. It couldn't be better. I kept pictures of the Advik family. They had two girls, and I had pictures of them.

On road trips, did you travel by train on the North Shore and the South Shore Els?

We traveled on the bus. Did you see the bus in Rockford that they refurbished for the movie, *A League of Their Own*? That was the kind of bus we rode. We sang, and we told stories, and we read, just like they did in the movie.

What else do you remember?

I was just one of these people that liked my own way, and that was the main reason I left the league. I had run after a fly ball in the outfield, and I tripped on a rock, and I sprained my ankle. We were to go to Racine the next day, and I believe it was for the playoffs, the Scholarship Series. My ankle was swollen about three times normal size, and Marty McManus said, "You aren't going. You're going to stay right here and stay off that ankle."

I got on a bus and went back home, so that was the end of the league for me. That's what my stubbornness did for me. I wouldn't trade my life for anything else, but that was a mistake.

So you went home before the season was over?

I did, but I was really upset with myself. When my ankle healed, I went to Chicago and played a few games with the Blue Birds and other teams.

Did the league ask you to come back in 1945?

I didn't talk to anybody with the league after that. I stayed in Chicago for a while, but I ended up going back home.

I decided it was time to use some of my scholarship. World War II was still going on, and I wanted to join the WACs and get into a unit that would air ferry planes to Great Britain. I decided to go to school, and I went to Normal University [now Illinois State University] in Bloomington for a short while, until I learned I couldn't get the classes I needed to get into the WACs, and I went back to Springfield and worked in a defense plant. I was spot welder, and my mother came and worked on the same shift with me, midnight until eight o'clock in the morning.

In 1946, after the war ended, I went back to Chicago, and I got a job at a real estate office. I liked that, and I figured I would stay there. I told my mother, and she said, "Your uncle and aunt live in Sparta, Wisconsin, and you could get on the train and stay at their house and spend Thanksgiving with them."

I took the train to Sparta, and I liked it there, and my uncle and aunt offered me room and board, if I wanted to stay with them until I decided what I wanted to do. I got as job at a local pharmacy, and the girl working in the soda fountain had a brother coming home from the Navy. She liked me, and she wanted me to meet her handsome brother, and I did, and that was the end of me!

That's your husband?

Yes. His name was Edward, but he's been gone for years. Edward Powell was just getting out of the Navy, and I thought, "What a catch!" He didn't know what he was going to do for work, and he ended up working on the farm with his folks. We got married in 1946, and we lived in Wisconsin for eleven years. He kind of flitted around and did odd jobs. He drove the Army bus at Camp McCoy, in Sparta, and we lived with his folks and I had the kids. There were thirteen of us in the house, a nice houseful!

I had six children: Barbara Ann, the twins — Roger and Rita, David Joseph, Susan Marie, and Mary Ellen, the youngest. She was born here in Washington. My husband got a chance to drive a new car for a dealer, S.L. Savage, in Seattle. He could earn $300 if he would drive this new car to the sales company. He said, "If you want to go with me, grab what you can," and that's what I did.

The miracle is that my photo albums and scrapbooks got in the car with me. I never thought of them again until Penny Marshall was making the movie, and my son said, "Didn't you play in that league at one time?" I still have that scrapbook, and my pictures are very important to me. We ended up here in Carnation, Washington, and because I was raising children, I baby-sat children in my own home for thirty years.

Do you feel like the league made an impact on your life?

The All-American League did make an impact on my life. I learned so much, and when we get together at reunions, we always say, "We learned whatever morals we had, our way of life, and our thoughtfulness and consideration for others." All those things go together with playing ball. I was in Detroit last August [2010] for the reunion, and my two grandsons took me. They were so proud to be able to go with me — I had one on either side of me — and we had such a great time. They behaved like perfect gentlemen, and the All-American girls enjoyed them, and we had such a great time.

Mary Pratt
Rockford, 1943–1944, 1946–1947; Kenosha, 1944–1945
Interviewed on October 12, 2011.

Born: 1918
Height: 5'1"
Weight: 125
Positions: P
Batted: L
Threw: L
Career Batting Average: .144 in five seasons
Lifetime Pitching Record: 28–51 with 3.48 ERA

Mary Pratt was born in Bridgeport, Connecticut, the year the Great War ended. Her father had moved there to work as a draftsman in Groton, Connecticut, but after the war ended, William Pratt moved his family to Quincy, Massachusetts. Mary became an avid ballplayer in the neighborhood, mostly playing with the local boys. She graduated from North Quincy High in 1936, the midpoint of the Great Depression. Ambitious, determined, and studious, she wanted to attend college, and her parents encouraged her. Mary combined her lifelong thirst for education with her love for sports by attending Boston University and earning a bachelor's in physical education. Following her junior year of college, she was able to join a girls' softball team, the Olympets, and they played home games at the Boston Garden. Walter Brown, owner of the Garden, sponsored the Olympets during the summers of 1939 and 1940. The nine-player team (softball used ten players in that era) played mostly at the Garden, but they traveled at least once to play a girls' team at Madison Square Garden in New York. Mary, a spirited brunette who was 5'1" and 125 pounds, threw and batted left-handed. She couldn't be an infielder, so she became a pitcher, often practicing at home in the back yard with her father.

After graduation, Pratt taught for one year at Thayer Academy and two years in the Quincy Public Schools, and she also directed intramural sports and after-school programs. In June of 1943, she received a phone call from the office of Philip Wrigley, inviting her to travel to Chicago and try out for Wrigley's new four-team All-American League. Excited, Mary rode a sleeper train out of Boston to Chicago and took another train to Rockford, Illinois, home of the Peaches. She pitched the rest of the 1943 season for Rockford, returned home and taught during the 1943–44 academic year, and came back to the league in 1944.

A southpaw pitcher who began her five-year AAGPBL career with Rockford in 1943, Mary Pratt is pictured in the Peaches uniform (courtesy Mary Pratt).

She split her second season between the Peaches and the Kenosha Comets, managed by Marty McManus. A good teacher, McManus showed pitchers how to hold runners on base and taught them to throw a change-up. Improving, the determined little lefty, who depended on good control and a variety of breaking pitches, fashioned a career-best 21–15 record. She liked the Comets, and she made more friends in Kenosha. In 1945, Pratt returned to the Comets. Assigned to the Peaches in 1946, she was a good teammate who served as a mentor for younger players for two postwar seasons.

The league allowed sidearm hurling in 1946 and switched to sidearm in 1947, and Pratt, who couldn't make the adjustment, left the circuit, but she took many fond memories with her. Although she enjoyed being a professional ballplayer, Mary was devoted to teaching and to expanding opportunities for girls to participate in competitive sports. Thoughtful, kind, and considerate, she spent 48 years teaching every facet of physical education. For 30 of those years, she also officiated girls' softball and basketball games at every level, ranging from recreation to high school to collegiate. The author of an interesting memoir, *Preserving Our Legacy: A Peach of a Game* (2004), Pratt loves attending AAGPBL Reunions, beginning with the first event in Chicago in 1982. She became an outspoken member of the Players Association, and she served on the association's board. Over the years, she has spoken dozens of times about the AAGPBL. A longtime advocate of opportunities for women, Mary kept in touch with many former players from the league years, including Rose (Folder) Powell, her roommate and friend in Kenosha.

JS: I know you self-published a memoir about your life and the AAGPBL, Preserving Our Legacy: A Peach of a Game *(2004), but I would like you to talk about your many and varied experiences with sports.*

Pratt: I understand what you are doing, and I appreciate anything that is being written that enables people to know, in my opinion, that there hasn't been an activity involving girls and sports that can equate to what Mr. [Philip] Wrigley established back in 1943. I was fortunate enough to meet Mr. [Ken] Sells in 1988 at the Baseball Hall of Fame, and have him tell me what was in Mr. Wrigley's mind when he decided to create the All-American Girls Baseball League. That's why I admire the articles and books that are being written about a league I was fortunate enough to be part of in the 1940s.

Where did you grow up, and how did you get interested in playing ball?

I was born, in Bridgeport, Connecticut, in 1918. My father, William Young Pratt, moved there because he was a draftsman, and he was working on submarines in Groton, Connecticut. My mother was Daisy (Gore) Pratt, and my brothers were William and Donald. After the Great War was over, my father became a Certified Public Accountant. The Depression came, and my family moved to Quincy, Massachusetts. I was entering the seventh grade. I've remained here ever since, and I majored in Physical Education at Boston University.

When did you graduate from high school and go on to college?

I graduated from North Quincy High in 1936. I went to Boston University, and I graduated with a bachelor's degree in Physical Education in the spring of 1940. Later, I completed the master's degree and Certificate of Advanced Graduate Studies. I went into special education in my last ten years of teaching, and I realized that knowing physical education and your ability to know about your body was an important part of my educational background from 1936 to 1940.

I admired my opportunity to play in the All-American League, but I want to be remembered as a school teacher. I spent 48 years serving as a teacher.

Did you play softball in high school?

The only opportunity that I had began with the boys who let me play ball with them. Along the way, when I was a junior in college, I saw an announcement that Walter Brown, who then owned the Boston Garden, Boston's biggest sports facility, was going to have a summer team playing out of the Boston Garden. I tried out and made this girls' team, the Boston Olympets, and played for two years. I learned how to pitch underhand. My dad played catch with me in the backyard. One of the trips that we made was to Madison Square Garden, and I found out that Millie Deegan, who later played in the All-American League, was playing on the New York team. I was fortunate to hear about this opportunity, and we played at the Boston Garden and Madison Square Garden against teams that Walter Brown and his committee had scheduled. We also played at Braves Field and at Fenway Park. Most of my ball playing experience was with the boys who let me play.

You played softball inside the Boston Garden?

That's right. They set up the field on a diagonal basis. The way they placed the diamond, you could never hit the ball the length of the Garden. As you went down the first base line, the foul line ran into an upright post that stood in the stands. If you hit the ball there, it was a ground-rule single. They used softball pitching, and there were nine girls on a team. We played two summers, 1939 and 1940. Dottie Green, from Natick, Massachusetts, who later played for the Rockford Peaches and then served as the chaperone, was one of the girls I played with in the Boston Garden. That team, the Olympets, was my only softball team experience before the All-American League. I'm grateful to have been accepted in the AAGSBL because of my desire and ability to play, even with my limited experience.

Today I believe that women should have leadership roles in our sports, but I'm so indebted to the men who gave me an opportunity to play softball.

After you graduated from Boston University in the spring of 1940, what did you do?

I took a part-time position in physical education at Thayer Academy, a private school in Braintree, supervising after-school activities in the Country Day Program. In 1941, I got a position in the Quincy Public Schools, and I taught physical education classes at Point Junior High and Central Junior High. I also supervised the after-school program, all for $1100 a year.

How did you end up with the All-American League?

I was just finishing my second year with the Quincy Schools in June of 1943. I had a call that came from Mr. Wrigley's office about the All-American League. The day after school ended, I took a night sleeper from South Station in Boston and rode the train to Chicago. Mr. Ken Sells, president of the league, met me at the station. He told me about my new team, and I took another train to Rockford to join the Peaches.

When I arrived at the stadium on Fifteenth Street, I went inside and climbed up to the top of the bleachers on the third base side of the field. Marge Peters was pitching for Rockford, and the game was already in the second or third inning. I watched the game. Afterward, I was met by Dottie Green, a catcher for the Peaches who only lived about twenty-five miles from my home in Quincy. Dottie took me to the house where we roomed with a Swedish family, the Nyquists.

I played a fair amount in 1943. Olive Little, one of our Canadians, was one of Rockford's top pitchers, and Marge Peters was another. We also had Muriel Coben, another Canadian, for the last half of the season. I knew players like Dottie Kamenshek, our excellent first baseman, and the manager, Eddie Stumpf, who was a longtime baseball man, and he had minor league experience around the time of World War I.

I went back to Boston and resumed teaching after the season. In 1944, I was able to leave before school ended to attend the league's spring training at Peru-LaSalle, Illinois. People from the Helena Rubenstein Salon came in and provided glamour tips and training. The league wanted girls to play ball well but also to look and behave like ladies. About three weeks into the season, I was traded to Kenosha, where a couple of the pitchers, Lee Harney and Helen Nicol, were injured.

The 1944 season was a memorable one for me, because I learned so much. Marty McManus was the manager. The All-American League was different from softball, because in softball, runners can't lead off the bases before the pitcher releases the ball. In the All-American League, runners could lead off and steal. Pitchers had to learn how to hold runners on base, and it was difficult. That's why many of the girls stole so many bases. They stole on the batteries. We were playing baseball rules but using a softball. I was a lefty. I used the "slingshot" delivery, and I depended on control, not speed.

Marty McManus showed me the "balk" move. I got better at holding runners. He also taught me how to hold the bat with the thumb on top and four fingers under it to "deaden" the impact. He showed me how to add a change-of-pace pitch, and that helped me win 21 games in 1944. The girls behind me played so well that I was able to win many games. I admire Marty McManus, because he was a teacher and a very knowledgeable person. *[Editor's note: Mary enjoyed her best season on 1944, fashioning a 21-15 record with a 2.50 ERA in 41 games.]*

In 1945, I returned to Kenosha, and in 1946 and 1947, I was assigned to Rockford. During those last two years, the girls were throwing sidearm, and I couldn't hold my own with other pitchers, but the Peaches kept me. I didn't join the Peaches until after school was out in June, and I didn't return to the league after the 1947 season.

The league gave me a wonderful opportunity to play ball and meet girls from all over the U.S. and Canada. A few of the outstanding players that I competed against were Olive Little, Millie Warwick, Dottie Kamenshek, and Carolyn Morris. With Kenosha, some of the girls I respected were Ann Harnett, Shirley Jameson, Gertrude Ganote, Jerry O'Hara, Jo Hageman, Lib Mahon, Betty Fabac, Pauline "Pinky" Pirok, and Dottie Schroeder. I shared a room with Rose (Folder) Powell. Canadians that I remember were Mary "Bonnie" Baker, Doris Barr, Helen Callaghan and her sister Marge, Muriel Coben, Gladys Davis, Dorothy Hunter, Kay Heim, Helen (Nicol) Fox, Dottie Key, Lee Surkowski, and Arleene (Johnson) Noga.

I also remember many of the California girls. They were Louella Daetweiler, Faye Dancer, Dorothy Harrell, Thelma Eisen, Gloria Marks, Betty Luna, Annabelle "Lefty" Lee, Kay Shinen and her sister Dorothy, Kay Rohrer, Lavonne "Pepper" Paire, Alma Ziegler, and Dottie Wiltse, who married Harvey Collins and spent the rest of her life in Fort Wayne, Indiana, raising her family. Later, Dottie served on the AAGPBL Board. Joanne Winter and Carolyn Morris came from Arizona, and I remember others from the West Coast like Merle Keagle. Some of the best players I knew as opponents were "Maddy" English, Sophie Kurys, Betsy Jochum, Margaret Stefani, Connie Wisniewski, and Mary (Nesbitt) Wisham, who pitched and played first base. I crossed paths with many of these girls at the AAGPBL Reunions.

I had the opportunity to play at the professional level in a league that maintained the highest standards, and I'm grateful for that opportunity. The wonderful thing about sports is that it gives you the opportunity to combine your academic learning with the physical properties of your body. Boston University gave me a great opportunity to learn the value of physical education.

Obviously the league made a great impact on your life.

The league gave me opportunities that I would never have had. Mr. Wrigley organized and operated the league, at least for the first two years, on a top-notch level, and it was continued in top-notch fashion. When I speak to groups and organizations about the league, I like to point out how well it was organized and operated. I was honored to be part of such a first-class league. I remember Ken Sells telling me during an interview at the Baseball Hall of Fame in 1988 that he was given $100,000 from Mr. Wrigley and told to find the best girls to play ball in this new league.

Later, I served on the AAGPBL Board for two years. Sports can help girls in many ways, and I became an advocate for girls in sports by the end of the 1940s. The difference between girls playing sports today and those who played in the All-American League is that we had to dress, act, and look like ladies in addition to playing ball well. I believe our league elevated the level of competition in sports. Ken Sells made that point about looking and dressing like ladies in our talk at Cooperstown, and that's the way a girls' league should be operated. I value the opportunity to have played in the All-American League. I want to be remembered as a teacher. I spent 48 years of my life in that profession.

Do you have other memories?

We live with our memories. I do and it was one in particular that occurred in the latter part of 1943. When I was called out of a class that I was teaching in order to respond to a telephone call from the then schoolboy editor of the *Boston Globe*. His call was an invitation to try out for what was known at that time as the All-American Girls Softball League. The league was initiated by Mr. Wrigley's office in Chicago. I could not get home fast enough to tell my mother about the call. As soon as school was out for the summer, I boarded the night sleeper out of Boston for Chicago. I was met by Mr. Sells of the Wrigley office and directed to Rockford, home of the Rockford Peaches. It was the start of five years, 1943 to 1947, in the AAGSBL, later the AAGBBL and eventually the AAGPBL.

I always remember being very active and interested in athletic completion. I took advantage of every opportunity that was offered to me. The opportunities were few and far between. None were involved in high school interscholastic or intercollegiate competition. Outside of school, I had taken advantage of opportunities that were offered to me during the summer programs on the local playgrounds. It was during those summer programs when I took part in many of the opportunities to play baseball with the boys. When I came home and did not return to the AAGPBL, I can recall playing in the park league with the men.

It was during my high school days that I took advantage of a church league basketball program, held at the local YMCA.

When I entered Boston University in the fall of 1936, my interclass play was to be limited to volleyball, basketball, and softball. I was honored to receive the Senior Award given at the end of my senior year.

After graduation, I remained active in field hockey and lacrosse, played at Wellesley College under the supervision of the Boston Field Hockey and Lacrosse Association. It was during that time that I assumed the leadership role and hosted the British Lacrosse Touring Team during their trip to Boston.

It was also during those early years that I took advantage of the opportunity to play competitive softball at the Boston Garden. The program was initiated in 1939 by Walter Brown, then owner of the Garden. It was at that time that I first met Dorothy Green. We were both with the Rockford Peaches in the AAGPBL in 1943. One of the highlights of the Garden program was our trip to Madison Square Garden to play the Roverettes. Some years later I was to renew friendship with Millie Deegan, who had played at Madison Square Garden that evening. She was to become my teammate in Rockford in 1943 and again in 1946–1947. In 1944 and 1945 I became a Kenosha Comet.

I did not take part in the spring training in 1943, because I had to finish teaching school. I did attend spring training in Peru, Illinois, in 1944. I became aware of the desire, attempt, and follow-through that the Wrigley organization established. It certainly equated with the policies and practices that were initiated when I entered the teaching field.

From the very start, I was amazed at the skill level of so many of the players. I have always remembered what Olive Little said to me at our first league reunion in Chicago. She remarked that her granddaughters were playing in the same Lassie League she played in prior to coming to the States to play in Mr. Wrigley's undertaking.

In those early years of the league, it seemed to me that the largest number of players were from California and Canada.

I was fortunate to have met so many wonderful players. One stands out over all the friendships I made. It was with Audrey Wagner, from Bensenville, Illinois. On our trips on the way to South Bend, we would pass through this small town. I played with Audrey in Kenosha. She was an outstanding left fielder and hitter. After so many years, I was to meet Audrey at our first reunion in Chicago. She was then a doctor, working on the West Coast. She was also a registered flyer and promised to visit me the next time she flew to Boston. She never made it. Soon after that meeting in Chicago, she and her nurse were killed in a plane accident.

Because I was a pitcher, I feel that I fondly remember the number one and number two pitchers on the teams in 1943. On Rockford, it was Olive Little and Carolyn Morris. On Racine, it was Joanne Winter and Mary Nesbitt. On South Bend, it was Sunny Berger and Muriel Coben. On Kenosha, it was Helen Nicol and Lee Harney. Each team carried four pitchers and it was in 1944 that two Kenosha pitchers were sidelined. I was assigned to Kenosha to play for Marty McManus.

ELLEN (AHRNDT) PROEFROCK
South Bend, 1944
Interviewed on November 1, 2007.

Born: 1926
Deceased: 2009
Height: 5'4"
Weight: 120
Positions: 2B, IF
Batted: R
Threw: R
Career Batting Average: Played less than 10 games
Released: June 30, 1944

Ellen Ahrndt Proefrock (1926–2009), who seized an opportunity to join the All-American League in 1944, was born and raised on a farm five miles outside of Racine, Wisconsin. Family members and friends always called her "Babe," because she was the youngest of seven children, six girls and a boy. Kids in the area played ball, and Ellen, a quiet, good-hearted person, joined them when she was old enough. At William Horlick High, the energetic teen played basketball and tennis, but her favorite was pick-up games of ball on the

A utility infielder with South Bend in 1944, Ellen Ahrndt, on the right, posed at Bendix Field with her teammate and roommate, Lee Surkowski (courtesy Kipp Proefrock).

playground or at a homemade diamond on the family's farm. Her brother managed a town softball team, and at age thirteen in 1939, Ellen played for his Racine squad against teams from other towns. She graduated from Horlick High in 1941, but her brother's team disbanded because players began working at war-related jobs. Ahrndt secured a job with the Dumore Company, a Racine firm that manufactured heaters and engines. In 1942 and 1943, she was a standout second sacker for Dumore's team. Manager Norman "Nummie" Derringer was a famous Racine athlete who played shortstop on a team that won ten state softball championships between 1934 and 1946. Dieringer knew about the newly-formed AAGPBL, and, later, he managed the Racine Belles in the 1950 season.

In the summer of 1943, Dieringer called a scout with the All-American League, and the scout saw the 5'4" Ahrndt, a blue-eyed blonde infielder, play in the city tournament. In 1944, she was invited to the league's spring camp at in Peru-LaSalle, Illinois. That season the AAGPBL expanded from four to six teams, and two dozen rookies made the grade, including the strong-armed Ahrndt, who was allocated to South Bend. Her experiences mirrored those of many new players, and in South Bend, she roomed in a home with rookie Lee Surkowski, from Moose Jaw, Saskatchewan. Bert Niehoff managed the Blue Sox, and he had a set lineup, including Detroit star Marge Stefani at second base. Ahrndt, eager and skilled, received little chance to play, although she got into a few exhibitions. Stefani had a bad knee, so Ahrndt took over at second if Marge had to come out of a game. The Racine native recalled, "The regulars hated to come out of a game, so I didn't play much." She finally got an opportunity at Racine's Horlick Field on "Ellen Ahrndt Night," when Dumore's workers filled the stands and honored her before the game with a bouquet of roses and a war bond. Ahrndt walked in her first at-bat, the manager sent Stefani to pinch-run, and Ellen had to return to the bench. She was released on June 30, 1944.

Ahrndt treasured her professional experience, even though her time was short and ended in disappointment. For the remainder of the 1944 season, she attended games the Blue Sox played in Milwaukee, Racine, or Kenosha, and she visited with teammates like Betsy Jochum, Lucella MacLean, Dottie Schroeder, and Jo Hageman. Three years later, Ellen married Casey Proefrock, and the couple had two sons, Kipp and Kurt. A stay-at-home mother, she also helped with a clothing store her husband opened after they moved to Brodhead, Wisconsin, in 1973. Later, Dieringer located Ellen for the AAGPBL Players Association, and she attended the Milwaukee Reunion in the year 2000. Before the movie *A League of Their Own* was released in 1992, Ellen Proefrock had not talked about her professional summer for decades. Still, she kept the scrapbook from her ballplaying experiences, she began sharing memories with family and friends, and she valued being part of the Frisch baseball cards that helped keep the league alive.

JS: *I'm working on a history of the Blue Sox from the beginning to the end, and I need more information about the wartime years before 1946. Did you come from Racine originally?*

Proefrock: I was the youngest of seven children, six girls and a boy, and that's why I was always called "Babe." We lived on a farm about five miles outside Racine. We rode the bus to school, but if the weather was nice, sometimes I walked home. I graduated from William Horlick High in Racine in 1941. In high school I played basketball and tennis, but we used to play ball all the time. My brother managed a softball team, and I began playing on his team when I was thirteen. We played other teams from towns around Racine. But in 1941, after World War II started, the team disbanded.

I took a job with the Dumore Company, and once I was hired, I became the second baseman for the company softball team. Two of my sisters already worked there, and they also played ball. Dumore manufactured electric heaters and engines. I played for the Dumore team in 1942 and 1943. A scout for the All-American League talked to Dumore's manager, Norman "Nummie" Derringer. The scout saw me play in the city tournament, and I was asked to try out for the league.

In the spring of 1944, I went to the spring camp in Peru-LaSalle, Illinois. They had a lot of good girls trying out at the camp, and later three of my sisters got a tryout in Milwaukee, but they didn't make it. After the tryouts, the league sent me to South Bend.

Do you remember any of the girls who tried out at the spring camp?

Lee Surkowski was one of the girls who made it, and she was also sent to South Bend. Lee had a sister, Anne Surkowski, but she played for South Bend in 1945.

Later that summer, a picture of me appeared on the cover of *Click Magazine*, in the *Milwaukee Journal* issue of August 27, 1944, and that's how people knew I played in the league. By the time the magazine appeared, I was no longer with the Blue Sox.

Did you live with three-four other players in a private house in South Bend?

I lived in a private home with Lee Surkowski. We roomed with Arnold and Nadine Bauer.

You know, the funny part about the league is that my kids didn't know I played professional ball until they made the movie, *A League of Their Own*.

Several players have told me that the movie made the league famous. Your baseball card says you didn't play a lot of games. You were a second baseman, right?

I played second base, but Marge Stefani was the second baseman. Marge had a bad knee, and I only played when she had to come out of a game. The regulars hated to come out of a game, so I didn't play much.

After I left the league, I married William "Casey" Proefrock. We got married on April 12, 1947, in Racine, and he passed away in 2006. We had two sons, Kipp and Kurt. For years we were partners in a clothing store, Just for Him and Her, in Brodhead, Wisconsin, where we moved in 1973. We used to go fishing together, and we were active in the Bethlehem Lutheran Church in Brodhead, and I really enjoy quilting.

Do you remember Betsy Jochum? She was a star player for South Bend in 1944.

The players I knew best were Betsy Jochum, Jo Hageman, and Lucella MacLean, and also Dottie Schroeder and Lee Surkowski. Betsy and Jo were Lutherans too, and we went to church together. They were all exceptional people and ballplayers. They all took me under their wings. Betsy and Dottie were fabulous. They were fast, and they were really good players.

Betsy batted .296 and led the whole league in hitting the year you played. Do you have particular memories about games you played?

The first game I played, I was at second base, and someone hit the ball toward the pitcher. I ran to second base instead of first, and Jo Hageman went after the ball. Everybody advanced, because nobody covered first base. We won the game, and I was glad about that. I was just so nervous, and I guess I couldn't get my wits together.

When we played in Racine, the Dumore Company had a "Babe Ahrndt Night." Everybody that I knew from Racine was there. They presented me with a gift [a bouquet of roses and a $50 war bond] before the game started. I knew the people from Dumore quite well, because I had played for them. The people that owned the company were so interested in the games. They were always there when we played in Racine. They were very supportive of the league.

Were you with the Blue Sox the whole season?

No, not the whole season. I left I think at the end of June, but I can't remember for sure. I know after I left, I would go and see the Blue Sox games, because I have pictures of the girls with me, and I wasn't in my uniform. I followed the Blue Sox always.

Did you stay in South Bend, or did you move back to Racine?

I moved back to Racine. I would go and see the Blue Sox when they came to Racine and to Kenosha, and also to Milwaukee. There was a team [the Chicks] in Milwaukee in 1944.

You mentioned a scrapbook. Do you have clippings of games that you played?

I just played in a few games, but most of what I have are pictures and stories where something was said in the newspaper about the girls.

Do you still hear from any of the players?

I still call Lucella MacLean, and she calls me, but I haven't heard from her in a while. I was waiting for a new phone directory [2007], because I called Lucella's number, and her phone was disconnected. She usually calls me at Christmas, and I didn't hear from her last year. The last time she called me was when the AAGPBL Reunion was in Milwaukee.

Who was South Bend's manager the year you played?

Let's see if I can think of it. The memory isn't so good when you get older. *[She laughs.]* It was Bert Niehoff.

I guess overall you felt like it was a really good experience.

Oh, yes, I did.

It sounds like you made some friends that you've had for the rest of your life.

That's right. It's always good to think of them, and my kids get out my scrapbook quite often. It's always a mess! *[She laughs.]*

Why did you not finish the season?

They let me go. *[Editor's note: South Bend released Ellen Ahrndt on June 30, 1944.]*

Probably because you weren't playing enough, because Stefani was playing all the time.

I don't know if that was the reason. I thought if they took me to play, I thought I was a pretty good player, but they let me go.

What did you do when you went back to Racine?

I found a job. I went back where I was working before I left, the George Morris factory. They made airplane parts for the war.

When did you get married?

I got married in 1947. My husband Casey Proefrock [pronounced: *pray-frock*] was in the service. He just died last year. We were married 59 years. It was a good marriage too. He died of Alzheimer's.

Do you remember the contract that you signed for?

I signed for $35 a week. My boss thought I was nuts because I didn't make as much money [in the league] as I did with the Morris Company. $35 then was a lot of money, but not compared to what you would make now. I was one of the lower-paid team members, because I wasn't a regular.

Do you remember traveling on trains?

We did travel some on trains. I know when I went to camp, I rode on the train. You might have to find out from some of the other girls about riding on the bus.

I know at South Bend [Center for History] they had my picture in there, but it's not there any more because I'm sure they changed it, but I was hitting the ball. They had it in there like I was hitting left-handed, they had it [the picture] backwards. I batted right-handed. The picture that was there was the one in *Click Magazine*.

Do you get letters from fans asking you to sign the Frisch baseball card?

Are you kidding? *[She laughs.]* As little as I played, every week I get letters. I have three shoeboxes full! They just keep coming and coming all the time.

I think that's because the girls in your league played because they wanted to play ball.

They played because they liked the sport.

Nummy Derringer, he managed me here in Racine, when at first they were trying to get everyone's name [for the AAGPBL Players Association]. He kept after me, "Send it in, send it in." After he went to Florida to a reunion, he came back, and he was a friend of our family, and he kept after me. Finally, I sent in the information that I was a player too.

The team picture that was taken in 1944, it was set up for the next week, and I left the week before, and I'm not in the picture from the 1944 team.

LUCELLA (MACLEAN) ROSS
South Bend, 1943–1944
Interviewed on November 20, 2007

Born: 1921
Height: 5'2"
Weight: 135
Positions: C, OF
Batted: R
Threw: R
Career Batting Average: .204 in two seasons

Lucella MacLean (1921–2012), one of the original Canadian players to join the All-American League in 1943, was born and raised in Lloydminster, a town of 1,500 on the Alberta-Saskatchewan border. The fourth of nine children of John and Anna Maria MacLean, she grew up loving fast-pitch softball. In Canada, talented players began competing on organized softball teams, and if younger girls showed the ability and skills, they played on teams with experienced players. Lucella played so well that at age fifteen in 1936, she was picked for Lloydminster's Nationals. Blessed with all-around athletic ability, she was taught to catch, and in 1937 she became the Nationals' regular catcher. Her ball club won the Estey Trophy, given to towns in the area that competed in a tournament, four straight times. When World War II began, MacLean, who didn't complete a class of Composition in grade twelve, couldn't qualify for training as a nurse. The Saskatoon Pats offered her a job and a spot on the company's team. In September 1940, she moved to Saskatchewan to play catcher and work as clerk-cashier for the Pats' taxi company.

Lucella, a brunette with blue eyes and an engaging personality, was one of the fastest players in the league. Although she could play the outfield, she had the quick hands, strong arm, and receiving skills needed for catcher. She spent two seasons with Saskatoon's Pats. A scout who was looking for players to join the All-American League, the women's circuit being organized in Chicago for the 1943 season, signed the Pats' star pitcher, Muriel Coben. However, Coben wouldn't go to Chicago for tryouts without taking a friend, and since MacLean was her battery mate, she also received a contract. Lucella was so excited that she couldn't sleep that night, thinking about the idea of being "paid for something you love to do!" The girls packed their bags, traveled by train to Chicago, roomed in the Belmont Hotel with other league prospects, and tried out at the Cubs' Wrigley Field. Lucella and Muriel made the league, both were sent to South Bend, but Coben was traded in mid-season to Rockford.

MacLean, at 5'2" and 135 pounds, was a dedicated, multi-talented athlete, and she adjusted to the AAGPBL. She performed well for the Blue Sox, but Saskatchewan star Bonnie Baker became the team's regular catcher. MacLean, the reserve, also helped her team by playing the outfield and subbing at first base. Always dependable, she was a timely hitter and a fine fielder for two seasons with South Bend, but an injury to her throwing arm limited her playing time in 1944. Disliking her 1945 contract as well as changes that would turn the league's game of modified fast-pitch softball into baseball, MacLean returned home and played one season for Edmonton. Late that summer, she received an offer to catch in the National Girls Baseball League, or the "Chicago League," a softball circuit. She moved to the Windy City and played seven seasons, starting in 1946 with the Chicks. At her request, she was traded to the Music Maids in 1949, to the Blue Birds (the catcher was injured) late in the 1950 season, and, in 1952, to the Bloomer Girls. Married in 1951 to Roger Moore, a

Shown at Bendix Field in 1944, Lucella MacLean, on right, is pictured with Blue Sox teammate Dottie Schroeder (courtesy Lucella Ross).

Kentucky native, she gave up softball after the 1952 season. Moore passed away in 1957. Lucella, who worked for two years in Detroit, returned to Lloydminster. She met Mervyn Ross, and in May 1960, they were married. The couple enjoyed 39 years together before he died in 1999. Lucella Ross treasures the golden years when she was a stellar catcher in the AAGPBL as well as the Chicago League.

JS: Can you tell me about your softball experiences in Canada before you came to the U.S.?

Ross: I started here in my hometown of Lloydminster. At that time there were only about 1,500 people here. It was a small town. I was playing when I was still going to school. I was playing for a Junior [amateur] team, but the coach for the Senior team wanted me to play for his team. It was different back then. Juniors were probably eighteen and under. So I started playing for the Senior team when I was fifteen years old. I didn't start in as catcher, but the coach wanted me to catch, so I did. I wouldn't wear a mask. Well, the first tournament I was in, I got a "bingle" on my nose, and got a nosebleed. So he put me in right field. The first ball that was hit went right my way, and I caught it, and that happened to be the end of the ball game. That was a good lesson, because I learned to use the mask. When I started with a mask, I was looking at the wires, instead of the ball. I finally figured you could see the ball without seeing the wires. *[She chuckles.]*

We played in tournaments in Saskatoon, and we won the Estey Trophy. That was a trophy that was up for the small towns and country teams to win, and we won the Estey four years in a row. The Nationals won it the following year after I left Lloydminster.

I finished [high] school, and then I played in Saskatoon. When I was playing there before, one of the owners of a ball team in Saskatoon saw me catching and liked my catching ability. So he offered me a job when I graduated. I told him I was going into training for a nurse. But when the time came, I was missing one subject, Composition, so I didn't go into nursing. I went to Edmonton and went to work.

The Saskatoon owner was watching the papers, and he didn't see my name as graduating. So he contacted the business manager of our team at Lloydminster. The business manager talked to my dad, and they contacted me in Edmonton. The owner offered me a job to come and play for his team in Saskatoon. I went there on September 13, 1940, and I played in '41 and '42 for the Saskatoon Pats.

During the 1942 season the All-American Girls League was scouting mostly for pitchers, because they had signed up a lot of girls in the south, at Regina and Moose Jaw. They wanted our star pitcher, Muriel Coben. But she wouldn't sign a contract unless someone else was going. The owner of the Pats took the contract to his lawyer, and the lawyer said, "Yes, the contract is good." The scout told our star pitcher that she could choose anyone she wanted to accompany her, because we all had to make it on our own, once we got to Chicago. Muriel picked me because we were battery mates.

It turned out that after the training season in Chicago, Muriel went to Rockford and I went to South Bend. I played in 1943 and 1944. In 1945 I didn't care for my contract, so I went to Edmonton and I played there. I worked for the Army and Navy Department Store and I played for their club.

You're talking about fast-pitch softball, right?

We used the 12-inch ball, but there was nothing "soft" about the ball, I'll tell you! In Alberta we call it fastball. We don't bother with saying "fast-pitch softball." But we're the only place in Canada that calls it fastball. The rest of the world calls it softball.

I played with Edmonton in 1945, and in the meantime, I was contacted by the Blue Birds in the Chicago League. They needed a catcher. I said, "Well, I can't leave the team. We're going into playoffs." When the season was over, I decided I did like pro ball better than amateur. They put me in touch with another team, because the Blue Birds found another catcher in California to finish out their season. So I signed with the Chicago Chicks in 1946, and I played right through 1952, but not with the same team all the time.

What were your teams?

I played with the Chicago Chicks from 1946 through 1948. Then I told the owner I didn't think he was ever going to have a winning club because he wouldn't put out the money. I didn't say that in so many words, but I asked for a trade. I was traded to the Music Maids, and I played for them in 1949 and 1950. Near the end of the 1950 season, the Blue Birds needed a catcher, because they had injuries. The owner asked me if I would take a trade, and I said, "Yes." I went to the Blue Birds and played through the playoffs, and all through the 1951 season.

The ball club was sold in the 1951 season, because the owner, Mr. Charlie Bidwell [who also owned the NFL Chicago Cardinals], had passed away, and the family didn't want to keep the ball club any more. But I wasn't going to play for them, because I didn't like my contract. I told them I wanted a trade, and I was traded to the Bloomer Girls. I played for them in 1952.

But I had married in 1951, and my husband didn't want me to play anymore, so I played the 1952 season, and that was it, for the Bloomer Girls. I married Roger Moore, a Kentucky boy.

How much money did you sign for with the Blue Sox in 1943?

I signed for $85 a week, and I was earning $17 a week at my job in Saskatoon, so that gives you a good comparison, because the value of money has changed. I was playing for the Saskatoon Pats. The owner had taxis, and I was a telephone clerk and cashier in the office. Muriel Coben, the lady I went to the States with, was one of the drivers. Two or three of the other ladies were driving cabs. It was wartime, and the ladies were doing lots of jobs. Muriel Coben died in 1979 of Lou Gehrig's disease.

Thinking about the Blue Sox, do you remember where you lived in South Bend?

I lived in a private home. There was one other girl and myself sharing a room, and we had kitchen privileges. It was a widow lady with a two-bedroom home. I had two different roommates. One was Betty McFadden, and the other was Bea Chester. She's a lady they have never traced as an All-American girl. Her mother was quite famous. She broke her arm, and the doctor told her she needed to carry something heavy to keep her arm straightened. She always went to the Brooklyn Dodger games and carried a heavy cowbell. And they used to call her "Hilda the Bell-ringer." Her name was Hilda Chester. But her daughter never came back the next year. The first roommate, Betty McFadden, was a pitcher, and she was released.

In the first year when you went to Wrigley Field, I think you lived in the Belmont Hotel.

Yes, the Belmont Hotel was close to the lakefront.

You were one of sixty selected. Do you know how many tried out?

I know there were eight catchers chosen, two per team. The league started with only four teams. There were sixteen or eighteen girls who were catchers trying out. There were lots of pitchers trying out. The other catcher who made it [with South Bend] was Bonnie

Baker. She's from Regina. That's a six-hour drive from Lloydminster. The Baseball Hall of Fame in Cooperstown has a file on each girl.

So you and Bonnie were the two catchers for South Bend in 1943.

Yes, and also in 1944. Bonnie stayed with South Bend for several seasons. Then one year [1950] she was manager with one team. I think she played through the 1952 season, the same as I did.

Do you remember some of the other regulars when you played?

We had Josephine D'Angelo in center field, and Betsy Jochum. Betsy and I were roommates in 1944. Jo Hageman played first base, and Marge Stefani played second base. Dottie Schroeder played shortstop. Lois Florreich played third base, but she wasn't always the third baseman. Betsy played left field. If I looked at a picture, I would know who else played the outfield.

In 1944, Lee Surkowski joined the team. Do you remember her?

Lee Surkowski played in 1944. She's from Moose Jaw, and so is her sister, Anne. Lee played outfield.

You played a lot more in the 1943 season than you did in 1944. According to the All-American League's official statistics, the figures for you in 1943 include 70 games, 228 at-bats, and a .206 batting average, but the figures for 1944 show 31 games, 66 at-bats, and .197 average. What happened?

I injured my right (throwing) arm in early 1944 in one game when I was sliding into second base. I was out of the lineup completely for two or three weeks. I went to a hospital in South Bend five days a week to get treatment for my arm. I sat on the bench for home games, but I didn't travel with the team. I remember late in the season I finally got into a game against Kenosha in August, but that's why I didn't play as much in 1944.

Do you have any favorite memories from playing for South Bend?

The people in South Bend were really nice to us. The owner or editor of the newspaper would gas up his car on a day off and let us take the car and go to the beach on Lake Michigan. He even had barbecues at his home for all the girls. Most of us were living in homes that weren't too far from the ballpark.

You played a Bendix Field, right?

That's right! What a hard old diamond Bendix Field was! It was hard clay.

Of course, you had to slide on the clay.

I wasn't much for sliding. I depended on my speed. I know I did slide some, but I didn't have many "strawberries," like some of the girls. Sophie Kurys, from the Racine Belles, slid a lot. She stole more bases than anyone in the league. The second year, 1944, they added two new teams, the Minneapolis Millerettes and the Milwaukee Chicks. But in 1945, the Chicks moved to Grand Rapids. They were a "traveling team," like the Millerettes in 1944. The Millerettes went to Fort Wayne in 1945 and became the Daisies.

You went to the Chicago League in 1946. Did they offer you more money?

Well, I didn't start out with more money. They weren't paying very big money. I was working a little besides playing ball. We played all night games, and once in a while on Sunday. But it was so hot, so we played night games under the lights. I told the owner, "I have to either quit playing ball and work, or get a better wage." So he paid me what I was getting when I first went to South Bend, $85 a week. When I went to the Music Maids in 1949, I got $100. That was a good salary at that time. But we had to pay board out of our salary. We had roommates, as the teams didn't want anyone being alone.

What about playing in the All-American League's uniforms with skirts?

The uniforms didn't bother me much. I think the dresses were harder for pitchers, because they had to put a fold in it and use fasteners, because the dress would be in the way. Some of them pitched "windmill," you know. Later, they pitched sidearm, but I wasn't playing then. Some of them didn't adjust. Some of the very best pitchers left the All-American League and came to the Chicago League. Connie Wisniewski couldn't adjust to the overhand pitching, so she came to our league for one year. But she was an excellent hitter, so she could play outfield and make pretty good wages.

It was so unusual then for women to earn money playing ball. Did you think about that at the time?

Yes, I did. When I got my first contract, I didn't sleep a wink that night. I was so excited. I thought, "How wonderful to get paid for something you love to do!"

We were a close bunch. We loved the game. We played at it very hard. We didn't have much social life because we were either playing ball, or practicing, or traveling. I do remember once when our whole ball team was invited to join officers from Notre Dame. We all went out as a group for the evening. We went for a meal, and we ate at a place where we could dance a little. It was very nice. But everything was ball. Of course, we had chaperones. They had strict rules, especially on the road. They had times you had to be in your room at the hotel. We weren't to be in the bars.

So there wasn't very much drinking and carrying on like they showed in the movie A League of Their Own?

There could have been some, but I wasn't a part of it. Not the girls I chummed around with. I don't know about the other teams, and I don't know what the other girls did when we weren't in the ballpark or together. But there were definitely chaperones checking on the girls. And I didn't know any manager who was a drunk.

In the movie, they had to put their flair to it. Our managers never came in the locker room, and if they did, it was only after the chaperones said they could. It wouldn't have been a very interesting movie without that.

Our manager was Bert Niehoff. He was from Oklahoma, and a former big leaguer. He was a very fine gentleman. His wife came to the games in South Bend. She was a nice lady. I didn't have any other manager in the All-American League. Bert didn't come back in the third year, and I don't know who the manager was for 1945.

It sounds like you had a very good experience playing ball for South Bend and also in the Chicago League.

I loved every minute. It was really great.

In Canada, you weren't being paid to play.

They gave you a job. When I got out of high school, I was offered a job to come and play for the Saskatoon (Saskatchewan) Pats. We probably played two or three games a week, not every night. We might have a double-header on Sunday. We have long days in Alberta in the summer. We could have evening ball games, and we would be all through playing before it got dark.

When I came out of school in 1940, I still had one subject to finish. In 1967, when we had our Centennial here in Canada, I decided to finish Composition. That completed my grade twelve.

What was your second husband's name?

My second husband was Mervyn Ross. We were married on May 7, 1960, and we were married thirty-nine years. He passed away on July 17, 1999.

It sounds like all of your experiences playing ball made a big impact on your life.

Playing ball did make a big impact on my life. I never expected to end up where I started, but I did. Lloydminster is a city of 25,000 people today, and it was a town of 1,500 when I left. We have oil, the heavy crude, and lots of mixed farming. They make ethanol out of the grain.

JOYCE (HILL) WESTERMAN
Grand Rapids, 1945; South Bend, 1946, 1952; Fort Wayne, 1946;
Peoria, 1947–1948, 1950–1951; Racine, 1948–1949

Interviewed on July 26, 2011, and October 18, 2010.

Born: 1925
Height: 5'5"
Weight: 140
Positions: C, OF, 1B
Batted: Left
Threw: Right
Career Batting Average: .228

Joyce Hill, later a standout player in the All-American League, lived in or near Kenosha, Wisconsin, almost all of her life. She first learned to play catch with her uncle, Lonnie Hill, who resided next door. By the time she reached elementary school, Joyce was playing baseball with the boys. Her father lost his job at Nash Motors during the Depression, and Joyce, the fourth of eight children of Cecil and Lillian Hill, moved with the family to a farm outside Kenosha that was owned by another uncle, George Clausen. Joyce, the youngest of four sisters, was older than her brothers, so she became her father's helper, handling chores like chopping wood and working in the garden. By 1937, the year she was twelve, Joyce played ball with her brothers and cousins and played softball on her Aunt Esther Clausen's county team. She attended a nearby one-room elementary school, a junior high in town, and Kenosha High, graduating in 1943. When Joyce was a ninth grader, Nash recalled Cecil to work, and the children rode with him daily to Kenosha to go to school. After graduation, Hill was hired by Nash, and she worked on airplane pistons for two years. In 1944, the Kenosha Comets needed two girls to fill in, and the team chose her and a friend, Ruth Radatz. Joyce batted once and fouled off a pitch, but she had never before seen women in any sport compete at such a high level. In the fall of 1944, when the AAGPBL held tryouts in Racine, she and Annastasia Batikis were chosen.

Hill began her eight-year baseball odyssey when the league sent her to Grand Rapids for the 1945 season. A right-handed catcher, first baseman, and outfielder who batted left-handed, the rookie hardly spoke all summer, playing in nine games but learning all she could about the players and the league. Allocated to South Bend in 1946, she was a reserve behind Bonnie Baker, the regular receiver, but she caught batting practice every day and worked hard to be ready for her opportunity. Loaned late in the season to Fort Wayne, she didn't play much. Sent to Peoria in 1947, Hill became the regular and played 90 games for the Redwings, mostly at catcher. In 1948, the 5'5" 140-pound brunette, a likeable athlete who was cheerful, friendly, and down-to-earth, split the season between Peoria and Racine. Playing for Racine in 1949, Joyce began wearing glasses after missing a fly ball in the outfield. Traded back to Peoria in 1950, she spent two seasons with the Illinois team, playing mostly first base. Following the 1950 season, she married Ray Westerman, and she played a final season in 1951.

Joyce Hill, who married Ray Westerman in 1951, played for the Redwings that season. Joyce, a Kenosha native, returned to play the last of her eight seasons with South Bend in 1952 (courtesy Joyce Westerman).

South Bend, however, beckoned in 1952, enticing Westerman out of retirement, thus giving the team a steady fielder and a good left-handed bat at first base. Despite a season of turmoil marked by a six-player walkout in late August, Joyce helped the Blue Sox on the field and at the plate, hitting a career-high .277. Being married, she lived alone and missed the players' usual social life. In the playoffs, she enjoyed one of her greatest thrills, hitting an RBI single to give her team a 10-inning 2–1 victory over the Rockford Peaches in game four—and tying the best-of-five series. South Bend, led by the pitching of Jean Faut, won the finale and the 1952 championship, and Westerman returned home for good. When AAGPBL Reunions began in 1982, the Kenosha heroine renewed old friendships, recalled fun experiences, and promoted the Players Association. Joyce, who kept scrapbooks and memorabilia for each season, loves talking to individuals and groups about the remarkable league that allowed her to fulfill her girlhood baseball dream.

Interview on July 26, 2011

JS: *How did you get started playing ball when you were growing up?*

Westerman: I was about five years old, and my uncle, Lonnie Hill, lived next door to me, and he was a ballplayer. I would go out with him, and Uncle Lonnie would toss me the ball. He didn't toss it that hard, but sometimes my thumb would get bent back, catching the ball, but I'd go right back out there and play ball again. I just loved the game.

By the time I started first grade in Roosevelt School in Kenosha, which was just down the block, I used to play ball with the boys. There weren't many girls who played ball in those days. I would play the outfield, and do whatever, but when I got up to hit, I used to be embarrassed, because I could hit better than the boys. Being embarrassed, I didn't want to go up and hit, because you weren't supposed to be better than the boys. But from then on, playing ball was my whole life, until now—and it still is.

What was your high school?

I graduated from Kenosha High School in 1943. But I didn't grow up in Kenosha. I lived there with my family until I was six, and my father, Cecil Hill, lost his house during the Great Depression. He didn't have a job. He was laid off from Nash Motors. My other uncle, George Clausen, had a farm next to his out in the county that he rented, and he told my dad, "Maybe we could make it livable for you there." I had four brothers and three sisters, so there were eight kids. We moved into the old farm house that was run down. We lived in two small bedrooms, a living room, and a kitchen, and that was seven of us, because one of my brothers had passed away. The house had no electricity, no running water, and a pot-belly stove. My mother, Lillian (Clausen) Hill, used to have a bottled gas stove, and she was a great cook. That's how we lived.

Name your brothers and sisters, from the oldest to the youngest.

They were Marguerite, Evelyn, Lorraine, and myself, Wallace, who was one year younger than me but had died of the flu at age two, and Richard, Cecil, and George. When Wallace, the oldest son, died, my dad almost went crazy.

You know, living in that old house was hard on my parents, but as kids, we loved living on the farm. I was my dad's helper. The boys were younger, and I was a tomboy. We cut down trees and split wood for the stove. We'd go over on the railroad tracks, not too far from us, and pick up coal to burn in the winter. My mom scrubbed clothes with a scrubbing board. The thing that supported us was my dad grew a big garden, and Uncle George sometimes gave us meat. Dad wasn't able to find work for several years. Life was rough on my parents, but not on us as kids. We always had enough to eat, and we never thought it was bad.

About the time I was twelve, I was playing ball with my cousins and my brothers. I went to a one-room school, Star School, with eight grades for one teacher. The school was located right near my grandparents' farm. I had four people in my class, and I graduated from that school in 1939. In fact, my mother had graduated from there. I went to Lincoln Junior High for the ninth grade, and to Kenosha High for grades ten through twelve.

Did you ride a bus into town to attend high school?

We rode with my dad when he went to work, because by that time he was working again for Nash Motors. We rode with dad when he left at six-thirty in the morning, and we stayed at my aunt's house until it was time to go to school.

Did they have any girls' teams?

When I was twelve, I played off and on in the county on my aunt's softball team, the Lincoln Stars. My cousin played on the team, and they were all kids that were about eighteen years old, but they let me play. When I turned eighteen in 1943, I began working at Nash Motors, and I worked on airplane engines. I polished pistons. Nash had a kind of fun team. They weren't real good ballplayers, but I played for them in 1944.

So in 1944 you were working for Nash and playing on Nash's team. How did the league find out about you?

I knew Kenosha had a team in the All-American League, but I hadn't seen the Comets play. It turned out for one series they were looking for two girls to fill in, because they had injuries. They picked two girls to substitute, and luckily, I was one of them, and Ruth Radatz was the other. I practiced with the team, and I got to play in one game. I got up to bat once, and I fouled off the ball, and I considered myself lucky. I had never seen girls play ball or pitch as well as the All-Americans. We didn't have any competitive sports for girls in any of the schools. We had after-school gym at Lincoln Junior High. That was the only sports I played in school.

After that game, I thought, "Oh, man, it would be great to be a professional ballplayer." That was my big dream. I loved the Chicago Cubs, and I thought, "Maybe I could make the All-American League." I figured the only way I would make the league was if I played catcher, because they needed catchers, and I did catch a little bit when I was twelve on my aunt's team.

That fall the league had tryouts in Racine. They sent the girls they wanted from Kenosha to Racine to try out, but to make a long story short, Annastasia "Stash" Batikis and I were the only ones they picked at Racine in 1944. They sent us to Chicago, and spring training was held at Waveland Park. We stayed at a hotel there and tried out again. That was the second time I'd been out of Wisconsin. It was scary to take the train to Chicago and try out, but I made it. The league sent me to Grand Rapids for my first season.

I didn't play very much for Grand Rapids, but I learned a lot. I didn't expect to play much, because I didn't have much team experience. The girls from California played year around out there, and they had all kinds of game experience. Mickey Maguire was the catcher for Grand Rapids, and she was one of the best catchers in the league. I only played in nine games.

What was it like for you in your first season in the All-American League?

Believe me, if I said ten words that year, it would only be if somebody asked me a question, and I answered! I was so in awe of thee girls wearing those uniforms, with me coming from a farm. I got used to the uniform, but I never liked it. I was very shy, and I didn't make a whole lot of friends. My first year was a learning experience.

You were sent to South Bend in 1946, after spring training.

We had spring training in Pascagoula, Mississippi, and the league sent me to South Bend. I didn't play much for the Blue Sox, just 21 games.

What was the difference in playing for South Bend rather than Grand Rapids?

There wasn't much difference, but I was more outgoing by then. I liked South Bend, and I liked the girls, and I made some friends. I worked really hard. I caught batting practice every day, because I was trying so hard to make it with the Blue Sox. I always had trouble picking off runners at second base. When I went to Grand Rapids, they wanted you to throw directly overhand, instead of sidearm, and I lost time trying to bring my hand up and throw overhand. But I'm surprised none of my earlier coaches had ever corrected me on that. But when I threw overhand in Grand Rapids, I got a sore arm.

The last two weeks of 1946, I was loaned to Fort Wayne. That's when I was practicing throwing to second, without a mask. They told Faye Dancer to stand up there at the plate but not to swing at the ball. Well, Faye took a half swing, intending to miss, but she tipped the ball, and it broke my nose. Later, I was playing catch and I broke my finger. That ended my time in Fort Wayne!

In 1947, everybody went to Cuba for spring training. What stands out about going to Cuba?

The plane ride and the food stand out. I didn't like the food, alligator steak and stuff. I would eat a lot of ham sandwiches. On the corner, the vendors would sell pineapple, and I ate a lot of pineapple. On May Day, we couldn't go out of the hotel, because the Cubans liked to celebrate their national holiday. Also, I have a picture of us leaning out of a hotel window and lowering a basket with money, and the Cuban guys would buy us Cokes. Another time, we were supposed to meet the president, but there was a coup, and they were shooting up the palace. We never did go to the palace to meet the president! We did eat several times at a place called Sloppy Joe's. I took some good pictures in Cuba. As for rules, we were told when we were on the streets to have three or four of us together. I was too shy for wandering around alone, but it was all fun. We practiced for a week, and we played a round-robin tournament the next week.

In 1947 you played for Peoria.

I was sent to Peoria after spring training, and that's where I began to play as a regular. I played 90 games for the Redwings.

What was it like living in Peoria?

I liked Peoria really well. I lived with a nice family, Art and Hazel Kurach, and I got to be friends with several girls. I spent time with "The Gang," Mary Wisham, Dottie Mueller, Jo Kabick, and Jerre DeNoble. We had the best time.

The league was pitching sidearm that year, and in 1948 they went overhand. I liked overhand pitching. I liked hitting the overhand pitching and also catching it.

You changed teams again in 1948.

I was with Peoria all of 1947, and partway through 1948, the league sent me to Racine, and I was heartbroken. I liked living in Peoria, and I thought, "Oh, gosh—I'll never get used to the girls in Racine." But after I got there, it was fun playing in Racine.

I got to stay at home when I was in Racine, because my family still lived on a farm. I'd go into Racine for the practices and ball games. When we were on the road, they'd pick me up on the bus, and we would leave.

You mean it was so close that you lived on your family's farm outside Kenosha?

After we lived in that old broken-down house when I was in junior high, we moved over to my grandparents' house, and we lived upstairs there when I was in high school. We had all the modern conveniences on my grandparents' farm.

Just before I got traded to Racine, I bought a new 1948 Nash Ambassador. I had to drive to meet the Belles on the road at the team's next game. I followed Racine on that trip, and then I drove home. In the movie, *A League of Their Own*, they said there's no crying in baseball, but I cried on that trip. But once I got settled in with Racine, it was fine.

I played all of 1949 with Racine, and I started wearing glasses that year. One night when I was playing right field, I looked up and got the ball in the lights, and it hit me in the head. I looked up to catch the ball, and I couldn't see it. The team sent me to an eye doctor, and I did get glasses, and I always wore glasses after that.

In 1950, the league sent you back to Peoria.

I returned to Peoria, and I made a lot more friends. Edie Perlick and Anna May Hutchison were two of my best friends in Racine. I got to know Hutch after the league ended, and some of her friends lived in Racine. So we got together, and we did everything together. One year Hutch and I took a boat trip down the Suez Canal, and we met Ted Williams on that trip. We had our pictures taken with him, and he said, "Don't call me Mr. Williams. Call me Ted."

In these later years, were you the team's regular catcher?

I became the regular with Peoria in 1947. At Racine, I did some catching and played the outfield, and sometimes I played first base. I also played regular with Peoria in 1950 and 1951.

When did you and Ray get married?

I married Ray Westerman in Kenosha after Peoria's 1950 season ended. A lot of the girls from Racine came to our wedding. When I went back to Peoria in 1951, Ray stayed in Kenosha, because we were building our house. He worked at American Motors and worked on the house. We started by building the garage, and we lived in the garage until we could afford to build the rest. We built a small building, later to be the garage, and we divided it into a small kitchen, a living room, a furnace room, and a bathroom. Then we lived there until we got the money to build another five rooms on to it, so we never owed money on our house. We built the first part in 1950, and we finished it by 1955.

In 1951 in Peoria, I stayed again in the home Art and Hazel Kurach, and my roommates were Maggie Russo and Noella Leduc. We used to chat about the games at night, and one time Art told Hazel, "You have to tell those girls to tone it down a little. I can't get any sleep!"

In 1952, I signed late with South Bend. I played mostly first base and I had a room by myself.

When you talk to groups about the league, do you have favorite memories?

We talk about the league and how it started and how we played and some of our experiences. The most meaningful thing to me was meeting all these girls and making friends, like staying with the girls in Peoria and Racine. I made lasting friendships with girls like Maggie Russo and Anna May Hutchinson. I got to know Stash [Annastasia Batikis], but not until after we played baseball. I read in a book that we went to spring training together in 1945, but I never knew it. I met Stash through Anna May. I heard that Anna May taught school in Racine, and I went to Racine and met her at a dry cleaning place. After that, we did everything together and with Stash too. To have all of these friends is so meaningful, and most of my best friends from the league have passed away. But I still know girls like Audrey (Haine) Daniels. We all bring part of our families to the reunions.

Interview on October 18, 2010

Tell me about your experiences playing baseball for South Bend. You played for Peoria in 1951, but the Redwings left the league after the season.

I got a letter from South Bend asking me to come back to the league. They made me a good offer, and I decided to go back, but I didn't get there until the last day of May.

Do you remember the manager, Karl Winsch?

I liked Karl a lot, but he was strict. Ray drove down to see me play one of the South Bend's away games. I asked if I could ride home with Ray, because we'd been married for a year, but Karl wouldn't let me. I said, "You're kidding!" He said, "No, you have to go on the bus." He said it was because of the team's insurance, but he was strict. But I respected him, because the rules are the rules. We got along real good, and I thought he did a good job.

Do you remember Shorty Pryer?

Shorty was a really good player, and a good hitter. Her batting average went down some in 1952, but she was a good player, fast on the bases. I didn't chum around with Shorty, but I knew her.

Later Pryer was suspended, and five others left the team — Lib Mahon, Dottie Mueller, Jeep Stoll, Shirley Stovroff, and Barbara Hoffman. Do you remember that?

I remember the suspension and the girls leaving, but I wasn't involved in any of that. Being married, I roomed by myself. I would go back to my room after the game, so I didn't run around with the other girls. For me, it was play ball and go home. I didn't have a car, so that was a tough season for me.

I do remember the incident near the end of the season where Karl asked Shorty to run for Betty Wagoner, and Shorty had her shoes off. She said, "Wagoner's as good a runner as I am." That's not what Karl wanted. He called to Shorty from third base, where he was coaching, and she didn't go right away, so afterward he said, "You're out of here." The next day, two girls walked out, Dottie Mueller and Barbara Hoffman. I remember there was a commotion in the locker room that evening, some shoving and pushing, and I heard a "Bang! Bang!" My back was turned, and I didn't see what happened, but it got quiet. Finally I said, "We've got a ball game to play."

What do you remember about Jean Faut?

Jean is a great person, and she was a great ballplayer. I always thought she was the best pitcher in the league. As a ballplayer, she could play any position, and she could hit any pitcher. We always get together at reunions.

But at the time, when the six girls left the team, I thought, "How in the world are we going to win these ball games?" For the playoffs in 1952, we had pitchers playing in the infield or the outfield, and it was just remarkable. We won, first, because we had the desire to win, and, second, we were determined to show the players who left that we could win without them.

What do you remember about the final playoff series with Rockford, when South Bend won the championship?

I remember the game before the last game, because I felt great about it. I had a chance in the tenth inning with runners on base, and I hit a single and drove in the winning run. Otherwise, we would have been eliminated. That was a big thrill for me.

That was an unusual year for me, being married, rooming alone, and not getting to chum around much with the other girls. Ray had our car, and I took the bus to the ballpark.

Did you play much first base?

I was mainly a catcher until the last two years. I played mostly first base for Peoria in 1951 and South Bend in 1952.

Do you have favorite memories?

The greatest thing that happened to me in the league was when South Bend won the championship in 1952. I had good seasons with other teams, but we never won a championship. Just making the league was a big thrill, but winning that championship with twelve girls was the greatest thrill!

We got our uniforms from Peoria, because the team left the league after the 1951 season. I've got two uniforms and eight signed balls, one from each season, showing the baseballs getting smaller. I also have eight scrapbooks, one from each season.

You saw the league go from underhand to sidearm to overhand pitching.

I remember Anna May Hutchison, a pitcher with the Racine Belles, starting the sidearm pitching in 1946. She started as a catcher, but used to throw batting practice all the time, and when they saw that, they made her into a sidearm pitcher.

Looking back, I came from a farm, and I was very shy, and I didn't say much for the first couple of years. I didn't get to play much, but I sat back and did what I could, and finally I got a little more outgoing. It was hard for me at first, but the girls were so good.

The only problem I had with another girl was with Dottie Mueller. She was one of my good friends in Peoria, but she was traded to South Bend. When I came to South Bend in 1952, the manager put me at first base, and Dottie was a pitcher and a first baseman. She got mad at me, but I was only doing my job. We hardly spoke after that. Afterwards, at the reunions, we talked about it and ironed it out. I was just doing my job and giving the team my best effort. That was the only problem I ever had in the league.

Looking back, you're glad you played in the league.

Playing in the All-American League was the greatest experience of my life. The first reunion in 1982 was the most exciting thing that ever happened to me. About the time spring training would have begun, we got a letter that had a picture of an All-American. I said, "What the heck is this?" I opened the letter, and they were having a reunion in Chicago. I was thrilled to death! Then they started having them every two years, and later they had reunions every year. In 2000, we had one in Milwaukee. I always look forward to the reunions.

Baseball was my whole life. I played until I was sixty, and after that, I coached in Milwaukee. My daughters played ball, and my granddaughters play ball. My youngest granddaughter is seventeen, and after next year, she will be in college. We've always gone to all of these events, and I love it.

Part II: The Postwar Years, 1946–1949

Isabel "Lefty" Alvarez
Colleens on developmental tour, 1949, 1950;
Fort Wayne, Battle Creek, 1951; Kalamazoo, 1953;
Grand Rapids, Fort Wayne, 1954
Interviewed on October 26, 1997, and May 30, 2012.

Born: 1933
Height: 5'4"
Weight: 125
Positions: LHP, OF
Batted: L
Threw: L
Career Batting Average: .195 in four seasons
Lifetime Pitching Record: There are no statistics for the 1949 developmental tour, but for the 1950 tour, her record was 6–6. Isabel posted a 2–0 record with Fort Wayne in 1951

Isabel Alvarez, who was born and raised in Havana, Cuba, saw baseball as her opportunity to emigrate to the United States, and after her arrival, playing ball led to meeting several families, notably in Fort Wayne, where the Blee family later sponsored her for American citizenship. A dark-haired beauty who once was runner-up in a Miss Cuba contest, Isabel had a brother, Tony, who was one year older, and together they played games ranging from baseball to roller skating to marbles on the streets near their home in the El Cerro district. Isabel, a talented girl who had good hand-eye coordination, and Tony were raised in a strict family. The Alvarezes were poor after the father, Prudencio Alvarez Leon, lost his job as a policeman when the

One of the Cuban Americans who played in the league, Isabel Alvarez spent two seasons with the developmental tour before being selected by Fort Wayne in 1951. "Lefty" is pictured in Daisies uniform (courtesy Isabel Alvarez).

military-backed dictator, President Fulgencio Batista, was ousted in the election of 1944. None of that mattered to Tony and Isabel, who grew up with a love of baseball, the favorite sport of Cubans since American sailors introduced the game in the 1860s. The Cuban League was organized in 1878, the Spanish-American War brought more opportunities to play U.S. teams, black players from the U.S. were accepted by 1900, and Cuban amateur baseball was booming in the 1940s.

Isabel was supported by her mother, Virtudes, who encouraged her daughter to try out for the new Cuban girls' team when the All-American League planned its spring training for Havana in 1947. When AAGPBL teams arrived, Isabel was playing for a team organized by wealthy Rafael Leon, who wanted his team to compete with American teams. The league's ties to Leon, improved by a fall tour, gave the All-American League a Latin presence. One Cuban traveled briefly to the U.S. to join the league in 1947, but several made the trip in 1948 when the AAGPBL expanded to ten teams. The minimum age was fifteen, so Isabel had to wait another year. Young and inexperienced, she was assigned to the league's developmental tour in 1949 and again in 1950, but baseball deepened her desire to return to America. The dream continued in 1951, when she was sent to the Fort Wayne Daisies, but traded to the Battle Creek Belles midway through the season. A southpaw at 5'4" and 125 pounds, "Lefty" posted a 2–0 record in 13 games, mostly in relief.

Alvarez didn't receive a contract for 1952, but her mother sent her to the airport, and she passed customs with the Cuban girls returning to the All-American League. Isabel returned to Fort Wayne. Oscar and Mildred Schelper, the family hosting her in 1951, welcomed her again and helped her find a job as a car hop. By chance, one day at a local ballpark she met Nancy Blee, who took Isabel home to meet her parents. Robert and Agnes Blee offered to sponsor the newcomer for citizenship, and after the application process and the seven-year wait, Alvarez became a citizen in 1959. Before that, she received a contract and spent the 1953 season as a reserve outfielder in Kalamazoo. Afterward, she returned to the Blees' home. The likeable Alvarez, who was friendly, hard-working, and learning English one word at a time, never again lived in Cuba. She played the outfield in 1954, the league's final season, starting with Grand Rapids and, several games later, returning to Fort Wayne, which was now her home. The AAGPBL ended after 1954, but the Cuban-American was happy. "My first job was a car hop," she recalled. "Then I worked for the Fort Wayne Tailoring Company, and later, I worked 37 years for GE." Retired and living on her own, Isabel Alvarez appreciates the opportunities that improved her life, particularly that her love of baseball led to her becoming an American citizen.

Interview on October 26, 1997

JS: How did you first find out about the All-American League?

Alvarez: My mom was interested a lot in baseball, and in the streets in Habana, I used to play baseball and things like that. She got me thinking about it. In 1947, the Cuban girls' team started getting organized, and she took me down to the manager for tryouts. Rafael Leon, who built up two teams, especially for touring in South America, made some kind of connection with Max Carey. Rafael Leon was a very important figure in my life, because I played for his team. There were other Cuban teams, but they weren't organized well. Leon was a very rich man, and he had connections with the U.S., and he was friends with Max Carey.

My mother said, "You better try out for that team, because they're going to play in South

America with the American team." My mother wanted me to come to America. I was very lucky. I tried out, and they told me I was going on the trip.

So you made the trip to South America with the Cuban team in the fall of 1947, after the All-American season ended.

Yes, when I went to South America, I was only fourteen, and I had to be fifteen to go to the U.S. That's why a group of Cubans came in 1948, because they were older, and then another group came in 1949.

Who were the first group of Cubans to go to the U.S.?

I have it written down on a piece of paper. Six came in 1948: Gloria Ruiz, Georgina Rios, Zonia Vialat, Mirta Marrero, Migdalia "Mickey" Perez, and Luisa Gallego.

When you came in 1949, you played on the tour that traveled around the country.

In 1949, Ysora Castillo came, and Mirta and Migdalia came back, and I came. I think Ysora played two years, and Mirta Marrero, I don't know where she's at, she played three more years.

I played in 1949, 1950, 1951, and 1953 and 1954. I didn't play in 1952. I was on the tour two years in a row, and I played for the Colleens. In 1951, I played for Fort Wayne. I was very lucky, because some of the girls who played on the tour never got to play in the league. In 1952, I worked at Hall's Drive-In. In 1954, I applied for citizenship papers, and I stayed. Then I got a contract from Kalamazoo, and I pitched and played the outfield.

Did you go back to Cuba after the 1949 and 1950 season was over?

Yes, but I don't remember exactly about 1952. See, I was changing addresses a lot. I was not in Cuba. I was in Fort Wayne, so I was just as happy as could be, running around and pretty free, without the obligation of being on a team and playing ball.

You did play the 1953 season, and did you apply for citizenship after 1953?

I applied for citizenship in 1954. I did not have to go back to Cuba after baseball was over because I had my papers to become a citizen. I became a citizen on October 7, 1959.

I waited many years to go back, until 1979, and see my mother, father, and brother, because in 1959–1960, that's when Fidel Castro came to power. I thought things were going to be different in my home and my culture, but everything was bad, even the relationship with my mom and my brother and his family.

My mother had all the collection of my baseball things from day one in Cuba and the USA. I used to send her things from the USA. When I was home in Habana, I packed everything with the purpose of making copies and sending it all back some way. When I arrived in Miami, I had no suitcase. I stayed in Miami two days trying to inquire why my suitcase didn't arrive, but I learned nothing. I was sick for a long time about losing my baseball things.

Do you have some favorite things that happened to you in baseball?

What I mostly remember is the tour. We had very close friendships, and we rode on the bus together. You can't forget the beginnings. It's just when you're a child, and that was my childhood. We were all together. We rode together.

So my first time in this country, and the first people I met, that's what I gathered from watching the game. We [Cubans] talked the same language, we grew up, we joked, we laughed, we had a good sense of humor. I can't forget that. When I came into the other league [AAGPBL], it was different. We were all separated. We all lived in different places. We all lived with a family. I found many outside friendships with fans. They picked me up to go to games.

I'll never forget the touring. We had tryouts, and we picked up new girls all the time.

The league was quite an experience for you. You must enjoy the AAGPBL reunions.

Oh, yeah. This is the best, this is the best. I'm going to be sixty-four [in 1997], and I'm going to retire, so I will have more time for the league.

Interview on May 30, 2012

You understand that I'm doing a book of interviews with former players, and that's why I first called you last year.

You asked me about Sue Kidd. I played on the [1949] touring team with her. We picked her up at a tryout in Arkansas, and she was pretty good. She was sitting on the same bus with me. We were sitting together. She didn't know me, and I didn't know her. She probably was wondering about my accent, you know, but she had a little bit of [southern] accent too! In those years, I was probably bad in my English, but we became good friends. She's a very nice person, and caring, you know.

Do you still live in Fort Wayne?

I've been here since the end of playing baseball, and I became a citizen. I played for the Daisies, and families, they get attached to the ballplayers, you know, and a family asked if I wanted to become a citizen, and I said, "Yes." They sponsored me, and I was very lucky in that. The Blee family, Mr. and Mrs. Blee, sponsored me, and they had a daughter, Nancy, and she knows about me living with her family. I became a citizen on October 7, 1959.

You first came to the U.S. in 1949 to play baseball.

I don't know how I made the touring team, because I was fresh from Cuba, and I could hardly speak English. That was my first year in the United States, and I didn't know anything. It's funny how Sue Kidd and I kind of communicated, but I don't know how she understood anything I said. When a rookie comes into the league, it's quite hard to get acquainted with everybody. When we picked her up after the tryout, she sat in the same seat where I was, so we had a good relationship.

Where did you grow up in Cuba?

I grew up in a district of Habana called El Cerro.

Did you play baseball in Cuba before you came to the U.S.?

Yes, I was on a Cuban team, and the Americans came to Cuba in 1947. At that time, we had an organized [girls] baseball team, and the manager, the owner of a wine distillery, was Rafael Leon, and he was a very wealthy man. He decided he wanted to have a team, and the American teams went there to train in 1947, and I had a chance to pitch one game, and I can't remember too much about it, but that was the first time my mother saw me pitch with a team with a uniform.

An American team came back in the fall of 1947 and played a Cuban team, but what it was, they mixed up the Cuban and American girls to make the teams strong, you know.

I could have come to the U.S. in 1948, but I was only fourteen, and I had to be fifteen to come to the States to play ball. In 1949, the manager came to my house, and he said,

"Well, you're going to America now." Max Carey was the American manager. He came to my house to ask permission from my mother if I was gonna come to the United States. I didn't have any English schooling when I came to the U.S. in 1949.

You were a left-handed pitcher, right?

It helped that I was a pitcher, because they needed them. The thing I remember about the touring team is we stuck together on the bus, and we also had good friendships.

It was different when the touring teams ended in 1950. In 1951, they [league] had me come to Fort Wayne, and it was a different atmosphere. I was on my own. I had to find my way. You live with families, you know, and that's how I met the Blees [in 1952]. A beautiful family, and they loved the Daisies.

You played for Fort Wayne in 1951, but you didn't play in 1952. What did you do in 1952?

The only way you could get in the United States was to have a contract. I didn't have a contract in 1952, but I got away from Cuba. My mother was pretty smart, so I got through the airport. I came with the group that was going to play, like Mickey Perez and Mirta Marrero, and they let me through, so I came to Fort Wayne, but I didn't have a contract.

I had to find my way. In 1951, I already met the Oscar Schelper family, who lived on Lille Street so I went to them and asked if I could stay, but I wasn't going to be playing, and they let me stay with them.

When I was staying here in 1952, the family helped me get a job as a car hop. Mr. Schelper said he was calling Mr. Don Hall, who was the owner of a drive-in restaurant. Mr. Schelper told him, "I have a Cuban girl, and she doesn't speak English well, but she needs a job." Mr. Hall said, "Bring her over," and I did get a job as a car hop. I met a lot of people doing this job. I had an accent, so I would go inside to write out the order. The manager, Mr. Lester Price, raised his hand and said, "You give me the order faster than I can read!" It was true, but it was the rush hour, and I liked him.

Later, I worked at the Fort Wayne Tailoring Company. The league called me in Fort Wayne, and they asked me if I wanted to play ball, and I told them, "No!" I was having a good time, working and not playing ball. I was free, with no pressure of baseball, and the first family, the family of Oscar and Mildred Schelper, was helping me get around in their car.

One time I went to a local ballpark, and I could walk to the ballpark to see girls, the kids, playing ball. For some reason, I had some money my mother gave me, about $100, and she told me to keep it in my bra, so that's what I did. My mother made me a pouch to put the money in.

The girls knew that I played for the Daisies in 1951, and they asked if I had any pictures with me. I had some, and I had the money, and for some reason, the pictures I had in my hand and the money got lost. I don't remember how. One girl came up, Nancy Blee, the daughter of Mr. and Mrs. Blee, and she said, "We'll call the police." She took charge. She said, "We got to find your pictures and your money." We found the pictures and everything in the outfield, and that's how I met Nancy Blee.

Nancy asked where I was living, and I told her I walked from the Schelper family's house, but I couldn't tell her where it was. She said, "I'm going to take you home to meet my mom and dad," and that how I met Robert and Agnes Blee.

It's a long story about growing up here in Fort Wayne. I had the help of everybody, and being a Daisy for one year, and all that happened to me in 1952, and I moved to the

Blee family's home. They got to know me and asked if I wanted to be a citizen. They probably thought I was just an orphan. That was all through Nancy. She played softball too, and she was there at the ballpark.

In 1953 you played for Kalamazoo.

Right. I was traded a lot. I played for five teams. I played for Fort Wayne, and I went to Kalamazoo and Grand Rapids and Battle Creek too, and I ended up in Fort Wayne.

I applied for the citizenship papers in 1954, and you have to wait five years. When I came to the U.S., I came as a ballplayer. In 1954, when the league ended, I didn't have to go home, because I had applied for citizenship. You see how lucky I've been? You cannot get into any trouble if you apply to be a citizen. But I was not that type. I was raised pretty strict, to obey and respect. My mom and dad taught me to respect.

What were the names of your father and mother?

My mother was Virtudes, and my father was Prudencio. My one brother, he's a year older than me, Antonio, but for short they call him Tony.

Did Tony play baseball too?

Yes, he played team baseball. I remember he took me out to grounds that were empty, and he was with me on the street, together, playing, and he'd find a place where he could throw and I could hit a ball. We were running around the street, but we didn't go far. When my mother wanted us to come back home, she clapped her two hands, and we could hear her a block away. That's how we got home.

We had to behave. When she called, we'd better come home. My brother and I were always together, running and playing, marbles and everything, like kids do. I used to roller skate a lot in the street. You strap them on, and they're hard on your foot, but when you're young, you don't feel anything — you just roller skate. I was pretty famous on the block for my roller skating, and people used to watch me. I was a little like a tomboy.

One of my uncles was a taxi driver, and he had a car. When he went by my house, I wanted to hang on the back of his car, and he said I could. I was hanging on the back fender, you know, but we went slow. I was a real rascal, but not nasty, you know what I mean?

What did you father do for a job?

My father was an orphan, and he was raised in Cuban orphanage. La Case de Beneficiencia was the orphanage. After the orphanage, he was in the Marines, and he met Batista, the dictator. The reason he got out of the orphanage is they have Cuban priests, and the orphanage was Catholic. My dad was not a good student, and the nuns used to pull his ears. You know, years ago they used to do that.

My dad was not good at all in school. In the orphanage, there was a priest there, and the priest adopted him. The priests always have a home, and I don't know how old dad was, but he went out there and lived with the priest in the house next to the Catholic Church. The priest adopted my dad, and the priest was wealthy. We had a lot of rich people in Cuba, but we had a lot of poor people too.

The priest adopted him and gave him his name, Alvarez de Leon. I shortened my name, because it was too confusing when I became a citizen. They thought Leon was my last name and Alvarez was my middle name, so I shortened it.

Anyway, when the priest died, the priest left him all his money. When my mom met my dad, she was bored, and he was rich, and anyhow, they got married. And they went to

Spain for a honeymoon, and they stayed there a long time. My father, with the money he had, started a construction business, like apartments and housing. The year was a bad year [during the Great Depression], and he lost all his money, and they had to come back home. My brother was born in Spain in 1932, and I think everyone was losing their money then.

I was born in Cuba in 1933, and my parents were poor. When my father was in the Marines, he met Fulgencio Batista, and he knew him. My dad needed a job, and Batista gave him a job as a policeman. My dad was a policeman for many years, and then there was a change of government, and Batista was out. My dad went to where he worked, and they stripped him of his uniform, and he lost his job. They knew Batista gave him the job.

[Editor's note: Fulgencio Batista, a sergeant in the Cuban army, took over the government on September 4, 1933, in a coup known as the "Revolt of the Sergeants." Batista controlled the Cuban government as well as the army. On January 14, 1934, he forced President Grau San Martín to resign and replaced him with Carlos Mendieta, who was followed by two other subservient presidents. Batista won election as president in 1940 under a new Cuban constitution. The Batista regime was corrupt, organized crime was encouraged, and the police were widely feared, but the U.S. recognized it as Cuba's official government. In 1944, however, Batista lost the election for president to Grau San Martín, and shortly afterward, Alvarez, along with Batista's other policemen, lost his job. Eight years later, on March 10, 1952, Batista took over the elected government in a coup, and he ruled Cuba until resigning on January 1, 1959, because the Castro forces were succeeding in their revolution.]

We were living pretty good when he was a policeman, but from then on [1944], we were poor, because my dad didn't have an education, and it was hard for him to get a job. Later, Batista forced himself back in as dictator [1952]. Batista was a "bad guy," and anyone who knew Batista was a bad guy, too. I was in the United States when Batista took over, and my father said he wanted to be reinstated and get a pension. My mom and dad wrote me asking if I could write a letter to Batista asking for my father to be reinstalled in the police force. I think Batista wrote me a letter and said he had to be reinstated in the police force and wear a uniform again. By that time, Cuba had a revolution, and people were getting killed. My dad refused, so he didn't get any retirement.

Once you got to the U.S., you didn't go back to Cuba, right?

I didn't go back to Cuba for a long time. I never missed my family, and a lot of people do miss their family. They're more family-oriented. I was raised that way. There was love, yes, with my mother, but my mother wanted my future to be good. She said, "You go to the United States and you don't worry about it." So I took advantage of that. My family, my brother, my mom, and my dad, and our life was pretty strict, and we didn't cry. My mom was pretty strong.

When I became a citizen in 1959, I knew my mom was happy. I took them for granted, and I did wrong for not wanting to go back home and see my mom, because she went through some bad times.

Looking back on it, you must be happy that you played baseball in the All-American League.

Yes, that's right. That was one of the biggest opportunities that anybody could have, because we had a whole girls' team in Cuba, and I was picked. I was very lucky. The opportunity to play baseball and to become a citizen, that was it. How can I get to the United States? We had baseball, and I got to play on the tour.

In Fort Wayne, we had a good reputation, and people liked us. People loved the Daisies.

In Fort Wayne I met tons of people, and I just loved the Daisies too. That's how I was trusted by the families. If you played for the Daisies, you're good people, even if you're Cuban. In those years back, people helped people. Well, you can't do that nowadays, to let somebody live in your home. I met the Blees' daughter at that ball game, and thanks to her family, I became a citizen.

After living with the Blees, I lived on a farm with the Schaeffers, and they lived about 20 miles southeast of Fort Wayne in the country near Decatur. I met Donna Schaeffer, and she was working at the Indiana Michigan Electric Company. She had a car, and she would drop me off at the Fort Wayne Tailoring Company, where I was working. She worked an eight-hour day, and she picked me up after work. After applying many times to work at General Electric, they hired me in 1962. I turned 65, and I retired from GE in 1999, and I had 37 years of service with them.

So I always had a job in Fort Wayne. My first job was a car hop. Then I worked for the Fort Wayne Tailoring Company, and later, I worked 37 years for GE. Once I started working at GE, I bought my own car. A friend who worked at GE co-signed so I could get a loan from the GE Credit Union to buy the car.

During all those years in Indiana, I moved from one place to another, and today, I don't know how I did it all. I am 78 years old now, and it feels good to have a home of your own. I enjoy the most living by myself.

Mary "Wimp" Baumgartner
Colleens on developmental tour, 1949; Peoria, 1949;
Kalamazoo, 1950; South Bend, 1950–1954
Interviewed on September 7, 2010.

Born: 1930
Height: 5'5"
Weight: 145
Positions: C
Batted: R
Threw: R
Honors: Played for South Bend against the All-Stars, 1952
Career Batting Average: .177 in six seasons

Mary "Wimp" Baumgartner grew up in Fort Wayne, Indiana, the youngest of five daughters in a working class family. Their father owned a small grocery story, and the older sisters delivered groceries on their bicycles. Mary Louise began working in the family store when she was in elementary school. Betty Jane, the oldest of the Baumgartner daughters, realized her youngest sister's favorite food at dinner was hamburgers, so she tagged her with the nickname "Wimp," after Wimpy, the popular Popeye cartoon character who lived on hamburgers. Wimp liked playing ball, and when the All-American League's Daisies (formerly the Millerettes from Minneapolis) came to Fort Wayne in 1945, she decided to be a professional baseball player. One year later, Lenna "Sis" Arnold, a local physical education teacher, made the Daisies, and her example inspired other girls. After graduating from high school in 1948, Baumgartner, who was too bashful to try out, worked in the family's store. In the spring of 1949, Fort Wayne manager Harold Greiner held tryouts in town, and three girls were sent to Chicago. Wimp, now eighteen, made the league. In Chicago, Lenny Zintak, who supervised the touring teams, suggested she switch from the outfield to catcher, where the need was greatest, and Wimp's greatest adventure began.

Baumgartner, who stood 5'5" and weighed 145, was assigned to the Colleens, one of the league's two rookie traveling teams in 1949 and 1950. "I loved catching," she recalled, "and besides, I had a front row seat to see the whole game." In late July, Zintak, who traveled with the touring teams, informed Baumgartner that she was needed in Peoria. She boarded her first-ever plane, a Piper Cub, and flew to join the Redwings. A reserve for Peoria, she caught batting practice and learned more about catching. In 1950, Baumgartner and the Redwings trained at Cape Girardeau, Missouri, but she was soon traded to South Bend. She spent most of the season backing up the regular receiver, Shirley Stovroff, but Wimp was loaned briefly to Kalamazoo. Altogether, she averaged .176 in 36 games. In 1951, the Blue Sox, managed by Karl Winsch and still led by the stellar pitching of his wife, Jean Faut, won the league's regular season title and also defeated the Rockford Peaches for the Shaughnessy Playoff Championship. Baumgartner hit .205, but played fewer games as the team's backup catcher.

Part of the group of younger Blue Sox, notably Sue Kidd and Janet Rumsey, both pitchers, and shortstop Gertie Dunn, Baumgartner watched in 1952 as dissension on the ball club led Winsch to suspend "Shorty" Pryer, and five veteran players left the team in support of their teammate. Baumgartner, colorful, outspoken, and hardworking, became South Bend's regular receiver. She kept improving, helped by tips from Faut, the league's best pitcher. Also, the remaining twelve Blue Sox, despite long odds, won a second straight Shaughnessy Championship, defeating Rockford in the best-of-five playoff. Wimp improved her skills during two more seasons, but the Blue Sox fell to fifth of six

A catcher who began with the Colleens on the developmental tour of 1949, Wimp Baumgartner, pictured in 1952, was traded to South Bend in 1950. Later, Wimp became the team's regular receiver (courtesy Wimp Baumgartner).

teams in 1953 and finished second of five teams in the circuit's final season of 1954. She loved baseball. "Just about the time we learned the game enough to play intelligent ball, the league folded up," Baumgartner observed. After graduating from college, she taught physical education and coached several sports for 28 years. Later, she became a dedicated leader in the AAGPBL Players Association and continued to preserve her friendships, camaraderie, and memories from the league through letters, phone calls, and visits.

JS: How did you get interested in baseball when you were growing up?

Baumgartner: Being from Fort Wayne and watching the Daisies in 1945, I decided I could play professional baseball. My PE teacher, Lenna Belle "Sis" Arnold, tried out and made the Daisies in 1946, along with some other players from the Fort Wayne area. At that time, I was a sophomore in high school. I graduated in June 1948. The season had already started, and Daisies held tryouts at their home park, Memorial Field. Maybe 15 girls tried out, but none of them made the Daisies' team, and at that time, I was too bashful to ask for a tryout.

In 1949, Harold Greiner was hired to manage the Daisies, and he was in charge of the tryouts in Fort Wayne in the spring of 1949. Quite a few people attended the tryout. Three of us were selected to go to Chicago to try to gain a spot on the two rookie teams that would be touring the southern states. Lenny Zintak was in charge of selecting personnel and deciding who would play at various positions in the field. Four Cubans tried out, but only one could speak English. In Chicago, Zintak had me work out as a catcher, and I really took to catching. I had a front row seat to see the whole game. Catching worked out fine, because I doubt if I would have made the league otherwise.

I played on the Colleens' touring team, and while we were on tour, Zintak would hold tryouts before every game, and I would warm up and catch the would-be pitchers. While in Little Rock, Sue Kidd, who was fifteen, came with her family to try out. Afterward, Zintak questioned me about Sue's pitching. I told him she had good control, good curve, a drop pitch, and adequate speed. Zintak talked to her father, Marvin Kidd, and asked if she could join the tour. He agreed. The Kidd family drove back to Choctaw and returned the next day. Sue had her bag packed and joined the tour.

In the last week in July, Zintak informed me that I would be flying to Peoria to play that night. The team sent a Piper Cub airplane to Jackson, Mississippi, to pick me up and take me to the game. But on landing, the pilot was informed that the Redwings were playing in Fort Wayne. The pilot and I got back on the plane and flew to Fort Wayne, and I arrived at the ball park a half hour before game time. I put on a uniform that was too small and warmed up the pitcher (I don't remember her name). That game was the first time my parents saw me play as a professional player. I survived my "introduction" to the AAGPBL, and I did finish the 1949 season with the Redwings.

In 1950, the next year, the league sent four teams to Cape Girardeau, Missouri, for spring training. The teams were Muskegon, South Bend, Fort Wayne, and one more. At the end of spring training, I was traded to South Bend. I got on the South Bend bus and rode north with the team. We played some exhibition games on the way. Sometime during July, I was loaned to the Kalamazoo Lassies, as their catcher injured her knee. I caught for about a month, and I was sent back to the Blue Sox.

South Bend's manager in 1950 was Dave Bancroft. Do you remember him?

Dave Bancroft was a good manager and a nice guy. He was busy most of the time talking to the older players, because they were the main players. Rookies were there to play if needed, but mainly we got to carry the catching equipment, carry the first aid kit, carry the bats and balls, do the important things, like push the bus! For rookies to meet some of the best players in the league, we were fortunate. South bend had Jean Faut, an exceptional pitcher, Shirley Stovroff, the catcher, Helen Filarski, at third base, Shoo-Shoo Wirth, the shortstop, Shorty Pryer, at second base, Betty Whiting, the first baseman, Lib Mahon, the left fielder, Jeep Stoll, in center field, and Betty Wagoner in right field. They were all excellent players.

In 1951, South Bend had a really good year. The Blue Sox came in first in the second half of the season, and they won the playoff championship. Karl Winsch was the manager. Can you tell me about Winsch as a manager?

In 1951 the Blue Sox had an excellent year and won everything. We were league champions and playoff champions. We had new pitchers, Sue Kidd and Janet Rumsey, a new shortstop, Gertie Dunn, and the younger players were starting to blossom. Karl Winsch was a pitcher who could instruct the young pitchers. He could not, or would not, help the position players, I think because he did not have the knowledge. Our team was very talented at every position, and our back-up people were competent. Winsch's teaching skills were limited, mainly because his own career was learning to pitch. Karl didn't teach us anything, but he had good players. The players helped their teammates become better players. The players' rapport was excellent, and we had good team play.

The year 1952 started out to be a good year. It ended up being a good year for the "Dutiful Dozen." Right before the playoffs, things began to come to a head. A few of the players decided that things would be better if some changes could be made. One player decided that she was run-down and therefore needed pep pills. A few people became more vocal about things that didn't go their way, and dissension started to raise its ugly head, primarily between Shorty Pryer and Karl, and the players began to take sides. Eventually words were exchanged and some players decided to walk out. With twelve players left, Jean Faut was the moral leader to get the younger players to wake up to the fact that they had to band together and they could win the playoffs, no matter what. We all bought into her state of mind that we could win. We wanted to show the ones that walked out that we could play ball without them. They told us we would be sorry if we didn't go with them. Karl had the most problems with Shorty Pryer. She'd let you know if you did something wrong, but she wasn't the manager.

What kind of catcher was Stovroff?

Stovroff was a good catcher. Any time she thought she picked up a signal from manager at third base, she'd come in to the bench and be sure and tell everybody. She was better than I was. I was on the bench in '51 and '52, as I was new at catching. With the little experience I was getting, I felt like I was getting more comfortable behind the plate.

Sue Kidd, Janet Rumsey, Gertie Dunn, and myself ended up rooming together at McGowans in Mishawaka, which was less than half a mile from Playland Park, where we played ball. I can't say enough about four young girls getting along and enjoying each other's company so much. We had a bathroom to ourselves, kitchen privileges, and two bedrooms. Most of the other players were envious of our living conditions. I can't say enough about my roommates, and we became lifetime friends.

We almost had two separate teams. We played together on the field. But as far as socializing, the younger ones didn't have much to say about anything. We had two teams socially. We played together on the field. We didn't talk to Karl. He had Sue Kidd pitch a double-header one time, and she won both games. He didn't say much, but what else could Sue do? Karl didn't have much to say to me, and I didn't say much to him.

What do you remember about the pitchers?

Lil Faralla and Dottie "Sporty" Mueller were both sidearm pitchers. In '50 and '51, I caught Faralla. She threw a low sidearm pitch that surprised some batters because it was coming from a different angle. She had good control, but she was not fast, and she also had a small curve and a change-up. Many times she would come in to relieve a pitcher. Faralla was a slow-working pitcher, so the base runners could take off and steal.

Dottie Mueller had a strict sidearm pitch, and it was fast. Her control at times became a problem. Her curve was exceptional, and she had a good change-up.

Jette Vincent was an average pitcher as far as speed, curve, change-up, and control. At times she was more on the wild side, and she liked to throw to first base and try and pick off the runner. Jette always knew what she wanted to throw, so we worked that out.

Sue Kidd had the most choice of pitches, and she had the most control. Sue was easy to catch because of her control. She was a workhorse, and she didn't waste any time between batters. Sue was also one of the better fielders.

Janet Rumsey had the best drop pitch on the team, and she had an excellent fastball. Her control was good, and she was a good fielder. She threw a "heavy" ball that sunk into the catcher's glove. She was the only one who threw like that.

I don't need to tell you that Jean Faut was the best pitcher.

When you look back on it, what are some of your favorite memories?

What I liked about being in the league is that I got to play, and I was a young kid. In 1950, I was a rookie and didn't know too much. But we had a really good team in 1951, and the only year we had any trouble was in 1952. Shorty Pryer was in the dugout when Karl Winsch called on her to pinch-hit in that game near the end of the season. She was in the dugout and had her shoes off, and Karl wanted her to pinch-run, and she didn't want to do it. A couple of them on the bench said, "Shorty, you need to get out there." I don't remember much about it.

My favorite memory was when we beat Rockford in the championship playoff in 1952. We had to go clear past Rockford to Freeport, that town next to Rockford, to finish that season. After that, I stayed in Rockford, and I slept at the bus station. I rode home on the bus to Chicago and then to Fort Wayne, and I got home late that night.

What else would you say about the league in those later years?

A lot of the older players were leaving the league, and the younger ones were coming on. The new players just weren't as good. By 1954 the caliber of play wasn't there anymore. Everyone knew it was the final season. Players right around our age for South Bend, like me and Gertie Dunn and Sue Kidd and Jan Rumsey, and some of the other younger players on other ball clubs didn't have enough time to develop. The teams were all getting younger players, and the caliber of play just wasn't there anymore. Everyone knew that 1954 season was going to be the end of the league. We weren't drawing fans any more, and we felt sorry about it. Just about the time we learned the game enough to play intelligent ball, the league folded up. We felt like we got gypped out of a good thing.

In the fall of 1953, I started college, because I knew I was going to go sooner or later, so I might as well get started, because I knew the league was only going to have maybe another year.

I want to say about Jean Faut that when I was catching her, she did more to help me and the other pitchers than the manager. Jean always told you how to do it better in a nice way, but she got her point across. Jean was a terrific person. Of course, her game was at stake, and therefore she had some good points to tell me. She knew what she wanted to do, and she knew what she wanted me to do.

After catching Jean a while, and in 1953 I caught her most of the time, I learned a whole lot. With her Pennsylvania Dutch voice, you could hear her all over the field. After she said what she had to say, she'd just stand there and grin. She was a people person, and her personality was truly optimistic.

When the players walked out, I was glad. The dissension was gone, and we were determined to win. We got to play without the rest of those players. We were glad some of them left, because they were all the time complaining amongst themselves. The rookies just sat there and looked, you know, the ones that had only a few years in the league under their belts. We talked about it a lot, the four of us that roomed together.

Lou Arnold was our cheerleader on the bench. She did win eleven games that one year, but she didn't have anything on the ball. I'd call for a curve, and that thing didn't even wrinkle, let alone do anything else. She got through a lot of those games due to how many runs we scored for her. But she did make a lot of noise. She was a cheerleader on the bench, and Karl liked that. He'd say, "Get something started," and she would do a good job of it. Lou was a very nice person, but not the greatest ballplayer.

South Bend did so well in 1951 because you probably had the best players in the league.

That's basically true, and they all got pretty close from playing together in 1951. South Bend was a good solid team all the way through at that time. Those of us on the bench did everything we could do to help the other players win, as far as practice and everything went. We had enough young players so we could challenge some of the regulars, and that made them play better. We had a good team, and that's all there was to it. I was very fortunate to be part of it.

When the six walked out, I was glad. I got to play. I was bound and determined we were going to win, and so was everybody else. Sue made up her mind, Gertie made up her mind. We had good pitchers in Faut and Rumsey and Kidd. It was fun playing that playoff series. I don't think any of us wanted to beat anybody worse than Rockford.

I was very fortunate to be on that South Bend squad, because we had good players, especially in 1953 and 1954. When you get to play, you feel better about everything. We were holding our own most of the time, but that's about it.

"Fearless" Froning, Mary Froning, we used to call her "Fearless." She used to run into the fence or do anything to get to the ball. She was a good player, and she had a great sense of humor. On the ball field, you never knew what she was going to do next. *[She laughs.]*

What did you and your roommates do in your spare time?

First of all, when we came off a road trip, we'd have to do laundry all day between the four of us. I know one time we went to a lake over by Elkhart. We went in the morning about ten o'clock, and we stayed out, lying in the sun. Sue Kidd got burned up, and she was supposed to pitch that night. She had to come back and tell Karl, and boy—did he hit the ceiling, and he probably should have. For about a week, Karl was mad at Sue.

We were always together. Mostly we used to go swimming, or we had practice. We all got along real good. We never had any fights. We didn't mouth off, except in a fun way.

Those were some of the best times of my life. Where else could you go and get paid for playing ball? I saved every penny I could. Mom and Dad had a grocery store, and their names were Les and Bernice Baumgartner. They sold groceries on credit, and they got paid when people brought in their checks to get them cashed. I always knew I'd go to college, but I wanted to play ball first.

Where did you get the nickname Wimp?

There were five girls in our family, Betty Jane, Marge, Millie, Deloras, or "Teen," and me, and I was the youngest. My oldest sister, Betty Jane, was seven years older than me. Remember the cartoon *Popeye*, with the character "Wimpy"? At the dinner table, Dad would go around and ask everybody what they wanted to eat, regardless of what was in the dish, which is what you were going to get. Dad would get to me and he'd say, "What do you want?" And I'd say, "Hamburgers." Betty Jane started calling me "Wimp," because if they wanted me to eat something, they'd say it was a hamburger. So the name stuck. I went through school with Wimp, and the teachers called me Wimp.

One time one of my girl friends called up and asked for Mary Baumgartner. Dad didn't like us to tie up the phone because it was for business only, and he said, "There's nobody here by that name." My job in the store was to wipe off every can and dust off the shelves. My older sisters had to deliver groceries to people who phoned in an order. We walked, or if we didn't have too much to carry, we rode our bikes. That's how our family made a living back in the 1930s and the 1940s.

What about some highlights of your life after baseball?

Starting in 1953, I attended Indiana Central College (now the University of Indianapolis), and I graduated with the bachelor's degree in Physical Education and minors in Biology, English, and Health. I taught PE for 28 years, and I also coached girls' sports, mainly track and field, basketball, gymnastics, softball, and volleyball. In the 1950s, I played basketball with the South Bend Rockettes, and later, I started playing golf and competed in several tournaments. In 1988, I went with many of my old friends to the National Baseball Hall of Fame in Cooperstown to see the dedication of the permanent display on Women in Baseball. I've been active in the AAGPBL Players Association, which was created in 1987 under the leadership of former player June Peppas. I was voted president of the Players Association from 1992 to 1998, and I'm still involved in the baseball association.

ERMA BERGMANN
Muskegon, 1946–1947; Springfield, 1948;
Racine, 1949–1950, Battle Creek, 1951

Interviewed on June 1, 2011.

Born: 1924
Height: 5'7"
Weight: 155
Positions: P, OF (13 games in 1946)
Batted: R
Threw: R

No-Hitter: Defeated Grand Rapids, 4–1, on May 22, 1947
Career Batting Average: .201 for six seasons
Lifetime Pitching Record: 182 games, 64–91 record, 2.56 ERA

Erma Bergmann, who grew up in a Jewish family in St. Louis, Missouri, liked playing ball with her brothers, Otto, the eldest (named after his German-born father), and Victor, the youngest, as early as she could remember. Her mother wanted her only daughter to take piano lessons, but when Erma said she wanted to go outdoors and play ball, Sophie Bergmann was wise enough to give her the daughter the chance to do what she loved. At age fourteen in 1938, Erma joined an amateur softball league, and she honed her skills by playing on regular diamonds with official rules and umpires. In 1942, during World War II, the enthusiastic young woman, a hard worker, graduated from McKinley High School. In softball, Erma often played third base because of her strong throwing arm. She caught the eye of an Amateur Athletic Union official for the long-distance softball throw, but the war and transportation limits caused cancellation of the national meet in New Jersey. Learning office skills for a year at a business college, Erma worked for two years as a stenographer. All the while she improved as a ballplayer, competing at the St. Louis Softball Park on three different women's teams during her eight amateur seasons.

In 1945, a scout for the All-American League, Al Nicoli, saw the 5'7" 155-pound brown-eyed brunette play, and he asked her to try out. Bergmann, worried about turning professional in a league that might not last, declined. Nicoli contacted her again in 1946. Although league officials in St. Louis warned her that pro status would mean she couldn't play softball in her home town, the determined Erma decided to give the girls' league a shot. Arriving at Pascagoula, Mississippi, for the circuit's two-week camp, she made the grade and was assigned to Muskegon. Manager Buzz Boyle needed a pitcher, and he taught the curly-haired right-hander to pitch submarine style. As the season progressed, Bergmann, like several other hurlers, shifted to sidearm, a natural motion, and the league (which had used underhand pitching since 1943), adjusted the rules and continued to evolve toward overhand pitching, authorized in 1948. "Bergie," tall, strong, and easy-going, highlighted her 1946 season by hitting her only career homer in the 2–1 win she pitched over Peoria, a victory watched by her family after they drove from St. Louis. On May 22, 1947, Erma hurled a no-hitter to beat the Grand Rapids Chicks, 4–1. She kept contributing to the Lassies' pennant-winning season in 1947, but she was allocated in 1948 to expansion Springfield. Pitching for the weak Sallies, she struggled to a 9–19 mark.

Bergman, a barrier-breaker like other women who played professional baseball in the 1940s, bounced back with two 11–14 seasons for Racine. She capped her AAGPBL career with Battle Creek, posting a 7–18 ledger for the last place Belles when the franchise moved to Michigan in 1951. A fine all-around ballplayer who fashioned a lifetime ledger of 64–91 with an ERA of 2.56, Bergmann shifted to Chicago's National Girls Baseball League in 1952. She hurled one season of fast-pitch softball for the Blue Birds and two for the Match Queens. The league was ending, so she made another pioneering choice, securing entrance to the St. Louis police academy. Graduating in September 1956, she became one of the city's first female officers. Enthusiastic, personable, and talented, she served with distinction for 25 years, after playing pro baseball and softball for nine seasons. A real team player, Erma Bergmann's contributions to women's sports and to St. Louis' civic life were boosted by the support of her devoted mother.

Warming up in Havana's Gran Stadium during spring training of 1947, Erma Bergmann, on left, throws sidearm pitches with Muskegon teammate Nancy Warren (courtesy Doris Sams).

JS: You were born and raised in St. Louis, Missouri.
Bergmann: Yes, but my dad was born in Germany. He served in the German army as a young man, and then he came over here. His older brothers were here and ran a bakery. He served in the American army after he got drafted in World War I. Pop served under two flags. I was his oldest child, and I had two brothers, Otto, named after my dad, and the youngest was Victor.

Can you talk about getting involved in softball and baseball?
I played amateur softball. I'm in the Amateur Softball Hall of Fame. We're all in Cooperstown for playing in the league, that's number two. I was put into the Missouri Sports Hall of Fame in 2007, and that was number three. This November I'm going to be put into the St. Louis Sports Hall of Fame, and that will be four halls of fame. It doesn't buy me anything, but it's an honor. *[She laughs.]*

How did you get started playing softball? Did you play with your brothers?
We had a piano, and my mother wanted me to take piano lessons. I said, "Mom, I'd rather go outdoors and play ball with my brothers in the neighborhood." So I played ball in the alleys and on sandlots with my brothers and their friends. I wound up playing on an organized softball team. The man who ran a junkyard in our neighborhood asked me to play on his team. We used to go "junking" sometimes when we were kids. We'd pick up junk and sell it and make a nickel or a dime. The man who owned the junkyard was the manager of an amateur softball team, and I played eight years of organized softball with lights, white bases, and umpires. That was really an upgrade from playing in the sandlots.

My mother let me do my thing, so I realized that if I ever had children that wanted to do something maybe that I didn't suggest, I'd let them try it.

One time when I played in Muskegon, the golf professional at the Muskegon Country Club was playing in a two-ball foursome, and he asked me to be his partner. He said, "Erma, if you play golf for five years, you could be a pro. You've got that much natural ability."

I said, "I'm playing ball in the All-American League. I can't be practicing golf for five years." You can't do everything at once in your life, but that's a little story to add to my baseball career.

How did you get involved with the league?

When I was playing amateur softball in St. Louis in 1945, a scout named Al Nicoli asked me to play in the All-American League. When I told them at the amateur ballpark, they wanted to bar me for two years so I couldn't come back and play amateur softball. Instead of congratulating me and saying, "I hope you make it," they told me they'd bar me for two years. That stopped me in 1945.

The next year, Al Nicoli asked me again. I thought it over and I said to my mother, "You know, I enjoyed playing organized softball for eight years, but I'm going to try the All-American League. If I don't make it, Mom, I'll come home on the first train or the first bus."

I took the train to Pascagoula, Mississippi, and I was rated one of the top rookies in the camp. Max Carey was president of the league, and I played for some good managers in the league.

The league sent you to Muskegon in 1946.

I played for Muskegon in '46 and '47 on the same team with Doris Sams. In 1948, they put me on the new Springfield team, and I cried. The league didn't tell me anything about it ahead of time. They said the new teams needed some veteran players. They couldn't have all rookies. I could agree with that, but why didn't they tell me before spring training at Opa-Locka, Florida? I was real satisfied with Muskegon, and I had pitched well there. I got picked by the chaperone, Mrs. Kessler, to stay at her home. She had a beautiful home. I loved Muskegon.

Do you remember much about your no-hitter against Grand Rapids on May 22, 1947?

It was raining lightly, and I hated the rain, because I used to play third base a lot in amateur softball, and I knew that when the ball is wet, you've got a chance of throwing it away. I never liked to pitch when it was raining. I think Arleene Johnson was at third base, and she made one error, and that's how Grand Rapids got one run, but we won, 4–1, and I pitched a no-hitter.

You pitched sidearm in 1946. Can you tell me about that?

Ralph "Buzz" Boyle, who was an outfielder for the Brooklyn Dodgers, was my manager in Muskegon, and he needed a pitcher. He started me out pitching "submarine" style, which meant your arm came about six inches from your knee. I could do that, because we used to play around when we were kids to see if we could throw submarine.

But as the 1946 season moved along, the league gradually raised the rule until you were throwing sidearm, and that was real easy for me. I never had a sore arm throwing sidearm, and the first thing you know, the league was pitching overhand [in 1948].

Who was your catcher with Muskegon?

Mickey Maguire was our catcher. I played two years with Mickey Maguire and Doris Sams and two years with Sophie Kurys. I played with some good ballplayers.

So when you pitched the no-hitter against Grand Rapids, you were pitching sidearm?
Yes.

You had some pretty good teammates and two good seasons with Muskegon. What was the difference when you went to Springfield?
I lived in a woman's house in Springfield that was so clean you could eat off the floor. My brothers came from St. Louis to visit me, and they had to take off their shoes to come in her house. I didn't like that too well, but I was only in Springfield for one year. Springfield wasn't bad, but I'd rather be with my friends in Muskegon. But when you're a professional, you have to play for whoever pays you.

You were traded to Racine in 1949.
I played for Racine in '49 and '50. Leo Murphy, the manager, wanted me in Racine.

What was it like being in Racine?
I liked Racine. It was really nice. I had friends there. I had a friend whose father was a corporate lawyer for one of the firms. They used to invite me to their home for dinner. I really liked Racine and the Belles' players, like Sophie Kurys and Edie Perlick and "Tuffy" Hickson. I loved the players I knew in Muskegon and in Racine. They called me "Bergie."

In 1951, the Belles franchise was sold to Battle Creek, and you went to Battle Creek. What was the difference between Battle Creek and Racine?
Battle Creek was a group of players from different teams. It wasn't like Racine or Muskegon, that's for sure. Guy Bush was my manager. He was a nice guy. I liked him.

I liked all of my mangers, Buzz Boyle in Muskegon, Carson Bigbee in Springfield, Leo Murphy in Racine, and Guy Bush in Battle Creek.

What are some of your favorite memories from the All-American League?
In 1946, my father and mother and my two brothers came to a game in Peoria when Muskegon was in town. I was pitching, and I hit a home run. I used to be a fairly good hitter when I played third base in amateur softball, but when you're pitching regularly, your hitting kind of falls off. You don't get the times at bat as the other players do.

My brothers brought my mom and dad to Peoria, and I hit that home run and won the game, 2–1, during my first year in the league. I was hoping we were going to hold them in the last of the ninth, because we were the visitors, and we did. My brothers brought my mom and dad down on the field after the game.

I said, "Mom, you understand what went on out there a little bit, don't you?"

She didn't know a ball from a strike, but she said, "You stand out there and throw for a while and they swing, and they stand out there and throw for a while and you swing."

I said, "Yeah, Mom, that's the general idea, only sometimes I'm out there a lot longer than they are!" *[She laughs.]*

My dear mother got the general idea of the game, even if she didn't know a ball from a strike.

I had a good arm, you know. Back in St. Louis, they were going to send me to the AAU women's long distance softball throw during World War II. At the amateur softball park, they measured how far I could throw the ball. They cancelled the National AAU Meet in New Jersey because of the war, but my team thought I could compete in the women's softball throw. I always played third base, so I must have had a pretty good arm!

The year with Battle Creek was your last season in the All-American League, but you also played three years in the National Girls Baseball League in Chicago.

I got the idea that if I could play with these All-American girls, I figured I could play with these Chicago professional girls. In 1952, I played for the Chicago Blue Birds, and in '53 and '54, I played for the Chicago Match Queens. Freda Savona was my manager. She had a voice like a man and she cried, too, because they called her names out on the field. Freda went to her priest and told him about it. The priest said, "Don't cry, Freda. You've got a heart just like they have." I thought that was a good answer.

Do you have other favorite memories from the All-American League?

I always just enjoyed myself. I didn't try to set a lot of records. It was such a great thing for me to get to play pro baseball, after they were going to bar me from playing amateur softball in St. Louis. I loved playing professional ball. I was always satisfied and happy with what I was doing at the present time. Wherever I went, I was able to hold my own with the good players.

Do you feel like the league made a big impact on your life?

I think the league helped me so much. Penny Marshall asked me that when they were making the movie, *A League of Their Own*. I was a pioneer in women's baseball, and after that, I was a pioneer for policewomen for twenty-five years in St. Louis. I met people from bag ladies to millionaires. I'm glad that my mom let me do my thing when I told her I'd rather go outside with the boys and play ball. She let me do it, and I wound up being in four halls of fame. That's quite an honor.

WILMA BRIGGS
Fort Wayne, 1948–1953, South Bend, 1954
Interviewed on January 28, 2011, and May 9, 2011.

Born: 1930
Height: 5' 4"
Weight: 138
Positions: 1B, OF
Batted: L
Threw: R
Honors: Led league in home runs with 9 in 1953
All-Star Team: 1954
Career Batting Average: .258 in seven seasons

Wilma "Briggsie" Briggs, born and raised in East Greenwich, Rhode Island, was the fourth eldest of twelve children. She worked on her family's dairy farm, milking cows, doing chores, and playing with her seven brothers, especially baseball. At age thirteen in 1943, Wilma was the only girl playing alongside her two older brothers on her father's baseball team, the Frenchtown Farmers, in a Sunday amateur league. In 1947, the summer after her junior year, the brown-haired teen with the hazel eyes, good coordination, and sweet swing played on the school's all-male team in a twilight league. As a senior, Wilma played left field for the East Greenwich boys varsity, but with a new coach, she didn't like it as well as playing first base in summer ball.

The school gained a great deal of publicity from the state's first female baseball player, and as a result, a sportswriter from Providence contacted the All-American League. He convinced the circuit's president, Max Carey, to let Wilma's parents take her to try out in the nearest league city, which was Fort Wayne. In such fashion did the seventeen-year-old get the greatest opportunity of her life, and loving baseball, she made the most of it. The Daisies needed a left-handed batter, and manager Dick Bass was impressed with her hitting. Wilma signed for $60 per week in June 1948. In her first game against Chicago, she grounded out as a pinch-hitter, but she also launched a successful seven-year career in the AAGPBL.

A good hitter who threw right-handed and learned to play the outfield, the 5' 4" Briggs averaged .258 lifetime, beginning with a .228 mark in 1948. The Daisies had a set lineup featuring the likes of Dottie Collins, Dottie Schroeder, Helen and Marge Callaghan, Tiby Eisen, and Vivian Kellogg, but Briggs played immediately on an established team, an unusual circumstance. Also in 1948, the circuit increased to ten teams by adding the Springfield Sallies and the Chicago Colleens. Like many other first-year players during the postwar years, Briggs grew up playing baseball against boys. As a result, she was unaffected by the AAGPBL's evolution toward baseball, which arrived with the adoption of overhand pitching in 1948.

Pictured in Fort Wayne uniform, Wilma Briggs played six seasons with the Daisies before being traded to South Bend in 1954 (courtesy Wilma Briggs).

Quiet, serious, and hard-working, Briggs blossomed under the tutelage of Max Carey, who managed the Daisies in 1950 and 1951. She learned strategies of the game from Carey, including protecting the runner, hitting to the opposite field, and bunting skillfully. She batted behind Tiby Eisen, and the two developed an intuitive understanding of each other's moves. Also, Wilma learned the ropes of life in the league from her roommate, Dottie Schroeder, the Daisies' classy shortstop and one of the league's most popular players. Gaining experience, Briggs led the league in home runs with nine in 1953, the last full season of the 10-inch ball. Traded to South Bend in 1954, Wilma blasted the regulation baseball, producing personal highs in homers with 25, which ranked third in the circuit, and RBIs with 73, also third best, and she helped slug the Blue Sox into second place. Overall, she ranked fourteenth on the league's all-time RBI list with 301 and second on the career homer list with 43. An excellent teammate, she always loved the league. In 1992, the 1969 graduate of Barrington College retired from a 23-year elementary teaching career. Reflecting on her AAGPBL experiences, she credited Max Carey's coaching with helping her become an All-Star in 1954, the final season of her most memorable years.

Interview on May 9, 2011

JS: Can you talk about your background and how you got involved with baseball?

Briggs: I grew up on a dairy farm near East Greenwich, Rhode Island, and I learned to milk cows, hoe the garden, pitch hay, and shovel a lot of— you know what. *[She laughs.]* My father Fred loved baseball. We had twelve children in our family, and I had seven brothers (one died as an infant), and two brothers were older. My brothers and I all worked in the barn, instead of in the house. My oldest sister didn't do much housework, and she didn't do any barn work.

My father loved baseball, but he wasn't available to play ball on a team, so he had his own team. Eventually, the team was called the "Frenchtown Farmers." Frenchtown was a suburb of the town of East Greenwich, and we lived in that rural area. My two older brothers played on my father's team.

I grew up doing stuff with my brothers, and my father allowed me to play ball with the boys. He used to hit ground balls to us in the back yard, which is really my fondest memory of baseball. We spent hours and hours doing that. My father hit grounders to my two older brothers, and at first I would back them up. They didn't miss very many, so it wasn't much fun being the one that chased down the balls they missed. So I crowded up in the front row with them, and that's how I got my start in baseball.

My father's team played every Sunday afternoon. When I was thirteen, my father would put me in the game for one inning, and he'd make sure I had one at-bat. That was a lot of fun for me, and I got to be a halfway decent ballplayer.

When I was in high school, our high school baseball coach was the past governor's father, Nick Carcieri, and I had him for a couple of subjects in school. Nick Carcieri coached the football, basketball, baseball, and gymnastics teams at East Greenwich High School. He also played on my father's team during the summer after my junior year. I played on the team, and so did our high school principal. Coach Carcieri was the pitcher and the principal, Rufus Brackley, was the catcher. That was the first opportunity Coach Carcieri ever had to see me play ball, and he realized I was a good ballplayer, equivalent to the high school guys.

The high school put a team in the summer league. I was going to play on the team with my brothers, the Frenchtown Farmers, and Coach Carcieri asked me to play first base for the high school team. This was just after the war years, and the first baseman was in the Sea Scouts. So I played first base for the high school team that summer. The coach asked me, "Why don't you go out for the high school team in the spring?"

You should never assume, but I thought Coach Carcieri would continue to coach. I went out for the school team the next spring, and I made the team, but we had a different coach. I had the feeling that he really didn't want me on the team. He never said anything, and the school got a lot of publicity with a girl on the boys' high school team. That past summer was a lot of fun with Coach Carcieri, but that senior year wasn't a lot of fun, but I did stick it out.

My brothers used to buy a little "Facts and Figures" book [Dell's *Major League Baseball: Facts, Figures, and Official Rules*, published annually in the 1940s] that came out about the facts and figures of the major leaguers, a 25 cent book. That book's back section had the All-American Girls Baseball League in it, and I had not heard of that league until I was a junior in high school.

I thought, "Gosh, maybe I could play professional baseball with a girls' team." *[She laughs.]* I really didn't know the caliber of ball they played, but I figured since I'd grown up only playing with boys and men's team, I shouldn't have any difficulty making a girls' team.

A local sportswriter found out there was going to be a tryout camp in New Jersey on Saturday, June 12, 1948, and I was graduating from high school on June 11 in the evening. Now I had a choice. I could miss graduation and make the tryout, or miss the tryout and go to my graduation. My parents wanted me to graduate from high school, and I would be the first in my family to graduate, so I chose to graduate with my class.

The schoolboy sportswriter from the *Providence Journal-Bulletin*, Dick Reynolds, found out that I was missing the tryouts. He said, "I will write to the league and I'll try to arrange a tryout for you in one of the league cities." It just happened that Max Carey was the league's president in 1948. Carey told Dick Reynolds the league was no longer having players come to the team cities, because most of them would get there and not make the league, and they wouldn't have any money to get home, so they figured the league would keep them. At that time, the league was paying the players' expenses home, and they were no longer willing to do that.

Finally, Dick Reynolds said to Max, "Look, her parents will drive her out to the nearest league city. If she doesn't make it, they'll drive her home." That was the circumstance under which I got my tryout, and Fort Wayne happened to be the closest league city.

I think we arrived in Fort Wayne around the twenty-first of June, and I had my tryout. I don't know who the Daisies were playing, but both teams were out there in uniform at Memorial Field, and they really looked sharp. They really played very, very well. I watched the visiting team take their batting practice, and then Fort Wayne took theirs. I had my tryout at first base. At home, when I wasn't a first baseman, I was the catcher.

When I batted, Dick Bass, who was the manager of Fort Wayne, came in to pitch, rather than have one of the girls pitch, like they had with the Daisies. He threw me pretty good stuff, but I'd been playing against men, so I figured he wasn't going to throw me anything I couldn't hit. I think it was my hitting that impressed him. Not only that, but I batted left-handed, and Fort Wayne didn't have any left-hand batters.

Dick Bass didn't tell me afterward one way or the other, if I made it or didn't make it. My cousin and my parents and I sat right behind home plate and watched the game that night. After the game, we went to the Hotel Van Orman. Harold Van Orman was president of the Fort Wayne Daisies at the time. We sat in the lobby of the hotel, and that's when Dick Bass said I had made the league, and I could stay.

My parents were going to leave. I was seventeen years old and right out of high school. I had never been away from home before, and I was thinking, "Oh, oh. Mother and father are leaving, and I'm not going with them." Suddenly I became fearful of staying. I remember my cousin saying to me, "Let's go in the Java Shop and get some ice cream." So we did.

In the meantime, Dick Bass called Max Carey in Chicago and said, "We've got this kid, and she's good enough to make the league, but she doesn't want to stay. She's scared."

Max Carey said, "Well, give her more money." That's why instead of starting at rookie pay of $55 a week, I started at $60.

While I was in the Java Shop, my cousin said to me that a good friend of my father's had said about Dad, "If I [Wilma] ever got the opportunity to play, he wouldn't let me, because he really wanted my brothers to play pro." But I said to myself, "That doesn't make any sense. Why would he drive a 2,000-mile round trip and then not let me stay?" I made up my mind right then that no matter what, I was going to stay.

When I went back out to the lobby, they said they were going to give me more money, but that didn't have anything to do with my decision. I said, "Yes, I will stay." My father said, "Just remember, if you don't like it, you can always come home." I did stay, and that was one of the best decisions I ever made. That's how I had my tryout for the All-American League.

Fort Wayne was leaving, I think on a nine-day road trip. I know they went to Chicago, and that was one of the first cities where they played. At seven-thirty the next morning, the bus was leaving for Chicago, and I had to take everything I had with me, because I wasn't assigned a place to stay yet.

We went to Chicago, and lo and behold, Dick Bass put me in the first game as a pinch-hitter. I was amazed! I finally dribbled one back to the pitcher, but before that, I hit two that were foul, but they would have been out of the ballpark. If they'd been fair balls, they would have been home runs. Max Carey, who was at that game as president of the league, was pretty impressed. He came down out of the stands afterward, and I met him.

Max Carey wanted me to stay in Chicago with their team [the Colleens]. Dick Bass said, "No, she's staying in Fort Wayne," because they needed a left-hand batter. That's how I happened to stay with the Daisies. I played for Fort Wayne the next six years, and the seventh year I went to South Bend [in 1954].

When you first began with Fort Wayne, who were some of the main players for the Daisies?

They had Dottie Collins, Tiby Eisen, Dottie Schroeder, Marge and Helen Callaghan, Evie Wawryshyn, and the only one I don't remember is the third baseman. Vivian Kellogg was the first baseman, and the catchers were Mary Rountree and Ruby Heafner. When I first came up, Mary Rountree was in college and hadn't arrived yet, but she was the main catcher.

In that first year, did you get to play very much?

This is unbelievable. I played immediately. You know what? I'm the only rookie that I know that played immediately. The rookies usually sat on the bench for a season or two. But Fort Wayne needed a left-hand hitter, and they didn't have one. I batted left-handed, and right from the start I was a fair hitter. That got me in the lineup, and I played right field. I actually learned to play the outfield and got halfway decent at it.

I never sat on anybody's bench, so I don't know what would have happened to me if I'd been sitting on the bench for a year or two.

I take it you always played first base or catcher when you were in high school.

I played first base all that summer [after my junior year], but, as I said, when I was a senior, I didn't think the new coach really wanted me, and he played me in left field. I remember one ball went way over my head, and the guy had an easy home run. I was very discouraged. I felt like I had made some kind of a mistake, but I couldn't have caught it. No one could have caught it.

Do you remember about spring training?

Later, we went to Angola, Indiana, for spring training. I went to spring training in Newton, North Carolina, Arlington, Virginia, and Cape Girardeau, Missouri, and the last two years were in Pokagon State Park in Angola, Indiana. I missed Opa-Locka, Florida, in 1948.

The Daisies always had good-hitting teams, but I don't believe you ever won a playoff championship.

The Daisies never won the playoffs. But we had good teams with Max Carey as the manager. He managed in 1950 and 1951. He was a teacher. He really got us running. In '50 and '51, I had more stolen bases than ever, and that's because Max Carey was the coach.

Max taught us so many different little things, like how to play a ball that rolls up against the fence, or how to play a fence so that you don't slam into it, how to slide, and how to slide away from the position where the ball's being thrown, and how to take a lead.

Max taught me how to bunt for a base hit, and how to bluff a bunt to protect runners when they were going to steal, because I blocked out the catcher. He taught me how to hit to the opposite field. I learned so much in those two years when Max Carey was there. After those two years, I was just coming into my own as a ballplayer.

I felt like 1949 was a total waste. I'm playing the outfield, and I don't really know how to play the outfield. The manager was a local Fort Wayne guy, Harold Greiner. I don't remember him ever telling me how to catch a fly ball in position to throw. I never knew where I was going to bat in the lineup. I remember batting fifth or sixth, something like that, with Dick Bass, but the next year, 1949, it seemed like every night I was in a different spot.

With Max Carey, I batted second. And I was still the only left-handed batter on the team, until Betty (Weaver) Foss came in 1950. Then Max started teaching me all these things, like how to protect base runners and bluff bunts, and how get out of the batter's box in a hurry by dropping the bat on the ball. It was very exciting to play for him when you could execute a play that he taught you. My best years were with Max Carey.

In 1952, with Jimmy Foxx, we won the pennant. I always said to myself, "It wasn't Jimmy Foxx's team. He had nothing to do with our winning. It was Max Carey's team." Max had instilled in us the will to win and ways to do it. It was a whole different ball game with Max as manager.

It was fun playing for Jimmy. He was a Hall of Famer! You can't beat that. I had a brother named after James Emory Foxx.

In 1953, we played for Bill Allington, but Max Carey was always Bill's biggest rival as a manger. I never really felt comfortable playing for Bill. That's probably why he sent me to South Bend in 1954. I like South Bend now, but when I was sent to South Bend in 1954, I thought it was the end of the world! *[She laughs.]*

The Weaver sisters were well known in Fort Wayne.

There was Betty (Weaver) Foss, Joanne Weaver, and Jean Weaver. Betty and Jean were the two oldest, and actually Joanne was the best ballplayer.

I wish Dottie Schroeder was still here to give you some comments. I can remember Dottie saying, "They were good. They were fast. They were strong. They were so fast, Jo and Betty, but the thing was, they'd run right over you."

Dottie played like a real ballplayer. Don't misunderstand. She was a tough ballplayer, but she was never dirty. She didn't like players who were like that. Every once in a while, Dottie would say, "Yeah, I know, Betty this, Betty that, but do they ever tell you how many runs she boots in, compared to how many she drives in?"

Most people didn't think about that. They liked the fact Betty Foss went into bases hard, and got strawberries, and slid hard, and ripped the bandage off. Fans like that kind of stuff.

Dottie always told this story. I was the runner on third base, and Betty Foss was a runner at second base, and the batter dribbled one back to the pitcher. Am I going to score from third base? I would have been out a mile. I moved off third base to make sure the throw went to first base, but there was no way you could score. Betty Foss comes tearing around from second base and passes me, and she goes home, and she's out by forty feet. Dottie Schroeder was playing for Kalamazoo by then, but she just could not get over that.

Dottie didn't like players who didn't have good heads. She always felt like the Weaver sisters got a lot more credit than they earned. That could be true, but the sisters were great. They could run. They got a lot of hits because they could run. Like they said, "Don't stand in their way," because if you did, they will run right over you.

It was novel to have three sisters on a team. I guess at one time Fort Wayne wanted to trade Jean, and there was a big fuss about, "If she goes, we go." The sisters pretty much had their own way.

Dottie Schroeder was such a good person. She didn't talk about people, unless something really bothered her. We were roommates for four years, so I got to know Dottie pretty well. She helped me a lot. During my second year, she said to me, "You know, if you get a good hard line drive on the hop in right field, you can throw that runner out at first base, like Rosie Gacioch does for Rockford."

That thought had never occurred to me, but Dottie was very helpful. I was one of the luckiest players in the league because I had helpful teammates, like Marge Callaghan, who played left field, and Tiby Eisen, who played center. Tiby and I always knew which one could get a ball that was hit between us. We had a system, "If you go after it, I'm going to back you up, so don't worry about it." Whoever was going to get the ball, the other outfielder stopped and found the play, so they could say exactly where to throw it.

Tiby Eisen was just phenomenal in helping me, and we never had a collision. Part of the helping each other was Max Carey, but part of it was Tiby Eisen, because she had played for Max when he managed the Milwaukee Chicks [in 1944]. She used to tease Max all the time. He had the National League record for stolen bases, but she used to say, "Yeah, but Ty Cobb was a better base runner!"

I remember everybody so clearly on my rookie team, but I don't remember the third baseman. I think Arleene Johnson played third base, but she was gone before I got there in June. She played part of the 1948 season with Fort Wayne, but I never met her until the AAGPBL Reunions. I met her when we played in the Old-Timers game. As old as she was then, Arleene had the softest hands for fielding ground balls. I can't imagine why Fort Wayne ever got rid of her. It seems like every year they had a different player at third.

You and Dottie Schroeder were pretty good friends.
We became good friends. I was always in awe of her as a ballplayer. To this day, I can't imagine why she asked a rookie to room with her in 1949. The reason I roomed with her, because I didn't know her very well, was because she said, "If we room on Bevel Avenue,

we'll have transportation to the ballpark." I thought, "Oh, my gosh. I don't have to ride the city bus."

When Maxine Kline and I were rookies together in 1948, we had to take the city bus to the ballpark. We didn't know our way around [Fort Wayne]. Sometimes we'd ride the bus to the end of the line because we were talking. It was so entertaining!

I roomed with Dottie in '49, '50, '51, and '52, and she was traded to Kalamazoo in 1953. We never had a disagreement, probably because I always looked up to her for being such a popular player and a good player. She was a really superb person. She was one of the nicest people I ever met.

What are some of your favorite memories, other than those you talked about?

One time Max Carey was coaching at third base, and Tiby Eisen was on first base. He had said to me, "I want you to bluff a bunt on the first pitch, just to make sure Snookie Doyle (she was Harrell then), the shortstop, is covering second base. Then on the next pitch, you're going to hit-and-run, and Tiby's going to take off and steal, and I want you to hit right through that hole the minute Snookie moves to second base."

And I did it! *[Laughing.]* That was one of the most exciting plays in my entire career — to be able to execute what your manager wants. It was absolutely perfect. I hit the ball right through that spot where she had been. That was an exciting play for me.

I was a left-handed batter, and I remember three pitches. Jean Faut threw me a ball, a big hanging curve ball that was coming right in to me, when I was playing with the Daisies. It was letter high, and I hit it to the opposite field, and I think it was the longest fly ball I ever hit to left field. For some reason, the left fielder was playing way out there, way out by the fence, and she backed up to the fence at Memorial Field, just under 300 feet — and she caught it! I thought I had a double or a triple, but I remember that pitch that Jean Faut threw me.

Marie Mansfield played with Rockford, and she wasn't much of a pitcher. You couldn't relax too much in the batter's box, because she might throw one right at you. She was very wild. Marie threw me a curve ball, and it was going to hit me on the front knee, because it was also going to come across that front corner of the plate. I had to back up, the umpire called it a strike, and it was a strike, but there's no way I could have hit that ball! I can see that pitch coming right now, just as plain as day, and I can see that ball break.

And I remember, when I played for South Bend [in 1954], Katie Horstman was pitching for Fort Wayne, and she had fair control, but she was not really a pitcher. Some of those girls were good pitchers, but some of them could just throw more strikes than balls. Katie threw me a change-up on a 3–2 count, and that was the only change-up I ever had on a 3–2 count. I swung and missed. I couldn't believe it. I thought, "Holy cow, a change-up on a 3–2 pitch!"

I was pretty good at hitting change-ups. If they threw me a change-up in Rockford, most of the time I'd put it in the right field bleachers. But I was really surprised to get that change-up from Katie Horstman on a 3–2 pitch.

Those are the things I remember more than anything else. I also remember the fun things. One time in Kalamazoo we were blowing bubbles out the window of the hotel. Max Carey goes by and said, "Stop doing that. You're going to be all out of breath for the game." I remember silly things like that.

I didn't break the rules, because I was too young for that, but the California players did. They had the bellhops at hotels letting them in the service entrances, so they wouldn't get caught. I remember one time when Pepper Paire and Jaynne Bittner were rooming together, and I was with Tiby Eisen. For some reason, I was with them, and we were in the hotel, and the keys fit different rooms. Somebody's key fit Bill Allington's room, and we short-sheeted him. If he got in that bed in a hurry, his knees must have been right in his mouth!

If he knew players were out after curfew, Bill would always call an early meeting, like a nine o'clock meeting the next morning after the game. The next night was when we short-sheeted him. Pepper and Jaynne were always up to something. They were fun to be around.

I got my first car in 1950 when I was twenty, and I remember Dottie Schroeder going with me to the Coca-Cola plant to get a case of Cokes for our landlady, which was really for us. On the way home, Dottie was yelling out the window at everybody, and I said, "Who are those people?" And she said, "Oh, I just want to see if they'll wave back!"

Dottie was usually very reserved and quiet, and very serious. But I remember one time when we were stopped somewhere on a road trip for a rest break. Wally Fidler was our bus driver. Dottie said, "Let's pull the bus forward." She wasn't much of a prankster, but she could be devilish. She knew I could drive a truck, and I guess she could too. Dottie got the bus in gear and moved it forward, and she said to me, "You put it back where it was." So I backed up the bus and put it where the driver had it parked. Dottie didn't do things like that very often, but when she did, it was so out of character that it was lots of fun.

I gather Dottie was widely respected among all the players.

Dottie Schroeder was probably one of the most respected ballplayers in the whole league. She was very graceful and very good at shortstop. Dottie Kamenshek was also widely respected, and she was the best first baseman. Jean Faut was also very respected, and she would have been good at any position, but she was by far the best pitcher.

Who was the greatest player? They played different positions, and I'd have a hard time deciding between Jean, Dottie, and Kammie. They were all such really outstanding ballplayers. I'd have to go with all three of them.

You know what? They all three had the best heads on their shoulders for the game. They were very savvy ballplayers. You had other ballplayers like Betty Foss who could run faster than anybody in the league, but they didn't always run at the best times. Some players made a lot of mental errors, but I think the respect went to those ballplayers who didn't make mental errors. We all make physical errors, but it's really the mental errors that cost you games. Kammie and Dottie and Jean Faut did not make mental errors. To me, that's the difference between a great ballplayer and a good ballplayer.

Interview on January 28, 2011

Can you tell me about your experiences with the Blue Sox in 1954?

In my seventh season I went to South Bend, and what a different experience it was. The fences were shorter there and I could hit it out of the ballpark, which was kind of nice. I didn't really want to go, because I had played my entire career up to that point with Fort Wayne.

The handwriting was on the wall that 1954 would probably be the final season. So I went to South Bend, and I had a good year. I had probably a better year than I would have in Fort Wayne, because I didn't really like Bill Allington, maybe because he was usually with the Peaches, and they always won so much.

South Bend was a good experience, and I know we would have won the pennant if Jean Faut had been pitching. There's no doubt about it. You would figure Jean for at least twenty wins, and we ended up [in second place] four games behind Fort Wayne.

One thing that was very different playing for South Bend compared to Fort Wayne. I almost always batted second in the line-up, not the first two years so much, but after Max Carey became manager in 1950. Jimmy Foxx tried to move me [in 1953], but it didn't really work, so he put me back in the second place.

However, in South Bend, I don't think I ever batted second. I batted third, fourth, fifth, anywhere along there, which gives you a much better chance to drive in runs.

What was the difference as managers between Max Carey or Jimmy Foxx and Karl Winsch?

Max Carey was a teacher, and I learned so much from him. Max was one of the very best managers I ever had, and I think he was one of the very best in the league. Bill Allington was a know-it-all, and I never really liked him. Maybe I was prejudiced, because I learned not to like the Peaches from day one. He just figured he was right and nobody else ever was.

Karl Winsch was strange. He was good to me, but I really don't know how to explain him. Sometimes he over-managed, and sometimes he under-managed. I tolerated him, but not as much as I tolerated Bill Allington. I never really liked either one. But I should say, at one of our reunions, Karl Winsch did say to me he thought I had one of the prettiest swings he had seen. He was quite complimentary. But I only played for Karl one season, and I didn't get to know him.

I did hear a lot about Karl Winsch, and he's one of the reasons Jean Faut didn't play in 1954, and that really, really bothered me.

Do you remember some of your Blue Sox teammates from 1954?

Sue Kidd was one, and the others were Betty Francis, Betty Wanless, we called her "Duke," and Mary Carey. I can't remember whether we roomed together, or we roomed next door. I knew Duke. We'd been teammates, and she was a good ballplayer. I pretty much hung around with those four girls.

One day Wimp Baumgartner said to me, "You're pretty quiet in the clubhouse." I said, "I've always been quiet." Wimp said, "Oh, come on! You and Maxine Kline used to run the Fort Wayne Daisies." I told her, "Maxine Kline and I never opened our mouths."

Maxine joined the Daisies the year that I did, so we were there for six years together. We used to sit there and listen and be intimidated by the stars, Dottie Schroeder, Dottie Collins, the Callaghans, Vivian Kellogg. We didn't have anything to say. I think Wimp got the idea because we were the only two still on the Fort Wayne team all these years later, because Maxine and I were going on our seventh year together. We never said anything in the meetings. I told her, "Wimp, you've got that all wrong." I was very, very quiet.

I think because I played so many years with Fort Wayne and I only played one year with South Bend that I don't have the same memories for South Bend.

For the first few weeks after I went to South Bend, I would look at the newspaper and automatically go to Fort Wayne in the standings. I'd think, "I don't play for them any more. I play for South Bend." That was kind of tricky for a while.

The best thing I can say about playing for South Bend was I could hit the ball out of the ballpark in any field. I couldn't do that in Fort Wayne. You could hit it out for a while, when they put the "home run" fence in, but that wasn't there the first five or six years. They might have put in that short fence in 1952. It was something like 293 and 300 feet down the left field and right field lines in Fort Wayne, and you didn't hit that 10-inch ball out of the ballpark. When I played at Playland Park, especially when they used that 9-inch ball, I thought, "If I played here my entire career, I would have hit a lot more home runs!" In 1954, I think I had only three or four home runs when they switched to the 9-inch ball. That was at the All-Star game, and I ended up with 25.

You said you knew several of these players. How would you describe Betty Francis?

Betty Francis was congenial, but I never really go to know her. She was kind of funny, always joking. I think she played center field.

Was it Betty Wanless that played with Fort Wayne? Can you describe her?

Betty Wanless was wiry, a little heavier than what you'd call wiry. To look at her, she looked like she might not be an exceptionally graceful ballplayer, but she certainly handled herself well. She played a solid third base, and she was a relatively good hitter. Betty Wanless was smart. She had a good head on her shoulders. She didn't throw the ball away, or throw to the wrong base. She was a good teammate. I really enjoyed playing with her.

How about Mary Carey?

Mary Carey was another one that was kind of joking all the time. I didn't know her before I went to South Bend, and I didn't really pal around with her in South Bend.

Why do you say when that last season came around, the signs were there that it would be the end of the league?

The schedule was different. We had fewer games scheduled. We had double-headers against two different teams.

What happened in 1954 was that the Muskegon Belles finished as a road team in 1953 and they didn't return, so you had this unusual five-team league.

It was strange. We really thought the league was going to fold at the end of the 1953 season. Each team was allowed to keep so many ballplayers, and the rest would go into a pool, so they could balance the league in the 1954 season, if, in fact, there was a '54 season. And they asked the players to take a cut in pay, and most did, because they wanted to play ball. South Bend gave me back what Fort Wayne cut, which was sort of an incentive to go to South Bend.

Do you remember your pay and the cut?

I was making around $100 a week, or $400 a month. I think they asked us to take a $50 a month cut, which I did, and I got it back when I went to South Bend. I also think some of the members of the board of directors may have put up that money, so it didn't show up. That was always a possibility. At that time, no ball club had ample money.

Can you talk about Jean Faut as a pitcher?

Jean Faut was a great hitter, a great heads-up ballplayer, and I think the best pitcher the league ever had, especially throwing overhand. I don't think anybody came close to her overhand. She had great control. You had to worry about getting a hit off Jean, but you didn't have to worry about getting hit by Jean, because she wasn't wild. She could throw strikes, and a lot of different strikes.

Do you remember Sue Kidd as a pitcher?

Sue Kidd threw the ball very hard. She was fast, and she didn't have the control Jean had, and she didn't have quite as much "stuff" as Jean had. Sue could throw hard. Every once in a while, one came at you. You couldn't be as relaxed batting against Sue as you could against Jean. You weren't very relaxed against Jean, but you could be more relaxed at the plate against her. If Jean threw a ball that might hit you, it was because she was telling you, "Back off." If Sue threw at you, back off, because you might get hit. *[She laughs.]*

How about Janet Rumsey?

Janet Rumsey was like a "Steady Eddie," consistent, and she threw a lot of strikes. She was a very good pitcher, because she did have good control. She was kind of fun to play behind. Some pitchers took all day to throw the second pitch. Janet had a good rhythm, and she was easy to play behind. You like to play behind pitchers like that. Jean, Sue, and Janet all had good rhythm. Maxine Kline was another one that had good rhythm. Maxine was more a thrower than she was a pitcher, but she threw strikes.

Janet was a very consistent pitcher. She was consistent about everything in her life, and she was a very nice person. So were Jean and Sue. They were good people.

I wish I could have played with Jean Faut, instead of against her. I got to know her at one reunion, and that was the most I ever got to know her. We had a good time. I'm thinking how much fun it could have been to be on the same team with Jean, but it didn't happen.

Do you have other favorite memories?

I hit a home run in South Bend when my parents were visiting. That was kind of neat.

In Fort Wayne, the first time my father ever saw me play, I was playing right field as a rookie, and I made a shoestring catch. I didn't see him, but I knew he was at the game, because I saw our car with our license plate, which was Z-7988. I said, "Hey, somebody's here from home."

During the game in right field, I made a shoestring catch. My father was not one to rush out. He was still sitting behind third base when I came into the dugout, and I saw him sitting there. He didn't say, "Hello." He said, "Lucky catch!"

Now that was his way of saying, "Good catch!" He'd use reverse psychology. He said the same thing when I hit that home run. He said, "Lucky hit!"

Those were good times, and good memories.

SHIRLEY BURKOVICH
Muskegon, 1949; Colleens-Sallies on developmental tour, 1950; Rockford, 1951
Interviewed on February 13, 2012.

Born: 1933
Height: 5'8"
Weight: 150
Positions: Utility OF
Batted: R
Threw: R
Career Batting Average: .229 in two official seasons

Shirley Burkovich was born and raised in Swissvale, Pennsylvania, a few miles east of Pittsburgh. The youngest of three children of Michael and Mary Burkovich, Shirley grew up in a time and place where girls had few opportunities to play competitive sports. However, her father and her brother Walt were ballplayers, so Shirley hung around with Walt and played ball with the boys. In 1948, the year the All-American League expanded to ten teams, she was fifteen and a freshman at Swissvale High. Walt told her about a newspaper story saying the All-American League was holding tryouts in Pittsburgh. He encouraged his athletic sister to attend, and finally, she agreed to go with him (he took a day off work) to sit in the stands and watch. After a few minutes of observing, Shirley took her glove, walked onto the field, and entered the tryouts. She was told she would hear later from the league. Finally, in the spring of 1949, Max Carey, the circuit president, sent a telegram asking her to report to West Baden, Indiana, for spring training.

Like the parents of most teenagers who received the All-American opportunity, the Burkovichs at first doubted the idea of trusting their daughter to a girls' baseball league located several states away. Finally, they agreed to let their daughter play, and since Michael had to work, Mary Burkovich accompanied her teenager on the train trip to Indiana. Shirley was allocated to the Muskegon Lassies, and her mother returned home, but only after receiving suitable assurances from the chaperone and the manager. Shirley embarked on the adventure of her life, spending the 1949 season with Muskegon as a utility player. "I had only played on sandlots and in the streets," she remembered. "To be able to be on an organized professional team and get a real uniform and play with the best women baseball players in the country was great!"

An inexperienced but versatile player, Burkovich was sent to the Fort Wayne Daisies in 1950 for spring training. The Daisies had an experienced team with a set lineup, and the league assigned Shirley to the touring Colleens and Sallies. A 5'8" brunette with blue eyes, she was quiet but eager and energetic. Right-handed, she could play any position, and that's what she did for most of the 1950 season. League statistics show the Pennsylvania native played 20 games and ranked eighth among

From Swissvale, Pennsylvania, Shirley Burkovich played most of the 1950 season on the developmental tour. Pictured in Fort Wayne uniform, Shirley spent the 1951 season with Rockford (courtesy Shirley Burkovich).

the 37 women who toured the country playing exhibition games against each other. However, she broke her ankle in August, and her glorious summer came to an abrupt end. In 1951, the eighteen-year-old was assigned to the Rockford Peaches, but Rockford, like Fort Wayne, also fielded a seasoned, talented team, and she only played in a handful of games.

Burkovich saw telltale signs that the league was going downhill, and she needed a full-time job. In 1953, she took advantage of a new career with Pacific Bell in Pasadena, California. She spent thirty years with the telephone company before retiring in 1983. As professional ballplayers realize, the baseball dream dies hard. Several All-Americans, who kept their league experiences to themselves for many years, organized the first of many AAGPBL Reunions, and old friends and teammates met in Chicago in 1982. Shirley seized a new opportunity, serving with the Players Association, most recently as treasurer. She loved participating in the making of the famous movie, *A League of Their Own*. She enjoys helping others, she likes working with the Players Association, and she encourages young girls to play baseball through the RBI Program.

JS: Where did you grow up, and how did you first start playing ball?

Burkovich: In my era, there were no sports for girls, so if you wanted to play ball, it was with the boys. That's where we started out, playing baseball in vacant lots and on streets. I grew up in a small town just outside Pittsburgh, in Swissvale, Pennsylvania. My dad and my brother were both ballplayers, and I hung around with them, and I played ball with the boys. I was one of three children. My brother Walt was the oldest, and my sister Phyllys was older than me. My parents' names were Michael and Mary Burkovich.

In 1948 our local newspaper carried an article saying there would be tryouts for the All-American Girls Professional Baseball League. I didn't see the article in the paper, but my brother did, and he brought it to my attention. Walt said, "Why don't you go down and try out?"

I was only fifteen, and I was kind of scared. I said, "Gee, I don't think I want to go down there. There will probably be a lot of girls trying out, and I don't want to go."

Walt took the day off work, and he said, "Well, let's just go down and sit in the stands. You don't have to try out. Let's just go down and look it over and see." Going with him, that was fine with me. We took the trip and we sat in the stands. But I think he knew that once I sat in the stands, there was no way I wasn't going to try out.

That's exactly what happened. I sat there in the stands for a while and watched, and he said, "Well, what do you think?" I said, "I think I'll go down and try," and I did.

The tryout was one of those things where they would let you know later, and I waited for several months. Since I wasn't going to be sixteen until the following February, they told me I couldn't be signed because I was underage.

When I turned sixteen in 1949, I got a telegram from Max Carey saying to report to West Baden, Indiana, for spring training. I was still a junior in high school. My mom and I went to the principal to see if I could miss school in April and May. School got out in June, but I would miss two months. The principal looked at my grades and said, "What we can do is send assignments with you for two months, and you can do those assignments and send them back. That way we can let you go." That was fine.

The next problem came up with my mother. She and my dad talked it over, and Mom said, "Shirley has never been out of state. I've never heard of the All-American Girls Baseball League, and I don't want to send her down there on her own." My dad was working and couldn't go, so my mom bought a train ticket, and we took the train to Indiana.

My mother met Helen Campbell, who was the chaperone, and she met Carson Bigbee, who was the manager. They assured her that everything was on the up-and-up. Mom stayed for two days. I stayed for spring training, and I spent the 1949 season with Muskegon.

Did you go all the way through the school system in Swissvale?

I was playing ball for Rockford when my Class of 1951 graduated, so I didn't go through the graduation ceremony, but I did graduate.

What do you remember about that first year in Muskegon?

That year with the Muskegon Lassies was the thrill of a lifetime for me. Just having the opportunity to play organized sports was different for me. I had only played on sandlots and in the streets. To be able to be on an organized professional team and get a real uniform and play with the best women baseball players in the country was great!

Who were some of your teammates?

I played with Mickey Maguire, Dodie Barr, Julie Gutz, "Shorty" Pryer, Amy Applegren, Jo Lenard, "Sammye" Sams, Betty Francis, "Blackie" Wegman, Sarah Lonetto, Dottie Stolze, Tex Fischer, Doris Tetzlaff, Norene Arnold, and "Sis" Waddell. I'm looking at the 1949 team picture. Helen Campbell was the chaperone, and Carson Bigbee was the manager.

Did you get to play very much?

I wasn't a regular player. I was a utility player, so I only played sporadically.

You returned to Swissvale after the 1949 season and went back to school. What happened in 1950?

In 1950 I was assigned to the travel teams, the Springfield Sallies and the Chicago Colleens. I toured with them until somewhere in August, when I broke my left ankle, and that ended my season. The players switched back and forth between the Sallies and the Colleens. They tried to keep the teams evenly matched. Because I was a utility player and I could play different positions, they moved me wherever they needed me.

What positions did you play?

All of them except catcher — wherever they put me!

You traveled by bus, right?

We traveled by bus to many different cities. I was just sorry I broke my ankle, because after that, the teams went up and played at Yankee Stadium, and I missed that game. But I did get to travel with the teams and play the first half of the season, and it was just a great experience. We were a close-knit group. We all traveled on one bus all of the summer.

How many players were there?

We had about fifteen on each team.

I've always said that was the best time of my life. My three seasons were just the best. I thought that was going to be my career. I planned on playing baseball forever. I didn't think I needed any other education. I never went to college.

The league got to where I thought it wasn't going to last much longer, and I got the opportunity to get a good full-time job. I was single, and I thought I needed to take advantage of that opportunity. I didn't know if I was going to get married, and I thought, "Gee, I'm going to have to support myself."

Did that opportunity come in 1951?

The job opportunity came after the 1951 season. During that season with Rockford, I think we all knew the league wasn't going to last much longer. It was slowly declining. The

1951 season was kind of sad for me. The league did last for three more years, but you couldn't tell at the time.

Looking back today, I think I made the right decision. I went to work for Pacific Bell in Pasadena, California. I went in as an entry-level operator. I ended up in the Engineering Department, and I spent thirty years with the company.

After the 1951 season ended, I spent one more year at home in Pennsylvania, just kind of floating around, but my family was moving to California. My sister and my brother moved in 1949, and my mom moved to California in 1957. I came to California in 1953 and started with Pacific Bell, and I retired in 1983.

The back of your baseball card says you had a part in the movie, A League of Their Own. *Can you talk about that?*

In 1988, when our league was recognized by the National Baseball Hall of Fame, Penny Marshall was there at the dedication of the permanent exhibit on women in baseball. She talked to a number of the gals, and we learned she was interested in making a movie about the league. After she got her funding together, she invited anybody who signed a contract with the league to have a part in the movie. They were filming segments at Cooperstown. I was one of the players who spent ten days in Cooperstown filming the ending part of the movie.

You mean where the women are playing an old-timers game?

Yes, near the end of the movie, when the credits are running. They're showing the older ladies, and they were all former ballplayers. Anybody who wanted to come was welcome, and some of us went.

Segments of the movie *A League of Their Own* were filmed in Cooperstown, New York, home of the National Baseball Hall of Fame, in the fall of 1991. More than two dozen former players participated. Shown here in the first row are (left to right): Shirley Burkovich, Jean (Geissinger) Harding, Wilma Briggs, Helen (Filarski) Steffes, Norma (Whitney) Dearfield, Joyce (Hill) Westerman, Ginger Gascon, Joanne McComb, Claire (Schillace) Donahoe, Bea Kemmerer, and Mary Moore. Standing in the second row: Dottie (Key) Ferguson, Salty (Sands) Ferguson, Lorraine (Fisher) Stevens, Sue Kidd, Maybelle Blair, Wimp Baumgartner, Katie Horstman, Angie Amato, Jaynie Krick, Anna O'Dowd, Shirley Weierman, and Lee (Surkowski) Delmonico (courtesy Shirley Burkovich).

I had a little line at the end. When Dottie Hinson, played by Geena Davis, comes to the reunion, several of the girls talked with her. In the movie, I came up to her and said, "Dottie, having you here is good luck." I spoke my line and scooted out of the picture. It was just one line, but it was fun!

That's pretty cool, because the movie really made the league famous.

The movie did make the AAGPBL famous, and we thank Penny Marshall every time we see her. If it had not been for Penny Marshall, we would still be obscure, unless you lived in one of those league cities at that time.

Most of my friends that I keep in touch with are from the reunions. When we played ball, we were not allowed to fraternize. So you knew the gals on your team. When I played with Muskegon, I knew those players. Where I met the other girls and got to be friends with them was at the reunions. You met gals who played for South Bend, or Fort Wayne, or Racine, or whatever. The reunions have been a big deal for all of us. It's a chance to see the gals. Now that we're getting older, it's imperative that we go to the reunions. We hope that everyone, if at all possible, can attend the reunions and renew their friendships.

It looks like the league made a big impact on your life, even though you had a short career.

Definitely. I was sixteen years old, and I'd never been out of Pittsburgh, except when I traveled to see other families in the area. To have that opportunity to join the league and travel around the country, and to have the opportunity to play with gals who were superstars, it was really great.

I was an ordinary ballplayer. I was just glad to have the opportunity to play in that league. I could hit-and-run, and lay down a good bunt. They always had me sacrificing, hitting to the opposite field, and moving the runner. That was my role, and I was happy with it. I had to get those runners in scoring position, so when the Dottie Kamensheks and the Snookie Doyles came up to bat, they could drive in the runs.

What do you do with the league now?

I serve as treasurer, and I'm on the board of directors. If and when we're asked, we go to schools and speak to kids. We do clinics for the RBI Leagues. Those initials stand for Revitalizing Baseball in the Inner Cities. It's for boys and girls that can't afford to play Little League baseball. We have a lot of girls who participate in the baseball clinics. You would be surprised at the number of girls who participate. We give the girls moral support, and we let them know it's fine to play baseball if you're a girl. Some of the girls don't want to play softball. They want to play baseball like the boys.

Marge (Villa) Cryan
Kenosha, 1946–1950
Interviewed on March 7, 2010.

Born: 1925
Height: 5'2"
Weight: 110

Positions: C, 3B, SS, 2B, OF
Batted: R
Threw: R
Career Batting Average: .209 in five seasons

Marge Villa, the third of four children of Jay and Eva Villa, grew up on the ranch of her parents near Montabello, a few miles east of Los Angeles. "Maggie," as her dad used to call her, thrived on outdoor life and sports, including swimming, hunting, fishing, and baseball. She particularly liked playing ball with her younger brother Tony, who was a good shortstop. Before World War II energized the home front in 1942, Marge played three seasons of softball for the Orange County Lionettes, a fast-pitch team. Talented, agile, and blessed with good reflexes and a strong arm, she played a lot of shortstop, and she also caught a few games. A tomboy at 5' 2" and 110 pounds, Marge didn't graduate from Montabello High. Instead, she worked at a wartime job for U.S. Rubber in nearby Los Angeles. At age twenty in 1946, she left the job (but returned to work in the off-season) because the All-American League came calling. A scout had seen Villa play for the Lionettes, and she was invited to the league's spring camp at Pascagoula, Mississippi. Allocated to the Kenosha Comets, the right-handed batter was dubbed "Poncho," based on her Spanish surname. Enthusiastic,

Marge (Villa) Cryan, a versatile infielder from Montabello, California, played five seasons for Kenosha. The Comet infielders shown are (left to right): Dolly Brumfield, Marge Villa, Ernestine "Teeny" Petras, and Fern Shollenberger (courtesy Dolly White).

eager, and versatile, the curly-haired Californian found the team needed catchers. The result was inevitable, once she blurted out, "Any dummy can catch!"

Villa did serve as catcher for Kenosha, but she was happy to play where she was needed, including shortstop, second base, and the outfield. In 1946, she played more than 100 games (the first of four 100-game seasons), batting .197. She roomed in the home of a retired English professor, and he tutored her so she could finish her credits and graduate from Montabello High. The league allowed sidearm pitching in 1946 and switched to sidearm in 1947. Poncho could hit sidearmers, and she slugged two homers and set a record with 9 RBIs in one game in 1946. She batted .207 in 1947, the year the league held spring training in Cuba. Reminiscing about daytime practices and night games at Lakefront Stadium, situated on the shore of Lake Michigan, she said, "I thought I was in heaven!" Businessman Gib Lantz had a daughter, Ginger, who identified with Villa, and Marge was able to drive one of his cars during her years in Kenosha. She enjoyed boating, fishing, and swimming, and she made friends easily, but she didn't drink. The Comets, like any professional team, had players who enjoyed partying. Instead of joining in, Poncho drove to and from get-togethers, serving as a designated driver to keep her friends safe.

Villa loved her five seasons with Kenosha, and one big league highlight came in the fall of 1949 when she embarked on a Latin American tour featuring an all-star team of Cuban girls and a team of All-Americans. The Americans had a stronger team, so the players mixed the lineups. Poncho, who grew up in a home where both English and Spanish were spoken, enjoyed meeting foreign leaders and dignitaries on the tour, and she was invited to many upscale events because she understood and spoke the language. She liked keeping journals and scrapbooks of her travels and games, and she kept a journal on the South American trip. Later, her father's ranch burned, and Marge lost the cherished scrapbooks and journals. A dependable all-around team player, she averaged .256 in 1950, finishing her AAGPBL career with a lifetime .209 mark. Returning to Montabello, she married Daniel Cryan, a dentist, in 1954, and they had two children, Renee and John. An active grandmother who still has fun golfing and pitching batting practice for her teenage grandsons' team, Poncho Cryan has no regrets about her life or her baseball career.

JS: Where did you grow up and begin playing ball?

Cryan: My parents were born and raised in Montabello, California, and I grew up a couple of miles outside town. My parents, Jay and Eva Villa, were from here, and grandparents were also born in California. My mother came from Bakersfield, but my father was born in Montabello. I was the third of four children, and in the order of age, they were Eleanor, Ernest, myself, and Tony. My younger brother Tony was about a year and a half younger than me, and we used to play ball together a lot. Tony was a great shortstop, but he got married and he was never able to pursue a professional career. When World War II came, my brothers went into the service, and I tagged along with my dad, hunting, fishing, anything to get out of the kitchen!

Did you play ball in school?

I didn't play in school, but I started playing for the Orange County Lionettes when I was a teenager. They were a great fast-pitch softball team. I played with them for two or three years. During World War II, the All-American Girls Baseball League got started. I never graduated from high school in Montabello, but after I joined the league, I was homeschooled in Kenosha, Wisconsin. I was living with the family of an English professor, and he was retired.

A lot of us from California used to play softball against each other here. We knew each other and we knew a lot of the managers, like Bill Allington and Johnny Rawlings. I played against them here. Later, Bill Allington was with Rockford, and Johnny Rawlings managed Grand Rapids. That's how I found out about the league.

When you moved to Kenosha, what position did you play?

I played shortstop for the Orange Lionettes, and every once in a while I played catcher. In Kenosha one day I opened my mouth and said, "Any dummy can catch!" Well, guess who the dummy was in 1946! *[She laughs.]*

For the rest of the season, I caught, because the first-string catcher broke her arm, and the second-string catcher had elbow problems. That's when I said anyone could catch, so I was the catcher, but shortstop was my regular position. I also played some games in the outfield.

I take it you had a pretty strong arm.

You have to have a strong arm to play baseball. My sister was the knitter and crocheter in the family, and I was out with the boys playing ball.

What was it like playing for Kenosha in 1946?

It was fascinating. I'd pinch myself quite often. I'd say, "Here I am, playing twice a day; we practice in the middle of the day and play that night, right across from Lake Michigan." I thought I was in heaven!

The Comets played in Lakefront Stadium at that time, right?

Yes, we did. Let me tell you, the humidity in the Midwest was something. We didn't have that in California. I kept thinking, "The evenings are going to be nice." At home, we goofed off in the evenings. Well, there was no way. The evenings were just as humid as the days.

On a road trip, we'd take the top mattresses and go up on the roof of the hotel to sleep, because it was so hot and humid.

What was Lakefront Stadium like?

It was an interesting place to play ball. There were times when the humidity was so great, but the weather could change. It was right on Lake Michigan. The lake was right behind center field. When the wind would change, and the cold breeze would come off Lake Michigan, you could hear the echo from the fans in left field. They would go, "Wooooooh." That meant the wind was shifting and the cold breeze was coming off the lake, and sure enough, it would get cold. It could also get foggy.

Lakefront Stadium was like our softball stadiums in California. Lakefront wasn't a big stadium, but it was a nice stadium. Left field seemed long enough, and right over center field was Lake Michigan. It was quite an experience.

Did you live with a family every year?

I lived with the retired English professor's family, and I lived with the postmaster's family for about three years, and they moved. After that, I lived with the fire chief's family. Sometimes several girls would get together and rent a home, or part of a home. Gib Lantz, a businessman in Kenosha, had a daughter named Ginger who took a liking to me and followed me around, and I took her under my wing. Her father would say, "If you need a car, Poncho, just let me know." I didn't have a car in Kenosha, so I'd use one of his cars and take some of the players and Ginger on outings away from the ballpark.

What are some of your favorite memories about playing baseball?

Just being able to play baseball was the big thing. I looked forward to spring training, because that's when you saw a lot of the country, and you got to meet a lot of different types of people. I really enjoyed playing in Havana, Cuba, in 1947, because we had carte blanche over there. May Day was a big deal in Cuba, and we were isolated in the hotel that day, and every store closed. They made a bunch of sandwiches for us to eat. We paid one of the bus boys to wait on us, and he was quite delighted.

Did you make good friends on the team in Kenosha?

I made friends, but I wasn't a social person. I respected my dad and mom for allowing me to go to Wisconsin and play ball. I don't say I was isolated, but for me to go from bar to bar or party to party, I never did that. My job was to play the best ball I could.

Did you know Helen Fox?

I played against her later when she went to Rockford. I caught her with Kenosha a few times. She was rather quiet, as far as I was concerned, not boisterous at all. "Nicky," they called her, threw a good rise ball. She had her own catcher, and the only reason I caught her a few times was the other catcher hurt herself. They both came from the same town in Alberta. Nicky Fox wasn't much of a mixer, and I wasn't either. If it was wrong, I didn't do it.

We had a good group in Kenosha. We all dressed well, like ladies. Bill Allington would tell his girls in Rockford, "Why don't you be more like the Kenosha Comets? They dress like ladies!" And we did. Sometimes you would see other girls from other teams wearing jeans, but none of us did that in Kenosha.

Your nickname was "Poncho," right?

Yes, it was, because of the Villa. They tagged me with that name in the All-American Girls Baseball League. They didn't call me that when I was playing softball in California. They called me "Maggie," and I hated that name! I guess in those days, the nickname for Margaret was Marge, or Maggie.

Your record looks like you had good years, and you played a lot of games each year.

The only time I didn't play was when I got hurt. I collided at second base with a friend from California, and that was about the only time I ever got hurt. That was probably in the 1950 season. Like I said, I was not a mixer, and I never drank. The only time I even thought of taking a drink was when I got married in 1954, and that was a glass of champagne.

What did you do in the winters?

I came back to Montabello right after the season, except I came later the times we had a winter tour. Twice they picked two teams, and we barnstormed in Latin America. When I came home, I had a job with the U.S. Rubber Company, and that was in East Los Angeles, which is adjacent to Montabello.

After I retired from the league, my dad had a little accident at the ranch, and he didn't want me to work. He wanted to pay me a salary to take care of them, and I used to chauffer them around, and I took care of his business at the 250-acre ranch. The ranch was about 65 miles above Montabello, and it only has about six oil wells now. We sold the ranch after my parents passed away, but we kept the mineral rights.

What do you remember about the Latin American exhibition tours?

I went on a shorter trip in 1948, but I really liked going on the South American tour in the fall of 1949 and meeting the dictators from those countries, like Juan Perón from

Argentina. It was supposed to be an all-star American team playing an all-star Cuban team, but there wasn't enough competition, so we mixed up the teams. I could speak the language, because I learned Spanish at home when I was growing up, so I got to go to palaces and fancy restaurants and meet dictators and other officials.

When they sent us to South America, we started out at Caracas, Venezuela, and we traveled down to the bottom of South America, and we flew back to Cuba. I used to keep journals of my playing time in the All-American Girls Baseball League, and my father wanted to show them off to friends at his ranch. But a fire started at the ranch, and all of the journals burned, along with everything else. I kept those journals from the time I played with the Orange Lionettes. I think my father was more hurt by the loss of my journals than he was about losing his ranch house.

Knowing Spanish was the big thing. We went to homes of leaders of the countries, the dictators, and they lived like kings. The crowds at our games were 90 percent men, and we'd have thousands come to the games. They would be crowded all around the outfield. The men just couldn't get over how well we played baseball. We interchanged some of the Cubans with players on the American team to have more balance, but it was fun.

You have to stay active. Today I still pitch batting practice to my grandsons, who are ten and thirteen. In the league, lots of the girls would put suitcases across the aisle so they could play cards on the bus trips. I thought that was a waste of time. I liked reading a good book. I would check my batting average, and I would write in my journal about what pitches I hit and what I missed. That was something for me to do instead of playing cards.

What do you remember about your managers?

One thing I really enjoyed was having good managers in the league, with the exception of one. At Kenosha we had Press Cruthers at first, and then Ralph Shinners for a year, and both of them had been big leaguers many years ago. In 1948, we got Chet Grant, and he was the best manager we had. After him, we had Johnny Gottselig for a couple of years.

Chet Grant knew the strategy of the game. He was great, but he didn't take anything from any of us. He wasn't boisterous, or anything like that, but he'd take you aside and point out what you were doing wrong. There was only one time he got to me, because I ignored his signal. When you're a base runner, you study the pitcher, and you know when you can take a bigger lead and steal the base. Chet didn't want me to steal one time, but I did. Even though I was safe, I got told off.

Chet Grant was the only manager we had that really knew the game. He knew how to win games, if you could execute what he wanted you to do. He was a disciplinarian. If you partied and he got wind of it, you heard about it. He would stay up until about two o'clock in the morning studying the game, and he knew what was going on with the girls. I might go out boating or fishing or swimming with friends. I didn't party, although a lot of the Kenosha girls did party. I'd be the chauffer, because they knew I wouldn't drink, so I'd take them wherever they wanted to go, and I'd pick them up when they needed a ride.

Our team had great gals. Many of them did party, and they'd play poker at night. All I wanted to do was play ball. I'd pick up a game with the kids in the neighborhood. They'd call me Poncho. "Hey, Poncho — Do you want to come out and play catch with us?"

I also liked swimming. One time I took a run and a dive into Lake Michigan on one of those days when it was about 95 degrees. Oh, my God, the water was ice cold! I thought I was going to die! My joints were aching like I couldn't believe. You can run and dive in the ocean out here, but you don't do that in Lake Michigan.

Do you remember a game in 1946 when you got 9 RBIs?

I remember the game vaguely. When you're a batter, there are times when the ball seems so big that you just can't miss it, and that was one of those days. I could hit to right field as well as to left field. I could hit-and-run, and I usually batted second or third in the lineup. One year I batted fourth, because I was hitting some long balls. I decided to see how hard I could hit the ball, but I preferred to bat second or third. That's what I told Chet Grant, and he accommodated me. "I don't want you to be unhappy, Marge," Chet said.

From the day I went to the first spring training until the end of my career, I had it all in scrapbooks. But the ranch burned down one year, and I lost all of that. At that time, I was still driving my parents around, and I hated losing all that stuff. But I took up golf. I got to be a scratch golfer. It came natural to me, like hitting a low outside pitch — and I still play golf.

I married my husband Daniel in 1954, a few years after I left the league. Today he's a retired dentist. We had a daughter, Renee Sotoquest, and a son, John. Renee has two sons, Dallas and Drew. John lives in Nebraska. He was a diver in college, and his son is a musician.

You know, the league years were a tough time, but they were a great time. You'd have lonely hours on the road in hotels or at home in your room all alone, and then you'd have fantastic times with the games and the other girls and the fans and the outings.

I can honestly say I have no regrets about my baseball career and my life. I loved my life, and I lived it to the fullest. I listened to my parents, and they said, "If it's wrong, don't do it," and I followed their advice. I drove the girls around in Kenosha, but I first learned to drive on the ranch when I was seven years old. It was about a mile and a half up to the cabin in the mountains, and I'd sit on my granddad's lap and steer the truck. The only bad part of my life was when I lost my parents. I had two brothers and a sister, and I've lived a fantastic life.

TERRY DONAHUE
Peoria, 1946–1949
Interviewed on February 17, 2012.

Born: 1925
Height: 5'2"
Weight: 125
Positions: Utility IF, OF, C
Batted: R
Threw: R
Career Batting Average: .127 for four seasons

Terry Donahue, who was born and raised in the small town of Melaval (population 100) in southern Saskatchewan, had fun playing ball as early as she can remember. Her parents were sports-minded folks who lived on a farm outside the town. Her father worked the farm, but after a long day and after Terry and her brother Tom finished the day's school work, Jack and Rosie Donahue took their children out in the yard to play a pick-up game of ball. In 1942, when Terry was sixteen, the Donahues took the two-hour drive to Moose Jaw. The city had a good fastball organization sponsored by the Royal Theater. A right-handed teenager who was blessed with good coordination and quick reflexes, Terry made the Royals, but she had to finish the school year first. She played softball in the summer of 1942, and she graduated from Melaval High in 1943. A sure-handed infielder and a good right-handed hitter, she enjoyed three more seasons with the Royals. Moose Jaw reached the semifinals for the Western Canadian Championship in 1945, and a scout from the All-American League saw her play. With her father's support, Terry packed for the train trip to the AAGPBL's two-week spring camp in Pascagoula, Mississippi.

Donahue, with her blue eyes and wavy black hair, was filled with desire, energy, and hustle, and she made the league. Allocated to Peoria, she spent four seasons with the Redwings. She began playing the infield,

From Melaval, Saskatchewan, Terry Donahue played four seasons with Peoria. Pictured circa 1947, Terry increasingly played catcher (courtesy Terry Donahue).

but an injury to the team's catcher late in the 1946 season caused her to fill in behind the plate. Thereafter, the versatile athlete, who was 5'2" and 125 pounds, caught more and more games. Like most girls in the AAGPBL, Donahue roomed with a family in her team's city. The Lloyd Turnbulls took an instant liking to the pleasant Canadian rookie, and before long, they wouldn't accept room rent. They came to Terry's first game to laugh at a sport featuring women playing baseball in skirted uniforms, but they quickly became ardent fans. Good-natured, upbeat, and outgoing, Donahue made her mark with Peoria and her teammates. The manager, however, altered her batting stance, and she compiled a .127 lifetime mark. Still, she was happy to handle any position (she played them all, except first base and pitcher), and she was adept at fielding every position. A timely hitter, she totaled just 31 hits in the 1948 and 1949 seasons, but she drove in at least one run with each hit.

Peoria never fielded a first-place team during Donahue's four seasons, but like other teams in the women's glamour league, the Redwings had their share of good players and exciting games. For Donahue, highlights included catching her first game in 1946 and Dottie's Mueller's 20th win in 1948. The league kept changing, adopting overhand pitching as well as base paths of 72 feet and a pitching distance of 50 feet in 1948, and in mid-1949, a livelier, red-seamed 10-inch ball and a 55-foot pitching distance. In 1950, Terry rejected her contract with Peoria. Concerned about throwing the longer distances, she moved to the Chicago League and played two seasons of fast-pitch softball with the Music Maids. In 1952, she began working with an interior design firm, and she worked and lived in Chicagoland for 38 years, before retiring. A friendly person who likes the AAGPBL Reunions, starting at Chicago in 1982, Terry Donahue remains proud of her ten seasons of hardball, ranging from Moose Jaw to Peoria to Chicago. She cherishes the lifelong support from her parents and her family, and she appreciates the movie, *A League of Their Own*, because it meant the once-glorious All-Americans were alive again on the silver screen.

JS: Where did you grow up, and how did you get started playing ball?

Donahue: I grew up on a farm in southern Saskatchewan, Canada, in a little town of one hundred people, Melaval. My parents' names were Jack and Rosie Donahue. They were very sports-minded people, and as long as I can remember, we were playing ball. My dad would work a long day on our farm, and, after we finished our homework, he'd take us out in the yard and play ball with my brother and my mother and me. My brother's name was Tom. When I played ball at school, my parents both came to all of my games.

We had a sports day in Melaval, and I was playing on a team and pitching that day. There were two teams from the city watching us play, and they were going to be the main attraction in the second game. A week later, my dad got a letter from the manager of one of the teams asking me to come in for a tryout. I was sixteen at the time, and my mother said, "No way." But Dad said, "Oh, yes."

We drove into Moose Jaw, Saskatchewan. They had a very good organization there, the Royals, and I made the team. At sixteen, I had to finish school first. As soon as school was over, I would go into Moose Jaw and play ball. That was in 1942. I played with the Moose Jaw Royals from 1942 through 1945, and we won the Western Canadian Championship in 1942 and 1943.

Where did you graduate from school?

I graduated from Melaval High School.

In 1945, our Moose Jaw Royals got to the semifinals of the Western Canadian Championship, and apparently there were scouts there from the United States, which I didn't know. A few weeks later, this man came up to me and said, "Would you like to come down in the spring for a tryout with the All-American Girls League?" I said, "Yes, I would."

When spring training came in 1946, I received a train ticket to go to the U.S., and I went to spring training in Pascagoula, Mississippi.

What was spring training like?

My poor mother! I'd never been more than 100 miles away from home, and she was pretty upset. I took the train to Chicago, and I rode another train to Pascagoula, Mississippi, which is where they trained in 1946. The league was adding two new teams that year, and they needed some more gals. It was tough, and it was hot. It was cool in Canada, but it was hot in Mississippi. I worked very hard in spring training, and then came Allocation Day. There were hundreds of girls in that room waiting to hear their names called saying they had made the league. When I heard my name called, I can tell you, I was the happiest girl in that room!

They sent me to Peoria, which was one of the new teams, and the other new team was in Muskegon, Michigan. They sent me to the Peoria Redwings, and I played four years for Peoria. I was never traded.

Did you live with someone in Peoria?

We all stayed in private homes. They put me with a couple, Mr. and Mrs. Lloyd Turnbull, and they were wonderful to me. I called them my "United States parents." I don't think she knew anything about ball, and her husband said, "We're going out to the game, and we'll have a good laugh about women playing ball in skirts!" When they came out and saw how well we played, they never missed a game. The Turnbulls were wonderful people. If I stayed in the States over Christmas, I went there. They had no children, and they just took me over.

We paid our room by the week. After the first month, I went in to pay for my room, and she said, "We don't want your money. We're just happy to have you here." They wouldn't take my money! They were wonderful. I saw them often, until they died.

At first, there were two of us, and the other girl, Dottie Ferguson, was traded. After the trade, the Turnbulls told me that if I wanted someone to come in and room with me, that would be fine. But if not, they didn't need the money, and I could stay by myself.

After my four years in Peoria was up, and I played for the Chicago League, and that was fast-pitch softball.

The 1946 season was when the league first allowed sidearm pitching. How did that affect you? Were you a catcher at that point?

I played mainly in the infield, but I played every position except first base and pitcher. In 1946, when sidearm pitching came into the league, we were using an 11-inch ball, and I like that size. The next year, it was underhand and sidearm, and in 1948, the league began overhand pitching.

So it didn't bother you to hit overhand pitching, after playing softball?

No, not at all. The ball kept getting smaller and smaller, until they reached a 10-inch ball in 1949. By the time they gave me my 1950 contract, I was doing more catching, and I thought maybe my arm wasn't strong enough to make the long throws.

I had an opportunity to sign a contract with the Music Maids in Chicago, so I thought it was what I'd better do. The All-American League was using a smaller ball, and the distances were getting longer, so I moved to Chicago and played fast-pitch for the Music Maids for two years. When I got my job, I decided I'd better quit ball.

What kind of job did you get?

I worked for a very fine interior design firm in Chicago, Watson and Boaler, Inc. I worked for them 38 years, and I retired from there. I loved my job, and I loved the people I worked with. I was very fortunate.

Did you make good friends in Peoria?

When we weren't playing ball, we were traveling on the road, so we didn't get to know a lot of the people. Fans would come up to us after ball games, and want autographs, and talk to us. They would offer to take us out to lunch, when we weren't practicing or getting ready for a trip. The fans in Peoria were great to us.

Did you make friends on the Redwings?

Absolutely! They were a great group of gals. My teammates included Betty Tucker. Dottie Mueller was a great pitcher, and Audrey (Haine) Daniels, and Twi Shively, and Joyce (Hill) Westerman were a few of my friends. After the league was over, we kept in touch.

Joyce Westerman was also a catcher.

Joyce was a very good catcher.

What did Twi Shively play?

Twi was an outfielder, a very good ballplayer, and she was very fast. I remember one night she was sliding in to second base, and she broke her leg. We asked to be taken to the hospital after the game to see her.

Do you have some favorite memories with the Redwings?

It was such a great group, and I was lucky that I was never traded. I loved Peoria, and it was a great place to live and play ball.

Can you describe the Peoria Stadium where you played?

It was a nice stadium, and it had good lights. We drew good crowds in Peoria, and the league drew almost a million people in 1948. The teams drew good crowds throughout the league.

I can remember one August game in 1946 in Peoria, I forgot who we were playing, and our catcher, Mary Rountree, broke her finger. The manager, Bill Rogers, said, "Terry, have you ever caught?" I said, "No," and he said, "Well, you're going in to catch." I said, "Okay, I'll do the best I can."

He handed me this great big catcher's mitt, and I said, "I can't use that. The ball will just bounce off it." He said, "What are you going to do?" I said, "I'll use my infield glove." He said, "Well, you're going to have a mighty sore hand!"

They put some padding into my glove, and it was a Sunday, and the game lasted 19 innings. It had to be called because of the curfew. It was the first game I caught. The next day was my birthday [August 22], which is why I remember the date!

They put sponges in my glove, and I started doing a lot of catching. The game is in front of you, and I enjoyed that.

Did you ever catch when you were playing with Moose Jaw?

I did catch one inning, because they were having a "Terry Donahue Night" in 1943 or 1944, and I played one inning at each position. But in the States, I did a lot of catching.

Did you get a catcher's mitt when you began catching more games?

I finally got a catcher's mitt, and it worked out really well.

I really didn't know how I would do at catcher, with the batter swinging the bat in front of me, but I really enjoyed the position. We had some good pitchers, like Dottie Mueller. I remember catching her twentieth win, maybe in 1947.

We'd win these games, and sometimes we'd lose, and we'd have to take a shower and get ready to travel, and we'd be on the bus most of the night to Kenosha, or wherever we were playing next. If we won, we'd sing for hundreds of miles, but if we lost, we'd be pretty quiet. *[She laughs.]*

I never heard any of the girls complain about riding those old buses.

As you know, we had to wear dresses or skirts. We couldn't wear slacks in public. We could wear jeans on the bus, but if the bus stopped in the middle of the night and we were getting off, we had to put on our skirts. We had to look like ladies! The league was very well run, and it was a great time in our lives.

I never heard anybody complain about the rules. That was what you had to do if you wanted to play professional baseball. Earlier they had a charm school, and I didn't get into that, but the chaperones would make sure we had lipstick on and we looked right. We had wonderful chaperones.

Those chaperones played a big part in the league. We were all very young. The mothers didn't want us to come to the States and play. When my mother found out the teams had chaperones, that helped. I wrote letters home to my parents, and they kept track of me.

At first, your father was in favor of you playing ball, but your mother wasn't?

They were both really behind me all the way, but my mother was concerned that I was going to another country. Travel at that time wasn't as easy as it is today. Dad said, "You'll go. You'll have your chance." I don't know if Mother thought I'd make it or not, but I fooled her, and I did make it. They were great parents and very sports-minded people. They were very loving and behind me all the way.

We played more than 100 games a season. We played games every night and doubleheaders on Sunday. And I can tell you this: Our pitchers went nine innings, not like today's major league pitchers, who can't last nine innings! *[She laughs.]*

Your batting averages were never high. Was hitting hard for you?

I was a good hitter in amateur ball, a very good hitter. I came down here and they tried to change my stance, and I never was as good a hitter as I was in amateur ball. I still hit a few good ones.

Your baseball card says that in 1948 and 1949, every time you got a hit you drove in a run.

I wasn't a great hitter, but I did get a few great hits! *[She laughs.]*

I was a good fielder. I loved my infield glove, and I still have it. I could pick up those grounders with that baseball glove.

What else did you enjoy about the league?

It was a great opportunity for all of us. When the league folded, it was a very sad day. We thought it would keep going on and on. When we found out a movie was going to be made about our league, that was really wild!

Did you see any of the filming of the movie, A League of Their Own?

Fifty of us players went to Skokie, Illinois, in 1992, and we met all the stars, and we told them about our experiences, and we tried to show them how to throw a ball. Poor Madonna threw like a girl. We thought, "How are they going to make a movie and have the stars throw the ball and hit the ball like we did?"

We were upset when we found that Madonna was going to be in the movie, because there were no Madonnas in our league. They assured us she was going to have a minor part and things would be fine. We were worried, but when we saw the movie, it was very well done, and Madonna did very well in her role.

If it had not been for that movie, we would be all dead and buried and nobody would have known about us. I worked at my job for 38 years, and I never told anyone about playing professional ball. They probably wouldn't have believed me. People found it hard to believe that girls played baseball when the movie came out.

In 1987, I was inducted into the Saskatchewan Baseball Hall of Fame, and Saskatchewan was my home province. In 1988, our league was recognized by Cooperstown [the National Baseball Hall of Fame]. In 1998, the 64 Canadian girls who played in the league were individually inducted into the Canadian Baseball Hall of Fame. It was really very touching. That was a wonderful day.

In 1995, Cooperstown asked me to come and read a story to children. It's called, "Players in Pigtails." I went to Cooperstown and read the story. Now you can go there and push a button and hear me read the story.

Do you get letters from people asking for your autograph?

Oh, yes! I get them from countries all over the world. In November 2005, I went to Japan with a team from a town outside of Boston, and they wanted to take two All-American girls with them when they played, and I was lucky to be one of the two All-Americans chosen. That was a wonderful time, and I enjoyed seeing those girls play ball.

All these things have happened because of the league. We can't play ball anymore, but all these wonderful things have happened to us!

When we were playing, we had no idea that we were making history in women's sports, or that someday a movie would be made about us, or that we would be welcomed in Cooperstown.

In 1982, we had our first reunion in Chicago. We hadn't seen each other for 30 years. The reunion was held at a Holiday Inn just east of Michigan Avenue. That was so exciting to see the girls you played with and played against. We had never seen anything like it. We had to wear name tags, because we didn't know each other, but we had a wonderful time. They decided we should have more reunions, and now we have them every year. It's a wonderful group of women, and I'm very proud to be associated with them. The San Diego Reunion this year was very nice. The sad thing is there are those who can't make it to reunions, and those who are gone. But it was a great experience, and a great life, and I feel very fortunate.

You're saying the league made a big impact on your life.

The All-American League made a big impact on all of our lives. Being from Canada, I always skated. I kept myself in shape in the wintertime by playing girls' hockey in Canada. So when I came down to the States in the spring, I was in good shape. The California girls had nothing over on me — I kept myself in good shape too!

So you went back home to Saskatchewan after every season in the AAGPBL, but after you got the job in Chicago, you stayed in Illinois.

Yes, I did. I liked the job and I liked the company.

Do you have other favorite stories?

We had an outfielder in 1949, June Emerson. She played right field. One night, one of the other team's batters hit a high fly ball to right field, and she lost it in the lights. The ball hit her on the head, and the center fielder was backing her up, and she caught the ball, and that's how the out was made. After that, we called her "Venus," you know, no hands! [She laughs.]

Another funny thing happened around 1948 to Phyllis Koehn, but we called her "Sugar." She was a good outfielder and a good hitter. We had a runner on third base, and she got up, and she hit a home run. Sugar was rounding the bases, and when she got to third, the manager said, "that's going to cost you $5." She got to the bench and said, "What is he talking about? I hit a home run."

The game goes on, and the score is tied, 2–2, and Sugar comes up to bat in the eighth or ninth inning, and she hits another home run. When she comes around third, the manager said, "Forget the $5!"

What happened the first time was the manager wanted a squeeze play, and Sugar missed the sign. Sugar and I often laughed about that time!

I remember that the league held spring training in 1947 in Havana, Cuba. The Brooklyn Dodgers already had trained there. We played exhibition games and outdrew the Dodgers!

LILLIAN "LIL" FARALLA
Peoria, 1946; Fort Wayne, 1947;
South Bend, 1948–1951; Kalamazoo, 1950
Interviewed on November 17, 2009.

Born: 1924
Height: 5' 6"
Weight: 160
Positions: P, 2B, 3B, OF
Batted: R
Threw: R
Honors: Pitched two no-hitters, both in 1948: Faralla stopped the Racine Belles, 2–0, in the seven inning opener of a double-header at Horlick Field on May 15, and she no-hit the Muskegon Lassies, 4–0, in a nine inning game at Playland Park on June 17, 1948
Career Batting Average: .209 in six seasons
Lifetime Pitching Record: 55–55 with 2.00 ERA

Lillian "Lil" Faralla was born in Brooklyn, where she attended elementary school. At age eleven in 1935, her family moved to sunny California, and she played softball in San Pedro, a small town a few miles south of Los Angeles. Lil attended San Pedro High, and by the time she graduated in 1942, she had played professionally for the San Pedro Saints, the Dr. Pepper team in nearby Los Angeles, and Woolworth's team in neighboring Long Beach. At 5' 6" and 150 pounds, the pretty blue-eyed brunette, gifted with good skills, a strong arm, and a love for the game, usually played shortstop and batted clean-up. Softball in California during those years was played at night, but after World War II erupted at Pearl Harbor in late 1941, the West Coast was subject to a blackout that lasted for most of the war's duration. As a result, Lil worked at a variety of jobs, including as window trimmer in a San Pedro dime store and later on the assembly line at a local aircraft plant. Feeling the need to contribute to the war effort, she joined the Coast Guard in 1944 and served for two years. Lil also played service softball. A scout saw her playing for the Coast Guard team in Long Beach, and when she was mustered out in mid–1946, she received a telegram from the All-American League inviting her to try out.

Faralla, who threw and batted right-handed, dropped her plans to go to college and rode the train to Chicago. She was sent to Peoria, where she tried out for the Redwings, signed a contract, watched the first game of a twin bill, and played third base for Peoria in the nightcap. A regular for the second half of the 1946 season, when sidearm pitching began, the twenty-two-year-old averaged .181. Allocated to the Fort Wayne Daisies at the Havana spring camp of 1947, Lil learned to pitch and play the outfield. A sidearmer, she threw mainly fastballs for a weak Fort Wayne nine that finished seventh out of eight teams. In spring training at Opa-Locka in 1948, the league allocated Faralla, who was independent-minded as well as friendly, to South Bend. She made new friends and became a standout, winning big in the 1949 and 1951 seasons. She missed spring camp in 1950, and in June, the team loaned her to the Kalamazoo Lassies. The Californian won her greatest fame as South Bend's second pitcher behind Jean Faut, the best overhand hurler in league history. Lil enjoyed many highlights, including two no-hitters in 1948 and 19 wins in 1949, the season South Bend and Rockford tied for first place with identical 75–36 records.

South Bend won the league's Shaughnessy Playoff Championship in 1951, and Faralla helped by fashioning a 15–4 mark, but her hitting prowess suffered when manager Karl Winsch wouldn't let pitchers take batting practice. Regardless, Lil thrived on being a member of the Blue Sox team that featured many other talented professionals. She enjoyed the camaraderie and the routine of pro baseball, including the overnight bus trips, card games in the hotel rooms after games, movies in the afternoon when on the road, and driving friends around South Bend in her car. In 1951, she remembered rooming with Jeep Stoll and living on East Caroline Street with the Warners, a family that even brought the girls fresh clothes at away games. Also a golfer, a swimmer, and a rock collector, Faralla later worked for the Army's Counterintelligence Corps in Los Angeles, before she served as a deputy sheriff for LA County. After retiring from the Sheriff's Office in 1976, the onetime star enjoyed the AAGPBL Reunions and renewing friendships with many of the women who shared the league's historic baseball experience.

Born in Brooklyn, Lil Faralla grew up in San Pedro, California. Lil is pictured with South Bend circa 1949 (courtesy Lil Faralla).

JS: Can you tell me how you got involved in baseball and with the league. You're from California, and I know you played softball first.

Faralla: I was born and raised in Brooklyn, but we moved to San Pedro, California, in 1935. I did play professional softball in California with the Dr. Pepper team up in Los Angeles at Fielder Field, which no longer exists. "Snookie" Harrell played in the same league. She was the shortstop later for the Peaches. This was during high school.

I started playing softball when I was fourteen for the San Pedro Saints. From there, I played with the Dr. Pepper team. I played with both teams, and sometimes I played in Long Beach for the Woolworth's team. I was a real good shortstop, and people wanted me to play for them. I always played shortstop in softball, and I was the clean-up hitter too.

Where did you go to high school?

I graduated from San Pedro High in 1942. World War II was going by that time, and there were no more night softball games in California because of the blackout. The war effort was on, and softball was out.

What did you do during the war?

I worked in local aircraft plants, and I worked for the JJ Newberry Dime Store in San Pedro. I was a window trimmer. I used to do their window displays. I also worked in the basement tagging everything, but I didn't clerk. I spent most of my time in San Pedro, up until I went east to play in the league.

How did you find out about the league in 1946?

I didn't. The All-American League found me. I went into the Coast Guard from 1944 to 1946. I knew nothing about the league. I played softball for the Coast Guard. A scout from the league came to see me in Long Beach when I was playing for the Coast Guard. After I got out of the service, I got a telegram asking me to come and try out. I wasn't working, because I had signed up to go back to Santa Barbara State College to become a teacher. But I wasn't going yet, so I figured I may as well go and see what the league was all about. In July, I traveled to Peoria and met the team. I tried out behind the stands when the team was warming up, and they signed me to a contract, and I watched the first game of a double-header on Sunday.

They put me on third base in the second game. In my first time at bat, I had never seen such fast pitching in all my life. The first pitch came too close and bounced off my shoulder and hit me in the nose, and I went down. They took me to the hospital to make sure I didn't have a broken nose. That was my introduction to the game as played in the league. I think the seams of the ball are still on my nose! *[She laughs.]*

You played 55 games in 1946, so you must have played most of the second half of the season.

I did. I played second base and I played third base, but I didn't pitch in 1946. In the second part of the season, the league went to that sidearm delivery. I threw mostly sidearm, and I had such a strong arm throwing from third base that they used to complain about me throwing curves from third base to first! The manager decided to try me out as a pitcher, because of my arm. I went home after the season, and I practiced pitching at home. I never had my foot on the pitcher's rubber the whole time I played softball. I didn't know the first thing about pitching.

You became a sidearm pitcher in 1947.

Yes, I did. I came back as a pitcher. When the league went to Cuba, that was my first spring training.

What was Cuba like?

Spring training in Havana was wonderful! We really enjoyed it. What I didn't know about baseball and this league was the allocation system. I came in the middle of 1946, and I knew nothing about allocation. The next thing I knew, I was in Cuba going through spring training. At the end of spring training, they sent me to Fort Wayne. I thought I was good enough to stay with Peoria. Like I said, I didn't know the politics of the game, or the workings of the game.

I went with Fort Wayne in 1947, and they had me pitch, and they had me play second base, and they put me in the outfield. When they went to trade me to South Bend, I was told the reason they were trading me was that they needed more help, because Fort Wayne was down near the bottom, and they were going to trade me for a pitcher that could help the team.

I told them, "Well, I think you're making a mistake, because who they're sending [Viola Thompson], I'm a better pitcher." I didn't see how that trade would help the team any, so I refused to go. I didn't know that South Bend wanted me because they wanted someone better to help them get into the playoffs. I was suspended for one day, and I sat out that game. Both of us that were supposed to be in that trade sat side-by-side and watched the game. After that, she went home.

I've always felt that if you're good enough, you stayed with one team. I knew that I was a good enough ballplayer, and I couldn't understand why they wanted to trade me when I was good enough to stay on that team. The next thing I knew, we went to spring training in 1948, and the league sent me to South Bend. Boy, did I have hell to pay! Some of the players kept bringing up the fact I had refused to go the year before, but of course, I wouldn't say anything.

In 1948, the league went to overhand pitching, but that would not have made much difference to you, because you were already pitching sidearm.

I was strictly a sidearmer. I can't throw overhand, but my pitching worked.

What was the difference in being on Fort Wayne's team in 1947 and South Bend's team in 1948?

I don't know about a difference, but it got so I became part of the Blue Sox team, and after a while I felt like I belonged, just like I felt like I belonged in Fort Wayne. When you go with a team, you're with the *team*. But it took me a long time before I won a ball game. It seemed like I was losing by scores like 1–0 or 2–0, and I just didn't seem to have much support at first, but then it all came together.

What was it like to play for Marty McManus?

I liked him a lot. Marty McManus was a gentleman. He was a great manager. He treated us with respect. I enjoyed playing for him. The two worst managers I ever played for were John Gottselig and Karl Winsch. They didn't know how to treat women.

What was it about Winsch you didn't like?

I guess I didn't have full confidence in him. I never remember him teaching me anything about pitching, even how to grip the ball. Karl also hurt my batting average. He never let me take batting practice. You play for a manger, you know, but you don't have to like them. I didn't like Johnny Gottselig either. I thought he was an animal! *[She laughs.]*

Then I found out Johnny Gottselig was a hockey player, and I realized why he was such an animal. He didn't know how to treat women. When I played softball, they had mostly women coaches, and they knew how to treat another woman.

Did you get to know Jean Faut very well?

Oh, yes. We're very good friends. I have a lot of respect for her. She's a super person. Jean Faut is tops. She was a wonderful ballplayer. She was our ace. She was always number one, but I was proud to be number two on her team.

[Editor's note: Lil Faralla enjoyed two great seasons when she ranked second for South Bend behind Jean Faut. In 1949, Faralla fashioned a 19–9 record with a 1.36 ERA, and Faut went 24–8 with a 1.10 ERA. So Faut ranked third in the league's ERA statistics, and Lil ranked fourth. Lois Florreich of Rockford won the league's ERA crown (22–7 record, 0.67 ERA), and Rockford's Helen Fox was second (13–8 record, 0.98 ERA). In 1951, Faralla finished with a 15–4 record and a 1.85 ERA in 22 games, and Faut produced a 15–7 record with a 1.33 ERA in 23 games. Jean's ERA placed her third overall behind Kenosha's Dottie Naum (5–4 record and 1.14 ERA in 12 games) and Grand Rapids' Alma Ziegler (14–8 record and 1.26 ERA in 22 games). Faralla's stats meant she was the league's seventh-best pitcher in the important category of earned run averages.]

Not only that, Jean was an all-around player too. She was a third baseman, she had a great arm, she could hit, she could run, she could do it all.

I'll tell you something I have in my notes. In 1949, I pitched in the most games, 34, with a record of 19–9. *[Editor's note: Faut also pitched in 34 games.]* In 1951, I was the best fielding pitcher. I didn't make an error in 22 games, and I fielded 1.000. But you have to remember, first I was a shortstop, and that makes a big difference.

In late June of 1951, South Bend listed you and Lou Arnold and a few others on waivers. In his journal, Doctor Dailey quoted Karl Winsch as calling you a "clubhouse lawyer." Do you remember that?

I never heard that term, but I always spoke my mind. I knew Karl Winsch and Doc Dailey didn't like me. It looks like they kept me for trading purposes. But I did what they asked me to do, and I won 15 games for them.

One thing I remember about those years is that we rode a chartered bus to and from games. It was even fixed up with a poker table so we could play cards. Also, when we were on the road, if you were going to pitch the next day, Karl would let you lie down on the back seat of the bus. It was a long seat, and it was more comfortable than the others. At the hotels, we could play the pinball machines in the lobby. That's one thing we could do. We also played cards in our rooms at night after the games, and we went to movies in the afternoon.

In 1951, South Bend won the championship. What do you remember about it?

I remember pitching in the championship round, and we won the game I started, but Jean came in and pitched in relief for most of the game. I pitched so many games that it's hard to remember, and they used me in relief too. I also played in the outfield sometimes.

One reason you never stayed long on a team is the league's policy was each team could keep about nine players, and everybody else had to go into a "pool" for other teams to pick. That's why you never stayed on a team so long, unless you were a top player. In 1950, they "loaned" me to Kalamazoo for part of the year, but I came back to South Bend.

Where did you live in South Bend?

I lived on East Caroline Street right across from Lib Mahon and Shoo-Shoo Wirth. Jane "Jeep" Stoll and I were roommates, and Lib and Shoo-Shoo lived across the street. The people they rented from, Swen and Jen Warner, were wonderful. We took all of our meals there, and Mrs. Warner did our laundry. We were on the same side of town as Playland Park. The four of us used to go to the practices and ball games together, and the Warners would come to the ball games to watch us play. They also went on some of the road trips, and Mrs. Warner would bring clean clothes for us. She would take our dirty clothes home afterward, and she would wash them for when we got back in town. After home games, the Warners would have us over for poker. Lib and Jeep and Shoo-Shoo and I would stay up and play poker.

Why did you leave the game?

Because I felt that I had played with the best people in the United States and Canada. Once you reach the top, there's only one way to go, and that's down. I could see the caliber of play was going down. I figured I may as well quit while I'm on top. Later, I worked for the Army in the Counterintelligence Corps here in Los Angeles, and after that, I worked as a deputy Sheriff for Los Angeles County. I retired from the Sheriff's Office in 1976.

I've never regretted it, but it was a difficult situation. Here I am being a secretary making $40 a week, and all I had to do was sign a contract for $100 a week and do something I really enjoyed doing. I'll tell you that's a tough decision. I really enjoyed the game. I enjoyed playing. You love the game. I still watch games.

Did you make a lot of friends in the league?

Yes, because I was with so many teams! *[She laughs.]*

The league had this rule that you couldn't fraternize with members of other teams, but I was on so many teams and knew so many people, and it's difficult to snub somebody that you played with. It was stupid rule. I had a lot of friends on every team.

Do you have favorite memories?

I just really enjoyed playing the game. I enjoyed being a baseball player. I'm glad I got the opportunity to play with the best. That's quite an accomplishment in my life. I also had certain accomplishments in the league, like my two no-hitters in 1948.

The All-American players achieved so much and overcame a lot of obstacles.

You know, we were playing in the league because we enjoyed the game. We weren't playing baseball for the money, or the recognition, or because we were making history. We were all doing something we loved doing when we played the game.

JEAN FAUT
South Bend, 1946–1953
Interviewed on July 15, 1995, and September 16, 2009.

Born: 1925
Height: 5' 4"
Weight: 135
Positions: RHP, 3B, OF
Batted: R
Threw: R

All-Star Team: 1949, 1950, 1951, 1953, all as Pitcher
Player of the Year: 1951, 1953
Lifetime Pitching Record: 140–64 with 1.23 ERA in eight seasons
Career Batting Average: .243

Jean Faut (rhymes with "out"), who came from a working class family in East Greenville, Pennsylvania, grew up with a love of baseball that developed into a eight-year career in the All-American League where she was recognized as one of the circuit's all-time great pitchers. Jean, the second oldest daughter — she had two sisters and three brothers — of Robert and Eva Faut, was a personable, attractive, and modest girl who loved sports. As she observed, you had two choices during the summers of her youth: go swimming or play baseball, and she played ball. An athletic-minded girl who was bright, serious, and talented, she liked watching the East Greenville Cubs, a semipro team, practice and play games. The ball club's second baseman taught the blonde, blue-eyed teenager the fundamentals of the game and also how to pitch. Jean never played softball, but she excelled in high school in the sports available to females, field hockey, basketball, and track. World War II was raging when she graduated in 1942, and she worked at a clothing factory in nearby Pennsburg making men's military trousers. Often she also pitched batting practice with the semipro Cubs, acquiring good baseball skills during the war years.

Faut never heard of the All-American League until a scout contacted her in the spring of 1946 with a train ticket to the league's training camp in Pascagoula, Mississippi. She jumped at the chance to leave her factory job as well as to play professional baseball. Two weeks later, when players were allocated, the 5'4" right-hander went to South Bend. Jean began as a slick-fielding, strong-armed third sacker, but midway through the 1946 season, the league allowed sidearm pitching, and manager Chet Grant sent her to the mound. Faut fashioned an 8–3 record in the second half of the season. Known for her sharp control and wide assortment of pitches, she went 19–13 in 1947, and she continued to develop into one of the league's superstars. Indeed, she often played third base when not pitching, rather than rest a day or

A talented ballplayer from East Greenville, Pennsylvania, Jean Faut pitched two no-hitters and two perfect games, and she was twice voted the league's Player of the Year. Jean is pictured as a rookie with the Blue Sox in 1946 (courtesy Louise Pettus Archives and Special Collections, Winthrop University).

two. Married to Karl Winsch after the 1947 season, Jean had her first son, Larry, at the end of March 1948, but she pitched herself into condition and produced a 16–11 mark. Blessed with excellent hand-eye coordination as well as a good fastball, several curveballs, and a changeup, Faut kept recording stellar seasons for South Bend. She peaked with a 20–2 record in 1952, also winning three out of four games in the Shaughnessy Playoffs and leading the Blue Sox to their second straight playoff title.

Faut's accomplishments in the AAGPBL were remarkable. She led the league in batting in 1949 with a .291 average in 117 at-bats, but Doris Sams, Muskegon's star outfielder and pitcher, batted over 400 times and won the title with her .279 mark. Faut pitched her first no-hitter in 1948 and another in 1949. She also hurled two perfect games, one in 1951 and one in 1953, the two years she was voted the league's Player of the Year, despite being a mother and a housewife off the diamond as well as being married to the manager, Karl Winsch, who was hired in 1951. Faut was respected by her teammates as well as players around the league. Dottie Schroeder, the circuit's only twelve-season player, recalled in 1995, "Jean could do it all and with excellence. A top pitcher with few equals; great hitter who was so good with the bat, she played infield or outfield when not pitching. I can't remember ever getting a hit off her pitching." Later a leader in the AAGPBL Players Association, Jean Faut, upbeat, friendly, and down-to-earth, enjoyed the reunions and seeing former All-Americans get recognition for their baseball achievements.

Interview on July 15, 1995

JS: *Where were you born and raised?*

Faut: East Greenville, Pennsylvania, which is near Allentown.

In Barbara Gregorich's book, Women at Play, ***she has a chapter on you, and she said there was a semipro team in your town.***

That's right. There were two things to do in those years in the summer. You went swimming or you played ball, and I played ball. Behind our row of houses, the fathers all went out there and cleared the whole field, and they made a baseball diamond. I never played softball.

How did you find out about the All-American League?

I didn't know about the league. The league started in 1943, and I was working in a clothing factory in Allentown during the war. Lots of sports got cut out during World War II.

I didn't try out or anything. A scout just called me up and sent me a train ticket to go to spring training in 1946. It was a train ride down to Pascagoula, Mississippi. The war was over, but there were still a lot of guys in the service, and we were all on the train together.

That year they were expanding the league by two teams, making eight teams, and they had about 200 rookies. Arthur Meyerhoff was head of the league, but the managers made the choices for the teams, and I was picked for South Bend.

Gregorich says that you threw several different pitches and you memorized your pitching pattern to each hitter.

Yes, that's right.

South Bend won championships in 1951 and 1952, right?

In 1952, we won the whole works, and that's when six players quit the team right before the playoffs, but we went ahead and won the championship. I am the most proud of

Jean Faut accepts the trophy on behalf of the team from league business manager Earl McCammon after South Bend, with only twelve players available, defeated Rockford in the best-of-five Shaughnessy Championship Playoff on September 11, 1952. Blue Sox players wearing their warmup jackets and standing in the first row are (left to right): Jo Lenard, Jette (Vincent) Mooney, Betty Wagoner, Sue Kidd, Faut, McCammon, Gertie Dunn, and Marge Wenzell. In the back row are Karl Winsch, manager, Lou Arnold, Joyce (Hill) Westerman, Wimp Baumgartner, Mary Lou Graham, Janet Rumsey, and Mary Froning (courtesy Louise Pettus Archives and Special Collections, Winthrop University).

our team for winning the 1952 championship than anything else, because we won that championship with only twelve girls.

I remember when I hit the two triples in the final game we won, 6–3, against Rockford. My second triple could have been a home run. I could have beaten the throw, but I was so exhausted after I rounded third base that I turned and walked back, and I sat down on the bag!

Sitting there, I heard Rose Gacioch's deep voice come booming out of the Rockford dugout, "My God, that girl is tired!"

Why did the six players quit?

Well, they were having a big squabble with the manager, who was my husband, Karl Winsch, but I don't know too much about it. The girls wouldn't talk to me, because I was the manager's wife, and he wouldn't talk to me, so I never knew what was going on in 1952. I just played ball.

The first year Karl was the manager, in 1951, he was for the girls. From the second year on, he was strictly for the board of directors. He wasn't for the girls at all anymore.

What about that baseball you have?

Faut [showing me a baseball]: This ball has the exact dimensions and is made exactly like when we played, except that now these balls are made in China. This ball came through DeBeer's. This ball is ten inches, and a regulation baseball is nine and a quarter inches.

Who were some of the managers that you played for? I understand many of the managers were former major leaguers.

Yes, and Dave Bancroft, who managed South Bend for two seasons, was one of them.

One night our manager talked Jimmy Foxx [manager of Fort Wayne in 1952] into taking batting practice, and he was really something. He hit several that flew past the lights, and the people loved it!

You knew your future husband, who was later South Bend's manager, when you came to South Bend. You got married and had your first son, Larry, in 1948?

Karl was also from my home town, and he was with the Philadelphia Phillies' farm system for a while, but he never made it to the big leagues. We got married, and Larry was born in 1948. Kevin was born in 1957.

The movie A League of Their Own *shows one of the women having a son with a uniform. That wasn't Larry, was it?*

The characters in the movie were fictional, and later on, my son Larry did have a uniform, but that had nothing to do with the movie. The movie changed a lot of things, and they didn't depict any real players.

You had a lot of good seasons, but you also played third base and you led the league in hitting in 1949. The 1951 season is one of the two years you pitched a perfect game.

I did that in 1951 and 1953. To have a perfect game, you have to have a darn good team behind you. There were some real good plays made in both of those games.

I read that in the your perfect game against Rockford at Playland Park on July 21, 1951, when the Blue Sox won, 2–0, you struck out Dottie Kamenshek twice.

Dottie Kamenshek was what I used to call a "punch hitter." She would hit the ball where you pitched it. The hitters who swung from the heels didn't scare me.

Who were some of your best friends with the Blue Sox?

Gertie Dunn was a good friend of mine. She grew up not too far from where I lived in Pennsylvania. Pinky Pirok was a good friend. Amy Shuman, who also came from Pennsylvania, started with me at Pascagoula in 1946, but her husband lured her home.

You finally retired after the 1953 season. What did you do?

You know, you're playing in a highly competitive league, and you stop cold turkey. There's a tremendous void there. You have that competitiveness in you, and I went to the bowling center, and later I turned professional. I still bowl a little! *[She laughs.]*

I remember going to see a few games the next season. But I couldn't take it. I would cry in the stands, because I wasn't out on the field.

Did you work too?

Oh, yeah, I always worked, but we never went back to Pennsylvania. My kids were born and raised in South Bend. I never took up golf until I moved here [Rock Hill]. I would have liked to play golf in South Bend, but I had to work.

What do you feel best about in terms of what you achieved when you were playing?

I always did the best I could. You talk to some ballplayers, and they say they could have played better and they fooled around too much. I didn't do those things. Our league was a part of history. It was an offshoot of World War II. I was a senior in high school in East Greenville when the war broke out, and some guys joined the service. They couldn't wait to go. Things are different today.

I'm surprised that you could pitch on a regular basis and also play third base.

I was fortunate. Not long ago I was speaking at an awards dinner for three counties in Pennsylvania. I said them. "You gals are lucky. You can get in shape. You can pump iron. I had to split wood to get my strong wrists." They didn't believe me! *[She laughs.]*

What do you remember about the 1948 season?

That's the year Larry was born at the end of March. The league went to spring training in Opa-Locka, Florida, and I missed spring training. I got started late in May. I remember running the track, which was outside the diamond at Playland Park, during a few night games to get in shape. It was a half mile track, and I would begin at the start of the game and keep running through the whole game.

I have a letter from Dottie Schroeder who said you were an awesome pitcher, and you had the ability to freeze batters at the plate.

Inez Voyce, who was a left-handed batter, used to say I'd wrap the pitch around her legs! *[She laughs.]*

Your second husband was Charles Eastman, right?

Yes, Charlie was a machine tool salesman for the Textron Corporation. The home office was in Vermont, but he worked out of the Detroit office. I met him in South Bend, and we were married in 1977. We lived in a suburb of Detroit for two years, and Charlie retired, and we moved to Rock Hill in 1979. He passed away in January of 1993. I was divorced for ten years when I met Charlie, and he was a salesman. He sold me on the idea of getting married again! *[She laughs.]*

What are some of your other league memories?

I remember one time that we were on the road in Rockford, and Bill Allington was the manager. They were way ahead of us, at least eleven runs, and he put a rookie pitcher in, and we started hitting her, and needless to say, we won the game!

The next morning, and I was always up early, I decided I was going out for breakfast. Nobody else was up. I walked down the street to this corner restaurant, where we usually ate breakfast, and who walked in but Bill Allington!

I was sitting at a table, and Bill sat down at the counter. The waitress behind the counter said to Bill, "What would you like this morning, a rookie sandwich!" *[She laughs.]*

Bill got all red in the face, and he didn't say a word!

Interview on September 16, 2009

I have a few questions about the 1946 season. The first time you pitched in 1946 was on July 29, when Viola Thompson was being batted around, and you came in for the last three innings. You finished the year with an 8–3 record.

We didn't have a good pitching staff, and I did some pitching.

Your first start was on August 6, and you beat Rockford with a two-hitter.

I don't remember that, but we needed pitching really bad. We had "Sugar" Koehn, and "Tommie" Thompson, and Lillian Luckey, who was from near South Bend, a softball pitcher, and we had Betty Luna.

Betty Luna won 23 games, and Sugar Koehn won 22 games in 1946. Do you remember Sugar Koehn?

Sugar Koehn was originally underhand, but she switched to sidearm. Viola Thompson was underhand and never went to sidearm, and neither did Lillian Luckey. Viola was strictly a softball pitcher, and not a fastball pitcher.

What kind of manager was Chet Grant?

Chet Grant was a football man from Notre Dame. In fact, he was quarterback when they introduced the pass play. He was the first quarterback to pass for Notre Dame. I liked Chet, but he got into trouble with some of the fans.

Do you remember Marge Stefani?

Marge Stefani was pretty much in charge of the infield. She and Bonnie Baker were in charge. That was the year Bonnie held out for more money. I understood she received just as much under the table as above the table, and that didn't sit well with the players.

Lib Mahon used to ask her, "Are you getting paid under the table?" Bonnie wouldn't tell her, but she rode my fanny all year long [in 1946]. She tried her best to get me sent home. Bonnie wanted someone else to play third base, Moe Trezza. But the board of directors came down to Pascagoula, and they insisted they wanted me on the team, not Trezza.

I liked the league a lot, because I never played softball. I had never played on a team before I went to tryouts. All I ever did was practice with the men's semipro team. Our school had softball, but they discontinued it because of the war.

Early in the 1946 season, they gave the steal sign to Shoo-Shoo [Wirth], and I bunted, planning to help her along. Afterward, Chet Grant asked me why I bunted. I didn't tell him I was green as grass, but I was. I told him I was going to help her with her steal, and he said, "You don't do that, unless I signal you to bunt."

I said, "You'll have to talk to me some more about your signals, because I have never played on a team before." Our whole team was shocked! *[She laughs.]*

Well, that's the way it goes when you're green, but I learned in a hurry.

You pitched sidearm, right?

You weren't allowed to go [the arm] above your shoulder.

Did you make some good friends in the league in 1946?

I was good friends with Pinky Pirok and Shoo-Shoo Wirth. Of course, I was a rookie, and we had quite a few rookies on our team, like Shoo-Shoo and Inez Voyce. Inez was in the Navy before she joined the league.

I roomed with Marie Kruckel with a family named Kahn, and I walked to the ballpark. Bonnie Baker, Marge Stefani, and Lib Mahon got an apartment, and they asked us to join them in the apartment. I was thinking to myself, "Lib's a drinker, and Bonnie's on my case all the time." So I decided, "Nope, I'm staying at the present home." Marie Kruckel went, but I stayed in the Kahn home by myself. I didn't have much time to do anything anyhow. We're either at a practice or a ball game. I was there to play ball.

When you reflect back on your years with the league and the Blue Sox, what kind of impact did baseball make on your life?

First of all, I must say that the eight seasons I played in the All-American Baseball League were the most exciting, most memorable years of my life. The league was extremely competitive, and more so as the years went by. The tougher it got, the more I liked it. The experience gave me self confidence that I needed to be successful in the jobs I had after baseball.

I grew up as a very shy little girl. I was easily embarrassed and not very outgoing with other people. Well, all that changed after playing baseball. I made many friends in the league and after the league.

I would have loved to further my education, but after I retired from baseball, I was raising two sons, Larry and Kevin. I definitely feel that I could have been successful in anything I attempted.

Whenever I give a speech and talk about my experiences in the All-American League, I always tell the young boys and girls to follow their heart. I say to make the choices in life that will lead you to the goal of doing what you love to do. That is what I did. My love of baseball took me to spring training for a tryout in 1946, and I have never regretted that decision.

The players in the All-American Girls Professional Baseball League experienced what Title IX is doing for female athletes today. May Title IX eventually reach its potential.

BETTY FRANCIS
Colleens on developmental tour, 1949; Muskegon, 1949–1950; Kalamazoo, 1950–1953; South Bend, 1954

Interviewed on March 7, 2011.

Born: 1931
Height: 5' 4"
Weight: 140
Positions: OF
Batted: R
Threw: R
Career Batting Average: .251 in six seasons
Best Season: .350 in 1954

Betty Francis, the youngest of seven children of Roy and Hattie Francis, was born in Maquoketa, Iowa, but grew up in nearby Monmouth. Her father was a barber, and her mother was a stay-at-home housewife who raised their children. Betty liked athletics, and she played the same outdoor games as most kids. Attending the Monmouth schools for her first nine years, she loved the halfcourt basketball that girls played at many schools across the nation in the 1940s. Her next oldest sibling, Paul, played varsity baseball, even though Monmouth High was so small that only eight boys played. Betty was good enough to be the ninth player, but girls couldn't play varsity sports with boys in Iowa. Following her freshman year in 1944, the family moved to Chicago. At nearby Ogden Park, she soon began playing what the local teenagers called "kitten ball," softball for girls using the usual rules but with a 14-inch ball. While at Harper High, the 5'4" brunette joined the track team at Ogden Park. She had good hand-eye coordination but not great speed, so she participated in events like the shot put, the baseball throw, and relay races. In late 1946, when the city held tryouts at Marquette Park for a minor league sponsored by the All-American League, the fifteen-year-old made it with the Blue Island Stars, and she played outfield.

In 1949, after displaying her talent and ability with the Stars for two summers, Francis was invited to AAGPBL tryouts. She was chosen and allocated to Muskegon. Following nine games, she was sent to the rookie developmental tour to gain experience, and she spent the rest of the season with the Colleens. Earning $25 per week plus expenses, she called it a "fantastic experience." In 1950, she returned to Muskegon, and the financially-strapped franchise shifted to Kalamazoo in June. Francis, a dependable outfielder, averaged a solid .256 in 56 games. She covered mainly left field, but played a few games in right, as All-Star Doris Sams played center. A right-handed batter, Francis, strong, agile, and a hard swinger at 5'4" and 140, often pulled the ball foul to left field, especially on pitches thrown on the inside part of the plate. She had a good eye at bat, and she always walked more than she struck out, for example, drawing 49 bases on balls compared to fanning 14 times in 1951. From 1951 through 1953, the Lassie stalwart posted averages of .231, .210, and .226. Although she hit 23 doubles in three years, she never hit a triple or a home run. Traded to South Bend in 1954, she took a tip from manager Karl Winsch, who suggested she use a heavier 35-inch bat. Conscientious, modest, and friendly, the Chicago athlete, who loved baseball's camaraderie, responded with a great season, producing career highs in batting at .350 as well as 13 doubles, two triples, eight home runs, and 58 RBIs.

Francis enjoyed her time in the league. She played the longest in Kalamazoo, so she knew the Lassies' players and the city better, but she liked her season in South Bend, where she once won two strings of pearls for hitting two

An Iowa native whose family moved to Chicago when she finished the ninth grade, Betty Francis rose from one of Chicago's girls' teams, the Blue Island Stars, to the All-American League in 1949. Betty is pictured in Kalamazoo uniform (courtesy Betty Francis).

homers in a single game. Given the opportunity, she would have played longer, but after the league failed, she returned to Chicago. Over the years, she worked at three manufacturing plants, mainly for Armstrong Paint and Varnish, where she spent 28 years before retiring in 1993. After the acclaimed movie *A League of Their Own* returned the All-Americans to the public eye, she participated in numerous events held to honor former players, and she still hears from the league's fans. Betty Francis, who attended the AAGPBL Reunion in nearby Milwaukee, treasures the value that baseball added to her life.

JS: Tell me about your family. Did you grow up in Chicago?

Francis: I know it says Chicago on my baseball card, and I did go to high school in Chicago, but I was born in Iowa. I was born in Maquoketa, Iowa, but I grew up in Monmouth, which is twelve miles away, but Maquoketa had the only hospital in our area. Monmouth is a small town in eastern Iowa between Dubuque and Davenport. My father, Roy Francis, who was a barber, and my mother Hattie, a stay-at-home mom, had seven children, and I was the youngest. My older brothers and sisters are Loren, Naomi, Gerald, Gail, Marvin, and Paul, the next youngest.

I was always interested in athletics. We played six-on-six girls' basketball at Monmouth, and I loved baseball. My brother Paul used to say that Monmouth had only had eight boys when he played on the baseball team, and if girls were allowed to play, I could have been the ninth player. I went to school for my first nine years in Monmouth.

In the early years my favorite sport was basketball. High school basketball was very big in Iowa, but we moved to Chicago, and the schools didn't have basketball. I was very disappointed, but I found out basketball was played in the Chicago park system, and I really loved that. Later, I got involved in baseball, and I didn't play any more basketball after I played in the All-American League.

In 1944, after my freshman year, we moved to Chicago. I was fourteen, and that's when I started playing "kitten ball," as we called it—slow-pitch softball with a 14-inch ball—at Ogden Park. In 1946, our Ogden Park ball team won the Chicago City Park Championship. Later in 1946, they had tryouts for a baseball team at Marquette Park, and I made it. The All-American League sponsored this minor league in Chicago. They had four teams, and my team was the Blue Island Stars. I played for the Stars in the summers of 1947 and 1948.

I went to Harper High School in Chicago, but I didn't graduate. My baseball card says I was an "all-around athlete" in track, but I wasn't a star. I didn't have any speed really, but I participated in the baseball throw, and the shot put, and I ran a relay, if they needed me. I love track meets. There's so much going on that they are really fun. That was in the years 1946 and 1947.

Later, in 1949, I spent a few games with Muskegon, and the league organized the rookie tour. We needed more playing time, because we weren't good enough yet. In 1950, I came back and played for Kalamazoo. The touring teams were called the Chicago Colleens, and I played for the Colleens, and the other team was the Springfield Sallies. Those were two new teams that were in the All-American League in 1948, but they faded out at the end of the season because of low attendance.

Did you have favorite teammates on the Colleens?

The girl I roomed with on the tour was Anna Mae O'Dowd, because we were on the same team, and later she went to the big league. Fran Janssen was on my team, and so was Wimp Baumgartner, and also Sue Kidd. When we were touring in Arkansas, Sue tried out, maybe in Little Rock, and they took her for the league. Later, when they made the movie *A League of Their Own*, Sue was the one who was pitching in that scene that showed the older players.

What was it like to be on the tour?

It was a fantastic experience. We made $25 a week, which was great, because we also got meal money, and our hotel rooms were paid. But if we weren't young, I don't know if we could have done it, because we did a lot of traveling. We'd stay two nights in a town, sometimes just one night, and then get on the bus and ride to the next town where we were going to play another game. The trips were long, but I didn't mind it at all — I liked it. I thought it was a piece of cake, but as I said, we were younger. The girls on the touring teams were not always the same. Some new players were picked up in the tryouts, which they held in every town where we played, and some girls were sent home.

In 1950 you went back to Muskegon, which became Kalamazoo in mid-season, after Muskegon lost the franchise. What do you remember about the Lassies?

After the tour, I went to Kalamazoo, and I remember the team's president, Lee Elkins, who owned the McNamara Trucking Line. Elkins had a nice cottage at one of the lakes, and one time he had the whole team out there for a picnic. He owned two race cars that ran at the Indianapolis Speedway. They had one of the cars out there, the "McNamara Special." Doris Sams sat in that race car when we were taking pictures, and Mr. Elkins didn't like that. The drivers used to consider it bad luck for a woman to sit in a race car.

In Kalamazoo, I had to compete with Doris Sams for center field, and I had no hope of beating her out. So with the Lassies, I played a lot of left field, and sometimes I played right field, but in South Bend, I played my favorite position, which is center field. Sammy was an outstanding player and an outstanding person, as were so many of the girls in the league.

When you played for South Bend in 1954, your batting average went way up. Why do you think that happened?

I'm a right-handed batter, and before I came to South Bend, I used to swing hard and pull the ball foul to left field a lot. Karl Winsch, South Bend's manager, got me to use an old 35-inch bat that nobody else liked, because it was a grungy, old, top-heavy bat. My first swing was a line drive to right field, and after that, I hit two home runs. I never used another bat, and I still have that bat today! I wasn't a home run hitter either. I was a line drive hitter.

I remember one time in South Bend, there was a jeweler that was giving a strand of pearls for a home run. I hit two that night, so I got two strands of pearls. After that, they discontinued the offer! *[She laughs.]*

At the same time, I got $2 from a fan for hitting the two home runs. I still have a letter dated July 8, 1954, I received from our team's PA Announcer, Vince Dayle, who worked for Station WJVA, and he enclosed the two dollars. The announcer told me, "I put it in my pocket and forgot about it, so here it is now." He also wrote, "Hope you had a happy birthday. I'm sure you helped make the evening very happy for many South Bend fans." That night we beat Fort Wayne, and it was right after the league started using the regulation baseball.

[Editor's note: South Bend's 10–4 victory, thanks to a pair of three-run homers by Francis, came in the nightcap of a doubleheader at Playland Park on July 7, 1954. Fort Wayne won the opener, 17–8.]

That night, July 7, my birthday, some family members drove from Chicago, but they were just at the gate when they were told I hit two home runs, so they missed it!

Another night I had a homer in Fort Wayne, and Fort Wayne had a longer fence — it was at least 300 feet. There was a jeweler there giving away a cultured pearl for a home run, and I still have that pearl. The girls in South Bend in 1954 were pretty good hitters, and we hit quite a lot of home runs, especially with the new regulation baseball.

Who did you room with in Kalamazoo?

June Peppas was one of my roommates, and one year I roomed with Mary Carey. One year there were four or five of us in a house in Kalamazoo. My roommates were June, Mary, Doris Sams, and maybe one more. Mary Carey used to play for Peoria, but she was traded to Kalamazoo in 1952, and we roomed together.

I played longer in Kalamazoo, and I remember more about the Lassies. We had a group of fans who didn't live in Kalamazoo, but they used to come to our games. I think they came from Grand Rapids. They used to call me "Betty May," but that's not my name. They were really nice. They gave me a hand-made lamp that was made by somebody in Grand Rapids, and the lamp had a figure of a ballplayer on it. The lamp was really cute, and it had my name on it. At that time, you paid $20 for a lamp, and that was a lot of money.

Did you have any idea in 1954 that it would be the league's last season?

There were some signs that the league might end. In the last couple of years, we weren't getting as many fans at our games. In 1954, they started taking stuff away, like our bus. We ended up traveling in our own cars, so several of us would ride in one car. That was near the end of the 1954 season. It seemed like there wasn't enough money.

I remember one time we came back to South Bend, and we were warming up in center field, and there had been a circus in town, and there were coins in the grass. We were all down on our hands and knees picking up pennies like crazy! They must have run one of those penny-pitching games at the circus.

After the league ended following the 1954 season, what did you do?

I came back to Chicago and worked in a factory called Autolamp, and they made hand-held spotlights for cars. I had been working there for a few years, and they would always take me back after the baseball season. After Autolamp, I worked at Hamilton Steel, where we made coaster wagons and garden equipment. After that, I worked at Armstrong Paint and Varnish for twenty-eight and a half years until I retired in 1993.

We had AAU softball in Chicago, but we were considered professionals, so I didn't play.

I spent time with my family members, and I have gone to one AAGPBL reunion. I also organized and ran many family reunions in Chicago, and, in later years, in Maquoketa, Iowa.

I went to the Milwaukee Reunion in the year 2000, and my nephew drove me up on a Saturday. It rained that day, and we were introduced on the field at the Brewers' game that night. What an honor!

What kind of impact did the league have on your life?

I didn't go on to college, but I worked in several manufacturing plants, until I retired in 1993. The movie *A League of Their Own* came out just before I retired, and the movie made an impact on my life that's still going on. We were noticed and honored, and people know us now. The movie helped make the league all over again. Once the movie came out, we started making appearances, and it brought back many memories. Making those appearances and being around other players, you'd be surprised how much we remembered. Talking to you about the Blue Sox, that made a lot of things come back. It's been really nice, and you don't realize what people think of you.

Gerry Clarke, who used to be the general manager of a minor league team, went to the Chicago Bandits professional girls softball team around 2005. One time he organized a whole weekend of events for the All-American women in the area. He has a reel of tape, original footage, about the league playing. We saw the tape once, and it must be priceless. Ken Burns made his documentary about baseball in "innings," and we're in one of those innings, I think the sixth inning. Those are the kind of things that came from our league and the movie, and I'm glad I had the chance to be part of the league.

The town where I was born, Maquoketa, Iowa, had me in the newspaper a couple of times. Jack Marlowe, a writer for the Maquoketa newspaper, interviewed me twice, and another time the newspaper in Merrionette Park interviewed me. That's quite an honor too.

Frances "Fran" Janssen
Grand Rapids, 1948; Colleens and Sallies on developmental tour, 1949; Peoria and Fort Wayne, 1950; Fort Wayne, Peoria, Battle Creek, and Kalamazoo, 1951; Battle Creek, 1952

Interviewed on July 17, 1997; letters of July 13, 1993, and September 14, 1997.

Born: 1926
Deceased: 2008
Height: 5'11½"
Weight: 155
Positions: P
Batted: Switch
Threw: R
Career Batting Average: .162 in four seasons
Lifetime Pitching Record: 13–18 with 3.41 ERA

Fran Janssen (1926–2008), a quiet but active redhead who grew up on a farm near Remington, Indiana, thrived on team sports like basketball and baseball. Her father, Fred Janssen, passed away when she was four, and her mother Anna later married Diedrich Ubbinga. The couple raised six children, including Fran. Nearly six feet tall and one of the best athletes in Gilboa Township School, she graduated in the ten-member class of 1943. Half of her classmates were girls, and they could play ball as well as the boys. The school offered no sports, so Fran and her friends played games like "work-up" baseball or pick-up basketball at recess or after school. Hoosiers thrive on basketball, and Fran was no exception. She graduated from high school during the peak of World War II, and in order to find a job, the pleasant, athletic, hard-working young woman moved to Fort Wayne and attended the city's business college. Several businesses sponsored city league basketball teams. Fran, going to school and rooming in a private home, played for two teams starting in the 1944–45 season: the Wayne Candies and, later, the Lincoln National Life Insurance Company. The All-American League's renamed Daisies moved to Fort Wayne from Minneapolis for the 1945 season, and Fran and some friends tried out in 1946.

Janssen, who preferred basketball and volleyball, chose not to play professional baseball. She continued working and playing basketball until 1948, when she seized the opportunity. Bright, friendly, and talented, she was invited to a tryout in Chicago, where she performed well, and the league sent her to spring training in Opa-Locka, Florida. "Big Red," a 5'11½" lanky right-hander, was allocated to Grand Rapids, where she posted a 4–4 record as a spot starter for the first half of the 1948 season. The Chicks, however, sent her home in late July, and Fran went to work for Lincoln Life. In 1949, Lenny Zintak, director of the league's new rookie touring teams, the Sallies and the Colleens, invited Janssen to try out, and she was chosen. She started pitching for the Colleens, but the savvy twenty-three-year-old had good baseball experience, and beginning on July 5, she pitched for and managed the Sallies. Altogether, the curveballing Hoosier posted a 16–5 record. Fran made the league in 1950, but she became a spot, or fifth, starter, splitting the season between Peoria and Fort Wayne. In 1951, her odyssey continued, and she pitched at least one game with four teams, Fort Wayne, Peoria, Battle Creek, and Kalamazoo. In 1952, she trained and hurled for Battle Creek again, but the Belles released her in mid-season.

Regardless, fun with sports, camaraderie with teammates, and activities with friends continued for Janssen. After moving to South Bend, she starred for the Rockettes' basketball team from 1954 through 1960, joining former Blue Sox standouts such as Betty Wagoner and Sue Kidd. Janssen also worked for nearly thirty years as an insurance representative. When the AAGPBL newsletter and reunions began, Fran got involved, and the Players Association was formed at her home in 1987. She helped with the association and the newsletter, *Touching Bases*, as well as with the league's archives, when those were deposited at the Northern Indiana Center for History (now the Center for History). A dedicated athlete who gave her best whenever she took the diamond or the hardcourt, Fran Janssen never tired of supporting the league, the players, and their activities. Always cheer-

From Remington, Indiana, Fran Janssen played five seasons with six teams. Fran is pictured with Fort Wayne, circa 1950 (courtesy Wilma Lewellyn).

ful, her personality, talent, work ethic, and love for the game made her the kind of "All-American" girl that inspired creation of the wartime AAGPBL in 1943.

Interview on July 17, 1997

JS: On the back of the flyleaf of Sue Macy's book, A Whole New Ball Game, **the picture shows a map of the eastern half of the United States. The caption says, "A page from Fran Janssen's scrapbooks showing the route taken by the 1949 rookie teams of the AAGPBL." One of the pictures (page 67) shows you and several players standing beside a bus used on the tour, and the picture indicates, "Courtesy of Fran Janssen." Did you meet Sue Macy at the Northern Indiana Center for History in South Bend?**

Janssen: I had put a notice in a magazine, maybe in *Women's Sports*, that we were looking for former ballplayers, and that's how Sue heard about the league, and that's how I got to know her. She came to several of our All-American Reunions, and she wrote that book and several articles.

How did you get involved with baseball?

I was living in Fort Wayne, where I went to go to business college, so I was working and playing basketball in the wintertime. I played some softball in the summer, and when the Daisies came to Fort Wayne, I got to know some of the players. I finally decided to try out.

You were born and raised in Remington, Indiana?

I was born on a farm near Remington. My father, Fred Janssen, passed away when I was three or four. My mother — her name was Anna, and her maiden name was Petersen — got married again a few years later. My stepfather's name was Diedrich Ubbinga. He and my mother both came from Germany. I have four sisters and a brother: Betty, Paul, and myself are Janssens, and Tinie, Wilma, and Anna are Ubbingas.

Where did you go to school?

A little township school out in Benton County, Gilboa Township School, and that's near Remington, although in a different county. I went there for twelve years, first grade through the twelfth grade, and I knew everybody. There were ten in my graduating class in 1943. *[She laughs.]*

After I graduated, I moved to Fort Wayne to go to the International Business College, and that was during World War II. At that time, I was living in a private home and helping with the house work to pay for my room and board. That was per an arrangement the business college made for a lot of students. They would go to these private homes, and they'd give us maybe a couple of bucks for spending money to help pay for meals during the week.

How long did you go to International?

I went for about a year and a half, before I started working. I had several office clerical and accounting jobs. Until I came to South Bend, I didn't work for any big outfit. When I played baseball, I had to take off in the summertime. I worked for a life insurance company for a couple of years, and they let me come back in the offseason. The office manager finally said, "You've got to make up your mind whether you're going to play baseball or work for us." I decided to play baseball. *[She laughs.]*

Did your high school have sports for girls?

No, we didn't have anything. The only thing we did every spring was we played a softball game against the team in town. That was it. Otherwise, we just played our own make-up games. We played work-up in grade school. We'd race out to the playground at recess, and we'd have three batters, and somebody would be yelling, "I'm pitcher," or "I'm first batter," and we worked our way up to bat. You learned a little bit of everything, the positions, the batting, the fielding, and boys and girls played it together. Our class happened to be a pretty good class. We were all pretty athletic, and the girls would beat the boys about half the time! *[She laughs.]*

Are you 5'11"?

I used to be! *[She laughs.]*

I was wondering how you got involved in playing basketball.

During World War II, a lot of businesses in Fort Wayne sponsored basketball teams. General Electric, Lincoln Life, and Essex Wire all had teams. General Electric Company built a gym, and we played in that gym, and we played in the schools. We had a regular city league. I played first for Wayne Candies and later for Lincoln National Life Insurance Company. A friend of my sister knew somebody that was starting a team, and I got acquainted with her, and that's how I got started. She had a car, and she picked everyone up for the games. I started playing in the 1944–45 season, and I continued playing after I joined the All-American League.

They had a tryout once for the Daisies in Fort Wayne, probably in 1946, and I went down. I was one of a half dozen girls that tried out, but I decided I didn't want to play professional baseball. I remember Bill Wambsganss was the manager. I told them I wasn't interested. After I got to know more of the gals playing on the Daisies, I decided they were having too much fun, so I tried out.

So you kept working and playing basketball in the winter, and in 1948, you got interested again in the All-American League.

I made the league at a big tryout in Chicago, and I was invited to go to spring training in Opa-Locka, Florida, down near Miami. The training was at an old naval base, and we stayed in the barracks. They had lots of land and lots of ball diamonds, and ten teams were there. I was allocated to Grand Rapids that summer.

Actually, I was assigned to South Bend for about three days, and camp was breaking up, and I pitched my first-ever baseball game for South Bend. They were taking two teams to Cuba to play exhibition games, and South Bend was going. That night, they had a reallocation meeting, and I didn't get to go to Cuba. I was assigned to Grand Rapids, and we traveled back up north with the Chicago Colleens.

You pitched in 11 games for Grand Rapids and had a 4–4 record for the 1948.

I was sort of the "extra" pitcher, but then I got released in July, I guess. I had to go back to Fort Wayne and go to work.

Where we you living then?

I was living in a rooming house. When I left to play ball, I was working for Walley Agricultural Service doing clerical work. I started there in 1946. When I left, he put an ad in the paper saying, "We Need Girl — To replace Frances who has gone to play soft ball with National Girls League." I still have the clipping. When I returned, I went to work for Lincoln Life.

In 1949, the league decided to start the touring teams to develop young players.

The two new teams, the Springfield Sallies and the Chicago Colleens, didn't do so well in 1948, and the Sallies folded partway through the season and became a traveling team, kind of like the Minneapolis Millerettes in 1944.

Yes, the Sallies lived in their bus as a traveling team. We called them the "Orphans." Then both teams folded at the end of the year, and they didn't have teams in Chicago or Springfield the next year.

How did you get back into the league in 1949?

I looked up my spring training camps. In 1949 I went to Pokagon State Park near Angola, Indiana, with the Fort Wayne Daisies, and I got a letter from Lenny Zintak in Chicago inviting me to come to tryouts in Chicago for the "rookie" teams. We had sort of a spring training there for about a week with the two teams that went on the tour.

After that training, you took off from Chicago and traveled around the country. You have this map that shows the route of the teams. Where did you begin playing games?

We played a couple of games in Quincy, Illinois, on the way south. We usually stayed two nights in a town. I don't remember all the towns where we played games, but I know we played in Joplin, Missouri, and Jefferson City, Missouri, and Memphis, Tennessee. I pitched that game in Memphis, and we played at a minor league ballpark. We played games in Oklahoma and Arkansas and Louisiana on the way to Austin, Texas, and then we played our way across the Gulf states before we went north through Georgia and South Carolina and North Carolina and Virginia on the way to New Jersey and New York, and finally traveled to West Virginia, where we finished up in Charleston. *[Editor's note: The players received $25 per week in salary and $3.50 per day in meal money, and all of their expenses were paid by the league.]*

You started out pitching for the Colleens and on July 5 in Austin, Texas, midway through the tour you switched to the Sallies and became chaperone-manager as well as pitcher, right?

That's right.

Do you have newspaper stories about those games?

Yes. Some of those stories are interesting in showing how the writers wrote about the girls playing baseball. You get some cute articles written by the guys! Most of them had never seen girls play baseball.

Is there a feature article on you?

Maybe it was in Oklahoma City they had a story with some information about me. After the tour, we came home right after Labor Day, and I went back to work.

Your baseball card says in 1950 you played for Peoria and Fort Wayne.

The league held a rookie camp in South Bend in 1950, and I was assigned to the Peoria Redwings. We trained in Peoria and played exhibition games against the Rockford Peaches. We played one game at the state prison in Joliet. One thing that made it difficult that season is that I usually didn't get to pitch in the regular order, and if it rained, I missed my chance. Later, I was sent to Fort Wayne.

You pitched your most games in 1951, 26 games, but you spent the season going between four teams. In 1952, when the league was reduced to six teams from eight in 1951, you pitched five games for Battle Creek, before they released you.

In 1951 I trained in Alexandria, Virginia, with Fort Wayne and a pickup team made up mostly of Battle Creek Belles. We were scheduled to play exhibitions at Griffith Stadium, but we got rained out both nights. In 1952, I went to spring training with the Battle Creek team, and we played exhibitions with the Fort Wayne Daisies. I remember staying at Mrs. Hewitt's boarding house, but I wouldn't eat grits for breakfast. Guy Bush was manager of the Belles that year, and Jimmy Foxx was the new manager of the Daisies. I wished I had gotten his autograph. Battle Creek released me fairly early in the season, so I decided it was time to go to work.

Recently I was checking figures on major league attendance, and the postwar major league total attendance peaked with nearly 21 million in 1948, and your league peaked in 1948 with about 910,000. After that, attendance for all baseball teams, the majors, the minors, and the AAGPBL, declined in the 1950s. The major leagues didn't surpass the 1948 total attendance until they reached a little over 21 million in 1962, the second expansion season.

Television was getting to be a big thing in the 1950s, and there were other things people were doing, so it wasn't just the girls' league. It was baseball.

The majors televised more games in the 1950s, and gradually the attendance went up. It seems like television promoted major league baseball.

To me, I was going through old scrapbooks, and I wasn't aware of the financial situation of the All-American teams. They never told us about finances, and I wasn't aware it was that bad. I've seen Doctor Dailey's "Notes" at Notre Dame's library, and he comments on the financial problems. I remember in one of Dailey's notes, he was complaining about Max Carey's "wild idea" about taking everyone down to Miami for spring training [Opa-Locka in 1948]. He said it was too expensive, and maybe he was right. He was against the ten teams from the beginning. *[She laughs.]*

I always felt that some of that national publicity we got was helping more than anything, and when they stopped doing that, it hurt the league. No matter if the league was only in the Midwest, if it was talked about in *Life* magazine, it was something more important.

There wasn't as much of that national publicity after 1948. In 1951 the league turned the teams over to the cities, and there were still eight teams for that season.

They also changed the name of the league to the American League. I wasn't aware of that until I started looking at the materials in the league's archives [in South Bend]. Any contract the players had, the league crossed out the All, and it was the "American Girls Baseball League." I never found a reason, but the guy in Chicago, [Arthur] Meyerhoff, maybe owned the "All-American" title. But you never heard that. Most people were never aware of that change.

When you think back, what were some of your favorite experiences?

One time in 1951, I was pitching for Kalamazoo against Grand Rapids. In the third inning, Alma "Ziggy" Ziegler, who played for the Chicks, was real good at working a walk with the umpires, and she walked and promptly stole second base, and she scored on a hit. I was disgusted, because the umpires always gave Ziggy a little bit of a "break," and she'd get that walk. But the score was 1–1 after eleven innings. In the twelfth, the manager took me out and put in Doris Sams. They finally lost that game in 19 innings, 3–2. I was upset because I felt it was my game to win, but after eleven innings, I probably was worn out.

Another game I was involved in was with Fort Wayne against the Peaches. We were getting clobbered by about 14–0, and I went in to relieve in the ninth inning. I pitched to one or two batters and got them out. When I got in the dugout, Wilma Briggs said they were going to win it for me, but I didn't think I wanted to stay there that long. But we did keep scoring runs and we won the thing in that last at-bat. I didn't even get to bat because they put in a pinch-hitter. Max Carey had let Tiby Eisen take over coaching at third base earlier, and he wanted to go back out, and we wouldn't let him (we were superstitious). The radio broadcaster had also given up on us and packed up. When things started happening, the announcer got on the phone and called in the play-by-play! It was the easiest game I ever won. I couldn't find an account of it, so I'm not sure of the details.

I had my best season on the tour. *[Editor's note: By her own tabulation, Fran was 16–5.]* Guess I was a little older and could throw a pretty good curve to strike out the younger ones. I did have a couple of two-hitters, but not a no-hitter. I got credit for one game on the tour because the right fielder fell asleep and let a ball drop — the girl keeping score thought it should have been caught and gave her an error.

I remember more of the good times we had, and even pitching games was fun. I just enjoyed the whole experience. I saw a lot of the country on the tour, and I enjoyed that a lot. We had a good group, and we'd get to a town and do some sight-seeing. When we played in Roanoke, Virginia, the people took us out to see Natural Bridge [35 miles north of Roanoke]. When we were in Jefferson City, Missouri, they took us out to see their state prison, and they had these old dungeons from way back when! *[She laughs.]* They took us to see the sights in most of these towns.

The 1949 rookie tour was really a unique experience. Did you have fifteen or sixteen girls per team on the tour, plus chaperones?

It was close to fifteen or sixteen players on each team, but it kept changing. Murray Howe was our publicist, our "front man," and he'd handle the publicity when we got to a town. I suppose he was from Chicago, but I'd like to learn more from him.

Did you usually stay in hotels on the tour?

We were always in hotels. Once, I think in Pensacola, Florida, they had us stay in cabins, but there weren't many of those around. We'd get in late at night to the hotel, and sometimes we'd have to wait for rooms that weren't ready. Sometimes we'd get in to the hotel early in the morning, and we'd have to sleep in the lobby for a while because the rooms weren't ready.

I sent postcards home from almost every town we played. I had stickers all over my suitcase by the time we got home.

Letter from Janssen, July 13, 1993, About Her First Pitching Experience in the Spring of 1948

As a rookie just trying out for the All-American Girls Professional Baseball League in spring training at Opa-Locka, Florida, in 1948, I was allocated to the South Bend Blue Sox.

The league had expanded to ten teams that year and also changed to overhand pitching, so managers were looking for pitchers. I was asked to try pitching and so my first game in the "big league" was as a pitcher, pitching for the Blue Sox in an exhibition game against the Chicago Colleens. The game was played in Miami.

My best memory of the game was of the umpire, Norris "Gadget" Ward, of South Bend. My catcher, Edith Barney, came out to the mound in about the third inning laughing because Gadget was grumbling about having to teach rookies how to pitch and even be bat boy. It seems I wasn't waiting to get a sign from the catcher or letting the ump get ready before I pitched. Gadget had to give me a few tips on how to pitch a game. Sorry to say I was the losing pitcher after five innings of work.

I was reallocated to Grand Rapids a few days later and never played for the Blue Sox in South Bend. Gadget Ward umpired for the league for many years and was respected as one of the best.

Letter from Janssen, September 14, 1997, About a Few Experiences on the 1949 Rookie Tour

We played a total of 71 games and ended up with the Colleens winning 36. We were promised a bonus if we won the most games, but there apparently wasn't any money for it. All we got was a uniform patch. Of course, I ended up on the losing team [the Sallies].

I made a few notes of things that happened at some of the cities. I pitched the game in Memphis that was televised, and when some of us went to church the next morning, several people came up to us to say they saw the game.

About ten of us went to New York City from Newark the night we played in New Jersey. The two chaperones went along — Pat Barringer and Bobbie Liebrich — and gave us strict orders to be ready to get on and off the train so we wouldn't got left behind. When we had to change trains somewhere en route, those two were the ones that got left! The rest of us stayed on the train and got off at Times Square and waited for them — of course, they got a good ribbing. That was the first trip to NYC for most of us, so it was a thrill to get out of the subway at Times Square and see the lights (it was just getting dark when we got there). Can you imagine a group of young gals doing that trip now?

The game at South Orange [New Jersey] drew the largest crowd since Babe Ruth had played there. Think I was starting to run out of energy at that stage, along with everyone else. I enjoyed our stay at the Shenandoah Caverns [in Virginia] where we had a little free time. It was pretty there. I stopped there about twenty years ago and found it was still there, but the top two floors had burned in the hotel. It was built right over the caverns. My niece was going to grad school at James Madison University at the time, so my sister and I were passing through.

I counted about 20 states and 46 cities where we stayed and played ball.

Since 1980, when one of our players [June Peppas] started a newsletter, we have had lots of All-American Reunions, had an exhibit placed in the National Baseball Hall of Fame in Cooperstown with our names on a roster of players, and watched the movie, *A League of Their Own*, become a hit. We did not realize we were making history at the time, but we are proud of it now.

GLENNA SUE KIDD
Sallies on developmental tour, 1949;
Muskegon, 1950; Peoria, 1950; South Bend, 1950, 1954
Interviewed on September 6, 2010.

Born: 1933
Height: 5' 8"
Weight: 165

Positions: P, 1B, OF
Batted: R
Threw: R
Career Batting Average: .201 for five seasons
Lifetime Pitching Record: 47–45
Pitched a No-Hitter: Sallies to defeat the Colleens, 1–0, on tour in 1949
Pitched and Won: Two complete games of double-header at South Bend's Playland Park against Grand Rapids Chicks, July 4, 1953, by scores of 2–1 and 6–1

The Choctaw, Arkansas, teenager joined the league's developmental tour in 1949, and she was sent to South Bend in 1950. Pictured in Blue Sox uniform circa 1953, Sue Kidd pitched and won both ends of a double-header (courtesy Sue Kidd).

Glenna Sue Kidd, who was born the year President Franklin Roosevelt took office during the low point of the Great Depression, grew up near Choctaw, Arkansas. Her father, Marvin Kidd, loved baseball and managed a town team in addition to running a store that contained the local Post Office, which he also operated. The six Kidd children took care of chores at home and duties at the store, but the boys also played baseball. Marvin's three sons attended a baseball school in Greenbrier, and they played on their father's Choctaw team. Further, Sue, who began playing with a rubber ball as a toddler, showed enough skill to play on Kidd's team by the time she was a teenager. Girls' games weren't for her. The tall, shy teen with the dark blond hair and gray-green eyes loved sports, and in high school she excelled in baseball and basketball.

Sue's baseball ability changed her life forever when two All-American League touring teams, the Colleens and the Sallies, arrived in Little Rock in June of 1949 to play a pair of exhibitions. "Doc" Williams, owner of Greenbrier's baseball school, got word to Marvin Kidd that his daughter should travel to Little Rock for a tryout. The Kidd family arrived and, Sue, then fifteen, tried out before the game. She made it, then rode home with her family to pack, and she rode back with them the next day to join the tour. Big and strong but socially awkward, the 5'8" right-hander with the hard fastball and an assortment of breaking pitches learned the proper behavior around teammates as well as how to get her hair done and buy clothes, and she made lifelong friends like Wimp Baumgartner and Fran Janssen. Not only did Sue pitch a no-hitter and prove herself worthy of the league, but she returned home and, on September 12, pitched Kidd's team to a victory over all the all-male Heber Springs All-Stars, a feat that became part of local legend.

Kidd graduated to the regular All-American League in the spring of 1950, but she bounced from the Muskegon Lassies to the Peoria Redwings and, on August 1, to the South Bend Blue Sox, where she spent most of the rest of her pro career. In 1951, the Blue Sox hired a new manager, Karl Winsch, once a minor league right-hander and now husband of the team's ace, Jean Faut. South Bend had good pitchers, so Kidd was loaned briefly to the Battle Creek Belles. Developing as a starter, the Choctaw hurler helped South Bend win Shaughnessy Playoff Championships in 1951 and 1952, the second title when 12 Blue Sox teammates outlasted the Rockford Peaches.

Like many young women who came to the league during the declining years after 1948, Kidd was anxious to play professional baseball. She cared less about money and more about playing ball. A determined competitor, she overcame shyness and helped South Bend win, especially in her last three seasons. Sue's greatest highlight came when she pitched and won both ends of a double-header against the Grand Rapids Chicks on July 4, 1953, before a crowd of more than 5,000 at Playland Park. A few days later, the team honored her with a memorable "Sue Kidd Night," and she tried to ride a mule onto the infield! Overall, Kidd posted double digits in wins from 1951 through 1953, and her 9–5 record in 1954 showed the country girl was a stellar performer. Afterward, she played basketball with South Bend's Rockettes, earned the bachelor's and master's from the University of Central Arkansas in the 1960s, and enjoyed teaching PE and coaching for years, but the baseball dream ended too soon for younger stars like Sue Kidd.

JS: How did you get into baseball?
Kidd: I was born into a baseball family. There were six of us, three boys and three girls. I've been told that I started playing with a small rubber ball when I was a crawling baby, and soon I would sit up, throw it against a wall, and it would rebound back to me. My dad, Marvin Kidd, managed a town team, and he let me play on the team when I was thirteen or fourteen, when they played weaker teams. It used to be that every little town or community in Arkansas had a baseball team back in the 1940s. That was about all there was for recreation, except going to church.

My brothers went to a baseball school in Greenbrier, Arkansas. That was run by Doc [Earl] Williams. I believe his son was a major league scout. Dad wanted to send me to the baseball school, but of course they didn't have facilities for a female.

Then in June 1949, these two traveling teams, the Chicago Colleens and the Springfield Sallies, came through Little Rock. Mr. Williams drove up to make sure Dad knew about it, because Little Rock is about seventy-five miles south of our home in Choctaw. We got the daily paper, so Dad knew about the teams, so he took me down to try out. I tried out before the game in the evening. We stayed and watched the game, but they said, "Go home and pack your clothes, and we'll have a contract ready for you tomorrow."

We drove back home, and my mother, Julia Kidd, washed and ironed all night. They found a suitcase for me. We had to go back to Little Rock in time to go to the Bureau of Vital Statistics to get me a birth certificate. Luckily, a gentleman who was born and raised up here in Choctaw worked for the bureau, and he walked me through, and got all the information, and he was a witness about where I was born and all, so I got my birth certificate. I was fifteen at the time.

I signed with the team, the Sallies, and they put me in to pinch-hit in the game that night. After the game, we left on our bus, and the next stop was New Orleans. We traveled through about twenty-five different states that summer, and we ended up in West Virginia, I believe on Labor Day weekend. Dad sent my sister and her husband and my brother over to pick me up, so I wouldn't have to try to get home on my own. I hated to see the season end, and I just hoped and prayed I'd get to play the next summer.

During that year, I was fortunate enough to pitch a no-hitter, and what kept it from being a perfect game was an error by the shortstop. You know, that happens. I came back home and that year I finished my school at Clinton, over in the county seat. It was a vocational high school back then, but now it's Clinton High School. I wasn't eligible to play basketball, because I'd played professional baseball.

On the twelfth of September, after I got back, Dad had a game set up in Heber Springs against a real good semipro team, the Heber Springs Merchants. I pitched that game over there, and I had good defense behind me and everything, and we won, 5–3. Dad tried to take me out in the seventh inning, but the fans wouldn't hardly let him. He talked to me and said, "Well, we'll go ahead and let you see if you can finish it." I was lucky enough to do that.

The next year, several of us rookies from that tour were assigned to the Muskegon Lassies. Lenny Zintak was the manager, and he'd been kind of the coach and manager on the tour. Mother and Dad took me to spring training at Cape Girardeau, Missouri, along with the Fort Wayne Daisies. Dad was pleased as punch, because he got to meet the big league star that was managing the Daisies, Max Carey. After about ten days, we headed north playing some exhibition games.

When we got to Muskegon, we went to our rooms in private homes. We went to the ballpark, and it wasn't a matter of a few days before they said there wouldn't be a team in Muskegon that year. [Muskegon later played until early June, when Kalamazoo bought the franchise.]

I was sent to Peoria, Illinois, to the Redwings. I went there, but of course I didn't know anybody there. I got along all right, and I pitched some good ball. I pitched a sixteen-inning game that we ended up losing about 2–1. It wasn't too awful long after that when South Bend traded for me. I went to South Bend, the Blue Sox, and finished out 1950 with them.

I had good stuff and everything, but I didn't win a lot of games. One of the things, of course, they bunted on me, so I developed more skill on fielding bunts and stuff like that. I got pretty good at pitching, and I stayed on with South Bend for several years [through the 1954 season].

In 1951, we had a great team, and that's when Karl Winsch came in as manager. Dave Bancroft was the manager in 1950. I was actually afraid of him [Bancroft], but I was only sixteen.

I know Bancroft wasn't real well-liked by a bunch of the ladies, because he was kind of grouchy. Some of the girls, like "Shorty" Pryer and Bonnie Baker, thought they had as much baseball knowledge as he did. Bancroft was there until the end of the 1950 season, and the next year they brought in Karl Winsch.

We had a real good team in 1951, and a lot of good pitchers. During that season at one time, Battle Creek, Michigan, the Belles, had some injuries. They borrowed players off other teams, and I was "loaned" to Battle Creek [on July 24, along with Gertie Dunn and Mary Dailey].

Guy "Mudcat" Bush was the manager there. He really gave me a lot of confidence, and in fact, he had me playing other positions [besides pitcher]. I stayed there about ten days to two weeks, and South Bend sent Jan Rumsey over and brought me back.

We went on to win the championship that year, and the next year, before spring training came up in 1952, I had a contract sent to me from Battle Creek. I signed that contract, and we went to Newton, North Carolina, for spring training. We no sooner got started with spring training than the manager said the trade [for Pauline Crawley] fell through, and I'd have to go back to South Bend. I went back to the Blue Sox for spring training, and I spent the rest of my playing career in South Bend.

Guy Bush really helped me a lot. He was a nice man, and he didn't beat you down, or anything. But I'm also glad I was with South Bend all the time I was, because they were a great team. I got along with playing ball fine, but it seemed like when I was tickled over something, Karl [Winsch], the manager, would always find a way to bring you down. I think that was his way, and I don't know why. Some of the girls bugged him, and that didn't go well.

Do you remember the incident when Shorty Pryer was suspended in 1952?

You know about the deal in 1952 when, around the last game of the season, Shorty Pryer wasn't playing, and Karl was resting her for the playoffs. But in the last inning, she had taken off her spikes and put on her loafers, or whatever, to go to the bus. Karl saw it. I don't remember whether it was Jan Rumsey or Betty Wagoner that was pitching and got on base. He called Shorty out to pinch-run, and or course, she wasn't ready. The words began. That time she talked back to him, and he told her she was done.

We got back to South Bend, and her good friends and other players decided to walk off. They tried to get the rest of us to walk off. At that age, I wouldn't do anything unless I checked with my folks. Dad said, "Certainly, do not leave. When it's somebody else's problem, you don't know the full details."

I hated to see those good players quit, but it did give me more chances, and I also got to play other positions some. The last two years, I played more first base when not pitching. I guess between Wimp, Jean, Betty Wagoner, Jette Vincent, and myself, to some extent, we were bound to win. Dad was a good aide also in telling us we could do the job.

I always tried to get along with all the players, but do know Shorty could tell you off good if you did something wrong, but she could also make me mad enough to do better. She was the ruler of that group. I don't think Lib Mahon really wanted to quit, and I think she really was sorry. I know she was sorry in later years, from visiting with her.

I wouldn't say Lib was a Pryer fan. I just think she got sucked in as did others, and they tried me. Luckily, I called my dad before I made any decisions. I think perhaps Jan and Gertie might have called their dads too. I'm not too sure on that.

What do you remember about Playland Park and the facilities for visiting teams?

The locker room at Playland was away from the stands, a separate building. I believe the umpires and managers shared that room next to the lockers. I guess they were attached, but there was no door into the locker room from there. The locker room was small, I doubt over twenty-five or thirty feet by fifty feet. Twenty or twenty-five, I would say. It had two long benches, and just passing room, the shower was to the left at the far end, no private shower, some four to six shower heads. It did have one or two toilets with doors.

Visiting teams dressed at hotels, but I've got to think there was a place they could shower to leave town after the last game of the series, unless they reserved a couple rooms for that at the hotel. I know we did that a few times when traveling.

I'm not sure when the fences were reduced for the last time, perhaps the last year. Dad put the ball over the fence toward all fields. He batted left-handed, but was not strictly a pull hitter. He could hit to the openings he saw in the defense nearly any time. Of course, he used to walk out of what would have been a batter's box, but country teams didn't worry about those things back then. One time at a practice between two playoff series, he had a "home run contest" with Karl, and Dad hit that ball out of there several times. I don't think Karl appreciated it!

Betty Wagoner got along with all players. She did not hang out with the group that went out drinking. We might all go out together on the road sometimes to eat good meals. Betty was also one of my best friends. She along with her mom and dad were a second home to me over holidays when I stayed on in South Bend to work, and play basketball. She was our player-coach, also another hillbilly from Missouri.

What else do you recall about that 1952 championship when South Bend has just twelve players?

Well, the Good Lord was with us, and we won that championship in 1952 with only twelve players. Jean Faut played her heart out, and so did the rest of us. She played third base when she wasn't pitching, and I usually played right field, when I wasn't pitching.

In one of the games I was pitching, Rockford had a runner on third base and two out, and the next batter hit me like she owned me. Karl came out and called "Time out," and for one play he put me at third base and brought Jean in to pitch to get that batter out, and we went on to win that game.

Talk about your knees knocking! I played third base when she pitched to that batter, and third base was one position I had never played. Karl wanted me to play in about halfway, and I could just imagine getting killed with a line drive, I did it, and Jean got the batter for the last out.

The league was going down by that time, and with those [six] good ballplayers that we lost, a few of them didn't even come back, and those that did went with other teams. Our team wasn't as good in 1953, and that's the year I pitched the double-header.

It was a great time in my life, and I really hated to see it end.

How did you get ready to pitch a game? I mean, what was your game-day routine?

I think most of the time by 1953, Karl would let you know the day before that you would be pitching. With less pitchers by then, you pretty well knew without being told.

I liked to trim my fingernails early the day I was to pitch. I didn't like to eat a large meal, maybe a grilled cheese sandwich, or a cheeseburger with some potato chips, or French fries, and a Coke. I just tried to take things easy in the afternoon, maybe go to a good movie.

I did more warming up to Wimp over the years, but it was Lois [Youngen] that year. I started slow, added speed as I got loose, and then threw the curves, and drops. When it was hot, it didn't take me long to get loose.

By 1953, I didn't have to run in the outfield as much after I had pitched, as I would often be taking some infield at first base, or fly balls in the outfield, and I loved to chase fly balls, so I got the running in doing something I liked. I was also a good fungo hitter, and I often hit fly balls to outfielders when I wasn't playing somewhere, or pitching.

Did you know Bonnie Baker?

Bonnie Baker was with South Bend when I first went there, but then they sent her to Kalamazoo. She was a good ballplayer, friendly, but I don't know what else I can say. As young as I was, she was naturally one of the older players, and she was quite a star. Bonnie was very serious about baseball, and later I believe she managed Kalamazoo for part of a season [1950].

Who became your friends in South Bend, like in 1951?

Wimp Baumgartner, because she had been on the tour [in 1949], and Betty Wagoner, because she was a hillbilly from Missouri. Betty's folks lived up there [in South Bend], and they became kind of like a second family to me. Gertie Dunn and I roomed together. She came there in '51. I liked Jan Rumsey and Jetty (Vincent) Mooney, she was a pitcher, and "Pee Wee" Wiley, and Lou Arnold was a big encouragement. She came back to play in '51.

Lou taught me some things about manners that she knew I appreciated. I had two older sisters, of course, but then I had three brothers, and it was always, "Fend for yourself."

In spring training, the first year Lou was there [1951], we'd get done running and everything, and we could get a ball and play catch. I'd run to the bag or the ball basket. Lou just took me by the arm and said, "Now, Sue, now there's plenty for everybody. You don't have to be in a hurry." She kind of taught me to excuse myself. My folks taught me manners, like, "Yes, Ma'am, No Ma'am," and that kind of thing, but I needed to learn to be less aggressive with my teammates.

When it came to playing ball, I guess it was kind of "Root, hog, or die" sometimes as a kid. But I appreciate Lou for that. She was older, I guess more than ten years older than several of us players, and she was like a "mother hen."

How about your time in Peoria?

I don't remember the manager's name in Peoria in 1950 [Leo Murphy was replaced by a player, Mary Reynolds, at mid-season], but I remember Faye Dancer from Peoria as much as anyone. She put Hadacol [a patent medicine] on her bat one time when she was in a batting slump. Faye was a fan pleaser, I'll put it that way. She turned her cap up, wore it backwards, but she was a good center fielder. I remember Joyce Hill, Maggie Russo, and Mary Carey gave me rides to and from the ballpark, and that was real nice.

How about Jean Faut? How would you describe her?

Jean was willing to help anybody out, to advise them. She was a quiet person in one way, but always friendly and nice. I've always kept in touch with Jean, and we enjoy our time together.

Karl, I guess, had played professional baseball and hurt this arm, and he probably kind of had a chip on his shoulder.

I know after I started playing first base some, when I wasn't pitching, Karl would hit those grounders hard enough to knock you down in practice, but I'd just stop the ball somehow. I was determined not to let him beat me.

Can you talk about memories of the 1953 season?

We had fun, we were more relaxed, but we did not have nearly the talent as years before.

As to my great memories, it would have to be pitching, and winning, both games against Grand Rapids in a double-header. Then having a "Sue Kidd Night" the next week, getting several gifts, gift certificates. Next would be getting to play first base some, especially when Amy Applegren pitched. The one downer would be Karl giving me a rough time. Perhaps I was a little big-headed, or Karl just wanted to knock me down a notch after winning those two games.

I have thought about the line-up most of the time, and it had to be Wagoner, center field, Dolly Pearson at second, Gertie Dunn at short, Jo Lenard in left, Jean Faut at third, Donna Cook in right, Amy Applegren at first, Wimp Baumgartner at catcher, and the pitcher. That's not necessarily the batting order, as Jean would have batted [higher] up in lineup. Marge Wenzell hurt her knee and didn't play.

I've always known I could have been a good hitter with more batting practice and playing time. I hit quite well at fast-pitch softball a few years later.

Can you describe the way you pitched?
I could go sidearm, but I was usually pretty much overhand, or three-quarters. I loved to throw a "drop" ball, and I came straight over on that pitch. It's not called a drop any more, but my superintendent in high school had taught it to me, and it was one of my favorite pitches.

It's funny you say that about the drop ball, because I'm left-handed, and when I was in high school, I developed a drop ball too, and now they call it a sinker.
My high school superintendent taught it to me in 1948 or 1949, because I got to play with the boys' baseball team in '49, before I went on and played professional on the tour.

I give him a lot of credit, too, because he was the one that started girls' basketball back in Clinton that I got to play. I went on and played basketball in South Bend with the Usherettes from 1953 through the 1960–61 season. We won three national championships playing boys' rules against other women's teams in the Midwest and the East. When basketball was in season, it was my favorite. When baseball was in season, it was my favorite.

But I promised my father that I would go to college. After he passed away with a heart attack, I left South Bend and came back to Arkansas to go the college in the fall of 1961.

You threw most of your pitches overhand or three-quarters, mainly a fast ball and a drop, right?
Sometimes I'd like to throw pretty much to the side and get the ball to curve in to a right-handed hitter. But that curve was the only pitch that seemed to hurt my elbow a little bit. I could throw the drop and the regular curve ball all day, but that inside [sidearm] curve would snap my elbow the other way, or something, so I didn't throw that very often, because I didn't want to hurt my arm.

What kind of pitcher was Lou Arnold?
The year she won all those games, she was strictly a reliever. She was a "junk" pitcher. I was a lot that way too. I could throw very hard, too, and that was one of my troubles with Karl. When I got two strikes, he wanted me to kind of throw at the batters' heads and "dust" them back.

But Dad had managed a Pony League team, and my brother played on it, and this other kid, Jackie Whillock, that ended up playing some in the majors, was a terrific pitcher. One day in Morillton, a little town maybe forty miles from here, they were playing, and he hit a kid in the head, "dusted" him back like that, and it killed him.

I just never could throw at a batter's head. Even if they'd hit a home run off me the time before, I just couldn't do it. You know, there were no helmets back then. I always remembered that, and I always thought Jackie would have been up in the majors sooner and would have done a lot better, if that hadn't happened to him.

Would you call your stuff hard, or a mixture?

A mixture. I threw different speeds, and I let up on the drops and the curves. I could throw a hard ball. It just wasn't my favorite, I'll put it that way.

Jean Faut could throw hard, right?

Oh, Lordy! Jean could throw hard. I hated to take batting practice against her, because she'd make that ol' bat sting your hands, especially in the cool weather. A lot of times you got it on the inside part of the bat.

Jan Rumsey could throw a hard ball, the "heaviest" ball I ever remember hitting against. I don't know why, but it just felt like it was a brick.

How about Lil Faralla?

Lil threw partly sidearm, partly three-quarter. I think she had pretty good control, but I don't remember her as well as I do the others, because she wasn't there by 1952.

You know, I didn't really didn't come out of my shell, so to speak, until 1953, because I took a lot of kidding. That's another thing I was thankful for to Lenny Zintak on that tour. I hadn't been out on my own, and I didn't know anything about professional ball. I really took a ribbing, and sometimes I was close to tears.

One day Lenny put his arm around me, and said, "Now, Sue, I want to give you some good advice." He said, "You just take this kidding and laugh it off, because that's a sign that they like you. If they didn't say anything to you, or were real derogatory, then that would mean they didn't like you." I've always tried to remember that.

I had my sixteenth birthday in early September, right toward the end of the tour, and I got on the bus that night. Lenny grabbed me and planted a big smackeroo on my mouth, kissed me big, and they began singing something like, "She's Never Been Kissed," but I was able to laugh it off. I always tried to remember what Lenny said, "When they kid you, they like you." I took a lot of kidding living up north.

At home, all I did in the summer was work around the house and in Dad's store, ride horses, play ball, and swim. So mother never bothered to get my hair curled in the summertime. On the tour, I looked like I had a bowl turned upside down on my head! So at one of the very first stops, the girls got permission from the chaperone and the manager and made an appointment somewhere, and they got my hair curled.

The girls also helped me pick out some better clothes that I could slip on, because we always had to put a skirt on, even if it was two o'clock in the morning when we got off the bus. I wore dresses to church, so they took me shopping and got my hair curled. The girls, like Wimp Baumgartner and Fran Janssen, and the bus driver, Walt Fidler, they were taking care of me. My folks were guaranteed it was a well-supervised organization and I'd be taken care of, and that was the truth. I remained good friends with Wimp and Fran, and we played basketball for the Usherettes later in the 1950s.

The bus driver, Walt, loved to sing along with those songs, he had a beautiful voice. We traveled at night, and Wimp would stand up in the front of the bus with him, and we'd sing songs all night. We had good singers on those teams!

We got to go to Yankee Stadium, right downtown in New York, and see five innings of the game, and we pulled out of there. Walt would have his window down and get those cops to stop the traffic, get out of there, make a turn, whatever. He just had that kind of personality.

How would you describe Shorty Pryer as a ballplayer?

She was a good second baseman. She and Karl did not get along. She was a little cocky, and I think he tried to take her down a notch, but she was not the kind you were gonna take down. She could come right back, and that was exactly what happened that night.

You know, there wasn't any sense of Karl putting Shorty in to pinch run. He only did it because he saw Shorty taking off her spikes with the last batter up and a runner on base. Why would he want her to pinch run, unless it was to start a ruckus?

Shorty was already perturbed a little because she wasn't in the starting lineup. She said something to Karl, and he said, "Well, I thought I'd give you a rest before the playoffs." Only Karl said it a lot stronger than that.

Karl did things like that. I remember sometimes in a game when I was pitching, as well as other pitchers, if he would have squeezed a run in, we stood a very good chance of winning the game. But he would hardly ever squeeze bunt for a lot of the pitchers. Now he would squeeze in a run for Jean. That's one thing he would do for Jean, because I guess he thought she could hold a one-run lead, and he didn't have confidence in the rest of us.

But I do remember the mumbles on the bench in certain situations, like when you've got a fast runner on third. The squeeze was a part of our game, when we had a tying run or a go-ahead run on base. Karl was funny like that sometimes. I would hear complaints from other pitchers and other players about, "Why didn't he do so-and-so," but I pretty well kept my mouth shut in those situations.

What would you say about your catchers with South Bend?

As to catchers, I would agree with Jean that Shirley Stovroff was one of the best, although she did not like my low curves, and drops, and she failed to get strikeouts for me because of this several times. Shirley did have a bad attitude, and she would get very mad at me shaking her off the fast balls, to throw a curve. She knew her weak point was the curves and low balls. Sometimes, after I kept shaking her off, she'd call time and come out to give me a rough time. Wimp was by far the best curve and low ball catcher.

Between Wimp [Baumgartner] and Lois [Youngen], Wimp was the better catcher, but not too good at throwing out runners. Lois, and Wimp too, probably needed more experience, and playing time. Shirley was also a better hitter than either of them. Wimp had an erratic arm, with the throw going into center field one time and landing behind pitcher's mound the next. I think she did have a bad finger on her throwing hand that year, which didn't help.

What about the league's final seasons of 1953 and 1954?

For South Bend, the team went downhill after the big break-up at the end of the '52 season, and I was fearful, especially in the '54 season, that it might come to an end. Even then I still had hopes into the winter that we would play again. However, that never happened.

I would have probably gone with Bill Allington's traveling team playing men's teams in the summer of '55, except Dad had his first heart attack, and I was needed at home to help run the grocery store and the small post office at Choctaw.

We still rode the bus in 1953, and I think most of 1954. However, funds must have become hard to find toward the end of the '54 season. I know cars were used some to travel to the closer games, Fort Wayne, Grand Rapids, and Kazoo perhaps. I don't think we traveled by car to Rockford.

I suppose, even though I didn't want to believe the league would end, I guess I could see it coming. As I look back, I don't remember Karl being too upset, or yelling too much, as I suppose he knew better than we that the league was coming to an end.

BETTY (PETRYNA/ALLEN) MULLINS
Grand Rapids, 1948; Fort Wayne, 1949; Muskegon, 1950
Interviewed on November 6, 2011.

Born: 1930
Height: 5'4"
Weight: 140
Positions: 3B, OF
Batted: R
Threw: R
Honors: Set new league assist record with Fort Wayne of 12 from 3B against South Bend, May 31, 1949
Career Batting Average: .139 in two seasons

Doreen Betty Petryna, who was born and raised in Liberty, near Regina, Saskatchewan, liked sports, but she didn't play fast-pitch softball before high school. The only daughter of George and Justina Petryna, both of Ukrainian descent, Betty (her mother used her middle name) grew up with three older brothers who loved baseball and hockey, two of the province's main sports. She tried softball once in the fifth grade, but girls usually didn't play ball. The family moved to Regina in 1940 when Betty was ten, so her father could take a job with the Canadian National Railway. Pert, bright, and eager, she did play softball as a freshman, because the school

From Liberty, Saskatchewan, Betty Petryna made the league with Grand Rapids in 1948, and she is pictured with the Chicks. Traded to Fort Wayne the next season, Betty set an assist record for third sackers with 12 on May 31, 1949 (courtesy Betty Mullins).

required everyone to play a sport. The coach, seeing her strong arm, put her at third base, but she had to learn the game. In the summer of 1947, after finishing grade nine, the 5'4" brunette, a right-handed hitter, and a girl friend played for a city softball team, Eilers Jewels. Betty played for the city's basketball team that winter. When the Eilers' ball club held tryouts in 1948, a scout saw the girls perform. Betty and Christine Jewett signed contracts for the All-American League, and a few days later, the girls rode the train to Opa-Locka, Florida for their great opportunity.

The league's spring training in the South was a whole new world for the young Canadians. Not only were they competing against seasoned professionals for a position in what magazines often called the "Glamour League," but they encountered a raft of new experiences, like being told on a bus ride that black people sat in the back and whites in the front. The league had ten teams in 1948, and Betty was assigned to Grand Rapids and Christine to Kenosha. Grand Rapids' starting third sacker was Pepper Paire, but later she hurt her knee, and Petryna became the Chicks' regular at the "hot corner." Not a strong hitter, she played 25 games and handled her position deftly. Blessed with her good reflexes and quick hands, she played in close, almost halfway to home plate, challenging batters to test her skills. At the end of the 1948 season, she met and fell in love with Roger Allen, who was working at a General Motors plant in Grand Rapids. Within a month they were married. After the Canadian infielder left baseball, the couple had three children and a happy marriage that lasted until Roger's death in 2000. Two years later, Betty married Don Mullins, whom she jokingly called her baseball "press agent."

Listed as Betty Allen in 1949, she was traded to Fort Wayne, but Roger kept his job in Grand Rapids, and three times he made the 200-mile drive to see his wife play ball. Playing third base for the Daisies against the South Bend Blue Sox on May 31, 1949, the Regina athlete enjoyed a memorable outing, setting a new record with 12 assists, mostly in the first four innings. Enjoying her season with Fort Wayne, she loved playing alongside Dottie Schroeder, the Daisies' fine shortstop. Off the field, Betty lived alone in a private house, and she missed her husband. She remembered playing briefly with Muskegon in 1950, but Roger was more important, so she left baseball. Afterward, the naturalized citizen coached a girls' team in her new city, DeKalb, Illinois; played on a co-ed softball team with her husband; and, starting in 1959, raised her children, Craig, Jane, and Justeen. Later, Betty earned further college credits and taught special needs children for 20 years. Still, baseball was on her mind: "I think of the league every day. Playing ball was the hardest thing for me to give up, but the excitement of being young and married took the edge off the excitement of going back, playing baseball, and living away another year."

JS: *Tell me how you got interested in playing softball when you were in school.*

Mullins: I actually started playing fast-pitch softball in grade nine at high school in Regina, Saskatchewan. One of my friends said, "Let's go try out for one of the Regina softball teams." There were two in Regina at the time. I said, "Are you going to try out?" She said, "Yeah," so I went with her. At that time, I had finished grade nine and I would go into grade ten in the fall. It was the summer of 1947. We both made one of the teams, Eilers Jewels, and I can't remember the name of the other team. We also played against two teams in Moose Jaw. I played for Eilers Jewels and went on with school, and I tried out again next year, the spring of 1948.

We were all there practicing and trying out, and unknown to me, a scout was watching our tryouts. After one game, the scout talked to three of us and offered us a chance to try out for the All-American Girls Baseball League in the States. I had never heard of that league. I was seventeen and had never really been away from home. It looked like a new world, and I was apprehensive at first.

The school asked if this gentleman could come and ask my parents about trying out in the States. My father and mother, George and Justina Petryna, who were of Ukrainian descent, thought it would be fine, partly because of how they were told the league was chaperoned. I had three brothers ahead of me that were avid sports guys — they played hockey and baseball. Those were the two big sports in Liberty, Saskatchewan, where I was born. We lived there until 1940, when I was ten, and my dad got a job in Regina on the railroad, and he thought we would have a better chance for jobs when we graduated from school. That's why I ended up in Regina.

My folks signed the form saying I could try out, and we tried out in Opa-Locka, Florida. At that time, we rode all trains. I was just in awe. The first time I ever played softball was in the fifth grade, because girls usually didn't play ball. But in high school, softball was one of the sports we had to play to get a grade. So I got another chance to play, but I had never even held a bat before the fifth grade. I got to be a third baseman, even though I didn't know anything about softball, the rules and everything, but I could throw the ball the hardest. We had a competition, and all of us had to throw the ball, and I threw the ball the farthest. Guess who got to play third base? *[She laughs.]*

When I tried out for the Regina teams with my girl friend, I wanted third base, because I was familiar with the position.

We went down to Opa-Locka, and it was a hard time for me, being away from home, but I was fortunate enough to make the Grand Rapids team. At that point, the league had ten teams, and they split the league up into two divisions. My girl friend, Christine Jewett, made the Kenosha team. I wanted her to be with me, if we made it, but she was put on another team. There were more than 200 of us there trying out, and I was fortunate to make the league.

Also in 1948, we had Cuban girls playing ball in the league. Coming from Regina, we were not used to seeing a black person or a person of any other nationality, except Ukrainian. The people were mostly English and Scottish, and I didn't know how to act around people who were colored.

One day in Opa-Locka, they gave us a day off, and the only place we could go was Miami, about 25 miles away. Opa-Locka was an old naval base. I went to Miami with my friend from Regina, Christine Jewett, and we got on the bus inside the base at Opa-Locka, where we were protected. We got on the bus first, and we went right to the back of the bus. At the next stop, a combination of all kinds of people got on the bus, black people and white people. The black people walked to the back of the bus, and they just stared at us. We were scared! We don't know what we did wrong. The seats in the back were theirs, not ours.

When we got back to Opa-Locka, the league officials told us the protocol: sit in the front of the bus, not the back. I was naïve. I thought everyone had a right to sit anywhere on a bus, and I never knew things were different in the States. We didn't have any black girls in the league, but we did have several Cubans.

How did your first year go with Grand Rapids?

I started out as utility third baseman, because the third baseman was Pepper Paire. She pulled her knee or something, because she had problems at times with her knees. So later

I got to play third as a regular, which was fortunate for me, and we won our division in 1948.

But we played Rockford for the championship. The Rockford Peaches in our league was like the New York Yankees. The league really stacked that team. Rockford had the best hitters, but the pitching was more equal, because all of the girls had to learn to pitch overhand in 1948. Grand Rapids won our division, and Rockford won theirs, and Rockford won in the playoffs.

It was just a wonderful time for me to be allowed to play in the league. It's true that you never think that what you're doing is something special. You do it because you just like to play ball. As years went by, people were bragging about the league. I never thought about it that way. I just had this warm feeling inside that I was able to play baseball, and I did it.

You know, these girls in the league were good ballplayers. What we didn't know, we were shown, I can't say really "taught," but we were shown how to make the plays right. I know for myself, I had to learn how to throw, and field, and hit. We got to be pretty good, but the only thing I couldn't do was hit the ball! *[She laughs.]*

When I think about it, I never had a bat in my hands until the fifth grade, and then how many times do you get up to bat in a game? I was never taught how to bat correctly, but I didn't really care, because I liked all the other parts of the game.

You played more than 120 games in your first two seasons, but do you remember one game above the others?

The biggest game I remember came against South Bend in 1949. *[Editor's note: The game Betty Mullins mentioned against South Bend was played at Fort Wayne on May 31, 1949, and she set a new AAGPBL record with 12 assists, at a time when the major league record for assists by a third baseman was ten. Betty threw out seven of the first eight batters on grounders to third.]*

Millie Deegan was pitching. We're just playing the game, and about the third inning, I was getting the ball hit to me all the time. In baseball, I played a very short third base. I would be in almost equal with the pitcher. I just loved it up there! I loved the drama of the batters hitting it to you. Of course, I was younger, and I could lean to the left or to the right better. I walked over to Millie and said, "Gosh, Millie — They're hitting the ball to me all the time. How come?" She looked at me and said, "Well, Betty, I'm throwing them inside!"

When Millie told me that, I started watching for the ball. If I had kept my mouth shut and just played, I would have been all right. After that, I made maybe three more outs, but then I started throwing them wide to first base, and I made two errors. I still set a league record, but I didn't realize that until the next day, when I was presented with roses at home plate. It was quite nice.

Also, I got married in 1948. I had met a gentleman in Grand Rapids who was a friend of my roommate, Barb Tetro. I met Roger Allen through Barb's sister-in-law in September. In October, I was supposed to go back to Regina, because my visa was up. Roger had gotten out of the Navy and he was working for a General Motors factory in Grand Rapids, because a friend in the Navy told him to come there for a job. Roger grew up in DeKalb, Illinois, and he moved to Grand Rapids in September, and I met him near the end of the season, and we were married for fifty-one and a half years.

We fell in love, and we didn't want to be parted, but I had to go back to Canada. I overstayed, and the government caught up with me. But they were so nice. They had a meeting with me and Roger, and we told them we wanted to get married. The man who interviewed us said, "Can't you wait?" We didn't want to wait. He said, "I'll get you one more stay, and if you get married within one month, you will get your green card." In one month, my folks came down from Regina, and his folks came from Illinois, and we got married. We lived in Grand Rapids.

When I tried out in 1949, I was hoping I'd stay in Grand Rapids, but the league allocated a lot of the girls. The teams were allowed to keep their established good players, and that was the league's rule, and that was all right. But it bothered me in 1949, because I had to leave Roger and live in Fort Wayne.

Fort Wayne had a good team in 1949, but Rockford won the championship again. The year I was in Fort Wayne, they had a problem getting a manager. They ended up getting a gentleman named Harold Greiner. He owned a tavern in Fort Wayne, and he owned a softball team. They enticed him to be the manager, and he was a good manager.

Also in 1949, the league went to a smaller ball halfway through the season. *[Editor's note: The AAGPBL switched from a 10⅜ inch circumference ball in 1948 to a 10-inch ball in mid–1949. The league's original ball in 1943 was 12 inches, and it was reduced in increment until a regulation baseball was introduced in mid–1954 during the circuit's final season.]*

I thought the change to a smaller ball would be my biggest adjustment, but it wasn't, because I could throw it better. I didn't have long fingers, so I could grip the smaller ball better and throw better. With a softball, my throws would tend to tail away, but it seemed every year the ball got a little smaller.

In 1950, we had a tryout in Indiana, maybe in South Bend. I made the Muskegon team at third base. I did play as a regular in 1949, and this was supposed to be a full year. I played two months, and all of a sudden, one day I was really missing my husband. You don't get to see your husband, because we were practicing and playing games at home or on the road seven days a week. I just said, "I can't do this again." I missed him too much in 1949. I went to the coach and said I needed to go home. Roger picked me up in Gary, Indiana, and that was the end of my baseball career. I really ached to go back, but I knew I couldn't do it anymore. I was still so young, eighteen, with no family around. About all we could do was write letters home, because it cost so much to telephone.

I still miss the league. I met a lot of nice ladies, especially Dottie Schroeder. She was like an idol to me, because of her playing ability and her sociability. At the time you often had "clique" situations, and it was hard to break into that clique, but not with Dottie — she was your friend. She had the gift of camaraderie with everyone, but she was her own person.

After baseball, I had three children with Roger: Craig, Jane, and Justeen. Our children were all athletic, especially in softball. They all three played ball through high school, and even after school, they played on city teams. Roger served in the Navy in 1946–1947, and they sent him to Panama. The New York Yankees used to train in Florida at Jacksonville, and that's where Roger was stationed at first. He was an excellent first baseman, and the Navy boys played an exhibition against the Yankees. The Yankees offered Roger a tryout after he left the Navy, but we got married, so he never tried out. You have to want to play professional ball, and he didn't want to do that. He wanted to be married and be at home. Roger passed away in the year 2000, and later I married Don Mullins. Don found out about my baseball career, and now he's my "press agent"! *[She laughs.]*

Where did you live in Grand Rapids?

The team found homes that were renting out rooms for the girls to live, and I was given a room by myself in a home. I can't remember the family's name, because I was never there enough to get to know them. You're practicing every day, and you're playing at night, and you're playing seven days a week. The room is a place to sleep in when the team is at home.

On the road, my roommate was Barbara Tetro, a Grand Rapids girl, and she may have gotten married in 1949 — I lost contact with her after I was sent to Fort Wayne.

I played for Grand Rapids that first year, and the next spring I tried out again, because you had to make the league each year. We tried out in South Bend, Indiana, and I made the Fort Wayne team as a third baseman. Dottie Schroeder played right next to me at shortstop. I felt good being able to think, "My gosh — I'm right next to Dottie Schroeder." She was a great player and a great person. It made me feel pretty important to be teammates with such a glamorous All-American League star.

Where did you live in Fort Wayne?

I also lived alone in a private house. The family had one son, and he worked for the Fort Wayne newspaper. I had a bigger bed that year, because I was married, and Roger might arrive from Grand Rapids. I believe he came three times to watch me play in 1949. It was a trip of almost 200 miles. Our car wasn't a good one, so Roger had to borrow a friend's car to make the drive. I used to be picked up to go to the games by some of the other players who had cars, but I didn't have a car. I was alone, and when Roger was there, we were just together.

The teams must have screened the homes quite well, because all of us who were put into private homes never had a problem with the owners. The people were so cordial. They would go above and beyond for the players. When you came home from a game, it would be late, and you hadn't had a chance to eat supper, so you would clean up and go to bed. The families would have "treats" for girls like me after the games.

I notice on the AAGPBL web site that your name is listed as Doreen Betty Mullins (Petryna). Is Doreen your first name and Betty your middle name?

Yes, that's right. I was born in the little town of Liberty, Saskatchewan, and all of us were born at home, and I was the youngest of seven children. After I was born, I contracted pneumonia. Mrs. Wintemute, a nurse in our hamlet, took me and two other children born the same day, and all of us had pneumonia. She took us from birth and tended to us for a month, and she named me Doreen Betty. I was well enough after a month, and my mother took me home. My nationality is Ukrainian, and dad and mom spoke Ukrainian in the home, but we all spoke English. My mother couldn't say Doreen, but she could say Betty, which she pronounced "Batty." That's all I knew through school, and when I was ten, we moved to Regina.

When I went to school in Regina, I had to bring my birth certificate. The school official who took the document said, "Your name is Doreen Betty Petryna." That's the first time I ever heard the word Doreen! Mom never was able, or wanted, to say Doreen. But as I got older and got married, Doreen Betty was my legal name, so I used it. But when I played ball, I went by Betty, because I didn't like Doreen. In our nationality, you're only allowed one name, but I had two! All of my uncles and cousins don't have middle names.

You indicated you still miss the league, so obviously your baseball experience made a big impact on your life.

I think of the league every day. Playing ball was the hardest thing for me to give up, but the excitement of being young and married took the edge off the excitement of going back, playing baseball, and living away another year.

I started to coach girls' teams here in DeKalb and Sycamore, and then we got on coed slow-pitch teams, because Roger loved to play ball. We didn't have our first child, Craig, until ten years after we were married, so we could enjoy playing ball together. But Craig came along in 1958 and Jane in 1960, and Justeen ten years later. Once we had Craig, I decided, "Playing ball has to stop. It's time to raise our family."

Thinking about Fort Wayne, the family's son who worked for the newspaper used to bring home the papers every day, so I have clippings of all of our 1949 games. Later, my daughter Jane organized all of the clippings into a wonderful scrapbook. I sent a copy to the National Baseball Hall of Fame and to the museum [the Center for History] in South, Bend, Indiana, where they have the AAGPBL archives.

I had all those clippings after I played in the league, and I put them in a box in the attic and forgot about them. As the years went by, more and more people began bringing up the league, so I went up there and looked at the old clippings. I sat there for hours looking through all of those things, like scorecards, that cost ten cents at the time. At Christmas, Jane and her husband Tom gave me this scrapbook as a gift. She looked at all of the clippings, without dates, and put them in chronological order. She laminated all the stories and memorabilia into a huge scrapbook with a wooden cover. I had copies made for all of my children, and I also sent copies to Cooperstown and South Bend. Don, my husband, carries around my baseball card. That's why I call him my press agent!

My kids didn't know I played professional ball until they were teenagers. It was just something I wanted to keep private and enjoy. The memories were mine. I love sports, and my family was sports-minded. It's in my blood. I grew up watching my three brothers ahead of me play ball. Later, I got the opportunity to play baseball professionally. I could watch baseball for ten hours and not get tired of it.

JUNE PEPPAS
Fort Wayne, 1948–1949; Racine, 1949–1950;
Battle Creek, 1951; Kalamazoo, 1951–1954

Interviewed on March 29, 2012.

Born: 1929
Height: 5'5½"
Weight: 145
Positions: 1B, P
Batted: L
Threw: L
All-Star Team: 1953, 1954
Career Batting Average: .273 in seven seasons
Lifetime Pitching Record: 18–31 with 3.54 ERA in five seasons, 1948–1951, 1954

June Peppas, a determined left-hander who came of age in Indiana, mainly in the Fort Wayne area, could have been a poster girl for the American Girls Baseball League, as the circuit was renamed in 1951. The daughter of Edna Glesing, who married George Peppas, June grew up during the Great Depression. Encouraged by her stepfather, she loved sports of all kinds, including baseball, softball, basketball, and volleyball. By the time she graduated from Elmhurst High in 1947, the teenager had played five seasons of fast-pitch softball for Bob Inn, a local restaurant owned by Harold Greiner, who also scouted for the All-American League. Greiner arranged for Peppas, a pitcher and a good left-handed batter, to try out in Chicago in the spring of 1948, and she made it. Sent to the league's spring training in Opa-Locka, Florida, the year overhand pitching was adopted, she performed well. Peppas was allocated to hometown Fort Wayne, soon managed by Greiner. At 5'5" and 145 pounds, the lefty was an attractive, multi-talented brunette who looked the epitome of the "All-American girl" playing baseball. Elaine Roth, a teammate and friend in Kalamazoo, remembered, "June had a good voice, played the piano, and when dressed up, she looked like a movie star." Always a good hitter, Peppas averaged .273 for seven years, peaking with marks of .333 and 16 home runs in 1954.

Peppas, however, traveled a rocky road to stardom. Three-quarters of the way through her rookie year, she injured her right knee, and she had surgery following the season. In 1949, she tore cartilage in her left knee, but she waited until after the 1950 season to have it repaired. Also, the southpaw had to work on improving her control. Traded to Racine in 1949, June was managed by Leo "Pop" Murphy, who allowed her to throw sidearm. The Belles moved from Racine to Battle Creek in 1951, and midway through the season, Peppas was traded to Kalamazoo. She played first base and continued taking her fifth turn in the pitching rotation, but the Lassies did not use her on the mound in 1952 and 1953. Instead, she improved her hitting and her fielding, and she was named the league's All-Star first sacker in 1953 and 1954. June's greatest highlight came in the 1954 Shaughnessy Playoffs. She had fashioned a 6–4 record in the league's final five-team season, and in the championship finals, a best-of-five playoff against Fort Wayne, Peppas won two of the Lassies' three games,

June Peppas, who started her seven-year career with Fort Wayne, joined Kalamazoo in 1951. Pictured in Lassies uniform, June became the league's All-Star at first base in 1953 and 1954 (courtesy June Peppas).

batting a sizzling .450. In the end, she pitched and won the league's last-ever game, 8–5, going 3-for-5 and driving home four runs.

However, the circuit folded after the season. Most of the players were dismayed, especially those who began in the 1950s. Peppas, energetic, outgoing, and unselfish, moved ahead, competing in sports such as golf, basketball, and volleyball, and enjoying activities like hunting, fishing, and water skiing. Soon she operated her own printing business, and later she earned bachelor's and master's degrees from Western Michigan University. Many years later, in 1980, the lefty began writing a newsletter and sending copies to former All-Americans for whom she found addresses. The newsletter grew into an AAGPBL reunion in Chicago in 1982. Five years later, June, Dottie Collins, Fran Janssen, and others formed an All-American Girls Professional Baseball League Players Association. Active in many ways, Peppas, who served one term as Players Association president, wanted to ensure that the historic league as well as the accomplishments of the more than six hundred talented women who played baseball would never again be forgotten.

JS: Where were you born and raised?

Peppas: I was born in Kansas City, but I grew up in Indiana in Marion and Fort Wayne during the Great Depression. My grandparents were from Indianapolis. My mother was born and raised in Indianapolis.

What were your parents' names?

My mother's name was Edna Glesing Peppas, and my stepfather, who raised me, was George Peppas. I took his name.

Where did you go first?

We moved to Indianapolis when I was just a baby, and we lived with my mother's parents. I remember living in Marion for a while, and then my dad and mother moved to Fort Wayne. My father was in the restaurant business, and he had a restaurant in Marion. He put one in Fort Wayne, and he decided we'd move to Fort Wayne to live. I was seven or eight when we moved there.

Where did you graduate from high school?

I graduated from Elmhurst High in Fort Wayne, and that was a county school. My folks moved out to a country place, and Elmhurst is a county school. I have one brother, George, who is twenty-three years younger than me.

Did they have sports for girls when you were in school?

Yes, we had basketball, because Indiana is a basketball state. We had basketball and softball and volleyball, and I played all of them. I was a left-hander, and I loved sports from the time I can remember, baseball, softball, or any sport I could play.

How did you first find out about the league, or were you already playing on an organized team?

From the time I was twelve until I was seventeen in 1947, I played for the Bob Inn softball team. I was a windmill pitcher. Bob Inn was the champion team in Fort Wayne, and we also won state a few times.

I graduated from high school in 1947, and I worked, and I played softball. I worked with my father in the restaurant business, and I helped Harold Greiner with the Bob Inn, which was a restaurant and a bar. In 1948 and 1949, Harold managed the Fort Wayne Daisies. He was like a father figure.

Do you remember how you first found out about the league?

Harold Greiner was a scout for the league, before he was a manager. *[Editor's note: Harold Greiner replaced manager Dick Bass, who was fired partway through the 1948 season. Greiner also managed Fort Wayne in 1949.]*

Harold got me interested, and he got me a tryout in Chicago in the spring of 1948. I made it during the tryouts, and they sent me to Opa-Locka, Florida, for spring training, and I trained with the Fort Wayne team. At the allocation, I was assigned to Fort Wayne.

What was that first season like for you?

I was a lefty, and I pitched the windmill style in softball. They wanted me to pitch overhand in baseball, and I had no control. What kept me going was that I had a good bat—I hit the ball well. About three quarters of the way through the first season, I busted up my right knee, and I missed the rest of the season. I had the knee operated on during the winter, and in 1949, I came back and played with Fort Wayne. I still had poor control but a good bat, and it was tough being a hometown player. Harold was the manager again in 1949, and he could see that my best bet was to go to another team. He traded me to Racine.

[Editor's note: Peppas played 11 games for Fort Wayne and 39 games for Racine in 1949.]

Fortunately, I had Leo "Pop" Murphy, who was a catcher in the majors, for manager at Racine. When I went there, Pop wanted me to pitch. I said, "Can't I throw the way I feel most comfortable?" He said, "I don't care how you throw the ball just as long as you get it across the plate."

I went to a sidearm motion, and I seemed to get my control better. Pop also wanted me for first base, because I had been working out with Fort Wayne as a first baseman. I took over for Marnie Danhauser, who had been the first baseman for Racine. But Marnie's bat wasn't as good, so Pop used me a lot. Sophie Kurys taught me to slide, and that really helped me. I did double duty like most of the girls. I took my turn pitching every fifth day, and the rest of the time I played first base.

You hurt your other knee, right?

I hurt my left knee with Racine in 1949, but I didn't have surgery. I played on it for a year the way it was. I had a piece of cartilage taken out of the knee after the 1950 season, and I kid you not—I have never had another bit of trouble with that left knee! After the league ended, I went back to playing fast-pitch softball, and I continued to play ball until 1968. I was also into all kinds of sports, like basketball, volleyball, bowling, hunting, fishing, downhill skiing, water-skiing, and flying. My right knee has been replaced, because I had several surgeries on it, but my left knee still maintains well.

The Belles' franchise moved from Racine to Battle Creek, Michigan, in 1951, and partway through the season you were traded to Kalamazoo, and you finished your AAGPBL career there. What positions did you play?

I played mostly first base, and I pitched a little.

Who were some of your teammates with Kalamazoo?

I played with Fern Shollenberger, and Dottie Schroeder got traded from Fort Wayne to Kalamazoo [in 1953]. We had girls like Nancy Mudge, Betty Francis, and Mary Carey. The Roth twins, Elaine and Eilaine, were there. Elaine relieved a lot, and she played longer in the league, and Eilaine played the outfield for about four years.

I believe you were an All-Star at first base in 1953 and 1954.

That was after Dottie Kamenshek was no longer playing. Nobody could play first base like Kamenshek could. She was outstanding. She was smart, and she knew the game. She was my idol. My last glove, Dot helped me break it in, and I still have that glove. Now it's bronzed. A couple of my friends decided I should quit playing ball, so they had my glove bronzed! *[She laughs.]*

You also played with Doris Sams.

Doris Sams was a real sweet person, and she would help anybody. She was also quite a golfer. In baseball, "Sammye" came in there and got things done when it was needed, and she had a good bat. She played center field when I played with Kalamazoo.

I remember there were four of us that roomed together in Kalamazoo, and Sammye was one of them. The landlady had four rooms upstairs, and each one of us would have our own room. We'd come downstairs in the morning and make our own breakfast, and Sammye would have us singing, "Good Morning to You." She had a great sense of humor! *[She laughs.]*

Starting in 1952, the league's first-place team as of July 1 played the All-Star team as selected by managers of the other teams. In 1954, the All-Stars traveled to first-place Fort Wayne's Memorial Park on July 9, and the Daisies won the game, 10–4. All-Stars pictured in the front row are (left to right): Jean Lovell, Kalamazoo; Rosie Gacioch, Rockford; Jean Smith, Grand Rapids; June Peppas, Kalamazoo; Nancy Mudge, Kalamazoo; Fern Shollenberger, Kalamazoo; Sarah Sands, Rockford; Ruth Richard, Rockford; and Wilma Briggs, South Bend. Standing in the back row: Barbara Liebrich, chaperone; Joyce Ricketts, Grand Rapids; Janet Rumsey, South Bend; Eleanor Callow, Rockford; Eleanor Moore, Grand Rapids; Dottie Schroeder, Kalamazoo; Gloria Cordes, Kalamazoo; Nancy Warren, Kalamazoo; Jeep Stoll (on crutches), Kalamazoo; and Woody English, manager of Grand Rapids (courtesy June Peppas).

The biggest highlight of your career was the 1954 playoffs when your Kalamazoo Lassies beat the Fort Wayne Daisies in five games for the Shaughnessy Championship. You averaged .450 (9-for-20) and pitched and won two of Kalamazoo's three games, including the final game, 8–5, where you allowed five hits and also went 3-for-5 with four RBIs. I covered that playoff series in my article for SABR, "June Peppas, All-American Star: Helping the Kalamazoo Lassies Win the 1954 Championship," published in The National Pastime *(2002), which is now posted on the AAGPBL web site. At that time, did you think the league was going to fail after the 1954 season?*

No, I didn't. All that winter I kept thinking, "It's coming back, it's coming back." I kept thinking I'd get a letter saying when spring training was going to start. I wasn't ready for it to quit. I was twenty-six when the league folded. It just fooled us. There was nothing there. I'm sure I was not alone in feeling that way.

You know, we had some outstanding players in our league. The Weaver sisters of Fort Wayne stand out, Betty (Weaver) Foss, Jean Weaver, and Jo Weaver, the youngest, and she was only eighteen when the league folded. Jo was phenomenal. She hadn't even reached her potential when the league ended. Jo was a great ballplayer. She scared you stealing bases— she was that fast!

As a batter, the pitcher I feared the most was Betty Wagoner of South Bend. She was a lefty, and she threw this big roundhouse curve, and as a left-handed batter, that was tough for me to hit.

Later, you went to college and earned a bachelor's and a master's degree, and you got into the printing business. You lived in Kalamazoo, right?

Yes. I worked for the Doubleday Brothers, a big printing outfit. They gave me a job in the wintertime when I was still playing ball, I think in 1952.

I didn't begin to go to college until fourteen years after I got out of high school, and I took a course or two at Western Michigan. I had been on a year and a half trip across the United States, and we got back from that trip in 1965. I came back to Kalamazoo, and I decided to go back to college. I had some credits when I attended in Fort Wayne, and I graduated with a bachelor's in vocational education around 1967.

During all these years in the 1950s, the 1960s, and the 1970s, nobody talked about the league, right?

That's about it. The All-Americans didn't get together or anything like that.

You're known as the person who organized the first newsletter and worked on the first reunion in Chicago in 1982—correct me, if I'm wrong.

We had our printing business at that time, and I got to thinking, "Whatever happened to these people?" I had a few addresses by 1980, and I knew some of the girls lived in Kalamazoo. Elaine and Eilaine Roth lived there, and Renae Youngberg lived there, and I probably had a couple of other names too. I wrote out a newsletter and sent it to the people I knew, and I said, "If you know the address of anyone who played in the All-American League, let me know." Before we knew it, we had quite a few people on our list, and I kept sending out different newsletters. I started getting contributions for the stamps, and it just escalated from there. We had our first reunion in Chicago in 1982.

Were you also involved in the formation of the Players Association?

Yes. We had a couple of people who were pretty good at that, and we decided we should start organizing. Dottie Collins was a major person in the Players Association, and

Fran Janssen was really involved. Joyce Smith, a roommate of Renae Youngberg, also worked on organizing the players. I missed an organizational meeting, and they elected me president. I served in that position for four years. We All-Americans are very proud of our accomplishments.

Did you participate in any of the making of the movie A League of Their Own?

The only time I was involved in it happened when six of us went down to French Lick, Indiana, when they were filming. We talked to Penny Marshall, and we talked to some of the actors, like Tom Hanks and Rosie O'Donnell. I never did meet Geena Davis. I think Karen Kunckel and her husband Jack did a lot of checking on whether things happened the way they showed it in the movie. I've attended some of the reunions, but the last one I went to was in Grand Rapids in 2001.

What kind of impact did the league make on your life?

Baseball and the league taught me a lot. It taught me that there are good friends around. The league is something that I'll never forget.

By the way, I remember when you gave the main presentation at our Myrtle Beach Reunion back in 1997. You brought tears to my eyes with your picture of Dottie Schroeder.

MAXINE (KLINE) RANDALL
Fort Wayne, 1948–1954
Interviewed on May 21, 2012.

Born: 1929
Height: 5'7"
Weight: 130
Positions: P
Batted: R
Threw: R
All-Star Team: 1951, 1952
Career Batting Average: .193 over seven seasons
Lifetime Pitching Record: 116–65

Maxine Kline, the ninth of ten children of William and Lily Kline, grew up in North Adams, a small farm community about ten miles northeast of Hillsdale in southern Michigan. The family lived and worked on a farm, and everyone in the little town knew each other. Active and athletic, Maxine, like other kids, played sandlot baseball during her early years. At North Adams High, the right-handed teenager, one of the tallest girls in school, excelled in basketball, and she led the girls' basketball team to three undefeated seasons. She also ran track, but North Adams had no softball team for girls, and she knew nothing about the All-American League. During her senior year, when she was playing on a local softball team, her basketball coach, Woody Wilson, heard about the league. That spring he and the school's principal drove Maxine, now 5'7" and 130 pounds, to Fort Wayne for a tryout, and she made it. Along with Wilma Briggs, a Rhode Island baseball star, Kline joined a Fort Wayne ball club that was loaded with good players but short on good pitching. Dottie (Wiltse) Collins was the team's longtime ace, but Dottie was pregnant in 1948, and she left the team after pitching her last game on August 1.

Kline, eighteen, played the outfield for Fort Wayne, because she had no coaching in softball or baseball. Partway through the season, after several injuries and with Collins planning to leave, manager Dick Bass converted Kline into a pitcher. Bass' switch worked, because the right-hander was blessed not only with a strong arm but also pinpoint control. Kline relied on her hard fastball mixed with a good changeup, and occasionally she threw a sharp curve. Jean (Geissinger) Harding, later the Daisies' second baseman, remembered that "Max" could almost always hit the catcher's glove, and that gave Daisy infielders an edge on the opponent's hitters. The tall, rangy brunette, who was normally quiet around veteran players, found it easiest to relate to teammates who grew up on farms, for example, Wilma Briggs, Dottie Schroeder, and Jean Geissinger, who was also a Michigan native. Kline worked hard to learn the techniques of pitching, including the windup and holding runners on base. She finished 8–13 as a rookie, but that was her only losing season along the road to becoming one of the league's best hurlers.

Kline matured as a pitcher in 1949, winning 14 games and no-hitting Grand Rapids, and she peaked in 1950 with a 23–9 mark and a 2.44 ERA, and she made the All-Star team

Maxine Kline, from North Adams, Michigan, began with Fort Wayne in 1948. Later respected as one of the league's best pitchers, Maxine, on right, is pictured circa 1952 with teammate Katie Horstman (courtesy Katie Horstman).

the first of four times. In 1950, manager Max Carey led the Daisies to the Shaughnessy Playoff finals, before Fort Wayne lost to Rockford in seven games. Kline continued her success, going 18–4 in 1951, 19–7 in 1952, 16–14 in 1953, and 15–7 in 1954. Considerate and respectful to teammates and fans, the standout right-hander pitched a fast-paced game, and she was tough to hit in the clutch. The ball club's president used to say, "Have no fear—Maxine is here!" After the league folded in 1954, she pitched three seasons with Bill Allington's touring All-Americans. Following baseball, Kline returned home and worked for an auto parts factory, where she met Bob Randall. They saved money for a house, finally marrying in 1973. Max enjoyed the AAGPBL Reunion in Fort Wayne in 1986, but back problems thereafter kept her from attending other reunions. She and Bob never had children, but they enjoyed working their Hillsdale farm together, until he passed away after 38 years of marriage. For Maxine Randall, her years in the All-American League changed her life forever and she treasures her friends and baseball memories.

JS: What were the names of your parents, and the names of your brothers and sisters?

Randall: My father and mother were William and Lily Kline. They had ten children, and I was number nine. Their names, starting with the oldest, are Kathryn, Celia, Nina, Viola, George, Frieda, Cora, William, Maxine, and Donna. We all grew up on the farm, and everyone in North Adams, Michigan, knew the Klines.

Where did you go to school, both elementary and high school?

I went all the way through school in North Adams. Our high school didn't have softball for girls. They had basketball and track, and I did both. We had some really good basketball teams, and we had three undefeated seasons. I also played on a local softball team. I graduated in 1948.

How did you find out about the All-American League?

I didn't know about the league, but my high school basketball coach did. His name was Woody Wilson. Coach Wilson and the Principal, Mr. DeWitt, took me to Fort Wayne for a tryout, and I made it.

What was it like being part of the Daisies? Did you have to adjust to overhand pitching in 1948?

The Daisies were a great team. As for pitching, I always threw overhand, so that didn't bother me. I started out as an outfielder, but the team had some injuries, they switched me to pitching. I always seemed to have good control. I had confidence in my ability, and I had a strong arm. I really liked throwing the fastball, but I also threw the changeup and sometime the curveball.

Do you remember where you lived in Fort Wayne and who your roommates were?

I lived at three different private homes in Fort Wayne, one on Central Drive, one on Harrison Street, and finally on Lillie Street. My roommates were Betty (Weaver) Foss when we lived on Central Drive, Wilma Briggs on Harrison Street, and Ruby Heafner on Lillie Street.

Dick Bass managed Fort Wayne in 1948. What was Bass like to play for?

Dick Bass was okay as a manager. He's the one that took me from the outfield and converted me into a pitcher.

Was the 1949 season much different from 1948, and what was Harold Greiner, a Fort Wayne man, like as the manager?

There wasn't much difference. Harold Greiner was a good guy, and everyone played hard for him.

In 1950, the Daisies had a very good record, 62–43, and they finished in second place, behind the Rockford Peaches. Max Carey was your manager in 1950 and 1951. Did Carey make a big difference in managing the team?

Max Carey was great. He was a good guy, and he sure knew how to teach baseball. We all played hard for him, and he did make a difference.

In 1950 and 1951, you had some big hitters, like the Weaver sisters and Wilma Briggs. What can you tell me about Betty Foss and Jo and Jean Weaver?

Everyone liked those girls. I liked them too, because they came from the farm, like me. They were great players. I sure was glad they played for Fort Wayne, because I would not have liked to pitch to them. They could really hit and run. Thank God they were on the same team with me! We would talk about farm life, but most of the rest of the gals didn't know what we were talking about.

In 1950, you enjoyed your biggest winning season with a record of 23–9. What helped you win so many games?

We had so many good players like the Weaver sisters, Vivian Kellogg, Tiby Eisen, Dottie Schroeder, and Wilma Briggs, to name some of them.

Who was your favorite catcher?

Rita Briggs. All of our catchers were good, but Rita was better, because she got right after you if you made any mistakes.

You were good friends with Wilma Briggs too. How would you describe her?

Wilma was one of my best friends. She came from the farm like me, and she was a good player and a good friend to this day.

In 1952, Jimmy Foxx managed Fort Wayne. How was Foxx different than Max Carey?

They were both good at teaching you the game, and I loved playing for both of them.

In 1953 and 1954, you had Bill Allington, the former Rockford manager, as manager of the Daisies. What was it like to play for Allington?

I didn't like him as well, but I always did my best for the team. After the league went out of business, I still loved playing baseball, and I joined Allington's touring All-Americans for three seasons.

How did you get around town and to the games in Fort Wayne?

I rode the city bus for a couple of years, and then I bought my own car.

Did it seem like the Daisies were losing fans and the league was going downhill during your later years?

I didn't think the league changed that much in the years that I played. In the later years, yes, the league did seem to be going downhill, maybe because of TV. But we always had our fans in Fort Wayne.

All of the Daisy players knew Dottie Schroeder. What was she like as a ballplayer and a person?

Dottie was my road roommate. She was a great person to know, and she also came from a farm. She was a good player and a good person. I'm glad that I knew Dottie and could play on the same team with her.

What can you tell me about Vivian Kellogg?

Vivian and I were the best of friends. I'd say the same about Kelly as I said about Dottie. They were both good as players and they were good persons. They were the two players I wanted to watch and be like.

You and Jean (Geissinger) Harding both came from Michigan. What about Jean?

Jean Harding lives about 18–20 miles from me. We talk often. Jean was a great ballplayer, a true friend, and a great person to know. I'm glad to have her as a friend.

How about Katie Horstman?

Katie was also a good all-around player.

Did you play most of your home games at Memorial Field in Fort Wayne?

We played all of our games at Memorial Field when I was with the Daisies. I never played at the [North] high school field.

The league played its final season with five teams in 1954. What was it like when they switched to the regulation baseball in the middle of the 1954 season?

The regulation ball was hard for me. The ball was nine inches instead of ten inches, and it made it harder for me to throw the pitches where I wanted.

Do you have favorite memories about the Daisies?

I have so many good memories that I couldn't tell you all of them. One time after a game we won, the whole team got me and threw me in the lake, and I came up under the dock and cut my nose! We were a close team.

Would you say the league made a big impact on your life?

Yes, it did. The league helped me learn how to get along with people, and most of all, being in the league and with the Daisies helped me learn how to dress. Remembering the league makes me think about all of the players, the fans, and the people I got to meet. The league did a lot of good for me, and it's something I will never forget.

What did you do after baseball?

I worked in an auto parts factory, Jonesville Automotive Products, making gas, oil, and brake lines for 20 years. That's where I met my husband, Bob Randall, and after we were married in 1973, we worked the farm together. We never had any children.

Bob was a true friend and husband. He was really a great person to know. Everyone loved him, because he was a really good guy. We were always together wherever we went. I surely was lucky when he came to the factory to work. From that day on we just knew we would be together. Our 38 years was too short.

Did you go to any of the AAGPBL Reunions?

We went to the one in Fort Wayne in 1986. After that, my back gave out, so I didn't go to any more reunions, but I sure miss seeing and talking to the gals.

I'm sure you have seen the movie, A League of Their Own. **What would you say about it?**

It's a good movie. It doesn't show what we really were able to do on the field, so I'd say some of the movie is realistic and some of it isn't.

EILAINE ROTH
Peoria, 1948–1949; Kalamazoo, 1950–1951
Interviewed on October 12, 2011.

Born: 1929
Height: 5'1"
Weight: 107
Positions: 2B, 3B, OF
Batted: R
Threw: R
Career Batting Average: .200 in four seasons

Eilaine Roth (1929–2011) and her twin Elaine, one of ten sets of sisters who performed in the All-American League, graduated from Isaac Elston High School in Michigan City, Indiana, in 1946, when Elston's graduating class had nine sets of twins! The second and third daughters of Herman and Elsie Roth, the girls had an older brother and sister, Harold and Althea. The Roth twins excelled at any game they played, including soccer, field hockey, volleyball, and basketball. For softball, Elston didn't field a girls' team, so they played recreation league ball, even after graduating. In 1948, Elaine, the elder sister by a few minutes, and Eilaine received their greatest opportunity when the All-American League invited them to spring training at Opa-Locka, Florida. Would-be poster girls for the league, the blue-eyed blondes were allocated to Peoria. Eilaine, 5'1" and 107 pounds, was a utility outfielder, playing 16 games and hitting .235. Elaine, one inch taller and the same weight, was a right-handed pitcher, and she fashioned an 18–15 record. Despite the league switching to overhand hurling, "E" Roth pitched underhand until mid-1949, when the 10-inch ball was introduced. In 1950, she was traded to South Bend.

The attractive sisters were talented, all-around athletes. "We used to have a lot of fun on the bus," Eilaine remembered, "going to the different cities. We'd get to the hotel, unpack, sleep a couple of hours, and then we'd be out on the diamond, practicing and playing baseball. We met a lot of good people, and we had a lot of good memories from the 'olden golden' days."

Eilaine, or "I," who played mainly the outfield, was versatile enough to play any infield position, if the team needed her to switch. She got into 91 games for Peoria in 1949, but her average slipped to a career low of .191, and Elaine's pitching ledger fell to 4–12 as she adjusted to the new red-seamed ball. A good team player, Eilaine was traded to Kalamazoo in 1950, and she spent two seasons with the Lassies. In 1951 Elaine was swapped to Kalamazoo, where she pitched four more seasons. Eilaine, however, found a job at a paper company in Kalamazoo after the 1950 season. Following the 1951 season, the company stated if

Eilaine, or "I," Roth, pictured with Kalamazoo in 1950, stands beside her twin and teammate, Elaine, or "E," who is on the left (courtesy Eilaine Roth).

she returned to baseball in 1952, she would lose the job. Eilaine's legs were bothering her, and knowing she had to support herself, she kept the job. Before long, the younger Roth twin found a better job with a pickle factory, and after 16 years there, she worked 21 years for Upjohn Pharmaceutical in Kalamazoo. Elaine, who hurled for the Lassies through the 1954 season, began working for Upjohn shortly afterward, and she helped her sister secure a position of her own with the firm.

The league made a big impact on the sisters' lives, and they cherished their baseball years. Indeed, they played industrial league softball for years in Kalamazoo, Eilaine for a few years and Elaine until she was seventy-five. Neither twin married, but later they enjoyed spending time at a summer home near Long Lake in Michigan's Lower Peninsula. "E and I were real close," Eilaine recalled, "but we were bashful and reserved, you know, when we started playing in 1948. Playing ball with these other women helped us grow up and develop. It was so nice to be able to get along with all the kids." Eilaine had a bit part in the movie *A League of Their Own*, which returned All-Americans to the public eye. The spirited sisters enjoyed hearing from fans, going to AAGPBL Reunions, and reliving memorable times from their endless summers together.

JS: I would like to get your baseball story, but I also want to ask about your sister Elaine, who passed away. You grew up together in Michigan City, Indiana, and you played ball together, right?

Roth: We played softball in high school, and a couple of years later, we got connected with the All-American League in 1948. We went to spring training at Opa-Locka, Florida, and Peoria took us.

We graduated from Isaac Elston High School in Michigan City, in 1946, and there were nine sets of twins in our graduating class! They didn't have softball in high school, so we played softball in a local recreation league for girls. Later, my sister Elaine played senior softball in a recreation league until she was seventy-five. I quit in the 1950s because of my knees.

But E and I did play lots of sports. We played on the high school girls' teams for soccer, field hockey, volleyball, and basketball, but no softball. We were into everything that girls could do. We kept going in sports, and later we played in the industrial leagues when we had jobs.

When we went to Opa-Locka in 1948, we were very bashful kids, me and Elaine. But we soon got into it with the league. We had a real good time. We used to have a lot of fun on the bus, going to the different cities. We'd get to the hotel, unpack, sleep a couple of hours, and then we'd be out on the diamond, practicing and playing baseball. We met a lot of good people, and we had a lot of good memories from the "olden golden" days.

What about the rest of your family members?

My father was Herman Roth, and my mother was Elsie. My brother Harold was the oldest, and I had an older sister, Althea. Elaine was born first by a few minutes, so I was the "baby" of the family.

Going back to the league, where did you live in Peoria?

Six of us lived in a big house, and we called it "Loudie Mays." Elaine was there, and Joyce (Hill) Westerman was there, but I don't remember all the others.

Did you play your games at Peoria Stadium?

Yes, we did play at Peoria Stadium. It was a softball field, and they turned it into a diamond for our baseball games.

I could play every position, but mostly I played third base and the outfield. In 1948, I only played when somebody was hurt. I wasn't a regular that first year.

Your sister Elaine was a right-handed pitcher.

Elaine was a real good pitcher. She started out as a relief pitcher, but soon she became a starter. She was a pitcher for all six of her seasons. We both batted and threw right-handed. We were identical twins, and I was a few minutes younger. Elaine was a little bit heavier than me, but we both had blue eyes and blonde hair. I'm still into watching baseball, and living in Michigan, I watch the Detroit Tigers. I live in Springfield, which is next to Battle Creek.

You played for Peoria in 1948 and 1949, and you were traded to Kalamazoo in 1950.

I went to Kalamazoo, and they had Bonnie Baker for the manager. Bonnie was perfect for the job. She did drink a lot of Cokes! She was really nice to play for, and we really liked her. We played in Kalamazoo at an old softball field.

Elaine was also traded in 1950, and she played that season for the Blue Sox. In 1951, she was traded to Kalamazoo, and she played for the Lassies through the 1954 season.

We got together again in 1951, but I quit after that season. I had a job in a paper company in the winter in Kalamazoo, and they said, "If you quit this job and go back to baseball, you're going to lose this job." My legs were getting bad, so I decided to keep the job. I did play softball after that in an industrial league for a few years. I worked in the pickle company for sixteen years, and I worked for Upjohn Pharmaceutical in Kalamazoo for twenty-one years. Elaine worked at Upjohn for thirty-two years before she retired. We worked in the same building, but not the same department. Today Pfizer owns that business.

Did you remember any differences in playing for Kalamazoo instead of Peoria?

The only difference was the manager. Leo Schrall was the manager we had in Peoria, and in Kalamazoo, we had Bonnie Baker the first year, and we got Norm Derringer in 1951. But they all did a good job.

Did you live in a private house in Kalamazoo?

We lived in an apartment building, but there were only two of us in a small apartment. We didn't have a house like we did in Peoria.

Do you have favorite memories from the league?

One day I was playing right field, and the batter hit me a fly ball with a runner on third base, and I threw the ball all the way over the backstop, instead of throwing it to the catcher. I remember that very well! I don't know whether we lost the game, or not.

Mainly what I remember is we all had a good time together. The girls got along great, and the chaperones did a fine job. They kept us going. The chaperones lined up the places where we lived. Otherwise, we would have had a real hard time finding a place to live.

Everything worked out real well for me. Some of the girls drank at the parties, and I never did much of that, but we all had a good time in the league.

Would you say the league made a big impact on your life.

Definitely. E and I were real close, but we were bashful and reserved, you know, when we started playing in 1948. Playing ball with these other women helped us grow up and develop. It was so nice to be able to get along with all the kids.

In my last year with the Lassies, I remember Jean Lovell, and she was a heavy-set person but a good catcher. Dottie Schroeder was our shortstop in Kalamazoo, and she was a really nice person. She was a real nice lady, and kind of funny — she'd bring up some jokes. Alice DeCambra was the real comic of the bunch. She was with the Redwings when I was there, and she came to Kalamazoo when I did in 1950. They're all gone now, but we really liked all of those people.

The bus rides seemed long to us, like riding the bus to Rockford, Illinois, was a long trip from Kalamazoo. Those buses aren't anything like the buses today. We used to sing on the bus, and we played cards. Quite a few of the girls played cards to pass the time. Dottie Mueller, who was a tall pitcher with us in Peoria, liked playing cards. She'd go to bars on the road to play cards. I have a lot of good memories from baseball, and I can't say a bad word about any of the girls.

Kids nowadays don't realize how nice it is to be able to play in a softball league in high school. We didn't have that when we went to school.

Did you have one of the parts in the movie, **A League of Their Own*?***

Playing in the league was a great experience for me, and the movie brought the league in front of the public. At the very end of the movie, when they're giving the credits, we were playing a baseball game, the "old-timers," some of the real players, and Jayne Krick, a big red-haired girl batting for the "Blue" team, kicked dirt at the umpire. I was the catcher on the "White" team, and I was the one who ducked away so she wouldn't hit me! You can only see me for a second, and that was the first time I caught. They said, "We need a catcher," and I volunteered, and I ran out there and put on the equipment. That movie was a lot of fun, too.

DORIS SAMS
Muskegon, 1946–50; Kalamazoo, 1950–53
Interviewed on July 1, 1997, in Knoxville at the home of Doris Sams.

Born: 1927
Height: 5' 9"
Weight: 145
Positions: P, OF
Batted: R
Threw: R
All-Star Team: As pitcher and outfielder, 1947, 1949; as outfielder, 1950, 1951, 1952
Player of the Year: 1947, 1949
Led League: Batting: 1949, with .279 average, and Home Runs, 1952, with 12
Pitched Perfect Game: Defeated Fort Wayne Daisies, 2–0, on August 18, 1947
Career Batting Average for 9 Seasons: .290
Career Lifetime Pitching Record: 64–47 for 6 seasons

Doris Sams (1927–2012) was a natural athlete as a young girl, and her great talent and folksy temperament, despite her shyness and humility, led to her successful career as one of the top stars of the All-American League. A down-home Southerner and the daughter of RJ and Pauline Sams, "Sammye" excelled at softball, marbles, badminton, and any other game girls could play. In 1938 at age eleven, she joined Nelson's Café in a league sponsored by Knoxville's Recreation Department, and the team won half a dozen state titles. After the first two championships, Pepsi Cola bought the team, and the bespectacled brunette kept proving she could pitch, hit, and field with top ballplayers, regardless of age. Also in 1938, she won the Southern Appalachian Marbles Tournament, making her the first girl to qualify for the national tournament in Chicago. She didn't win in Chicago, but her acclaim spread in Tennessee. Sammye also won the Knoxville singles and mixed doubles titles in badminton, and she was adept as a swimmer and a diver.

From Knoxville, Doris Sams, an all-around athlete who could pitch, play the outfield, and hit with power, became one of the league's perennial All-Stars and a two-time Player of the Year. Doris is pictured with Kalamazoo circa 1950 (courtesy Doris Sams).

Doris asked for a tryout when two teams toured through Knoxville in May 1946, following the league's spring training camp in Pascagoula, Mississippi. Sams, who was 5'9" and 145 pounds at age twenty, made the league and was allocated to Muskegon, a new ball club in the circuit's first eight-team season. Switching between the mound and center field, the sidearming right-hander, who also batted right-handed, posted an 8–9 record for the Lassies. But in 42 games, Sammye, who swung a quick bat during her eight stellar seasons, hit .274, a remarkable average for a rookie in the veteran-dominated AAGPBL. Loaded with young players, Muskegon finished in fifth place with a 52–60 record, but in 1947, the team improved greatly and captured first place with a 69–43 ledger. However, the youthful Lassies stumbled in the playoffs, losing to Racine, but Grand Rapids defeated the Belles to win the Shaughnessy Playoff Championship. The Lassies never won a playoff title. Declining fan interest led the franchise to shift to Kalamazoo, Michigan, in June 1950, but the hard-hitting Sams kept improving.

By the time she left the league after the 1953 season, Sams' achievements could have filled a highlights film. On August 18, 1947, she pitched a perfect game, defeating Fort Wayne, 2–0. Calling her performance far less than "perfect," Sammye credited the fielders with a host of fine plays. Still, the likeable Lassie finished 1947 with a 20–8 record, and she averaged .280, fourth best in the league. She made the postseason All-Star team, and she was voted Player of the Year. Sams won the award again in 1949 when she won the batting crown at .279, making her and Jean Faut the only two-time MVP winners in league history. A perennial All-Star, Sammye won the honor in 1947, 1949, 1950, 1951, and 1952, the year she set a new home run mark with 12 while batting .314. Aided by the livelier 10-inch baseball introduced in mid-1949, she batted more than .300 during her last four seasons, averaging an impressive .290 lifetime. Hindered by a lingering illness in 1953, her last season, Sammye batted .312 with just one home run, but she belted another homer off Beans Risinger of Grand Rapids in the Shaughnessy Playoffs. Risinger fanned Sams in her final at-bat. When Doris retired from the renamed American Girls Baseball League to work as a computer operator for the Knoxville Utilities Board, she knew the girls' circuit was about to end. Bright, talented, and witty, Sammye, who loved her years in the league, said after our 1997 interview, "Stick with me, and you'll be walking in tall cotton!"

JS: Why don't you tell me how you got started playing ball?

Sams: My dad played semipro ball. He got married, so he couldn't go any further with baseball. He had his family to take care of. I feel like I played ball since day one, out here on the fields with my brothers, Paul, and Bob Jr. (or RJ).

What were your parents' names?

My father was RJ [Robert J.] and my mother was Pauline Sams. I played ball with my brothers since the day I could remember. And I played football with a whole bunch of groups out here. I loved football about as well as I did anything. I got to be about twelve years old, and I quit football. *[She laughs.]*

A fella around here got groups of us together playing ball. He said, "Sams, you need to go to the city recreation with the city softball players, because you're a better player than most of these girls." Sure enough, one of those city teams picked me up, and I started pitching for them.

Is that where the picture was taken that you showed us?

Yes.

I started pitching when I was eleven to girls who were a good five, six, seven years older than I was. We ended up winning about six or seven state championships.

What was the name of that team?

I started out with Nelson's Café. Pepsi Cola Company took over the team after we'd won two or three championships, and I stayed with Pepsi Cola until 1946, and that's when I got into pro ball.

Did you play sports in high school?

No, I didn't play sports in high school, because I was involved with those gals in the city.

I got into badminton when I was about fourteen or fifteen. I won the city singles and the city ladies doubles and the city mixed doubles, all in the one year. I love badminton. If you get somebody that can play badminton, you've got somebody that can move. That's the fastest game I've ever played. I beat a few of those birds, you know! *[She laughs.]*

Where did you go to high school?

I went to Knoxville High School. That was another high school up the street, but I wanted to go across town, for some reason. We had city and county schools back then. If you lived in the city, you went to the city school. If you lived in the county, you went to Youngs High.

The way I got involved with the All-American League was that a kid who went fishing with my dad, he was about fourteen years old, came over here one day. He said, "Doris, I heard on the radio that there's going to be two professional girls baseball teams pass though here."

I said, "I never heard of it," and I hadn't. It turns out they were touring back after spring training.

"What you need to do, they said, is go over to the hotel and talk to the manager."

Well, I'm still kind of backwards, you know, and I thought, "Why, I won't do that."

This friend of mine was with me, and she said, "Come on, we're going over there."

I went over there, knocking on that door, and I took a big, deep breath. This guy comes to the door, and I introduced myself, and I said, "I play softball around here, and I want a tryout."

He said, "Well, are you any good?"

Now he swears I said this, but I don't believe I did. He claimed I looked him right in the eye, and I said, "I hit a home run about every time I get up." I never have forgotten him telling me that! *[She laughs.]* He was the Racine manager. Leo Murphy was his name.

It was raining cats and dogs here, and I knew there wasn't any way I could try out with them. Leo Murphy said, "Get on the bus with us, and come on down to Chattanooga." That's where they were playing next. I went down there and tried out, and he said, "Go back home and get you some clothes and meet us in Michigan."

I'd never been away from home in my life, and I still can't figure out how I just went right through it. Of course, I was homesick the first year.

So you got on a bus and went to Michigan?

No, I think I flew to Michigan from Knoxville.

That must have been the first time you flew on an airplane.

Yeah, that's probably true. I've forgotten how I got there. I may have walked, I was so excited! *[She laughs.]* I may have gotten homesick like everyone else, but I thoroughly enjoyed every blame day of it.

So you started out with Muskegon, the Lassies?

Yes, they were a brand new team in 1946. Later, Kalamazoo bought the whole Muskegon team. I played on the same team for the eight years I played.

When did you graduate from high school?

In January of 1945.

I got a good story for you. I didn't have a job, so I was looking for one in '46. I went into this studio, Manzer's Studio, and there was just the one girl there, and she was back in the back room trying to get a baby to shut up so she could take a picture. That was when they had these cameras sitting up, and you pulled the film out and stuck it in again, and when the kid looks good, you punch a bulb. But she couldn't get that baby to hush. She came out front and said, "Just sit down. I'll get with you after a while."

That baby wouldn't hush, so I started crying like a baby. When I did that, she got some of the best pictures of that baby, and she said, "Are you looking for a job?"

I said, "No, not really. I came up here to get my picture taken, but I'll take a job with it." So that's how I got my job, and I worked several years with her, after I came back here from playing ball. She's the one who called me "Sammye," so I carried Sammye up to Michigan with me. She said, "Come on back. You can work for me when you get back."

So you flew up to Michigan about the time the season started. Where did you live in Muskegon?

I don't remember the street, but you know they took us into private homes. There was three of us in that house, and I had a bedroom, and the other two girls had a bedroom. There was three of us off the team that went into one dwelling. One was Nancy Warren, and I don't remember the other one now.

Did you live with families the whole time, or did you move into an apartment later?

No, we lived with families. We were always in a private home. The room was about all you had, but then you weren't there half the time, and you were always eating out. You just had a room to sleep in, and we were gone just about every other week. I believe $5 a week was what it cost. That was big money. That was about like my salary!

What was your salary?

I think it was around $65 or $70 [a week] when I started.

That was a pretty good paycheck.

That was twice what I was making down here "crying like a baby"! *[She laughs.]*

What do you remember about that first season?

I thought I was a pretty good ballplayer, until I got up there. They sat me on the bench for about three weeks. All they let me do was pitch batting practice. I was getting a little perturbed. I thought, "I did pretty well back home. How come I can't pitch up here?"

Finally, I was sitting there on the bench one night, and we were getting beat, 7–0. Of course, I'm just sitting there watching the game. I felt like I ought to be out there playing.

The manager says, "Okay, Sams, warm up." I was shocked. I thought, "What the heck? We're already down seven runs. I don't have anything to worry about." I went out there and started pitching some pretty good ball, and we like to beat that team. I don't remember who they were, but from there on in, I got into my little pitcher's round. I realized maybe I could pitch a little.

Who was the manager?

It was Buzz Boyle. He was the first manager I had. Then I think Bill Wamby [Wambsganss] came in. I'm not good at talking about myself, but once you get me wound up, I'm full of it! *[She laughs.]*

I had three different ways of pitching underhand. I had the figure-eight, you know the one that comes around here [she demonstrated] and flips around. Then I had the sort of a submarine. I was a natural sidearmer. I came real low with that submarine, and I threw the "rise" ball. Then I had the windmill, and that's all they're pitching today.

One day we were playing Grand Rapids, and by the way, when I first hit that league, all I heard was, "Connie Wisniewski," and she was with Grand Rapids. I thought, "If you can beat Connie, you've got it made." We were playing the Chicks, and we were leading them by one run. I walked a batter, and she stole second, and she ended up on third with two out. We were about to get beat, and that was the last inning.

I thought, "Well, nobody's ever seen me really pitch this windmill, and I'm going to try it on this gal." I had two strikes on her, and I went around about six times and released it, and the ball just happened to hit the heart of the plate, and she's still standing there, holding the bat! *[She laughs.]*

Of course, I was a little dumfounded myself, but that sure was planned! I don't think I threw that windmill over three or four times, but every once in a while I'd catch somebody. I could never get it over all the time — that was my problem, because I didn't pitch it that often.

So mostly you pitched that figure-eight delivery.

When you come around with that figure-eight, you come around like this [she demonstrated again], and you get a lot of backspin, so you get batters hitting a lot of pop flies. That's what I pitched here in Knoxville all the time.

But I was a natural sidearmer, and when they put me in the outfield, my catcher just called me everything. When I was throwing from the outfield, I threw the awfulest curve you ever saw. That was my natural throw, but when they went overhand, they liked to kill me. That's when I quit pitching, because it liked to tore me up my arm. I just couldn't throw overhand. Of course, I got tired of pitching anyway, because I wanted to play all the time.

When you weren't pitching, you played in the outfield?

They started me out in right field. I was always pretty good at shagging flies, so I ended up in center field. In center field, you have to get a good jump on the ball.

Do you remember going to Havana in the spring of 1947?

I sure do.

Can you talk about what it was like to go to Havana?

It was hot as Hades, for one thing. It must have been 110 over there. *[She laughs.]* It was interesting. I'd never been everywhere, really, except for Muskegon. *[Laughs again.]* Havana was real good. Those people were just bug-eyed. They just couldn't believe women could play ball like that!

They sell this pineapple, halves and quarters, on the street. I'm standing there one day trying to get my money out, about quarter or fifty cents for this pineapple piece. One of those Cuban guys came by and took a big bite out of it and just kept going, while I'm fumbling around trying to get my money! *[She laughs.]*

I have one picture that shows all of the teams walking down these stairs in front of the University of Havana Library.

I do remember that.

You played some games there, right?

Yes, but the biggest thing I remember was the heat. I don't like heat.

Most of the women I've talked to say they had a lot of fans come out to watch them.

Oh yeah, we had huge crowds.

I've got a picture of little "Shorty" Pryer and Jo Lenard and myself there, and you know, we had knee socks. It was so durn hot in Cuba that I rolled mine down. They took a picture, and gosh, that thing went all over heck and half of Georgia in the news. Boy, Max Carey and a bunch of 'em weren't happy. I was standing there with my socks rolled down, and I was supposed to be in uniform. They had a few words to say about that, but it was a little late. They informed me it shouldn't be done. That scared me, you know. I thought, "Here goes my ball career!"

In 1947, Muskegon made the playoffs, right?

I'm thinking that was the year we were in the playoff and we were going to play Racine, and they beat us. We were so sure of that playoff, because we beat Racine down the road all year. We just fell apart, youngsters, you know, in the playoffs.

In that particular Racine game, one of 'em in which I got beat, somebody hit a line drive at me, and I threw my wrong hand, I'm right-handed. I threw my bare hand out there, and that ball hit it. And I'm not kidding, that hand swelled up in nothing flat, and they had to take me out of the game. Of course, I'd already lost it for Muskegon.

Racine beat Muskegon in the playoffs, but Muskegon had the best regular season record [69–43] in 1947.

We had beat Racine like a drum all year.

Grand Rapids won the playoffs. GR beat Racine in seven games. I think one of Racine's best pitchers at that time was Anna May Hutchison.

Right, she was a pretty good pitcher. She was an "iron horse" for them.

Who were the pitchers on your Muskegon team?

We had Nancy Warren, and Erma Bergmann, and Tex Fischer. Tex played shortstop, and then she'd pitch, once in a while. She and I pitched a lot alike. We just sort of had a fast ball and all that stuff. When we got into doubleheaders, we were in trouble. The teams would get used to hitting the same kind of pitching.

I told Tex, "It's your turn!" *[She laughs.]*

Tex was quite a fielder. The perfect game that I pitched, I believe it was in 1947. I was reading about that no-hitter, but they hit me like a drum. But it was just one of those days when everybody's on their toes. The batters were hitting line drives. The pitcher doesn't do it — let's face it. The batters were hitting line drives and everything else, and the girls were making unreasonable catches on that day.

The last ball that was hit, they put a little ol' pinch-hitter in there, and I knew I had a perfect game. And I thought, "Oh, no, watch this." I threw one in there, and she hit that thing back at me like a bullet, and it took one hop, and I couldn't get it. That ball ricocheted up in the air, and Tex come running in from shortstop, and caught it, and threw it to first base to end the game. I mean, we had everybody out there run to death!

Pitchers and quarterbacks get all the credit, but you're nothing without those people behind you.

What you're saying is your team played really good defense.

Everybody was on their toes. I mean, everything that was hit was caught. When you're getting hit hard, and the fielders keep coming up with the ball, well, golly! Everybody was clicking. Then you read it in the paper, "Look what a great game Sams pitched." It's a joke!

I've always said this: A lot of ball playing is luck. You just happened to be in the right place at the right time. The guy over here could have done the same thing, if he'd have been there. Everybody can be beat, one time or the other.

Were you surprised when they chose you Player of the Year in 1947?

Gosh, yes. I'm just up there playing. I wasn't trying to break records. Sometimes I can't believe the stuff I'm reading [about myself]. People get to writing this stuff, and pretty soon

Doris Sams, on left, watches as Alva "Tex" Fischer fakes a radio broadcast, with Jo Lenard smiling in approval. It turned out that the microphone was live, and folks in the stands heard Fisher's comments (courtesy Doris Sams).

they've stretched it so far, you don't know which is right and which is wrong. When you get older, you know, it sounds better! *[She laughs.]*

The Player of the Year in 1948 was Audrey Wagner. In 1949 you were Player of the Year. By 1949, you weren't pitching, right?

I pitched a year when they went to overhand, and then I said, "If you want me to play two positions, I want two salaries." You know what they did there. I went to the outfield.

Who do you remember as some of the better hitters while you were playing?

Audrey Wagner, she could put it out of there. Jean Faut was a good hitter. I'll tell you Jean Faut was a heck of a good third baseman too.

You played through the 1953 season.

The league was going. I could see that. You know, somebody wanted to buy that whole league and take it to Oregon. The league was just getting worn out there in the Midwest. The league lasted twelve years. Some "big dog" wanted to buy it, I believe in 1953, and he made a big offer, but I don't know what it was. He would take all the teams and take them to Oregon, out in that direction. I believe the league would still be going if that had happened.

By 1953, I believe the attendance was down.

The men [in the major leagues] were back, that's what killed it. Television was here. The men had the money, they worked in the factories. But we drew fans for a while!

We had a lot of little ol' girls, Junior Lassies, coming out, and we'd teach them on Saturdays sometimes. They had little uniforms like we did, with little skirts and little hats. Boy, they were mean looking, ready to romp! *[She laughs.]* They just worshipped you, really. They were six or seven years old, "Oh, I want to play, I want to play!" I really miss it.

What was it like to travel around? Did you go on a bus?

We rode a bus, and we pushed it, half the time — an old beat-up bus. It wasn't as good as a school bus. We'd be out there, two or three o'clock in the morning, shoving, trying to get that bus to go on up the road.

That's one reason I quit, and I could have quit two or three years sooner. I was so long-legged, I couldn't get comfortable on the buses. If you had any height at all, you couldn't get comfortable back then on buses. Half of the buses didn't run good. We had maintenance on them all the time. We had a great bus driver, and we had a lot of fun on it, but we fussed about it.

Then you would stay in a hotel when you went on a trip.

We all stayed in the same hotel, and they tried to get us all on one floor, if they could. It was easier for the chaperone. *[She laughs.]* We didn't want to run her to death, you know.

We had a great chaperone. They did have their jobs to do. You know, we used to sit in the dressing room before a ball game, and so-and-so's got a bad arm, and you got a bad leg, and somebody else is hurting back here in the back. You'd be sitting there rubbing each other, you might say, and the chaperone's back there working on somebody else. Somebody was hurt all the time. It was really comical. We'd just massage each other, trying to wrap ankles and all.

We had Helen Hannah, an ex–Marine. She was trained well. Helen is still around. She'll be at the 1997 All-American Reunion, I'm sure. Her dad was a big ballplayer in California. Now she'll have a story for you.

What are some of your favorite memories?

I got a picture in the scrapbook one time in Muskegon showing Tex Fischer and Jo Lenard and myself sitting there in the dugout, and the game was going on, you know. Some guy was right above us with a microphone, the radio, sort of broadcasting. He just dropped that thing down there, and we thought it was dead. Boy, you ought to have heard Tex, telling about the game and everything. They took a picture of us. We had a lot of fun!

I ended my whole career in 1953 like this. Three men on base, two outs, and I come up to bat. This girl, Beans Risinger of Grand Rapids, had not been pitching well. In fact, she'd walked the three that were on there, I think. Her first ball came in there so fast I didn't even see it. I wasn't planning on swinging anyway, you know, because she'd been walking everybody else.

So I thought, "Oh, boy, she's going to put me another in there like that." Well, she didn't, but I was swinging anyway. She struck me out. That's the way I ended: with three men on base, two out, and we couldn't get in the playoffs for that reason. Now how would you like to end your career with that?!

Dottie Collins was kidding me about it over the phone one day.

I said, "Hang on a minute, Dottie. How come they always remember that, but the time I batted before that, I hit one over the fence, and there wasn't a darn soul on base."

That's what hurt. I thought, "Why didn't I wait and save that home run with those three on base?" But that's a bad way to end a complete career, you know.

Did you just decide not to go back in 1954?

I got a good offer of a job, and I thought, "I better take it." I was twenty-seven years old, and the bus rides were killing me.

I had a feeling that league wouldn't go much longer. The league was going down by 1953. You could see it. It was getting to be the same old teams, over and over, and the same old players. It was time to leave.

And I thought, "If I don't take this job, I might not get it later." I worked for the Knoxville Utility Board, the power line company. I worked up there twenty-five years, and I retired when I was fifty-three years old. I retired too soon. My mother had been sick for about four or five years, so I retired, and I lost her six months later. But you never know those things. Dad died back in 1963.

How about your brothers?

They're both still around. One of 'em is down here at the power company, and the other one is in Chattanooga. The one in Chattanooga is the best PR man I got. He just whoops and hollers when something happens. They both encouraged me. My whole family has really been behind me.

Do you still have your old uniform?

I sent my uniform up there to the Center for History in South Bend, where they were checking things out to see what they were going to take to Cooperstown [to the National Baseball Hall of Fame], and where it ended up, I don't know. My number was 17, the Muskegon Lassies, and the uniform was sort of a gold color.

LOU (ERICKSON) SAUER
Racine, 1948; Rockford, 1949–1950

Interviewed on November 9, 2011.

Born: 1929
Height: 5'9"
Weight: 160
Positions: P
Batted: R
Threw: R
All-Star Team: 1949
Career Batting Average: .214 in three seasons
Lifetime Pitching Record: 37–17 (including 4–1 in playoffs of 1949 and 1950)

Louise "Lou" Erickson was born and raised in Arcadia, a town of 1,900 in western Wisconsin. Baseball was America's pastime, and Louise learned to play catch with her father, who worked as a technician for the local creamery and was a pitcher on the town team. Known as the town tomboy, she played pick-up ball games with her five younger brothers, other boys, and a girl friend. Like most kids, they used makeshift equipment like boards for bases, and they hit an old taped ball with a bat that had been fixed. In the 1940s, towns often had baseball teams that played each other, and Louise, a diamond in the rough at 5'9" and 150 pounds, hung around Arcadia'a ballpark, shagging fly balls the men didn't want to chase. In 1946, another team's manager sent her name to the All-American League. Erickson graduated from Arcadia High in June, after refusing her coach's requests for two years to be the only girl on the boys' varsity. She had few plans for the future, and she worked as the "hired man" on her grandparents' farms.

The AAGPBL changed Erickson's life forever. In 1948 she received a letter from the league's headquarters in Chicago inviting her to the Windy City for a tryout. The letter, a surprise, was welcomed, because what better living could a girl earn than by playing professional baseball? On June 2, her nineteenth birthday, Louise, after buying a ball glove and spikes, boarded a train for the 300-mile journey to Chicago. Arriving at Shewbridge Field, the inexperienced but talented and eager Arcadia girl met supervisor Lenny Zintak and

From Arcadia, Wisconsin, Lou Erickson is pictured with Racine in 1948. Traded to Rockford, Lou became a stellar pitcher and helped the Peaches win Shaughnessy Playoff Championships in 1949 and 1950 (courtesy Lou Sauer).

worked out, at first in the outfield but soon as a pitcher. Ten days later, after Zintak showed the right-hander how to change speeds on her pitches, she rode a train to Chicago's south side, pitched, and won an exhibition over the Blue Island Stars. Erickson was sent to the Racine Belles, and within a few days, manager Leo Murphy used her in relief. She worked 4.2 innings, the Belles came back to win, and Lou, as Murphy dubbed her (her nickname of "Toots" was out of bounds) had her second-ever victory. Traded to the Rockford Peaches in 1949, Erickson was developed into a starting pitcher by Bill Allington, a master of teaching the game. She spent two years with the Peaches, winning a total of 33 games, and Rockford won Shaughnessy Playoff Championships in 1949 and 1950.

"Playing professional baseball was really an eye-opening experience for me," Lou recalled. "We had never traveled any place." Her family didn't own a car, and Lou didn't own one until she married Burton Sauer two months after the 1950 season ended. The brown-eyed brunette had many highlight experiences, such as notching victory number eleven by outlasting Maxine Kline and the Fort Wayne Daisies, 3–2, in a 16-inning marathon on a muggy day in July 1949 with the temperature over 90 degrees. Erickson, with her fastball, different curves, and changeup, displayed sharp control, and she was one of the league's most effective hurlers for two seasons. Cheerful, down-to-earth, and hard-working, she loved the game and her teammates, but she disliked the endless bus trips, and she left baseball to get married. A fine ballplayer who returned to her roots in Arcadia, Lou Sauer enjoyed their two children and 57 years of marriage before Burton passed away. She didn't participate in making the movie *A League of Their Own*, but the 1992 film made the league famous. Arcadia's elaborate Memorial Park has monuments to honor American soldiers from all wars, tour buses come to town several days a week in warm weather, and the All-American pitcher often got aboard to tell her unique baseball story.

JS: How did you get interested in baseball when you were growing up?

Sauer: I was born in 1929 and raised in Arcadia, Wisconsin. I've lived here all my life. My parents were Orlen and Sadie Erickson. I had five brothers and one sister: Roland (Bud), Arlen Jr., Don, Sam, and Bob, and my sister is Sue. Our small town population was 1,900 when I received a letter from the All-American League asking me to try out in 1948, which was two years after I graduated from Arcadia High School.

Did you play ball in school or on a local team before the league contacted you?

I had no experience whatsoever. I didn't even have a glove. We just had a bunch of kids in the neighborhood, and we played out in the street. We put boards down for the bases and played pick-up ball.

Back in the 40s, every little town around here had a men's baseball team, and they'd play each other on Sunday afternoon. On the Arcadia team, I had an Uncle Jim, and on the team in Whitehall, about 15 miles northeast of here, I had an Uncle Basil — they were brothers. Whenever the Arcadia team had practice, and the ballpark was only a block away from our house, I'd go and be the tomboy in the outfield shagging balls the men didn't want to chase. That's all the baseball experience I had, until I received this letter from the league inviting me to come to Chicago and try out. I'd never heard of the All-American League. It was a total surprise to me.

You graduated from high school in 1946 but didn't join the league until 1948. What did you do in between those times?

I worked on the farm. My grandparents on both sides, the Hansons and the Ericksons, were brought up on farms near Arcadia, and I was the hired man, so to speak, doing all the hard work. You know in the movie, *A League of Their Own*, where the scout finds the girl milking cows? They could have found me there. That's what I was doing! *[She laughs.]*

You received the letter from the league around the beginning of the 1948 season?

I received the letter in the last week of May, and on June 2, 1948, my nineteenth birthday, I left for Chicago on my first-ever train ride. I had to buy a glove and spikes, because I didn't have either one. I started from scratch! *[She laughs.]*

What was it like when you arrived in Chicago?

When I reported to the tryout camp, located on 74th and Aberdeen Streets in Chicago [at Shewbridge Field], the man running the show was Lenny Zintak. He said, "What position do you play?" Well, how do you say, "Shagging balls in the outfield for a men's team"?

The first couple of days, I played the outfield, and I was shagging fly balls. I was wheeling the ball in to the cut-off person, and I guess I was throwing the ball pretty hard and pretty straight, and Lenny saw that. After two days, he said, "How would you like to try pitching?" Everybody always needs pitching. I thought, "Well, I'm down here. I might as well give it a try." For the next week we worked on control, and Lenny taught me how to throw a curve ball, and all that good stuff. After about ten days, Lenny said, "I'm going to an exhibition game tonight down in South Chicago, and I want you to pitch that game."

I went with Lenny and the team for about an hour ride, and we beat the Blue Island Stars, 24–2. I couldn't believe it, but I found the clipping in my brother's military stuff, and that's how I know the score.

That was my total experience when I was sent over to the Racine Belles in 1948.

Your stats show you got into three games, but you won once.

One night in Fort Wayne, the starting pitcher was hit for five runs, right off the bat. The manager, Leo Murphy, looked at me and said, "Lou, warm up!" That didn't take very long, because I had thrown batting practice, which I did about every day. So I went in and held Fort Wayne for 4.2 innings, and we came back and won the game. I have that clipping too. So that was my second win at that point, and the first win came in the exhibition in Chicago.

After the season, Rockford picked me up, and in spring training, Bill Allington said, "I'm going to make a starting pitcher out of you." That's the rest of the story, and it turned out pretty good, because the Peaches won championships both years. Counting the playoffs, I was 19–6 in 1949 and I was 17–11 in 1950. I've got two full scrapbooks from cover to cover, and I never put a clipping in either one. My mother and my brother in the military put those books together, and when I came home at the end of the season, I had a full scrapbook for each year. I never looked at those scrapbooks until the movie came out [in 1992].

Were you involved in the making of A League of Their Own *at Evansville?*

I received the invitation, and that invitation is still in my drawer. I did not go down there. Had I known then what I later found out from other ballplayers, I would have gone. But for me, just going alone was hard. I don't drive, and my husband Burton was working full time, and my son and my daughter were both working.

Burton and I were married fifty-seven years when my husband passed away in 2007. We got married in November 1950, two months after the end of the season.

Do you have favorite memories from Rockford in 1949 and 1950?

Playing professional baseball was really an eye-opening experience for me. We had never traveled any place. My family didn't even own a car. I never had a car until I got married. As far as any of us got was out to the farm, if Uncle Nick was going, and he lived in Arcadia. They didn't have any kids, but there were four of us kids and Dad and Mom, so we'd pile in the car and go out and visit my mom's family. That was the extent of my traveling before 1948.

All of those bus trips in the league, that kind of got me. After three years of bus travel and winning two championships, there was only one place to go, and that was down. Lois Florreich, Rockford's star pitcher, was quitting the same year I was, so that took half of the Peaches' pitching staff. After three years, at the ripe old age of twenty-one, I had enough. *[She laughs.]*

Did you go by Lou, or Louise?

The first time I was shipped over to meet the Belles in 1948, I had to meet them in Peoria, so I took the train from Chicago, after I signed my contract in the Wrigley Building. I joined the Belles in the lobby of the hotel at Peoria. The manager, Pop Murphy, and the chaperone, Willie Wilson, were waiting for me, and they said, "You must be Louise." I said, "Yeah." They said, "What's your nickname?"

I told them what my grandpa named me when I was four, and that was Toots. They said, "We can't call you Toots." They cut Louise down to Lou. There are old-timers in Arcadia who still call me Toots, but the ball club named me Lou.

What were the main pitches that you threw?

I threw a fastball, curve, and change-up. I changed speeds on the fastball and the curve. I threw fast curves, slow curves, fastball, and change-ups. A change-up is still the best pitch. You can get a major leaguer out on a change-up, the way they stand up there and swing.

Did you make some good friends in the league?

Oh, yes. At this year's San Diego Reunion, I had a real nice visit with Joyce Hill Westerman. If there are doings around the state, we meet at those events. I knew Sophie Kurys from the beginning, and I saw her.

We visited Joyce Westerman this past summer [July 2011], and she has a great deal of memorabilia — a full scrapbook from each season, and also a uniform from Peoria.

I have the scrapbooks for the two full seasons with Rockford, and I have several baseballs, the Rockford pennants, the team pictures, and the yearbooks from Racine and Peoria. Those will go to the kids at the right time.

I guess you would say the league made a big impact on your life.

Yes, but the movie made the biggest impact. My neighbors here didn't know I played ball. The old-timers knew, but the younger people never heard of the All-American League. When the movie came out, I started getting phone calls. Also, the tour buses started coming by my house, and now I talk to them all summer long.

We have one of the nicest veterans' parks in Arcadia. It's called Soldiers Walk, and it has the memorials from all the wars in which the USA has ever participated. People come from all over the U.S. and Canada to see it, and I live two blocks away. The tour director interviewed me one time for a TV program, and he asked if I would mind stepping on the buses and telling my story.

What I do is take a pack of baseball cards for each bus that arrives. First, I have to ask the folks if they've seen the movie. If they haven't, they don't know what you're talking about. But usually it goes over really big. Just before I went to San Diego, I had five tour buses stop in eight days, and that was the end of the season. Our "color" season ended about the time I went to San Diego, but the veterans' park is the big attraction. One of the businessmen put up a big plaque of me between the two local ball diamonds.

After the movie came out, I had to dig out my memorabilia, because everybody wants to see it. I still have my scrapbooks, my spikes, and a couple of my baseball caps, but not my glove. When Lois Florreich and I quit after the 1950 season, she gave me her glove, and I gave her mine, because we weren't coming back. I coached the high school summer league for three or four years, and I coached the ladies' senior softball team for three years. I coached and umpired also. I used to put my duffel bag with my glove and spikes and stuff on the bench when I was umping, and somebody stole the glove. So Lois' glove is gone, and Lois has passed away. Someone from Rockford searched it out and found that my glove was sold at a garage sale. I'll bet that glove is being used today.

The league was the best three years of my life, and I'll never forget those years. The hot, muggy days we had this summer remind me of one memorable experience at Fort Wayne, Indiana, in the summer of 1949. We were riding the bus to the ballpark from the hotel, and we went past one of those signs that had the temperature on the outside gauge, and it said 90 degrees. Guess whose turn it was to pitch? The game went sixteen innings, and Fort Waynne's Maxie Kline and I both pitched the whole sixteen innings, and we won! You think we threw only one hundred pitches? I thought I was going to die, but I didn't!

Bill Allington was trying to find a way to tie a towel on me, so I could keep my pitching hand dry. Everything on me was wet. Even my socks and shoes were wet. There's no way you can legally have a towel out there, but I got into a lot of dirt. Poor Maxie—she went all the way too. I pitched a couple of fourteen-inning games, and that's as far as I wanted to go. The sixteen-inning game was a double-header in our league—seven innings in the opener, and nine in the late game. But those years were the best thing that ever happened to me.

Pat Scott
Springfield, 1948; Fort Wayne, 1951–1953
Interviewed on March 15, 2012.

Born: 1929
Height: 5'7"
Weight: 155
Positions: P
Batted: R
Threw: R
Career Batting Average: .218 in three seasons
Lifetime Pitching Record: 48–26

Pat Scott, who possessed boundless energy, enthusiasm, and drive, grew up playing softball as well as baseball on her parents' farm near Burlington, Kentucky. The eldest of three daughters of Wilfred and Irene (Patrick) Scott, Pat always liked playing ball with

From Kentucky, Pat Scott made the league with Springfield in 1948, but her mother's illness forced her to come home. Pat returned to the circuit three years later, and she is pictured with Fort Wayne in 1951 (courtesy Pat Scott).

neighborhood kids. Fortunately for her, the family's farm had a ball field similar to the one shown in the movie *Field of Dreams*, except the Scotts' diamond was surrounded by tobacco fields, not corn. By age twelve, Pat was hurling in a fast-pitch softball league, and she proved herself a stellar pitcher for years. The country girl also enjoyed going to practices of the men's baseball team that played games on her family's field on the weekends. Several players taught the eager teenager what she needed to compete, and before long, Pat, who was caught by her mother, was pitching, as the saying goes, "like a pro." In the spring of 1948, a few months before she was scheduled to graduate from St. Henry's High School in nearby Erlanger, Kentucky, the teenager was contacted by the All-American League to go to spring tryouts in Chicago. She and her mother worked a deal for Pat to study for exams so that she could return and graduate with her class.

In Chicago, after two weeks of training, Scott was allocated to the expansion Springfield Sallies. Big and strong at 5'7" and 155 pounds, the quiet brunette with hazel eyes was ready to live her baseball dream. However, three weeks later her mother became ill, and she was called home to help her father with the farm and her three younger sisters. By the time her mother did recover that summer, it was too late to rejoin the Sallies, so Pat put baseball on hold. She went to work for the local extension office of the University of Kentucky's Home Economics and Agriculture Department, and she played softball in her spare time. In the fall of 1950, she was contacted by Max Carey, who, as president of the AAGPBL in 1948, had seen her pitch. Carey, now managing Fort Wayne, convinced her to join the league at spring training in 1951, and Scott happily returned to baseball. Backed by the hard-hitting, smooth-fielding Daisies, she became one of the league's best pitchers for three seasons, posting records of 15–7, 17–7, and 16–12.

Scott pitched and won the game that gave Fort Wayne the city's first league pennant in 1952, and she enjoyed the camaraderie of her many skilled teammates. She might have produced a near–20 win season in 1953, but Fort Wayne's manager, Bill Allington, altered her pitching style, and, before she returned to her faster approach, she hit a four-game losing streak. Blessed with good control, Scott, full of intensity, delivered a good fastball, changeup, and curveball, but when each season was over, she was happy to return to the farm and her old life. An opportunity to become a foreign exchange student took her away from baseball in 1954, and when she came back, she attended the University of Kentucky. After earning degrees in zoology and medical research, she worked more than thirty years as a clinical researcher. Baseball was never far from her mind, but until the advent of the players' reunions in 1982, the Players Association, and *A League of Their Own*, she kept active by pursuing varied interests, including training horses and training dogs. Honored several years ago by the naming of a local ballpark as Pat Scott Field, the All-American also shines as a talented woodcarver. Pat likes attending AAGPBL Reunions and renewing friendships with other onetime girls of the diamond, she embraces the league's fans, and she loves watching younger friends and relatives play her favorite game.

JS: How did you first started playing ball?

Scott: I played softball for many years here in Kentucky, and the high schools didn't have softball when I was growing up, so I played independent softball starting around age twelve. I was a fast-pitch pitcher for ten years. I pitched softball until I came up to the league to play baseball. The only experience I had playing baseball was with the boys on the farm. We used to go up on the school grounds, and if the boys didn't have enough for two teams, I got to play. That made it kind of nice.

My family owned a little farm near Burlington, Kentucky, not far from the school. On that farm, there was a baseball field. That's where the weekend minor leagues played, and men came up there to play. It was kind of like the movie, *Field of Dreams*, but instead of corn growing around us, we had tobacco. Those men in the minor league took me under their wing, and they taught me what I knew about baseball. They had some awfully good ballplayers in the 1940s. They loved to play the game!

What were your parents' names?

My father was Wilfred Scott, and my mother was Irene (Patrick) Scott. Not only was she my mom, but she was also the best catcher I ever had. She always had me ready for spring training each year. She could handle the pitches!

I had three younger sisters, Gloria, Mary, and Frances, or "Tommie," and she was the youngest. They're all two years apart. All three of them became catchers in softball, and I was the pitcher.

Where did you go to school?

I went to St. Henry's High School in Erlanger, Kentucky, which was a few miles east of Burlington, and I graduated in 1948. That's when I tried out up in Chicago, and I was lucky enough to make the All-American League with the Sallies.

My father was thrilled that I made the league. I went to spring training in 1948, but I had to promise that I would complete high school before I could go. We went down and talked to the principal, and they agreed that since it was only going to be three weeks, but it was exam time, I would have to take my books with me, study, and come back and graduate with my class. I did that. After high school, I went to play ball with the Springfield Sallies. I was only with the team for three weeks, and my mother became very ill. My father had to do all the work on the farm, so I had to go home and take care of my sisters. I forgot all about baseball. By the time my mother recovered, it was too late for me to go back to the Sallies, so I didn't play for two more years.

Did you work on the farm for those two years?

I worked as a secretary in the extension office, which was the field office of Home Economics and Agriculture for the University of Kentucky. In the fall of 1950, I got a call from the local newspaper saying they had a phone call from someone trying to locate Pat Scott. Dad took the phone call and he talked to the man from the paper. The man who called was a friend of his, and Max Carey had left his number at the newspaper for me to call him.

Max Carey was president of the league when I tried out in 1948, and evidently he remembered me from Chicago, and now he was manager of the Fort Wayne Daisies. I called him, and he said, "Pat, you should come back and play for me." I said, "I haven't touched a baseball since two years ago in Chicago."

He said, "It doesn't make a bit of difference, because I know you can play. Come and play for me." That was in 1951, and I went to spring training with the Daisies, and I continued there with the Daisies for three years.

Where did you live in Fort Wayne?

I lived with Mr. and Mrs. Bill Berger and their son Jerry, who was eight or nine years old in 1951. I stayed with them all three seasons with the Daisies. I came home in the offseason, and I worked as a clerk in a tobacco warehouse. That was a big thing in Kentucky in the wintertime. A friend of my father's owned a big company, the Richwood Tobacco Warehouse.

Did you have a problem getting used to pitching baseball, after pitching fast-pitch softball all those years?

No, I didn't. Back home, I already taught myself how to field a ball, and how to throw a ball. When I had time after getting my schoolwork done, I'd go outside by the barn. I had a rubber ball, and I'd throw that ball up against the barn, and I'd run back and field it like a fly ball, if it was in the air, or I'd play it like a grounder, if it was on the bounce. I put a bushel basket out there by the barn, and I'd pitch to that, and see how many times I could put the ball in there. I pretty much taught myself to pitch baseball.

Was Max Carey a good teacher? He was Fort Wayne's manager in 1950 and 1951.

Max Carey gave me some hints, but he didn't seem to work with me that much. He saw the way I did it, and about the only time he corrected me was when he saw I was doing something to hurt myself, or not getting the pitches where the catcher wanted them.

Accuracy was one of my things. I had good control. I don't know what the girls thought who batted against me, but I had a good fast pitch and a good change-up, but my curve wasn't worth a nickel! *[She laughs.]*

My pitches got me by. You know, they always talk about how important the pitcher is, and the catcher. They're probably in some ways the most important players, but at the same time, I always tell everybody, "If I didn't have eight good players behind me, I wouldn't have made the records that I did."

Another thing: I always wanted to be the best fielding pitcher on our team. I had a .990 percentage in 1953. I not only wanted to be a good pitcher, but I wanted to be a good fielder.

[Editor's note: Scott improved each season, fielding .961 in 26 games in 1951, .975 in 26 games in 1953, and .990 in 32 games in 1953. In each of her three seasons, she was Fort Wayne's best-fielding pitcher.]

You also had good winning records. You had records of 15–7, 17–7, and 16–12 in your three seasons.

Yes, I did. You know, never in my dreams did I think I could go up there to that league and do that, not having any more experience than I did. Once I made up my mind that's what I wanted to do for the team and Max, and whoever the manager was, I did my best—and I had good players behind me.

Did you have some good friends on the team?

I don't know how other team members felt about it, but I was kind of an introvert at the time. I was a farm girl, and the best I can say is that I was happy playing ball and going home, and that was it. I didn't do a lot of things with the girls, but we didn't have much time, other than playing time, to be with the other girls.

Do you remember your roommates?

The first year I roomed with Lois Youngen. We only roomed together for about half a year, and she was traded to South Bend. I lived by myself after that, but with the same family, and they had one boy, about eight or nine years old.

Did you have favorite games that you pitched?

The pennant-winning game when we won the 1952 pennant was the highlight of my career, and we won against Rockford, 5–1.

The other game was in Battle Creek, Michigan, on July 16, 1953, and I pitched an 11-inning game that Fort Wayne won, 3–0. We split a double-header. We won the first game, 3–0, and the Belles won the nightcap, 3–0. The newspaper called it a "pitchers' duel" between me and Mirta Marrero, and we scored our three runs off five Belles' errors. Marge Pieper hit two triples off me, but they couldn't score either time.

Was Jimmy Foxx much different as a manager in 1952 than Max Carey in 1951?

I don't think so. I never really paid attention to that. The Daisies were going good, and Jimmy Foxx never gave me anything different to do. Like they say, you don't change horses in the middle of the stream.

I can tell you a story about Bill Allington in 1953. I should have had a 20-game winning season in 1953, and as it was, I had a 16–12 record. I can't remember the town where we were playing, but Allington came out of the dugout to see me, and he said, "You're pitching too fast, you're pitching too fast. We're going to slow you down." I said, "What are you talking about slowing me down?"

Allington said, "Well..." and I said, "In other words, you want them to hit the ball out of the park?" He got as little mouthy with me, and I thought, "There's no sense in arguing with him." So, you know, I did what he said, and I lost the next four games.

After that, the team president, Mr. [Harold] Van Orman, called me into his office. He said, "Pat, what's going on out there? You've never lost four straight games since you've been here!"

I thought, "If I don't tell him, I'm going to catch the devil. If I do tell him, I'm going to be riding the bench." Well, I don't care about riding the bench. I've just got to say what I'm thinking, so I told him.

I said, "Mr. Van Orman, I'll tell you, I've been winning up to this time," and I said, "You don't change the color of the horse when he's drinking."

He said, "Why?"

I said, "Bill's been changing my style of pitching."

"Ah," he said, "I knew that when I first saw you pitch those losing games. When do you pitch next?" And I said, "Probably Tuesday night."

He said, "I'll be there. If Bill Allington crosses that third base line and comes to that mound, the game will be called for sure. He'll be riding the bench, not you."

I don't know exactly what happened, but Mr. Van Orman must have called Allington in to his office for a talk, because when I went out to pitch from then on, I won straight down the line, pitching like I did before. I had no problem with my style of pitching, so I think 1953 would have been my best season.

I've never told that story before, but I think Bill Allington realized later on that he was wrong. When the team owner calls you into his office, and he says he knew I wasn't pitching the way I always pitched, if he could see it, why couldn't Bill Allington see it?

That's a good question.

I mean, you just don't change things when you're going good. You can check my record, and I never lost four in a row before. If I'd won a couple of those games, I would have been close to 20 wins.

Why didn't you come back for the 1954 season?

When I came home in the fall of 1953, my dad said that Professor Jones from the University of Kentucky was here in town last week wanting to know when you were coming home. I told him, and he said he had something he wanted to talk to you about.

The professor said, "This is what it's about. Pat has a lot of travel experience, and a lot of farm experience, and a lot of 4-H experience." (We used to show cattle all over the country.) He said, "I'd like for her to fill out an application to go to Europe as an exchange student."

I said to Dad, "How am I supposed to apply? I haven't been to college yet, and most of those exchange students are already first-year students." Dad told Professor Jones that I didn't think I should fill one out, but he said, "You tell her that has nothing to do with it. It's what's on the application that counts." He told dad they were going to send me an application, and they would love to have me fill it out.

I talked it over with Mom and Dad. I said, "You know, I've reached my dream. I've played professional baseball, and I loved every minute of it. I still love it, and I always will." But you know, a farm girl doesn't have much of a chance for new opportunities, and we didn't make that much money on the farm to be able to save a whole lot. I said, "To go to Europe and live over there for five or six months is a dream come true." The idea was if you were selected, you worked on five farms and lived with the families. I went ahead and completed the application. I figured if I did happen to be selected, fine and dandy, but if not, I could go back and play another year of baseball.

At the end, I was one of twelve finalists picked to be interviewed, and they would pick six people to make the trip. I went up the university to the interview. I never will forget, they had several professors, one from the Home Economics Department, one from the Agriculture Department, and some others.

I looked at this one professor, who had been a student in the program, and I thought, "I'm going to be in trouble." He and this girl — she was also a professor after she was a student in the program — both had a chance to ask me questions. He said, "If you go over there to foreign countries, would you take a drink?"

I said, "If you're talking about drinking alcohol, they don't drink as much as people do here, but they have been brought up with drinking wine. So yes, if I'm with a family and they serve wine for dinner, I'm going to have a glass of wine with them."

When the interviews were all over, I was one of the six they picked to go. The Home Economics Department professor called me in and said, "Pat, I want you to know what won this for you. You were honest. Your experience with that baseball league won it for you, because you've traveled and met people, and that's something these other kids never do. They've never been out with the public."

Baseball to me was an education, not just playing ball. That's how I decided not to go back to the league and play another year. You have to move on with your life. I came back and I started to college at the University of Kentucky in 1955, and I graduated in 1959 with a degree in Zoology.

What did you do with the degree?

I went into medicine. I worked for a clinical laboratory doing medical research for thirty-two and a half years at a school and a hospital in Cincinnati.

It sounds like baseball made a big impact on your life.

I'm telling you right now, I owe a great deal to my time with baseball. I thoroughly enjoyed the girls that I played with, every one of them. I didn't associate with the girls as much as I would have liked, because of living by myself most of the time. The only times we got together was when we had a picnic, or some event. When you went to the park, you didn't have any time to fool around. But I loved every minute that I was with the league.

Have you gone to AAGPBL Reunions?

The last one I went to was in Houston in 2006. We've had a lot of illness in the family, and I haven't had much of a chance to go in recent years. Also, the last two years I have gone to the International Woodcarvers Conference out in Iowa. Oil painting was originally my favorite thing, but about twelve or thirteen years ago, I got interested in woodcarving. I've been to the international conference twice, and entered two pieces, and won two ribbons, and that's about as high a compliment as I can get in woodcarving.

You've done many interesting things in your life.

The opportunities were there, and thank heaven, I was able to think about the opportunities, and say, "Hey, make a decision now," and the choices have worked out to my success.

Back in 2006, the city of Walton built a new park for the kids, and they put in a good-sized softball field, and the Little Leaguers play baseball on it. They named the park Pat Scott Field. They had a big shindig for me.

One day a little boy who lives up the street saw me, and he said, "Miss Pat, we're going to go over and play baseball on your baseball field." I said, "Gosh, that's great! But I said, 'I'll tell you what. That's everybody's field,'" and he just grinned! *[She laughs.]*

About six months ago, somebody took the sign off the ballpark. They put up a new one, and this sign has Pat Scott Field and my picture on it! You never know what's going to come out of baseball.

INEZ VOYCE
South Bend, 1946; Grand Rapids, 1947–1953
Interviewed on August 28, 2009, and September 6, 2011.

Born: 1924
Height: 5'6"
Weight: 130
Positions: 1B, P
Batted: L
Threw: L
Honors: Second all-time in RBI with 422 in eight seasons — Dottie Schroeder had 431 RBI in 12 seasons
Career Batting Average: .256
Lifetime Pitching Record: 1–1 in four games in 1948

Inez Voyce was born in Rathbun, Iowa, the ninth of ten children, and her family moved to nearby Seymour two months later. She grew up playing sports in the neighborhood, mostly with boys, and kids in those days loved playing pick-up games of baseball. Inez's friends used makeshift equipment, usually a broken bat, and none of them owned a glove. The talented teenager played four years of basketball at Seymour High. In the summer of 1940, following her junior year but before she turned sixteen, she played in a

An Iowa native, Inez Voyce is pictured with South Bend in 1946. Inez was traded in 1947 to Grand Rapids, where she played seven stellar seasons, finishing second on the league's all-time RBI list with 422 (courtesy Louise Pettus Archives and Special Collections, Winthrop University).

girls' softball league in Lucas in return for room and board. Voyce graduated in mid–1941, just six months before the United States entered World War II. Inez wanted more education, so she attended a business college in Davenport, where she also played for the college's basketball team. Afterward, she worked as a secretary for a garage. Her mother and her younger brother, who graduated from Seymour High in 1943, moved to California to join her father, who, due to poor health, had moved to the West Coast two years earlier. Homesick, Inez joined her family in November 1943, and she found a job with the local Post Office. She worked there until serving in the Navy, starting in mid–1944.

Voyce, a brunette who was tall, strong, and athletic at 5'6" and 130 pounds, threw and batted left-handed. She worked in the Navy's Personnel Office near San Francisco, and she played service softball. Because she was seen playing Navy ball by a scout, Inez was invited to the All-American League's spring camp at Pascagoula, Mississippi, in 1946. Assigned to the Great Lakes Naval Station north of Chicago, she got leave, traveled to Pascagoula, and made the league. A hard-hitting but not fleet first sacker, she was allocated to South Bend, where she spent the 1946 season. Inez, a good clutch hitter, averaged .210 and drove in 43 runs for the Blue Sox, but both figures proved to be the lowest of her eight-year career. Allocated to Grand Rapids in 1947, the Californian spent seven seasons with the Chicks, averaging .256 lifetime and racking up 422 RBI, a figure that left her in second place on the league's all-time list. Dottie Schroeder totaled 431 RBI, but she played 12 seasons, compared to eight by Voyce.

In the postwar years, All-American League teams traveled by bus. Voyce remembers those overnight journeys, which could be 300 or 400 miles. In addition to their salary, the players received $3.50 per day meal money, Inez recalled, and a person could save a little by eating carefully. In Grand Rapids, she first roomed with Tex Lessing in a private home, and they lived within easy driving distance of the ballpark. In those years Grand Rapids played games at South High Field, a football field on which the city laid out a baseball diamond with the short fence in right field. She thrived as the circuit evolved more toward baseball, including lengthening the bases paths to 72 feet in 1948 and adopting a livelier 10-inch ball in mid–1949. Voyce remained a regular with the Chicks through 1953, earning the nickname "The Hook," because she seemed to snag every throw at first base. An excellent first sacker, she always reminded the pitcher about possible plays whenever one or more runners were on base. Down-to-earth, friendly, and sociable, she loved the life of a professional athlete, and she enjoyed making new friends. After baseball, besides working for a living, Inez took up golf, another sport at which she excelled. Like so many other women, the league made a big impact on her life. "In fact," Voyce recalled, "I didn't want to quit in 1953, but the league was going downhill and folding up."

Interview on August 28, 2009

JS: Can you talk about your background and how you got interested in the All-American League?

Voyce: I was born in Iowa, and that's where I was raised. I graduated from Seymour High School in 1941. I was born in Rathbun, but we only lived there for two months before my parents moved to Seymour. I was the ninth of ten children, and one older brother is the only one left. He and his wife live outside of Boston.

We did not live on a farm. Our house was in town, but we did have cows, chickens, and pigs. We planted a big garden, so we had plenty of territory. Seymour was a town of about 1,500, and we had a "Times Square," and we had a band concert every Saturday night in the summertime, and I played trumpet in the band.

How did you first get interested in baseball?

I started when I was old enough to walk. I played ball with my brothers and my cousins. There used to be a football field near where my cousins lived, and a lot of the kids would show up, and we'd play a pick-up game of baseball. It was always a pick-up game, and we didn't have any equipment. We'd have a broken-off bat, and I don't remember anyone having a glove. I've been athletic all my life.

During high school in Seymour, did you play any sports?

I played on the girls' basketball team. In my four years of high school, they used to have two-court basketball with two dribbles for each girl. You had the three guards at one end of the court and the three forwards at the other end. I played basketball for four years in high school, and that was a lot of fun, but they didn't have any girls' softball. When the movie *A League of Their Own* came out in 1992, the *Des Moines Register* put my picture on the front page.

Who were your personal friends in South Bend?

We were all friendly, but I didn't have any true friends in South Bend. I had a few true friends in Grand Rapids, but most of them have passed away.

You graduated from Seymour High in 1941, and later your family moved to California, but you didn't go into the Navy until 1944. What did you do?

After high school I went to Business College, the AIC, or American Institute of Commerce Business College, in Davenport, Iowa. I went mostly to play basketball on the AIC team. They played in tournaments with other teams.

I remember the first job I had was working as a secretary in the office of a garage that worked on cars. I earned $15 a week.

My father was a superintendent of coal mines, and because of his health, he had to move to California around 1941. About the time my younger brother graduated from Seymour High in 1943, he and my mother moved to California to be with my father. My family lived here for a long time. After my father passed away, my mother moved back to Iowa, but that was after I retired from the baseball league.

Later, I got homesick for my family, and I moved to California. When I got out here in November 1943, I walked the streets looking for a job. I tried the power company, the gas company, and all of that. The Post Office hired me for the Christmas rush, and I worked in the parcel post window. They liked me, and they kept me on. I worked in the money order department until I joined the Navy in 1944.

What did you like about being in the Navy?

I liked being in the Navy because I worked in the Personnel Office, and you got to meet all the people who came into the Navy. Hunter's Point, which was a dry dock just outside San Francisco, was the base where I served, and they had 100 WAVES to each 500 sailors. I even went out and played softball with the boys in the Navy.

In 1946, I was able to go to Pascagoula, Mississippi, to the league's spring training because of an accident. The tugboats were pulling a ship out of the dry dock, and they collided, and they had to find out the reasons for the accident. In those days, they used a Dictaphone, and at night I'd have to go into the office and transcribe what had been recorded on the Dictaphone. Because I put in that extra work, my supervisor let me go to spring training early.

I had to serve a certain amount of time, but I was about ready to get out of the Navy. I could have shipped overseas, but I didn't want to go. I wanted to play baseball. When I went to Chicago in May of 1946, they sent me to the Great Lakes Naval Base, and they discharged me. I immediately went to South Bend to play first base. We were playing with a softball at that time, and we had underhand pitching.

How did you first get interested in the All-American League?

I was always interested in sports, and the Chicago Cubs were my favorite team. My sister and her husband lived in Chicago in the summer of 1944, and in late August, I went to Chicago to see them and to see the Cubs play. My sister also took me to the Wrigley Building, and I must have inquired at that time about the All-American League.

At Wrigley's office, they said, "Well, the season is almost over. Why don't you contact us next year?" In the meantime, when I went home, I decided to join the Navy. I enlisted, and I was there for twenty-one months.

In South Bend in 1946, I remember Jeannie Faut and Marge Stefani and Betsy Jochum and Lib Mahon and Shoo-Shoo Wirth and Bonnie Baker. So we had a pretty good team, but I can't remember too much about the 1946 season. I didn't hit too well, and later I got to be a better hitter when the ball got smaller and the pitcher was moved farther away.

Where did you live in South Bend?

I had a roommate and we lived with a married couple all year, and we paid room and board. I can't remember their names, but they didn't live too far from Playland Park. One of the WAVES came up to visit me for a week, and we went on a tour of South Bend, and stuff like that.

I enjoyed my first year, but the league sent me to Grand Rapids in 1947. So I only played one year for South Bend. I remember at Playland Park the bleachers for the fans to watch the ball games were a long way from the field, and they had that race track all around the ball field.

Do you remember the manager in South Bend?

Our manager was Chet Grant. He seemed old at the time, but he was a good manager and a nice gentleman, but I don't remember much about him. Lucille Moore was our chaperone.

How did you travel?

We traveled by bus. We'd stay in a town two or three days and play games in that town two or three days, and we'd ride home after the last ball game, which might be three or four hundred miles from Racine, Wisconsin, through Chicago, all the way to South Bend or later to Grand Rapids. Those were terrible trips. I could sleep on a bus, but those trips were nice only when you got to the other town!

They paid us $3.50 a day for meal money, and you'd eat your meal and save a little money out of that. Those were the good old days! *[She laughs.]*

Interview on September 6, 2011

Can you talk about playing baseball in Grand Rapids?

At Grand Rapids, we played a lot of games at South High Field, and we played one year at Bigelow Field. I really enjoyed playing ball in Grand Rapids, but I had to retire after the 1953 season, because the league was folding up.

I enjoyed Grand Rapids very much. John Rawlings was the manager, and he was a good manager, not too harsh or anything like that. We had Connie Wisniewski, Sadie [Doris] Satterfield, Corky Olinger, Alma Ziegler, and Pepper Paire. We had a good team. We didn't win all the time, but we had a good team.

Did you live in a private home in Grand Rapids too?

Tex Lessing and I roomed in a private home on Prospect Avenue, and we had cooking privileges, if we had wanted to cook. Right across the street they had about six players living in a private home.

We were close to the ballpark, which I believe was on Michigan Avenue, but we didn't walk to practices or games. We drove our cars to the ballpark, which was at South High at first. The ball field was a high school football field which was marked off and fenced for softball, and there was a dugout on each side. I think the left field fence was 210 feet, and the right field fence was shorter. I was a left-handed batter, and I remember hitting a few home runs into the stands.

Who were the Chicks' pitchers?

We had Alma Ziegler, who pitched sometimes, and we had Mid Earp, who was an excellent pitcher. We had Connie Wisniewski at first, before we converted to overhand in 1948. We had Lorraine Fisher, and later we had Beans Risinger.

What was the difference between hitting against sidearm and overhand pitching?

There wasn't too much difference. The ball came in a little faster with overhand pitching, but the pitching distance was longer too. I had hit girls' pitching in high school. I remember one summer after I was a junior at Seymour High, a man that was running a girls' ball team in Lucas, Iowa, which was a very small town, wanted me to come up there and play for his team. I went to Lucas and played ball, and he paid my room and board that summer. I stayed there just one summer. So we'll put Lucas, Iowa, on the map!

The ball got smaller almost every year, and in the summer of 1949, the league went to a ten-inch ball. Was it better to hit the smaller ball?

I think so. It made our game closer to men's baseball, and the pitching mound was moved to around fifty-five feet away. It was fun to hit overhand pitching.

You batted in a lot of runs each year, and you finished second on the league's all-time RBI list with 422.

I batted clean-up most of the time. Connie Wisniewski used to bat third, and Sadie Satterfield batted fifth, but I don't remember a lot of the details of the games.

You were always a good defensive first baseman. One newspaper story said they called you "The Hook," because you caught almost every ball thrown to you at first base.

I wasn't too bad, but the field was not very good. I never liked to play on a skin infield, like in South Bend where they had an all-skin infield, no grass. There were a few things about the ballparks that made it harder for us to play real good, because the infields were definitely not baseball caliber. They had rocks and lumps, and what have you. That made it tougher than it would have been with a clean infield, but it would have been nice to play on better fields.

I believe you also played golf in Grand Rapids.

I remember the dentist in Seymour was the only guy I ever saw when I was in high school who had a set of golf clubs. At that time I wasn't interested in golf, but he was the only one in town who had golf clubs!

I started playing golf when I was playing for the Grand Rapids Chicks. They had a nine-hole course not too far from the ball field. It was called the Indian Golf Course, I think. I'd go with Alma Ziegler, and we'd play golf. Afterward, we'd go home and rest for the games. I remember Heinie Martin, the radio announcer in Grand Rapids. A lot of the Chicks that I knew have passed away.

Do you have favorite All-American memories?
I just look back on playing professional ball, and that part I really like.

I got to play professional baseball from 1946 through 1953, so that was my career in baseball. Since that time, I came home to Santa Monica and got a good job. Starting around 1978, my boss let me play golf every Tuesday morning on the women's club. It was the LA Women's Golf Association where I played golf. He probably thought it was a lark and I'd only play a few times, but I played golf until 1991 when I retired.

We used to go to some of the card shows, and I remember one time I got paid several hundred dollars for selling our signed cards.

Would you say the league made a big impact on your life?
The league made a very big impact on my life. In fact, I didn't want to quit in 1953, but the league was going downhill and folding up.

DELORES "DOLLY" (BRUMFIELD) WHITE
South Bend, 1947; Kenosha, 1948–1951; Fort Wayne, 1952–1953
Interviewed on June 2, 2011.

Born: 1932
Height: 5'6"
Weight: 125
Positions: 3B, 1B, 2B, OF
Batted: R
Threw: R
Honors: Led Kenosha Comets in hitting in 1951 with .273 average. Ranked second in league in hitting for 1953 by averaging .332.
Career Batting Average: .231 for seven seasons.

Born in Prichard, a small town just north of Mobile, Alabama, at the depth of the Great Depression in 1932, Delores, or "Dolly," Brumfield later attended Murphy High School in Mobile. As a girl, she liked playing ball on a nearby school playground, and a neighbor encouraged her interest, playing "pitch and catch" with her. In May 1946, shipyard workers, who often practiced on the same playground, saw the teenager's ability and encouraged her parents to contact the new All-American League, which was holding spring training at Pascagoula, Mississippi. Dolly's mother took her 13-year-old on the 60-mile drive to the camp, where she tried out for Max Carey, but she was too young for the league. Disappointed, Dolly returned home, and that summer she played softball with a women's team at Brookley Field in Mobile.

In 1947, Dolly, not yet fifteen, was invited on the AAGPBL's adventure to Havana, Cuba, where the circuit flew two hundred players and league personnel for two weeks of spring training. Although she worked out with Fort Wayne, the league allocated Brumfield to South Bend. After four two-team exhibition tours that blanketed the Southeast, the league's teams returned to the Midwest and opened the season. Dolly played third base and outfield on occasion in 1947, mainly if a regular was injured, but she spent most of her time playing catch in the bullpen down the left field line. In 1948, the league shifted her to Kenosha. Right-handed all the way, Brumfield spent four seasons in Kenosha, where she was often the team's youngest player. Steadily improving, she played first base. In 1950 she batted .264 and played a personal-high 108 games. In 1951, the final season for the financially-strapped Comets, she averaged .273.

From Prichard, Alabama, Dolly Brumfield played her rookie season with South Bend in 1947. Traded to Kenosha in 1948 and to Fort Wayne after four seasons with the Comets, Brumfield is pictured with the Daisies (courtesy Dolly White).

Brumfield's life was unusual, because being a professional athlete at a young age prevented her from having the same interests as other teens, even her brother and sister. Also, after 1947, she had to skip spring training to finish the school year, but she persevered, graduating in 1950. Mostly she socialized with the younger players, and she made friends in the towns where she played, especially Kenosha and Fort Wayne. Personable, bright, and outgoing, she came into her own with Fort Wayne, playing for Jimmy Foxx in 1952 and Bill Allington in 1953. Dolly made new friends, shared an apartment with other players, and, in her final season, the 5'6" first sacker hit a sizzling .332, second to the Daisies' Joanne Weaver, who led the league with a .346 mark.

In addition, Brumfield was exposed to a variety of travel opportunities and to people from all over America, including many girls who attended college, as well as to career choices that she would not have enjoyed at home. She completed her bachelor's degree at Alabama College (now the University of Montevallo), near Birmingham, and later she earned master's and doctorate degrees in Health, Physical Education, and Recreation at the University of Southern Mississippi. Married to Joe White, Dolly became a dedicated teacher at Henderson State University in Arkansas. Always an athlete, she served as a coach, an organizer of recreation activities, and an advocate of women's sports. Later, White became a force in the AAGPBL Players Association, serving on the board of directors and then as the organization's contact person. Her talent, desire, and determination drove her along the road from the South of the segregation era to the All-American League, to college teaching, and finally, to FanFest at major league All-Star games.

JS: Where did you go to high school?

White: I grew up in Prichard, and I went to Murphy High School in Mobile. I graduated in mid-term 1950. At that time, Alabama had only eleven years of public education. Because I quit school in order to go to Havana for spring training in 1947, I couldn't get certain courses in order, so I had to go an extra semester.

How did you first get interested in playing ball?

I lived near the school playground, and that's where all the action was, and I got out there and played with all the boys. I just liked to play. I actually lived between an elementary school, which had a big playground, and the junior high, which had a ball diamond. That's where the guys from the shipyards would come to play in their league during World War II. I'd be there when they got there to practice and play, and they put up with me. *[She laughs.]*

One of my neighbors in 1946, Grady Branch, worked at the paper mill, and he played on a church softball team. He was one of our neighbors who spent a lot of time with me in the afternoon playing "pitch and catch" between the houses. Grady was very special to me, because he gave me attention. I'm the oldest of three, but my brother, Earl Lamar Brumfield, was only sixteen months younger than me. I had a sister, Mary Helen, but my dad paid more attention to the boy in the family. My brother followed my dad's activities. My father, Earl Henry Brumfield, was a hunter and a fisherman, and those are the activities my brother liked.

Who encouraged you to go to Pascagoula in 1946 and try out?

The men from the paper mill who practiced on the junior high field in the afternoon. They saw the notice in the newspaper, and they went to my parents and offered to take me to Pascagoula. My mother said, "No, if you think she should go, I'll take her." My dad had to have the car to go to work, so we borrowed my grandmother's car, and Mother took me out of the eighth grade to drive about sixty miles to Pascagoula, Mississippi. That's where I actually tried out for Max Carey, who was president of the league. Mary Rountree was the one who caught for me.

Max Carey asked me how old I was, and I said, "I'm thirteen, but I'll soon be fourteen." He told my mother the league didn't take girls that young. She said, "I didn't want you to take her. I wanted to know what you thought."

Mr. Carey wanted me to come to Chicago and be put on a team, but my parents refused. I got hooked up with the Brookley Air Force Base women's softball team in 1946. I turned fourteen that May, and I played one year of softball with them. The team was named for Brookley Air Base, but the girls were from all over Mobile. Some of them worked at the shipyards and some worked at the air base. That was my first organized ball team. We traveled to Mississippi and Louisiana and over into Pensacola, Florida, to play other teams.

Margie Holgerson was the other girl from Mobile, and she played for the Rockford Peaches in 1946. Over that winter, I was contacted by the league again, and Max Carey sent Margie out to meet my family. It was because Margie Holgerson was there to chaperone me that I got a chance to make the league at Havana in 1947.

What was it like to travel to Cuba in 1947?

Margie Holgerson, who was the only other girl from Alabama, rode on the train with me to Miami. Girls came to Miami from all over the country and from Canada, and we flew to Havana for spring training. If you talk to many girls in the league, a lot of them started to play when they were fifteen or sixteen.

What was spring training like being in Cuba?

I was so young that I mainly did what they told me to do. Marge Stefani with South Bend was one of the older girls, and she used to give me a hard time. They were good to me, but they knew I was very young, and I just did what they told me. I didn't think too much about it at the time. We were training and playing ball every day. We had some time to walk around Havana, but we always had to go out in groups. The league didn't want us going out individually. We got to walk down the main street and walk over to the capital and do some sight-seeing.

You found out that you made the league and the Blue Sox while you were there.

We went through all of the spring training, and they had their meetings, and they decided who was going to be on what team. I was playing with the Fort Wayne team, and they assigned me to the South Bend team. My mother always got onto me because in the picture of the South Bend team, I didn't look happy at all! I had been playing with Fort Wayne, and I didn't know any of the girls with South Bend. I'd been gone about two weeks, and I'm on a different team. It was rather traumatic for somebody that young.

When you moved to South Bend, where did you live?

I roomed with Shu-Shu Wirth. Lucille Moore was the chaperone, and she did all the arranging. Shu-Shu was from Tampa, Florida. She thought Shu-Shu was from the South, and I was from the South, and that would be good. We roomed with a couple that didn't have any children, Mr. and Mrs. Swen Warner. She was a homemaker and he worked at Sears Roebuck, and he was an usher at Playland Park. They lived within walking distance of the ballpark, and they became my fans. I didn't have a car, and Shu-Shu didn't have a car, so we had to find ways to get to the ballpark.

Did you like playing at Playland Park?

It was an unusual park with that race track around it, but as far as playing ball there, I enjoyed it. In my rookie year, I did a lot of catching out in the bullpen area with the girls when they were warming up, so I didn't have to sit in the dugout all the time. Most of the girls were nice, like Jean Faut and "Sugar" Koehn.

How was Chet Grant as a manager?

Chet was a good manager. I enjoyed playing for Chet. He was all business. I thought managers were supposed to be like that, and being so young, I thought all of them were like Chet. We practiced in the mornings starting around ten o'clock, and we were usually out by one o'clock. Chet would send the other girls home, and he'd work with me, the rookie infielder, and "Red" Mahoney, the rookie outfielder, along with some local girls. After that, we'd get our lunch and go back to the ballpark. We got to know all of the girls, but the two rookies didn't have much contact with the other players away from the ballpark. We played at night six days a week and double-headers on Sundays and holidays, so you didn't have much time to get into trouble.

Who were some of the girls you got to know in your first year with South Bend?

Daisy Junor was one of the older players, and she was married. Daisy was Canadian. On the way back from Havana, Daisy was the one in the airplane sitting with me. Lucille Moore made sure someone was always taking care of me, because I was so young. When the airplane hit an air pocket, I thought it was fun, but Daisy didn't like it at all! *[She laughs.]*

I broke into the lineup in 1947 because Shu-Shu broke her leg sliding. Chet Grant moved "Pinky" Pirok from third base to shortstop. Pinky was the third baseman, so they needed a third baseman. When Shu-Shu got hurt, I played third base.

In 1948 you ended up with Kenosha.

At the end of the season, the teams were allowed to keep their starting lineups, and the rest of the players went into a pool. The teams that had the worst record the previous season got first choice. I guess Chet had spent a lot of time with me, because he'd keep me after practice after he let the other girls go, and I'd practice with some of the local girls. I actually had more friends with the local girls than I did on the team, because I was so young. When Chet moved to Kenosha to manage in 1948, he chose me from the pool. I played there for four years, until the Kenosha team folded.

What was it like being in Kenosha after playing and living in South Bend?

I was a year older, for one thing. We lived in a rooming house, three or four girls, with another couple that didn't have any children, and they lived right next to the Presbyterian Church. They had a big two-storey house, and I roomed with another girl on the sleeping porch. That was the main thing in the league — where you were living. We lived within one block of the bus stop, so I could catch a bus and go to the ballpark for the practices and the games, and I was also close to the town so I could eat. The couple also let us do laundry, and you had to be able to do those kinds of things.

Again I made friends out in the town. That's where most of my friends were, out in the town, and they had cars. One girl worked at Jockey Underwear in Kenosha, Stella Guzauskus, and she became my best friend, and she had a car. Stella couldn't help me going to practices and ball games, but after the games, she could take me home. Later, she married a teacher named Bob Bauer.

When you went to Kenosha, did the Comets still play in Lakefront Stadium?

No. I played at Lakefront when I was with South Bend. Kenosha played their games at Simmons Field when I was there.

What position did you play when you went to Kenosha?

The one the manager told me that he needed! That's the point I usually try to make with young people when I'm talking about the league. My idea was, "Hey, I'm a rookie! Give me one of those positions. I don't care which one."

Actually, I played infield and outfield. Kenosha traded away "Lefty" Hohlmayer in 1949, and I played first base after that. Lefty batted left-handed, and most first basemen were left-handed hitters. I played some center field. I played different outfield positions. The one infield position I never played was shortstop. I didn't play second base until I went to Fort Wayne in 1952 and played for Jimmy Foxx. I told him, "Jimmy, I never played second base." But Fort Wayne had traded the second baseman, and I ended up playing second base for Jimmy.

How would you describe yourself as a hitter?

I was a better hitter than I was a fielder. Ground balls were tough for me. I wasn't a base stealer. I wasn't a fast runner. But I was a better hitter.

Who were some of your teammates with Kenosha?

Fern Shollenberger for sure — she was a honey. Some of the other Kenosha girls were Audrey Wagner, Julie Gutz, Marge Villa, Dottie Naum, Betty Fabac, Lefty Hohlmayer, Marilyn Jones, and Jean Cione. I roomed a lot with Marge Villa on the road. Dottie Naum was always a character. But Fern Shollenberger was one of the best gals there. She was one of my closest friends in Kenosha. In later years, Jean Cione was one of my better friends, but not when I was there. I was one of the younger ones, and Jean was the star! *[She laughs.]*

One of the most important things to me was that I made friends not on the team but out in the community. After the games, those were the girls I went with. The other girls on the team were usually older than I was, and older players don't have much time for younger ones. When we were on the road and in the hotels, that was different. The same was true in South Bend. I made more friends outside and off the team than on the team.

Was Nicky Fox still with Kenosha when you were there?

No. I never played on a team with Nicky Fox. I've dealt more with Nicky more after the league was over. My first contact with Nicky came when I was with South Bend. We were playing an exhibition game on the way from Cuba to South Bend in the spring of 1947. Nicky was pitching one time, and she threw me that ol' knuckleball, and I like to broke my neck hitting it. That got her attention, and it tickled her. We've been friends ever since.

You went to Fort Wayne in 1952.

The Kenosha team folded after the 1951 season. After that first year with South Bend, I was always late going to the league, because I had to wait until school was out, and that was usually the early part of June. That's when I reported. Chet Grant was with Kenosha only that 1948 season, and he got out. Johnny Gottselig was the manager after that, but in 1951, that last year, we didn't really have a manager.

I enjoyed my time in Kenosha. I lived close enough to the bus and close enough to town to feel like I could get around, and I made good friends out in the community. I kept in touch with many of those friends over the years. We had a good ball team in Kenosha, and we got along together. Jo Hageman was our chaperone. It was just a good time.

What was the difference between Kenosha and Fort Wayne, where you played in 1953 and 1954?

Fort Wayne had the stars. The day I arrived after I finished school, Jimmy Foxx met me in the dugout and told me I'd play second base. I told him I'd never played second base, but that's where he put me.

I'm playing second base, and you know who was the shortstop? It was Dottie Schroeder, the only girl to play all twelve league seasons. Dottie was outstanding, a star wherever she played, and she was beautiful. Betty Foss was on first base.

One time in 1952, I was playing second base and not doing that good. I'd played first base in Kenosha most of the time. One night Betty Foss was sick and couldn't play. Jimmy Foxx said, "Well, you been wanting to play first base. Tonight's your night." He put me on first base, and I had a really good night, a particularly good night hitting. The next year, Fort Wayne put Betty in right field and put me at first base, and I had a much better year in 1953. In fact, I outhit her by eleven percentage points [.332 to .321 in 1953], and Betty was an outstanding hitter.

I was second in the league in 1953 when I hit .332, and Joanne Weaver led the league at .346. Joanne was the center fielder. She was one of the better ballplayers in the league, and she was a fast runner. Of the three Weavers, I thought she was the better player.

What was the difference between Memorial Field in Fort Wayne and Simmons Field in Kenosha?

At Memorial Field, you had outfield fences. In Kenosha, you didn't have an outfield fence. The lights were way out in the outfield, so if a ball got between the outfielders, there was nothing to stop it. Another thing I liked about Fort Wayne was the fans were close to you. In South Bend at Playland Park, that was a disadvantage, because the race track came between the ball diamond and the grandstand. The fans were further away in South Bend. In Simmons Field it was good. You had a nice grandstand and good bleacher areas, and they were pretty close to the foul lines. But in Fort Wayne, the fans were closer to the ball game. From the standpoint of the fans being close to the game, Playland wasn't as a good place to play.

Do you have highlight memories of Fort Wayne?

Fort Wayne was the first place I ever played where we had an apartment, instead of a room. We didn't live in somebody else's home. Five of us had our own apartment. Joanne Weaver had an old beat-up Chevrolet, and that was our transportation. And again, I made friends out in the community, and that was always a help too, because I never had a car while I was in the league. I had stayed in Fort Wayne's Van Orman Hotel when I played for Kenosha, so I knew a little bit more about the downtown area. Fort Wayne was just a good place to play.

I was very fortunate. I had three teams and three cities where I played. Everywhere I made more friends outside the team than I did on the team, probably because I was younger. I wasn't a party girl, and I didn't like to drink. Dottie Schroeder was a very pleasant person to be around. In South Bend, Marge Stefani was the mother figure. I remember in 1947 when I went to Havana and Marge was around, and I said to her, "Yes, Ma'am." That was the way I was taught to speak to older people, but Marge said, "Don't you Ma'am me!"

What kind of impact did the league make on your life?

The biggest impact, and I find it in my own family, is that my brother and sister were closer together, and they had those teenage years together, which I didn't have with them. They're much closer to each other than I am. I'm closer to my sister now, because my brother lives out in Washington state, because he was in the service and retired from the border patrol there.

At the time, the league was a negative experience as far as the family back home and going to school. I didn't really fit in with the other teenagers, until I went to college. I was three years in high school and four years in college that I was playing ball. I didn't talk much about the league, because nobody in high school or college knew what I was talking about. In my later years in college, only a few of the girls came up to see me play. It was rare that one of my friends from college would show up at Kenosha or Fort Wayne.

Where did you go to college?

First I went to Montevallo, which was the Alabama College, and it's near Birmingham. Everybody knew it was for women, but they never called it by that name. Now it's the University of Montevallo. Later, I earned my master's and doctorate at the University of Southern Mississippi at Hattiesburg. My degrees are in Health, Physical Education, and Recreation. I got my master's while I was in Mississippi, and I got my doctorate after I came to Arkansas.

In some ways because of your age, your experience with the league was more negative than positive.

As far as the social experience, I wasn't that close to many of the girls on the team that I played for. I got closer to many of the girls in later years than I ever did while I was playing ball, and that was because of my age, being younger than most of my teammates. Also, I was from the South, and most of the girls were from other parts of the country.

When you look back on it, how would you summarize your league experience?

The league changed my life. It provided opportunities that I would not have had otherwise. No one in my family had ever had a chance to go to college. I got the idea from being on teams with girls who were going to college. They were in college or they were college graduates. I heard a lot about that, but for my first three years, I was still in high school. The league was an unusual opportunity that made it kind of rough being a teenager, because what I'd been doing all summer was altogether different than being at home with others my age.

Overall, the league provided me opportunities to get an education, to travel all over, and to meet people from all over the country and from Canada. It was just a blessing. Even travel — most people didn't get much opportunity to travel in those days. I traveled mostly by train from Mobile to the city where I was playing.

The league must have been intended for my life. Maybe the biggest thing was the league gave me opportunities that were not open to girls from the South. And people in the communities where we roomed adopted me like I was family. Even later when I was teaching, people in communities where I lived treated me like family.

Part III: The Last Years, 1950–1954

Mary Lou (Studnicka) Caden
Grand Rapids, 1951–1953
Interviewed on November 5, 2011.

Born: 1931
Height: 5'5"
Weight: 160
Positions: P
Batted: R
Threw: R
Career Batting Average: .180 in three seasons
Lifetime Pitching Record: 38–30 with 2.49 ERA

Mary Lou, or "ML," Studnicka was born in Oak Lawn, just south of Chicago, in 1931. Five years later, after her father died in an accident, her mother moved the family — Mary Lou and her seven older brothers — into the south side of Chicago. Studnicka grew up playing with her brothers and their friends, and like most kids, they loved playing baseball. Around the age of nine, she began riding her bicycle a mile and a half to Marquette Park. Encouraged to get a glove, she saved her money, and her sister-in-law helped her buy a new ball glove. Mary Lou began playing practice games with boys at the park. In 1946, the year after World War II ended, the All-American League held a tryout at Marquette Park. Director Lenny Zintak supervised the event, the league sent former star Rogers Hornsby, and Mary Lou met him. Later, Zintak held tryouts for more than 120 girls and formed a four-team AAGPBL "minor league" in Chicago.

Studnicka played in the Chicago girls' league for four seasons. She was asked to go to Cuba with the All-Americans in 1947, but her mother refused. In 1949, Mary Lou graduated from Lindblom Technical High School with good grades and four years of perfect attendance. In 1950 she didn't play softball, because she had surgery to remove an inflamed appendix. The following year, at age twenty, Mitch Skupien, her coach in the Chicago league, moved to Grand Rapids to manage the Chicks, and he soon recruited Studnicka for his team. Zintak had taught the Chicago girls well in the early years, and Mary Lou adjusted to the strict rules of the AAGPBL, renamed the American Girls Baseball League in 1951. At 5'5" and 160, she was a strong, hard-throwing right-hander who fired a good fastball and a "heavy" overhand curve. Grand Rapids had a solid lineup, with Alma "Gabby" Ziegler as the on-field sparkplug leader. For the Chicks, Studnicka posted records of 15–5, 11–12, and 12–13 along with a lifetime ERA of 2.49.

The blue-eyed brunette enjoyed playing professional ball on a close-knit team with dedicated teammates like Ziegler, Beans Risinger, Mamie Redman, Marilyn Jenkins, Inez Voyce, Doris "Sadie" Satterfield, and all the rest. Sadie tagged her with the nickname ML, saying, "By the time we get Mary Lou out of our mouth, the game will be over!" ML, soft-spoken, easygoing, and friendly, liked the camaraderie they shared, the singing, and the high jinks on the bus trips. However, the Illinois hurler had worked for Chicago's First National Bank since she was a senior in high school, and she kept her job in baseball's offseason. When the league dropped from six teams to five for 1954 (there were eight teams when ML began in 1951), she was asked to move to Fort Wayne and take a salary cut. Instead, she left the game to keep her bank job.

Married to Adam Braze in 1956, ML got pregnant with her first daughter in late 1957, and she also found a better-paying position with the LaSalle Bank. In 1962, she began working for the Chicago Police Department as a fingerprint technician. Her husband passed

Mary Lou Studnicka, or "ML," as she was dubbed in Grand Rapids, is pictured with the Chicks circa 1951 (courtesy Mary Lou Caden).

away in 1970, and two years later she married Paul Caden. By then ML had three daughters, Pauline, Laura, and Elizabeth, and she continued to work for the city. Later, after retiring, she enjoyed the AAGPBL Reunions. ML moved to Arkansas and got involved in volunteer work. The former pitcher has enjoyed speaking to different groups, including the Kiwanis and senior citizens, about the historic women's league in which she played a meaningful part for three glorious summers.

JS: How did you get involved with baseball while you were growing up?

Caden: I was born in Oak Lawn, Illinois, just outside Chicago. There was a lot of land between Oak Lawn and Chicago when I was born, but it runs into Chicago now. We lived on a farm in Palos Park. My dad, his name was John Studnicka, was killed in an accident when I was five years old. Since we rented the farm, Marie, my mom, used the insurance money to buy a house in the city of Chicago. My brothers were John, Frank, Carl, George, Robert, Anthony, and Thomas, and I was the "baby" of the family.

We started school on Chicago's South Side. I didn't have any girl friends, because I was a shy kid, so I played mostly with my two youngest brothers and their friends. After school, we'd find a vacant lot and start playing baseball, and I turned out to be pretty good at it. In fact, I was better than my next closest brother, and he complained to my mom that I should find my own friends, because I always got picked for a team before him. So my mom said, "Why don't you find other friends to play ball with?"

I was around nine or ten, and I'd ride my bike up to Marquette Park, which was about a mile and a half away. The park had an island, and it was surrounded by a lagoon, and the island had several ball parks. I'd ride over the bridge to the island and watch the guys play ball. Every once in a while, I'd see someone I knew and play catch with him. Finally, they said, "Why don't you get a glove and then you could play ball with us?" I saved my money, and my sister-in-law helped me buy a glove, and I started playing with the fellows at the park. The men's coach at the park said I could play in the practice games, but when they had a league game, naturally I couldn't play. But I learned how to keep score and stuff like that.

One weekend the Chicago daily newspaper said the park district had hired former major leaguer Rogers Hornsby to go around to the various parks and conduct baseball clinics. He came to our park. Naturally, being the only girl out there with a couple of hundred guys, the neighborhood newspaper got involved and took pictures of me with Rogers Hornsby. He gave a little speech about how I could throw and hit and do all that baseball stuff.

After that happened, some girls who had been going to the women's section of the park playing volleyball and taking dancing lessons showed interest in playing ball, so the men's coach started a fast-pitch softball team. In the meantime, Rogers Hornsby had told Wrigley about me, and he also told Wrigley about Lenny Zintak, who was coaching the girls' team. Wrigley contacted Zintak and asked him if he'd like to start some farm clubs for the All-American League. This was the summer of 1946, and some of the girls in the All-American League were already going back home after a couple of years of baseball.

Lenny Zintak put out the word to all the parks in Chicagoland that there would be tryouts for girls' softball. They had one tryout on the city's North Side, and one tryout on the South Side. I don't know how many girls showed up on the North Side, but out of both districts, he called 120 gals and formed four teams for the summer of 1946, two for the North Side and two for the South Side. We played twice a week. We got sponsors, anywhere from taverns to bowling alleys, to pay for uniforms and equipment. They decided we should wear the same uniforms as the gals in the All-American League. Our league was allowed to pitch sidearm, just like the big league did in 1946. Finally, in 1948, when the big league switched to overhand pitching, the farm teams changed to overhand, and I was switched from the outfield to pitcher because I had a strong arm.

In 1947, I was invited to go to Cuba, but my mother wouldn't let me get out of school. She was forced to quit school in the third grade. She was still young, and she knew how important education was, so she refused to let me get out of school. I played on the farm teams in 1947, 1948, and 1949. I graduated from Lindblom Technical High in 1949, and I had four years of perfect attendance and no tardiness.

In 1950, I had surgery, and it turned out I had an inflamed appendix. I didn't play much ball that year. I had my appendix taken out in April, and toward August, I was allowed to play some ball. I got a bid to go to South Bend, but I didn't feel up to it yet. I was working at the First National Bank, and I turned down South Bend.

In 1951, the fellow that was coaching my minor league team in Chicago, Mitch Skupien, was invited to manage the Grand Rapids Chicks. I was approaching my twentieth birthday, so I didn't have to have my mother's permission to join the big league, even though I still lived at home. Skupien sent me a contract, because he knew I had the ability, so I joined the Chicks. Skupien had coached me for two or three years in Chicago.

What was the name of your team in Chicago?

We were the All-Stars. There were a couple of names, depending on whoever sponsored us. Marquette Park was our home park, but we played at Blue Island, which was a park with lights, and Thillen Stadium, which was on the North Side. A fellow named Cole Lenzi had a bowling alley and a semipro baseball team, and he had a field built behind the bowling alley. The only reason you knew it was a field, because the outfield and the infield were full of stones and potholes, was that he had lights, so we played a few games out there. Wherever they could find lights, they would book a game. We had chaperones. I forget what parks they practiced in, because I was a South Sider and I wasn't too familiar with the North Side parks.

You came to Grand Rapids in 1951, and you pitched for the Chicks for three years. What was it like to be in Grand Rapids?

Grand Rapids was real nice. I got to board with a widow, Inez Warmels, who lived in the southwest section of town. She had a daughter about fourteen and a son about nine, and she was real nice. I'd take the bus to the ball park, and sometimes I'd get a ride from a player who had a car. It was a minor league park, Bigelow Field, and later it burned down, and then we played at South High Field.

What was it like to play in the All-American League, or the American Girls Baseball League, as it was renamed in 1951, compared to where you had been playing in Chicago?

The All-American League's farm clubs were real strict with us. There was no fraternizing with the other teams. Lenny Zintak, the guy in charge of the farm clubs, ran baseball clinics all winter long inside the gym at the park where we played. We had a blackboard, and we had chalk talks, and we each had our own notebook, and we had to draw diagrams of the baseball diamond and what position the players were in, and he'd ask us questions. He'd say, "If the ball was hit between third and short and gets past 'em, where does the shortstop go, and where does the second baseman go?"

Lenny Zintak made sure that everybody knew which way to go on whatever ball was hit, where to throw the ball to keep the runners from advancing, what the pitchers did to back up the catcher or third base on throws from the outfield, and stuff like that. He was strictly baseball, and we learned a lot. We learned a lot more than some of the girls playing in the big league did about the technicalities of baseball.

What kind of manager was Mitch Skupien?

Mitch Skupien was great. He only managed Grand Rapids in 1951, and in 1952, Kalamazoo offered him more money, and he went and managed for the Lassies.

After that, we had Johnny Gottselig, the Blackhawks hockey player, for part of 1952. One of our gals, Alma Ziegler, they called her "Ziggy," kind of ran the practices. Gottselig would show up at the ballpark and be in uniform, and all that, but he'd be talking to the owners or somebody. Ziggy would be running the club. He would coach at third base during the game, but he wasn't too much of a manager.

They brought in Woody English about mid-season on 1952, and he managed the rest of 1952 and all of 1953. Woody was there in 1954, but I retired. I didn't go back to the league after the 1953 season.

In 1954, they sent me notice that they were pooling the players because they were balancing the teams. They were down to five teams, and I'd be playing for the Fort Wayne Daisies. My salary was cut, and it was hardly more than I was making at the bank. By this time, I had a real good job at the First National Bank downtown in Chicago. I didn't feel justified in taking off for a cut in salary, so I sent a letter to the league saying I was retiring from baseball.

Who were some of your friends on the Chicks?

Dolly Konwinski played with me in Chicago — her name was Dolly Niemiec then. We worked together in a flower shop in Chicago owned by a friend of hers. Other friends were Mamie Redman, Ziggy Ziegler, Beans Risinger, Doris Satterfield, Connie Wisniewski, Inez Voyce, and Marilyn Jenkins, who started as a bat girl and trained to be a catcher. I knew all the girls.

When we had a day off, we did stuff together, like go fishing or go to a beach on Lake Michigan. We had a pretty close group.

What kind of pitches did you throw?

I threw a fastball and kind of a slow curve. I threw a "heavy ball." I threw directly overhand, and the catcher was always shaking her hand. I'd throw to first base, and Inez Voyce, we called her "The Hook," would say, "You don't have to throw so hard!" Inez was a real good first baseman. She played the infield well, and she was a real good hitter.

Ziggy was the captain — she was great. One game I pitched, it seemed like everyone on the team decided if they were going to make an error that summer, they were going to do it in that game, like ground balls going between their legs and dropping fly balls. I was having a hell of a time! It was summer, and I remember it was real hot.

There were two outs, and it seemed like we couldn't get the third out. Ziggy walked up to the mound, and she said, "Hang in there, ML. We'll get them sooner or later." She had such a hangdog look! I was burning up, and it seemed nobody could do anything right. I forget the score, but I know we lost. *[She laughs.]*

Another incident that was funny happened when Guy Bush was managing the Battle Creek Belles. We were playing them in Grand Rapids one time in 1952, and I pitched, and we beat 'em. A couple of weeks later, we played 'em in Battle Creek, and it was cold. The temperature was 52 degrees, right around July 4. Dottie Hunter, our chaperone, said, "ML, you better go out a little bit earlier and warm up, because it's real cold out there."

I had a long sleeve sweatshirt under my uniform, and the catcher was Mamie Redman. We left the clubhouse and we're walking across the field, and Woody English and Guy Bush came out of the coaches' clubhouse. As they passed us, Guy said to Woody, "Is she pitching tonight?" Guy pulled a chaw of tobacco out of his pocket, and said, "Here, have a bite."

I said, "No, that stuff will make me sick." Guy said, "Have the whole thing!" Woody laughed. He said, "I don't think they want you to beat them again, ML!"

"Sadie" Satterfield tagged me with the nickname. She said, "By the time we get Mary Lou out of our mouth, the game will be over! Call her ML."

It sounds like you had a good time playing in the league.

We did have a good time. On the bus trips, we'd sing, and I'd play the harmonica. After a while, we had our card players who would go to the back seats and play cards. In my rookie year, Ziggy walked up one time and said, "Hey, ML, you want to play cards?" I said, "Do you play for money?" She said, "Yeah," and I said, "I don't gamble. I don't play cards for money."

Ziggy said, "Listen, fun's fun, but you can't laugh all night."

When it came to road trips, after we left the ball park, we'd travel all night. We'd bring our bags all packed, and we'd hurry up and shower, and get on the bus, and we'd try to find some place to eat. It didn't have to be fancy. Sometimes it would be a tavern that would serve sandwiches. A lot of times, we'd be on the bus maybe five hours, and someone would have to use the bathroom. And they'd yell, "Tee time!" We got a new bus driver who didn't understand, so Dottie Hunter explained to him what it meant. She told him when that happened, he should pull over to the closest place that was open, and if there wasn't anything, he should pull over close to a field.

One night the bus pulled over next to a corn field, and the corn was higher than our heads. Dottie let us get off the bus with blue jeans on, because it was pitch dark and way out in the country. Everybody found a different row, and began to squat, but all of a sudden, a farmer yelled, "Who's out there?" Dogs started barking and chasing us. You never saw a bunch of girls trying to run so hard, trying to pull up their blue jeans, and tripping over them! It was so funny the bus driver laughed all the way to our destination.

You had good records every year. You threw a heavy ball and a curve. Who caught you most of the time?

Mamie Redman was there all three years that I pitched, and Mary Rountree was there in 1952. Mamie left early each year because she was in college. When Marilyn Jenkins started catching in 1952, it was Marilyn Jenkins until Mamie showed up, and when Mamie went back to school, it was Marilyn doing the catching. Mamie did most of the catching when I was there.

In 1953, Grand Rapids got into the playoffs, and the Chicks won the Shaughnessy Playoffs over the Kalamazoo Lassies. I believe Beans Risinger struck out Doris Sams for the last out of the final game, but the time before Sams hit a homer off Risinger. Who were the other pitchers?

Beans pitched, and we had Jeanie DesCombes, and "Mobile" Silvestri, and Jaynie Krick, and Ziggy pitched too — she pitched and played second base. I can't remember all of them.

What happened after baseball?

I started working at the First National Bank in Chicago when I was a senior in high school. I worked on Saturdays until I graduated in 1949, and then I walked into a full-time job. My boss was very sports-minded. He arranged for me to leave early for spring training, and he arranged for me to return after the season, usually in October. I was a bookkeeper. The bank had 107 books, private and business accounts. They also had what they called "country books" for various banks. After six months of training, I could work any of the books. I could sort out the checks and post them on the machine, so if anyone was sick, I could take over her machine. I was good at it. All the supervisors were happy when I filled in under their sections.

At Christmas, they handed out bonuses and told you what your raise for the next year would be. The first year I got the lowest raise of anyone. I figured it was because I was only there one year. The second year, I got the lowest raise. Some fellow that only worked two books got a terrific raise. I went to my boss and complained about the raise. He said. "Well, Mary Lou, you're young, and you're not married, and you don't have many responsibilities. The men with families have responsibilities and they get the big raises." I thought, "That's a crock."

In 1956, I got married, and the same thing happened. I said to my husband, Adam

Braze, who was an iron worker, "I'm going to quit," and he said fine. In the first week of December, I went up to my boss, complained about the raise, and I said, "I've had it. I'm giving you two weeks' notice." On the last working day before New Year's, I went to my supervisor and asked for my check. He thought I was kidding, but he sent me downstairs to see another supervisor, and they finally gave me the pay. I stayed home about a week in January. The weather was bad, and my husband wasn't working. They were starting a new building downtown, and he went to check on that job, and I went with him. I was reading the want ads, and the LaSalle Bank needed a bookkeeper. I walked over to the bank, they interviewed me, and they hired me — for more than I made at the other bank.

I got pregnant, and my first daughter was born in January 1958. I worked up until the middle of November 1957, and I went back to work when my daughter was about six months old. I worked nights at the LaSalle Bank. I would go to work when my husband came home. Me and another gal would finish up the bookkeeping. If it took us five hours, we worked five, and if it took us eight hours, we worked eight, but we got paid for forty hours. It was a real good job.

In 1962, I read in the paper about a job for the city. I walked over to the address and found out it was City Hall. I got the application, and filled it out for a fingerprint technician. I turned in the application, and a month later I got a notice to report to Wells High School to take the exam. Over ten thousand people had applied for the job. After another month, I got a notice that I placed with the first twenty-five people, and I should report to the police academy on December 3. They took us to the Chicago Board of Health, and we did a blood test and a urine test. There were twenty-five of us ranging in age from twenty-one to a gal about forty-four. We had six weeks of training, and one guy was let go because he couldn't pass the physical, and one gal quit when she found out she had to do shift work at the Police Department. There were two groups. One worked days and one worked from four o'clock to midnight. We were on six months probation, and after that, I got on the midnight shift, which was 11:30 to 7:30 A.M. I was pregnant at the time, and I had to watch my weight. I got a leave of absence, had my daughter, and went back to work nights when she was three months old. I worked there twenty-eight years — the best job I ever had — and I retired officially on August 1, 1990.

What happened to your first husband?

My first husband died in 1970. In 1972, I got married to Paul Caden. He was a fireman, and I met him through a friend. He died in 2003, but we had thirty-one good years together. Paul went to a lot of reunions with me, until he got congestive heart failure in 1997. I have three daughters: Pauline, Laura, and Elizabeth. Laura is a schoolteacher in Chicago, and she presented me with a great-grandson in September 2011. I have two great-grandbabies living in Indiana.

Would you say the league made a big impact on your life?

Yes, it did. The league taught me how to be reliable, and it taught me how to get along with people. I made a lot of friends with the players, and I met a lot of the fans.

Last year a fellow from Grand Rapids interviewed several former All-Americans, and he sent us a CD of the interview. I spoke at an assisted living facility, and I showed the CD, and they really enjoyed it. After that, I began speaking at the Kiwanis and other clubs. On my 80th birthday in July, two of my friends from church had a birthday party for me, and they played the CD. We had about twenty-five people from my church, and they really enjoyed it. One gal told me, "We had more fun watching your CD than playing games!"

You know, during our era, we acted like professionals. Today in baseball, they give high fives and celebrate after every hit, every play, and every inning. Times have really changed.

JEAN (GEISSINGER) HARDING
Fort Wayne, 1951–1954; Grand Rapids, 1952
Interviewed on September 26, 2011.

Born: 1934
Height: 5'6"
Weight: 135
Positions: 2B, IF
Batted: R
Threw: R
All-Star Team: 1953, 1954
RBIs: Led league with 81 in 1953
Career Batting Average: .306 in four seasons

Jean Geissinger, like most girls who played in the All-American League in the 1950s, grew up playing ball with uncles, cousins, and neighborhood boys. In Huntingdon, Pennsylvania, she played ball almost every Sabbath in her "Sunday-go-to-meeting" dress. "The boys accepted me," Jean remembered, "and they were very kind." At West Chester High, she played the four sports usually available to girls in the postwar years, field hockey, softball, basketball, and track, but baseball was her favorite. In 1951, the spring of her junior year, Jean's sister Connie, whose husband Mike Bryant was serving in the Army in North Carolina, saw an All-American League exhibition game near the base. Connie walked up to Max Carey, who managed the Fort Wayne Daisies, and said, "I've got a sister who could play this game." Jean soon received

From Huntingdon, Pennsylvania, Jean Geissinger joined Fort Wayne after a tryout in 1951. Jean spent part of the 1952 season with Grand Rapids, and she is pictured in Chicks uniform (courtesy Jean Harding).

a letter from the Daisies asking her to come to Fort Wayne and try out. Her father and mother finally signed a contract for their seventeen-year-old daughter, and Jean rode a train to Indiana. Doris Tetzlaff, a six-year league veteran now serving as chaperone, met Jean at the railroad depot and took her to a room. That night the Pennsylvania teenager saw her first AAGPBL game.

Geissinger, a brunette who stood 5'6" and weighed 135 pounds, was talented and enthusiastic, and she loved playing defense. Right-handed all the way, she was a good infielder who could hit with power. In 1951, she roomed with Katie Horstman, an Ohio rookie, and together they learned the professional game from Max Carey, one of the loop's best teaching managers. The team practiced hard, but the players, recruits and veterans alike, didn't mind because, like Geissinger, they wanted to excel on the diamond. Jean, a modest, quiet player, got into 22 games, but in her first at-bat, she blasted the ball out of Fort Wayne's Memorial Field. In 1952, when Evie Wawryshyn retired, Geissinger started at second base, and she formed a fine double-play combination with Dottie Schroeder. In 108 games, Jean batted .280 with 56 RBIs. A big hitter as well as a graceful fielder, she usually struck out more than she walked. She made the league's All-Star team at second base in 1953 and 1954, and she topped the circuit with 81 RBIs in 1953.

Geissinger, traded to Grand Rapids after 19 games in 1952, came back to Fort Wayne in 1953. She made her greatest mark with the Daisies, peaking at .377 with 26 homers and 91 RBIs in 1954. Jean and her talented teammates played for manager Bill Allington in 1953 and 1954. The Daisies won the regular season title both years, but they failed to win either Shaughnessy Playoff Championship. When the circuit went out of business after the five-team 1954 season, Geissinger joined Allington's touring All-Americans, and they played men's teams—although switching batteries—for three summers. After that, she worked in an office as a "secretary-bookkeeper-gopher." In 1959, she married Blaine Harding, a catcher and an Army Special Forces vet. The couple raised three daughters, Ann, Karla, and Jana, and all three earned athletic scholarships under the Title IX Program. When the All-American League was recognized by the National Baseball Hall of Fame in 1988 and the movie *A League of Their Own* appeared in 1992, Harding took it in stride. She liked talking about her famous teammates rather than dwell on her baseball feats. Regardless, she worked with the AAGPBL Players Association for years, she maintained many of her baseball friendships, and she valued her opportunity to compete in the national pastime when few women were able to live their baseball dream.

JS: Can you tell me about your background and how you got interested in the league?
Harding: When I was growing up, my dad, Richard Geissinger, worked for UPS. I think they called it Railway Express at that time, but he traveled all over. My mother's name was Lillian. We left Huntingdon and moved to West Chester, Pennsylvania. That's where I began to play more than one sport in school: field hockey, softball, basketball, and track. I used to play baseball with my uncles and cousins and everyone else in the neighborhood. I was the middle one of five children. Their names were Virginia, who just passed away last summer, and Connie, and then me. Dick was two years younger than me, and I have a half-brother Tom, who is a lot younger. My older sisters weren't into athletics at all, but my brothers were. I think my dad wished I was a boy! *[She laughs.]*

I used to play baseball every Sunday morning in my "Sunday-go-to-meeting" clothes. I was at second base with the skirt of my dress almost at the ground. That's the way we played ball a long time ago. The boys were very good to me. The boys accepted me, and they were very kind.

As for getting into the AAGPBL, my sister Connie and her husband, Mike Bryant, who was a chef in the Army, were stationed down in North Carolina. She happened to see a league game in spring training. She walked over to Max Carey and said, "I've got a sister who could play this game." That's how I got started. They sent me a letter from the Fort Wayne team, and my mother and my father finally signed it. I think my mother was scared, but she agreed to let me go.

Did it matter to your parents that the teams had chaperones?

It sure did. I went on a train all by myself to Fort Wayne, and Doris Tetzlaff, the chaperone, met me and put me up in a hotel. I went to that first game, and that was the longest game I ever saw. Earlene Risinger was pitching for Grand Rapids and Maxine Kline went about twenty-one innings. That was my very first game in 1951. I was still a junior in high school.

Did you play other sports in high school?

I played field hockey, basketball, and softball on the girls' teams. We were playing the half-court basketball with three girls at each end.

You played second base and the outfield. Did you start the first year?

Dottie Schroeder sprained her ankle after I'd been there a while, and I took her place at shortstop, just for a short time. I went over to second base when Evie Wawryshyn retired after the 1951 season.

Who was your roommate with Fort Wayne?

I roomed with Katie Horstman. We were both rookies in 1951.

What was Max Carey, your first manager, like?

Max Carey was very, very into the game. He made us practice really hard, but I didn't care, because I loved the game. He'd hit the ball hard during infield practice all the time. Katie would be on third base and I would be at shortstop. He'd really drill us!

You played most of the 1951 season, but in 1952, 1953, and 1954, you were a regular.

I played second base after Evie Wawryshyn retired, and Dottie Schroeder was the shortstop. Jo Weaver was in center field and I'd be at second. We'd go out of the dugout after an inning, and we'd touch second base, and she'd keep on going to center, and I'd turn right to my position. It was just something we did.

Beside Dottie and Jo and Katie and Evie, at that time, we had Maxine Kline, and we had Tiby Eisen and Wilma Briggs in the outfield. Jean Weaver was also there. Our catchers were Kate Vonderau and Mary Rountree.

Was it hard to break in as a rookie?

No, I just went along with the flow. As I said, I loved the game. I didn't pay much attention to how well I did. I just played hard, that's all. Of course, Jo Weaver and I started hitting home runs. If she hit more than me or not, I didn't care — she was my teammate. I was never envious or jealous of her. We just played hard, and we played well.

Jimmy Foxx was your manager in 1952, right?

Yeah, but I didn't get to play for Jimmy Foxx very long. I was traded to Grand Rapids.

Who was the manager at Grand Rapids in 1952?

We had Woody English for manager. He was a "Good Joe." Grand Rapids had Beans Risinger, and Marilyn Jenkins, who started out as a bat girl, and Ellie Moore. They had

Alma Ziegler at second base, so I moved to the outfield. Grand Rapids was very nice. Mary Rountree, one of the catchers, went with me on that trade.

Grand Rapids won the championship in 1953.

But I wasn't with Grand Rapids then. I was sent back to Fort Wayne in 1953. They had the "rookie rule" after 1950. I was a rookie at first, and Katie Horstman was a rookie, and I got traded. Grand Rapids had that fire at Bigelow Field, and they lost all of their equipment. They had good people up in Grand Rapids.

So you spent 1953 and 1954 in Fort Wayne with Bill Allington as manager. What was it like to play for him?

Bill Allington was pretty much into baseball too, like Max Carey. Bill would give us "pop quizzes" on the rules and regulations. We really hit the rule book with him. I can still recite the infield fly rule! *[She laughs.]*

In 1954, your last year, you batted .377 and hit 26 home runs. I believe Jo Weaver batted .429 with 29 homers.

Jo Weaver nosed me out in the last week of the season with those home runs, but that was all right — no problem.

What were the Weaver sisters like?

They were strong. They kept to themselves pretty good. They talked all the time during the game. They were good people, and they were very fast! *[She laughs.]*

Do you have favorite memories?

Before my first time at bat, the Lassies kept saying, "How well do you hit?" I said, "I don't know." But the pitcher threw it right down the pike, and I hit it out of Memorial Field. They said, "Well, now we know how you hit!"

Do you remember unusual things that happened?

One time I pitched to "Babe" Didrikson. Babe, Patty Berg, Mickey Wright, and Jackie Pung all came to Fort Wayne to play in the Mad Anthony Golf Tournament in the fall of 1954, and they all came to the ball field. The Babe, who was a tall and skinny lady, wanted to bat, and everyone wanted her to bat. I used to be the batting practice pitcher, so I could throw strikes. They pulled me off second base to pitch to the Babe. Rita Briggs was catcher that day. I threw one right down the middle, but Babe swung low, like golfers swing. Rita came out from behind the plate and said, "You know, she's a low swinger, so let's put them down around the ankles." I said, "Okay, put the mitt down there," and I threw her some low pitches. Babe finally connected with some long hits, and everybody applauded! I got all the signatures of Babe and her friends, and I still have those in my scrapbook. Babe was dying with cancer, but I don't think anyone knew it at the time.

Would you say the league made an impact on your life?

It sure did. Everybody grew up a little bit in the league. I really did appreciate playing ball. I was not that worried about hitting, but I loved to play defense.

A lot of the girls that played in the 1950s were young. Many of them were not out of high school when they started with the league.

That's right. I was a junior in high school when I began with Fort Wayne in 1951. A lot of us were pretty young. By 1952, my dad lived in Jersey. I graduated from Lower Camden County Regional High School, and I went back to the league. Later, after the league ended, I played on the tour with Bill Allington's All-Americans, and that was fun too. We may not have been as fast on the bases, but we played baseball just as good as the men.

I met my future husband Blaine Harding on Allington's tour. Blaine was a catcher, and he was in the Army, the Special Forces, and he played baseball in the Army. Afterward, he was in the Detroit system for a while before he moved up here. We got married in 1959. He was a good athlete, so our daughters got their athletic ability from their father as well as from their mother. All three daughters all got sports scholarships to go to college, and they all graduated. Their names are Ann, Karla, and Jana. The federal government started Title IX just about the time Ann was graduating from high school, so our daughters were able to use sports to get a college education, and that was great.

KATIE HORSTMAN
Kenosha, 1951; Fort Wayne, 1951–1954
Interviewed on August 18, 2011.

Born: 1935
Height: 5' 7"
Weight: 150
Positions: OF, P
Batted: R
Threw: R
Career Batting Average: .286
Lifetime Pitching Record: 29–11 with 2.50 ERA in four seasons

Catherine "Katie" Horstman, born in Minster, Ohio, grew up playing baseball with her brothers, but she never heard of the All-American League until 1951, when she joined the circuit. Katie lived on a farm outside of Minster along with five brothers, four of them older, and two sisters, and they all liked sports. In the summer, the kids played baseball with boys from neighboring farms. In the winter, they played basketball, often inside the Horstmans' barn. Later, Jimmy Foxx said she had the strongest wrists he ever saw on a girl, and Katie attributed that strength to her daily chore of milking cows early in the morning. Raised in a German Catholic family, Katie, like her siblings before her, attended mass at eight o'clock before school started. Nuns of the Precious Blood taught at Minster's elementary and high schools. Also, the sixteen-year-old was playing for a Catholic Youth Organization softball team when she was spotted by a league scout during the spring of 1951, her sophomore year. Her father, John, had passed away a year before, and Alvina, her mother, gave her permission to try out after the school year ended on May 23. Horstman and another local girl, Joan Bernard, traveled to Fort Wayne to try out. Katie made it, signed for $50 per week, and launched a "miracle," her baseball dream.

The Minster teenager, a right-handed batter who was eager, strong, and talented at

From Minster, Ohio, Katie Horstman joined the Daisies as a hard-hitting rookie in 1951. Pictured in 1953, Katie, standing in the middle of four other Daisy sluggers, is flanked by Jean Geissinger and Dolly Brumfield on the left, and by two Weaver sisters, Betty (Weaver) Foss and Jo Weaver on the right (courtesy Katie Horstman).

5'7" and 150 pounds, roomed in Fort Wayne with another rookie, Jean Geissinger. When the Ohioan saw the girls had to slide in skirts, she recalled, "I really tried to hit that ball hard, so I didn't have to slide into base!" Uniforms aside, Katie enjoyed a good season, hitting .256 and filling in at different positions for the Daisies, who finished second in the first half of the season but lost the semifinal round of playoffs to South Bend (the league's season was split into two halves in 1951, the only time that happened after 1943 and 1944). In 1952, Katie traveled with the Daisies as well as the Battle Creek Belles to spring training at Newton, North Carolina, which was her first trip south of Ohio. That summer Jimmy Foxx moved her to third base, but again she also pitched for the Daisies. She liked all of her managers and learned from each one — Max Carey in 1951, Foxx in 1952, and Bill Allington in 1953 and 1954. But in 1954, the league's final season, when a regulation baseball was adopted in early July, Horstman emerged as a slugger, hitting a personal-best .328 with 16 home runs and 55 RBI.

Horstman hated to see the league end, but when manager Bill Allington assembled a team of traveling All-American girls who would play men's teams (the women's battery pitched against the women and likewise for the male battery), she jumped at the chance. The outgoing Katie spent three years on Allington's tour, enjoying the unique experiences and playing the game she loved. Afterward, she lived with Dottie Schroeder and her family in Sadorus, Illinois, and continued her education. In two years Katie became a registered medical record librarian, and, after joining the Franciscan Sisters of the Sacred Heart in 1959, she became a teacher. She taught and took classes at DePaul University, and in 1965 she was the first nun in the United States to graduate with a Bachelor's in Physical Education. Later, she left the convent and became a teacher and coach at Minster High, where she produced nine state champions in track and cross country. An All-American at heart who treasured her memorable seasons in the league, Horstman loved the game, her baseball experiences, and the AAGPBL Reunions.

JS: Where did you grow up, and how did you get interested in baseball?

Horstman: My father was John H. Horstman, and my mother was Alvina (Berning) Horstman. We grew up on a farm about two and a half miles east of Minster, Ohio, and I used to have to ride my bicycle into town to play ball. I had five brothers and two sisters. We had lots of cows to milk, but we also had a small field where, after our chores were done, we played ball in the summertime. We played baseball, because my brothers weren't going to play softball. You had to play baseball, and if you weren't any good, you would get teased. I made sure I was as good as my younger brother. I was the seventh child, and he was a year and a half younger than me. Everybody dominated me except my brother John, who was younger and much smaller.

We played ball practically every night, unless it rained. We played baseball in the summertime and basketball in the winter, because we had a basket in the barn. We had a pretty good wooden floor, and we'd move stuff like hay out of the way and practice for a couple of hours. By the time I was in high school, it was mostly John and me playing basketball, because my older brothers were in service or in college. But in the earlier years, on Sunday afternoons in the summer, it was a big thing to go around the neighborhood and get all the guys and gals to play baseball. We'd take turns going to each other's farm and playing ball. We were close to the same age, and all the families had five or more kids. It was a good time. I had a good childhood, except for milking those cows. I didn't mind when I was younger, but when you got into high school, you had to get up so early in the morning.

But the milking was good, because two good things came out of it. First, my mom never had a curfew on us when we dated or anything, because she knew we'd be home by midnight because we had to be up by five o'clock to milk those cows. If you were late getting up, you got another cow to milk, and normally it was one of your brother's cows. *[She laughs.]*

Second, when I played for Jimmy Foxx in 1952, I was batting one night, and he said, "Wow, you can really hit that ball! Were you a farm girl?"

I said, "My gosh, does it show?" Jimmy said, "No, I was a farmer too. It gives you a lot of wrist strength, but I've never seen more wrist strength in a girl than you."

So milking the cows paid off in baseball, and I was happy about it. Now I really thank my parents that I was raised on a farm, rather than in the city.

Where did you go to school?

I went to Minster High School. At that time, Minster was mostly a Catholic town, and the school was on the grounds of the church. The bus would come early, and we all had to go to mass every morning. Minster was a public school, but the church owned everything on that whole block. The region was German Catholic from Cincinnati all the way to Toledo, especially around Minster. The Miami-Erie Canal went from Cincinnati to Toledo, and that's why the Germans settled in this area. Normally to the right (east) of the canal, the people were mostly German Lutherans, and to the left (west) of the canal, they were mostly German Catholics. We have a beautiful Catholic Church in Minster, and the largest Dannon Yogurt plant in the USA. We have about 2,800 people living here now.

You went to mass before school every day?

Yes. Mass started at eight o'clock, so we got there about quarter to eight. We had mass from eight to eight-thirty, we ate breakfast, and we started school. The schools were an elementary with grades one through eight, and the high school had grades nine through twelve. We had nuns of the Precious Blood teaching us. Since the people were mostly Catholic, that was fine. I only knew one Protestant as a youth!

You must have started playing in the All-American League before you graduated.

I graduated in 1953, and I started with the league in 1951, after my sophomore year, when I was just sixteen years old.

Were you already playing on a local team?

That's how the league spotted me. I was playing on the CYO team, the Catholic Youth Organization. Father Schuwey, a young priest from Louisville, Kentucky, who just got out of the seminary, was a super-handsome guy. He thought the girls should have a ball team, so he started the CYO, a summer softball league. It seemed like the girls all tried out, because he was so handsome. But Father Schuwey took the girls who were the best ballplayers.

A scout from the league came from Fort Wayne visiting a real estate man, Tony Bernard, who was the coach of the St. Henry team, and Tony's daughter played on the team. He said to the scout, "Why don't you come to see the game? We've got a good softball team, and it's really going to be good, because Minster is tough." St. Henry and Minster were number one and two in the CYO, and this was April of 1951. The scout said, "Oh, yeah — We've got the Fort Wayne Daisies, a baseball team." Tony said, "A baseball team? I'm taking you to a softball game. I didn't know girls played baseball." The scout, said, "they've got a pro baseball team, but I'll come to the game and see if I see anybody that's good." He came to the game, and right away he spotted me and Tony's daughter.

After the game, the scout came up to Tony and said, "I think these two could make the team." The scout asked me, "Would you be interested in playing baseball?" I said, "I dreamed about that all my life, but I didn't know there was a girls' pro team." He explained they had a professional league with eight teams. I said, "I'm still in school." The scout said, "That's all right. We'll make amends for that. You can come after you finish school."

School ended around May 23, and the All-American League started the regular schedule around the middle of May. I told Mom about it — my father had passed away a year before, in 1950. She said, "Well, you're going to have to pay your own way, and make your own money." I said, "Mom, it's pro. They pay rookies $50 a week. I'm mowing lawns for 40 cents and baby-sitting for a dollar." I said, "I'll pay my way through high school, if that's necessary, but I haven't made it yet."

Mom let me go, and I went to Fort Wayne and had a tryout, and the team signed me. The other girl was Joan Bernard, but she had plans to get married in about a year, so she didn't want to stay. I went home and told the superintendent. They wouldn't let me out early the first year, but I only had to wait a week until school was out.

The chaperone came to visit my mother, and she told us about all the rules and regulations I would have to follow. My mom said, "Well, that's okay, as long as she goes to church every Sunday. If she misses church, she comes right back home." We were very strong Catholics. I promised to go to church, and the chaperone promised she would see that I went to church.

The league was like a miracle. I used to dream every night, "If I could only play baseball, I would be satisfied." Never in my life did I expect that dream to come true. I couldn't imagine that somebody would come and ask me if I would play pro baseball. I would have played for nothing, but $50 a week helped!

In fact, $50 was a lot of money at that time. We had everything paid, except we had to pay room rent, and you lived with a roommate in a private home. We couldn't just stay anywhere, so it was pretty strict.

When I saw the skirts, I thought, "Oh, my Lord — I'm not going to slide in that!" But you had to wear the uniform if you wanted to play. When I got my first "strawberry" from sliding, I thought, "This is not going to happen again. I'm going to hit a double, or anything but a single!" I really tried to hit that ball hard, so I didn't have to slide into base!

That's how I started. In 1951, I had a super roommate, Jeannie Geissinger, from Philadelphia, who was also a rookie. Jeannie was a long ball hitter too. Everything just worked out right, and I loved it.

The league had a regular season champion and a playoff series for the championship — we called it the World Series. The league had a five-game playoff, but we started school after Labor Day. So that year I wrote to the superintendent and asked if I could stay a week longer. He wrote back and said, "Take all the time you want, as long as you come back."

In 1952, my junior year, I told the superintendent that spring training was going to be in Newton, North Carolina, and I really wanted to go, but I'd have to leave around the first of May. He said, "I'll tell you what. If you get your conduct, you can go." I'd do ornery things in school, you know, but I got my conduct. I was as good as gold, because I wanted to go to North Carolina. I also stayed in Fort Wayne longer because of the playoffs, because the Daisies were in the playoffs every year, from 1951 through 1954.

I did come home for my graduation, the league let me off, but I went right back to Fort Wayne the next morning. My baseball dream came true, and that's all I wanted. But the league ended after the 1954 season, and I was devastated. I was only nineteen. But the next year, several of us went on tour with Bill Allington.

I have to say something about my managers. Max Carey, my first manager, was a super base stealer, so he taught us how to steal bases. Jimmy Foxx was a super hitter, and he loved the way I batted, and I learned a lot from him. In 1953 and 1954, we had Bill Allington. He was from California, and he was a semipro at one time. He taught us baseball. When we went on a road trip, he would have the rule book with him. You had to get up at seven o'clock in the morning, and at eight o'clock you had to be in one of the rooms of the hotel. Everybody came with a pad and pencil, and he asked you questions. We went from the first page of the rule book to the last page, and you better be able to answer the questions, or you would have to write out the rule and the answer. Today the major leaguers can make spectacular plays, but the fundamentals aren't there. Bill Allington taught us the fundamentals, like how to trap a runner in a rundown with two throws, not five or six.

After the league disbanded, Bill Allington decided to hire a "bookie" from Omaha, Matt Pascale, to book our games across the Midwest, the West, and the South for the next three summers.

We would play men's teams, but we would switch the batteries. The women would catch and pitch against the women, and the men would do the same against the men. The major reason for this was that we knew we were not as strong as the men, but we wanted the spectators to view our skills of throwing, hitting, running, and knowing the fundamentals of the game.

We traveled in two cars: Bill Allington's Studebaker station wagon and Joan Berger's Ford sedan. We had eleven ballplayers, one duffel bag and one uniform each, a total of four bats, and a dozen baseballs. We traveled and played in a different city every night beginning on June 1 and ending on Labor Day.

Matt would send posters to the businessmen of a town to display the date and the team we were going to play two weeks before we arrived. As soon as we arrived, we would ride on a truck following the fire truck with the siren blowing and announcing to the people that there was a game that night.

An official program that was sold at the games gave pictures with brief biographical sketches of each of the players. The number of league records listed by players was impressive. Compared to the glory days of the AAGPBL, the pay wasn't very good. But at least we could still play professional baseball, the sport we loved. We were making approximately $250 a month. That's not bad, but we certainly didn't play for the money, but for the LOVE of the game. Plus, we met many wonderful people and had a beautiful tour of twenty states from Ohio to Iowa to Montana to Texas.

I remember one time we were supposed to play a game in Jasper, Texas. We were scared to death that night. First, we didn't see our signs and posters in the town. We asked a fellow, "Where's the ballpark?" He said, "I never heard of that ballpark."

We stopped at the sheriff's office, and he was a little man about fifty years old. He was a real Texan, and he said, "You're not going to play these people." Bill Allington said, "Yes, we are. I've got a copy of the contract."

The sheriff said, "You're not going to play these people." Bill said, "Why not?" The sheriff said, "They're black." From the back seat, I piped up and said, "Who cares?" The sheriff said, "If you don't shut up, young lady, I'll send you across the border."

We finally got to the ballpark, and as soon as we got there, seven sheriff's cars drove up. It was a beautiful ballpark out in the woods, and we thought, "This is great." But the sheriff's men kept saying, "You're not playing ball against them." Bill kept arguing, but finally the man who arranged the game paid us. We were scared, but the sheriff finally cancelled the game, and we drove one hundred miles to stay overnight.

We had the same experience with "southern hospitality" another time when we played near New Orleans. When I rode the school bus at home, it was always best to get the back seat, because the driver couldn't see what you were doing. I got on this city bus, and I went right to the back, and everyone followed me and sat down. Well, the bus didn't move. I finally said, "When are we leaving?" The driver said, "As soon you move to the front of the bus." I said, "We paid. Can't we sit in any seat?" He said, "Didn't you read the sign, Blacks to the Back?" I said, "How come the whites can't sit in the back of the bus?" His reply was, "It's the law here, Yankee." We all got off the bus and walked.

What happened after the All-American tours ended?

After the barnstorming tour of 1957, Dottie Schroeder suggested I live with her family in Sadorus, Illinois, while I was looking for a job in the area. Within a week, I was working in the Burnham City Hospital in Champaign as an admitting clerk. While working there, I became acquainted with the medical record librarian who convinced me to further my education in becoming a Registered Medical Record Librarian. I had the prerequisite of two years of college, and all I needed was one year of library training at the hospital. I was very lucky to find St. Elizabeth Hospital in Danville, about twenty-five miles east of Champaign. The school was operated by the Franciscan Sisters of the Sacred Heart from Joliet, Illinois. I entered the school on January 5, 1959, and graduated as a Registered Medical Record Librarian on December 10, 1959.

Two weeks later, I joined the Franciscan Order in Mokena, Illinois. The Reverend Mother had other plans for my future. Instead of becoming a medical Sister, I became a teaching Sister. She wanted me to teach physical education at the new Sacred Heart Academy for Girls located next to the Mother House. I taught PE in the mornings and then hopped on a train to attend DePaul University in the afternoons. I finally graduated with a bachelor's degree in Physical Education in January 1965. I was the first nun in the USA to obtain a degree in PE. Of course, this made headlines in the Chicago newspapers, much to the chagrin of the Order, and I was dismissed from the convent after serving five years.

You roomed with Dottie Schroeder, and you knew her well. Can you talk about her as a person and a ballplayer?

I remember we corresponded about Dottie shortly after she died in 1996, and I have a lot of great memories about her. She was always willing to help you with your skills of the game.

I really got to know Dottie when we toured the country for three years. We had eleven girls traveling in two cars, and we stayed four, five, or six in a room after the games. We did that for three months in the summers of 1955, 1956, and 1957. Under those circumstances, a person gets to know everything about her teammates.

Everyone I associated with loved being around Dottie. The fans especially loved her not only for her beauty but also for her graceful movements playing shortstop. She was fast on defense, and she was a very intelligent player. I can't ever remember her making a mental error. She really knew the game of baseball, and she loved playing the game. She was the only girl who played all twelve years of the league, plus she played on the Allington tour for three years, which proves how much she loved the game.

Dottie's love of God and family and friends were just as precious to her as baseball. She was very religious. Singing in the church choir was also something she looked forward to every Sunday. Her mother was her closest friend, and they supported each other to the smallest detail. Her love for her brothers Don and Walt was just as great as her love for her mother. The family was exceptionally close. I never saw them argue when I lived with them in Sadorus, Illinois, when I was attending college.

Probably Dottie's greatest trait was her *kindness*. She was always nice to everyone, whether they were rich or poor. When people in the media talked about how great she was, Dottie would try to change the subject of the conversation. She was very *humble*.

Another trait was Dottie's dry sense of humor and her witty answers. You would think about what she just said for a couple of minutes, and then chuckle for five minutes! She was a very interesting and pleasant lady.

Do you have favorite memories from the league?

When I first started with Fort Wayne in 1951, I pitched a lot of batting practice. The very first girl I met spoke Spanish. It was Isabel Alvarez, who was a Cuban. I thought, "They've got Cubans on their team. I live sixty-five miles from Fort Wayne, and I never even heard of women's pro baseball!" *[She laughs.]*

The next girl I met came from Canada. Evie Wawryshyn was a good ballplayer, and again, I was thinking, "Sixty-five miles away and I didn't know about the league, but the Canadians knew about it!"

My first train ride was heavenly. We arrived at Newton, North Carolina, in the spring of 1952, and we had another team with us, the Battle Creek Belles. We were out there practicing against each other, and I was playing right field. A teenager in the stands looked at me and hollered, "Hey Yankee, go home!" I thought, "A Yankee — does he mean the New York Yankees?"

I said, "I'm not a Yankees fan. I'm a Reds fan!" I had no idea that southern people called us Yankees. The furthest south I'd been was Dayton, Ohio. I had no idea about being a Yankee, but the other girls on the team just roared! That was a culture shock for me.

I did love the southern fried chicken, but I'd never heard of grits and okra and hominy. At home we ate corn and beans and meat. I lost a lot of weight on that trip! *[She laughs.]*

What are some of your other memories about the league?

One main thing was the league had rules, and you had to follow the rules. Two hours after a game ended, you had curfew. If you didn't obey it, you got fined for being late.

We were traveling to Rockford one night, because it's an all-night trip. We always traveled on Trailways buses. We stopped at this little town because Wally Fidler, our driver, had to get gas. He said it was the last town where we could gas up. You couldn't get off the bus unless you wore a skirt. I was up in the front, and I said, "My gosh, this town is maybe 5,000, and nobody is awake." The chaperone said, "It will cost you $5, Horstman, if you get off that bus without putting on your skirt." I put on my skirt! *[She laughs.]*

A Coke used to cost twenty-five cents, so $5 was quite a bit of money. You just had to follow the rules.

We always ate as a team, and they don't do that now. Today the uniforms are different, but ours were all the same. We had to wear our hair about the same length, down to the neck. We had to look feminine. They don't do that now. To us, ballplayers were idols. We looked up to them. I think kids still look up to ballplayers, but the athletes today don't behave like we did.

Something else has changed. They taught us to play baseball. If you want to show off, go to Hollywood, Bill Allington would say. They also fined you for making mental errors. At the time, maybe we didn't like it. But I'm so glad the league enforced the rules like they did.

In 1952, I started out playing right field, but Jimmy Foxx moved me to third base. I also played second base for the Daisies, and on the tour, I played next to Dottie Schroeder at shortstop. I even played catcher. I think I played every position, including pitcher. Toward the end, they knew the league was going to dissolve, although I never admitted to myself that it would end. I thought I was going to play baseball forever, but it didn't happen that way. I did get to play. And I was very thankful.

The league made an important impact on your life.

The league made a very big impact on my life. I became a teacher and a coach after I left the convent, and I coached nine state champions in track and cross country at Minster High. I was strict with them too, just like it was in the league. There's no harm in discipline. My players had respect for each other, and they were always together.

The league really constructed a solid foundation for the rest of my life.

❖ ❖ ❖

JOAN (BERGER) KNEBL
Rockford, 1951–1954
Interviewed on January 30, 2012.

Born: 1933
Height: 5' 4"
Weight: 133
Positions: 2B, RF
Batted: R
Threw: R
All-Star Team: 1952
Career Batting Average: .250 in four seasons

Joan Berger, who was born and raised in Garfield, 20 miles north of Newark, New Jersey, soon learned to play ball with the help and support of her father. The older of two daughters of Steve and Angeline Eisenberger (her dad instructed her to shorten their surname when she joined the AAGPBL), Joan was playing on her father's girls' team, the Garfield Flashettes, by the time she reached the seventh grade. Featuring girls from around the town, the Flashettes played teams like the Stamford, Connecticut, Nutmegs. Eisenberger's team kept improving. When they finally topped the Connecticut squad, the Nutmegs' fans began rooting for the Jersey girls. Joan also played on her father's basketball team against girls' teams from New York, including Police Athletic League teams. The six-person teams competed under the girls' rules for the era that called for three defenders and three

Joan Berger, from Garfield, New Jersey, became a regular with Rockford in 1951. Joan was a starting infielder for the Peaches through 1954 (courtesy Joan Knebl).

forwards at each end of the court. A good all-around athlete at 5'4" and just over 130 pounds, Joan also played basketball at Garfield High. However, sports for females in schools weren't very advanced, and mostly girls played in recreation leagues.

In the spring of 1949, Eisenberger saw a notice in a New York newspaper about tryouts for girls to play in the All-American League. The tryout was held in Irvington, a half-hour drive south of Garfield. The sports-minded father took his athletic daughter to the tryout, and though she made it, he wouldn't let her join the league until she graduated from high school. He did relent during the summer of 1950, after Joan finished her junior year. The family motored to Grand Rapids, Michigan, and the sixteen-year-old tried out with the Chicks. Manager Johnny Rawlings encouraged the Eisenbergers, but the Chicks were going through a financial crisis, the girls weren't getting paid, and Steve's family returned home. Enthusiastic, competitive, and bashful, Joan responded to a letter from the league inviting her to spring training with Rockford in 1951. The Garfield native made the train trip along with another New Jerseyite, Carol Habben, and both made it with the Peaches. Thus, the big adventure began for Joan, as a right fielder (she was soon sent to the infield), and Carol, as a catcher. Improving her game with experience, Joan made the 1952 All-Star team as a rookie at second base.

Berger joined a classy Rockford ball club that already had won four AAGPBL titles. The tough-minded Peaches battled South Bend in the playoffs in 1951 and 1952, but the veteran, talented Blue Sox won two straight Shaughnessy Championships. Berger, in addition to becoming a regular at second base, helped her team in many ways, fashioning a career batting average of .250 in four seasons and demonstrating her toughness and skill in the infield, for example, gobbling up grounders, making tough catches, and completing double-play throws. Well-liked and respected by her teammates, the brown-eyed brunette also lived her dream by enjoying the social life of a professional ballplayer. She liked the team luncheons with local businessmen's clubs, the invitations to lunch or dinner at the homes of Rockford's dedicated fans, and the camaraderie between talented teammates who were united by the common bonds of baseball and friendship. After the league folded, she played with Bill Allington's touring All-Americans, but she found the league had been more fun. Married in 1959 to Andrew Knebl, the couple had three sons. After the cheering stopped, Joan was mostly a stay-at-home mom, but she appreciated her many Rockford teammates and loves her many baseball memories.

JS: How about telling me how you got started playing baseball when you were growing up?

Knebl: My father, Steve Eisenberger, was a great sports fan, and he played softball. He was a roundhouse pitcher. He used to take me to the games with him, and I used to go out in the outfield and shag flies. Later, when I was in the seventh or eighth grade, he started a girls' team, the Garfield Flashettes. We had girls from all around our area, and we lived in Garfield, New Jersey. My mother, Angelina, and my sister Janet, who is ten and a half years younger than me, supported me playing ball.

We weren't too good when my father's team first got started, and later we got better. We played against the Stamford, Connecticut, Nutmegs — they were pretty well known. At first, they'd beat us by big scores, but when we got better, we'd lose maybe 1–0. We finally beat them in a game. Their fans started rooting for us, because we were the "underdogs!" [She laughs.]

My father later started a basketball team, and we'd play against teams from New York, the Police Athletic League teams. One time we played against a colored team. We were beating them, and we had to leave by the window, because they got angry with us! *[She laughs.]*

Where did you go to high school?

I went to Garfield High, and I graduated in 1951. When I went to join the league, my father told me to play under the name Berger.

Did you play on teams in high school?

We had a basketball team, but not a softball team. Girls' sports were not very advanced back then. The Garfield Recreation Department had basketball teams, and we played by "girls' rules." We had three forwards at one end, and three guards [defenders] at the other end, and we could take two dribbles at one time. I played forward.

I also used to bowl a lot. I even helped set up pins, when they were stuck without a pin boy, and they used to call me to fill in. Bowling was very popular in those years.

How did you find out about the All-American League?

My father read an advertisement in the *New York Daily News* about the league having tryouts in Irvington, New Jersey, about half an hour drive south of where we lived. This was in the spring of 1949, when I was a sophomore in high school. My father took me to the tryout, and I made it, but he wouldn't let me go join the league until I graduated from high school.

That first year, 1949, I went to the Midwest with a school teacher, Mary Diane, from Middletown, New York. She picked me up and we drove to the Midwest. I got to watch some of the All-American League games.

In the summer of 1950, after my junior year, my father and mother took me and drove out to Grand Rapids. Johnny Rawlings was Grand Rapids' manager. We traveled all day to get there, and Rawlings told me to go out to shag flies. About the time we were going to quit, my eyes were so tired, and the last ball hit me right in the head. That's when we quit.

I said, "My arms are so tired," and Johnny Rawlings said, "You come to the game tonight and dress up." He gave me a uniform, and I got dressed, and Johnny and my father were talking. The girls in Grand Rapids weren't getting paid at that time, the team was short on money. My father said that I couldn't stay, because the girls weren't getting paid. So we went back home.

The following year, 1951, I got a letter to go to Rockford, Illinois, to the Peaches. I went out for the spring training, but I couldn't stay and play until after I graduated. Carol Habben went with me to Rockford, and she made it too. It was so cold on the train that we stayed in the bathroom until we got to Chicago, and then we had to transfer!

Where did the Peaches have their spring training in 1951?

It could have been Peoria, Illinois.

Carol Habben and I were accepted by the Peaches. I went as a right fielder, and Carol, who was from Midland Park, New Jersey, was a catcher. They kept me under the limit for games, because they had a "rookie rule," and I was considered a rookie in 1952. I made the All-Star team at second base in 1952. That was a thrill for me, because I played with girls that had lots of experience. I was the only rookie to play on the All-Star team.

I played with Rockford all of 1953 and 1954, up until the league ended.

What did you do after the league ended in 1954?

I played on the traveling team, Bill Allington's All-American Girls. In late 1954, we played a couple of games around Fort Wayne. After that, I played the whole three seasons with them. Traveling was kind of hard on us. We had to travel in a couple of cars almost every day. We went back and forth to games, east or west, north or south, for the games.

Who was the manager when you first went to Rockford?

The Rockford manager in 1951 was Bill Allington. He was a really good teacher. There weren't too many managers who could teach. When we were on the road, he would give us ten questions each night from the rule book, and we would have a meeting the next morning, maybe around nine-thirty or ten o'clock, to discuss the questions and answers and different plays based on the rulebook. At home, we would practice the plays.

You had some famous teammates with Rockford.

We had Dottie Kamenshek, Ruth Richard, Eleanor Callow, Alice Deschaine — they were all good hitters. We also had Snookie Doyle, Dottie Key, Rosie Gacioch, and she was our pitcher. Rosie was a good pitcher. We had Mickey Jinright, from Cuba, and Dolores "Pickles" (Lee) Dries, from New Jersey.

Was Mickey Jinright a pretty good pitcher?

Mickey Jinright was slow — you could see the seams on the ball! She was great for six or seven innings, and the hitters got used to her pitches, so we needed a relief pitcher. But Mickey had good control.

What kind of pitcher was Gacioch?

Rosie was one of the top pitchers, and she had good control. There was Marie Mansfield, and she had a terrific fastball, but she was on the wild side — she kept the hitters loose! *[She laughs.]*

Rockford had Nicky Fox and Amy Applegren too.

Nicky Fox was still pitching when you went to Rockford. Was she a good pitcher?

Yes, she was. Nicky had very good control, and Dottie Kamenshek was the best hitter.

You were a pretty good hitter too.

In the beginning, I was second batter, and we used to pull the hit-and-run. I was a right-handed batter, but I could hit to right field. Dottie Key was the leadoff batter, and I would have to take two strikes, just in case she stole a base. When I had two strikes, then I could hit.

In other words, Bill Allington, the manager, wanted you to take two strikes?

That's right.

What was it like playing in Rockford's Beyer Stadium, or the "Peach Orchard," as they called it?

The stadium was a football field with a running track made of cinders all around the field. Where it bothered you was mostly right field, because it was a football field, and right field was shorter than left field. In right field, you'd go back for a ball and run onto the track, and I turned a couple of ankles at the time, because I hit the cement outline, which was close to the right field wall. The cement edge kept the cinders inside the track. I twisted a couple of ankles my first year playing right field, and I remember playing with two taped ankles.

Where did you live in Rockford?

We lived in people's homes. The first year I remember staying with a family that had three little boys, a very nice family, but I can't remember their last name. They put me with

Carol Habben. We came in late, so they put us together. Carol came from New Jersey too, and she was a good catcher and a good hitter.

You got into the playoffs in 1951 and 1952 against South Bend.
Yes, and we lost!

How many championships did Rockford win before you joined the Peaches?
I think Rockford won four championships.

Do you have favorite memories from being with the Peaches?
The fans were great in Rockford. One little girl used to buy me a soda every time she came to a game. Everybody had one little fan that was a favorite.

The Pagel family used to invite the whole team out to their farm for dinner. We'd help them load the hay and shell the peas, and we did a little of everything, which was good. I never did that kind of thing, because I was from the city. They'd feed the whole team, and it was a nice outing. Those events made you feel like you were at home.

Before one game in Rockford, they had a fashion show. Some store supplied us with outfits, and the team picked some of us girls to model the clothes I happened to be one of the "lucky" ones. They brought in a huge flatbed trailer, with steps to go up and down. We had to parade across the flatbed and turn and turn around and cross over again, and then we went back down the steps, all the time wearing high heels!

In Rockford, we would be invited to businessmen's clubs for luncheons. We would sit at a round table with the men asking us questions galore, so we hardly ever got to eat! What impressed me one time was that I watched a fellow clean his chicken off the bone using a knife and fork!

Remember, I had just graduated from high school, and I had never done anything like this.

I guess I was kind of shy. When fans asked me for an autograph, I would blush and sign for them.

Did you have best friends on the team?
There was Al Deschaine, Ruth Richard, Marie Mansfield, and Eleanor Callow. Actually, everybody was friendly, but those were the ones I'd hang around with when we did the questions and answers on the road. We'd get together before the meeting with Bill Allington, and we'd discuss the questions and answers.

Did you like playing in the league better than being on the road for three years with Allington's All-Americans?
Yes, I did. Being on the road with the All-Americans after the league ended was more like a job. We started out with eleven girls and Bill Allington, our coach. We traveled in two cars, his Studebaker and I had a Ford. We each had one small suitcase and our duffel bag with our baseball equipment. Sometimes you'd travel all night, and we'd get into a town and have to wait for a hotel room, and we'd have to do our laundry. Whereas in Rockford, sometimes you'd have a good landlady, and she'd do your laundry for you. She'd take your laundry when you got home and wash it for you. We really had nice landlords and landladies in Rockford. They treated us special.

I remember one hotel where we stayed gave us a big dorm-type room. There was a rope with knots near the window. I said, "What the heck is this for? Some of the girls said it was our 'fire escape.'" There's a first for everything!

On the tour, we would ride in a flatbed truck in a parade in the town where we were going to play. Sometimes after the game we would have to take a cold shower. Instead, we would travel at night in our stinky uniforms!

It seems like the Peaches were really popular in Rockford.
Yes, we were.

When you look back on the league, did it make a big impact on your life?
Yes, I would say so. But when you came home after being away in the league, you kind of lost your friends that were at home. My father had the softball team, but it didn't last long after I went away.

Your parents must have been proud of you.
My father, mother, and sister were very proud of me, and so were my aunts and uncles.

After you got done playing professional baseball, what happened?
I already had a job, a good job. When springtime came, I said, "I'm going away to play baseball." When fall came, they'd take me back. I was a pinner in a textile printing business. I pinned the material down, and the men printed the design on the fabric. When they finished, we'd have to take out the pins and hang the fabric up to dry. When it was dry, we rolled up the fabric. We worked on tables that were 80 yards long.

Did you continue with that job after baseball?
I did, but I got married in 1959 to Andrew Knebl, and after that I didn't work.

Did you have children?
We had three boys: Andrew Steven (my husband's name is Andrew Joseph), Kevin, and Robert, and the youngest one died in a drowning accident when he was sixteen.

I was mainly a stay-at-home mom, but every now and then I'd go to work at one job or another, just to help our family get ahead.

Do you go to the AAGPBL Reunions?
I went at first, but not anymore. I have a macular degeneration problem in my right eye, and I have a hip problem, so it's hard to travel.

Those are what I call fringe benefits of maturity! *[We laugh.]*

Do you keep in touch with any of the girls you knew in the league?
I keep in touch with Ruth Richard and Al Deschaine, who lives on a lake in Michigan.

Do you have other memories from the league years?
I hit my first home run in Grand Rapids. We were playing the Chicks in Grand Rapids, and I hit my first home run over the right field wall. They had a factory there [the Dexter Lock Company].

The longest ball I hit for a home run was in Rockford. I really hit that one, and it went way out to left field. The stadium was a football field, with left field being the longest part of the outfield, and at the end it went up a slope. I remember the ball going up that slope, and the girl chasing it. I really connected with that ball!

Another time we were playing against Grand Rapids, and Bill Allington had showed us how to block the bag. I was playing second base, and I blocked the bag. Alma Ziegler was sliding into second, and she was out. She got up and said, "The next time you block the bag like that, I'm going to come in spikes high!"

I said, "Listen, I have the ball, and the bag is mine!" *[She laughs.]*

We had a little confrontation there, and I can remember it to this day. But she didn't scare me! Grand Rapids was good at trying to intimidate people, but it didn't work with us.

On Allington's All-American tour after the league ended, we played against men's teams ranging from all-star teams to Triple-A teams. We exchanged the batteries, pitcher and catcher, so the men pitched against the men, and the women pitched against the women. If the men gave us a pitcher, we had a good chance of winning. If they gave us an outfielder to pitch, they had batting practice!

Once we played two innings against a men's Triple-A team. I think it was in Omaha. I was playing second base, and this guy hits the ball really high in the sky. I'm watching it, and watching it, and backing up, and backing up, and wondering if the ball will ever come down. Finally, I put my arm back and caught the ball over my head, and the momentum sat me down. I never caught a ball that was hit so high!

We had more than one experience with guys sliding hard into second with spikes high. I said, "This is only an exhibition game. What are you, out to kill me?" *[She laughs.]*

I had plenty of memorable things happen to me over all those years of playing baseball.

Mary Moore
Sallies on tour, 1950; Battle Creek, 1951–1952
Interviewed on March 26, 2012

Born: 1932
Height: 5'5"
Weight: 145
Positions: 2B
Batted: R
Threw: R
Career Batting Average: .229 in three seasons

Mary Moore, who grew up in Lincoln Park, Michigan, loved baseball, the Tigers, and infielder Eddie Lake, who lived with his family a couple of blocks away. When Lake was traded to Detroit and took over as the Tigers' regular shortstop in 1946, Mary, active, outgoing, and athletic, was nearly fourteen. Already she was playing sandlot baseball and football as well as other outdoor games with the boys in the area. One of her girl friends from school lived next to the Lakes and babysat their children, and Mary often tagged along. In turn, Lake obtained tickets to Tigers' games for them, and the girls collected autographs of Detroit greats like Hal Newhouser, Hank Greenberg, and George Kell. Lake, home on an occasional day off, would hit fly balls to the neighborhood kids, and he taught them to judge and catch the ball. Mary had three brothers, but the oldest, John, cared little for sports. John did split his large newspaper route with his energetic sister, and their father made large baskets for their bicycles to help them deliver the papers. The Lincoln Park "paper girl" usually saved her money to buy sports equipment — thus ensuring the neighborhood boys would want her to play ball on the vacant lot.

Sports for girls in the Detroit-area schools were scarce in the 1940s, and in Mary's case, Lincoln Park had one girls' gym class. When Moore graduated in January 1950, jobs were hard to find. Her English teacher told her about Lincoln Park grad Doris Neal, who had played two seasons in the All-American League. Moore knew nothing of the league, but she began working out at the Kronk Gym downtown with other ballplayers, including Helen (Filarski) Steffes, a third sacker for South Bend. Moore, a brunette who stood 5'5" and weighed 145, was invited to a tryout in South Bend in the spring of 1950. At the suggestion of veteran players, Mary said she played second base. The upshot was a trip to Chicago where the right-handed batter competed against dozens of girls for a position on one of the two touring teams, the Springfield Sallies. Thus, Moore embarked on the greatest summer of her life, traveling the United States and playing the Chicago Colleens, including an exhibition at Yankee Stadium. One of the best girls on tour, Moore afterward found a job with an auto components firm near Detroit. But that winter, a machine guard failed, and she suffered damage to the first two fingers on her throwing hand.

From Lincoln Park, Michigan, Mary Moore played on the developmental tour in 1950. However, a work-related injury to her throwing hand limited the remainder of Mary's career to parts of two seasons for Battle Creek (courtesy Mary Moore).

Baseball was never the same for Moore, who was drafted for the 1951 season by the Belles, newly-moved to Battle Creek. However, her hand injury was so recent that the ball club, loath to incur the medical responsibility, sent her home after a few games. In 1952, still classed as a rookie, Moore played second base for Battle Creek, but she suffered torn ligaments and tendons while sliding into second herself. Mary's pro career was over. She turned down a contract with the Belles in 1953, because she knew her performance was no longer up to her pre-injury standards. She returned home and went to work for Michigan Bell, where she retired after 35 years. But in 1955, Moore had her amateur standing reinstated. For years she played fast-pitch softball and, after 1975, slow-pitch softball. She left the game in 2010, when she helped with the AAGPBL

Reunion in Detroit. One of her great thrills, besides appearing on a baseball card, was participating in the filming of *A League of Their Own*, where she slid safely into home in the "reunion game" as the movie's credits are rolling. Mary Moore is proud of her baseball career, and she values the recognition that the All-Americans have received from the movie.

JS: Can you tell me where you grew up and how you got started playing ball?

Moore: I grew up in Lincoln Park, Michigan (my baseball card mistakenly says the state was Illinois), which is a few miles south of Detroit. Back then, the girls didn't have any sports to play in schools. In my senior year, we were allowed to take one hour of gym, but we had to split the basketball court with the boys. That was our "sports" for girls.

Growing up in Lincoln Park, there weren't a lot of houses in our neighborhood. There were a few kids, and we'd go out to a field near the house with a scythe and cut down the weeds so we could play ball. That's how the boys played in the field, and I played sports with them, because there weren't any girls in the neighborhood. I had an older brother, but he wasn't interested in sports, so I got into playing with the toys and the outside stuff.

What are the names of your parents and your brothers?

My dad was Joe and my mom's name was Eva. My older brother was John, and my two younger brothers were David and Don. There was quite a gap between my younger brothers and myself. There was thirteen years between me and David, and seventeen years between me and Don, so I usually took care of them. That's the way it was in the 1940s. You had to help out, and you had a lot of discipline in families at that time.

John, my older brother, had quite a large paper route, so he gave me a section of it, and it was unusual to have a "paper girl." My dad made us great big baskets for our bicycles, and we had to ride quite a long way. I was about twelve when I started the paper route, and I earned money so I could buy sports equipment. I had bats and balls and footballs and stuff, so if the boys in the neighborhood wanted to play ball, they had to come and get me, or else they couldn't play! *[She laughs.]*

In those days your bats would crack, you know, and you'd put a little nail in the bat, and you'd tape it up, and after a while, you'd have electrical tape wrapped around the ball. Those were hard times at the end of the Depression and during World War II. In the war years, you had gas rationing and food stamps for stuff like coffee and sugar. I remember my parents could trade whatever stamps they didn't use to someone else for what they needed. Life wasn't easy.

I played ball with the boys, and later I played on a church team. One of the Detroit Tigers, Eddie Lake, who played shortstop for the Tigers in the late 1940s, lived about three blocks from us in Lincoln Park. My high school chum lived right next door to the Lakes, and she would babysit the kids. She'd go over there, and I'd go with her. Eddie Lake took us to a bunch of the Tiger games with him. He would come out in the yard and play ball with us. He'd hit the ball in the air to the kids in the area. He'd hit high fly balls, and most of them would go running in too far, but he taught us how to judge a fly ball.

I was very fortunate that Eddie Lake was there, because I got lots of autographs with the Tigers through him. I had Hal Newhouser, Hank Greenberg, George Kell, and all those guys from the late 1940s. I still have an autograph book.

That's kind of how I was playing ball, and I loved sports. When I graduated from Lincoln Park High School in January 1950, my high school English teacher, Faye Nelson, put me in touch with Doris Neal, this other Lincoln Park girl who had graduated and was playing professional ball. I had never heard of the All-American League, and it had been going since 1943. I got in touch with Doris in the winter of 1950, and we'd go down to the Kronk Gym in Detroit. A bunch of the Detroit-area girls would go there to practice baseball in the winter. You could practice sliding, and playing infield, and hitting. There were a few All-Americans who went there, like Jo Kabick, a pitcher, and Marge Wenzell, an infielder. I think Marge's father was a scout for the All-Americans. I met Helen (Filarski) Steffes back then, and we became friends.

Helen played for the South Bend Blue Sox at the time, and she took me for a tryout in South Bend in the spring of 1950. I can't remember who all they had on the team in South Bend, but the Blue Sox had one of the better second basemen in the league. After two weeks of training in South Bend, the team sent me on to Chicago to the league tryouts.

You were playing second base?

That's a funny story. When Helen took me to South Bend, they had all these veteran players, and they asked me where I played, and I said, "Any place, wherever they need someone." That's how I always played on the boys' teams, you know, if they needed a catcher, or a first baseman, or an outfielder.

The veterans said, "You can't do that. You gotta tell them you can play someplace, or otherwise, they'll think you're not that good." So they went through all these positions, and they said, "Well, third base, that's really the hot corner, and shortstop, you really need a strong arm for that, and we really don't know about your arm, and first base, you have to really stretch and be athletic and dig 'em out of the dirt, and we don't know about that, and the outfield, you really need a strong, accurate arm, and we don't know about that. Why don't you tell them second base?"

I was naïve, so when I went to spring training in 1950, I told them I played second base. I never really had any training at second base, but that's what they told me, and that's what I told South Bend. I ended up playing second base as long as I played ball, but it's funny how I started playing that position.

I went on to Chicago to tryouts, and they had quite a few girls there too. These were tryouts for the "traveling teams," as they called them, the Springfield Sallies and the Chicago Colleens. The league needed fifteen girls per team, and they must have had a hundred girls there. We had two more weeks of spring training, and I was fortunate enough to be chosen to play on the Springfield Sallies.

That spring and summer of 1950 we traveled, and we hit 21 states and Canada. We had a 90-game schedule, but we played 77 games, and the rest got rained out. We played a game at Yankee Stadium before one of the Yankee games, and we got to meet all of those guys. Casey Stengel was the manager. They had Joe DiMaggio, Phil Rizzuto, Whitey Ford, and we met all of them. We played our game before their game, so we played in some nice places. We also played in Washington, DC, at Griffith Stadium. We rode the bus and played all night games. They were all one or two-day stands. After the game, we'd get on the bus and head to the next town, and sleep on the bus, if you could, and maybe arrive in the town early the next morning.

The days were ours to do with whatever we wanted. We had to do laundry, and catch up on our sleep, and do letter-writing. But in a couple of places, like New York, we went to Radio City Music Hall and to Coney Island. It was a beautiful experience to get to do that and travel all over. We played through all the South, the East, the New England states, and Canada, so there are places I would never have gotten to see. To do all this and *get paid for it* was really nice.

I believe you were paid $25 a week plus meal money, and the league played all expenses.

Yes, the pay came to $46 a week, and the meal money was separate, because it wasn't taxable. Actually, that was good money at the time. In 1954, when I started with Bell Telephone, I started at $49 a week. That was later, and I was getting $46 to play ball. I liked that a lot better than working in an office! *[She laughs.]*

Actually, this was the tour, and I got drafted by Racine in 1951, but before the season started, they moved the franchise to Battle Creek. I got the rookie pay of $55 a week. It was an increase, but now you paid your own room and board. You took care of everything but the traveling and buying the uniforms. Fifty-five dollars a week was the rookie starting pay, but a lot of them, depending on who they were or what position they played, earned more, but $55 was good pay.

You had an injury in 1951, right?

In January 1951 during the offseason, I was working at a small automotive appliances company out on Plymouth and Telegraph Roads. I was working on the punch press, and the guard failed, and the press damaged all the fingers on my right hand. I was making Packard rings, and the press yanked my hand back, and it cut off the tip of my first finger, cut off the middle finger to the second joint, the third finger got split open, and the little finger was damaged.

I did go to spring training in the spring of 1951, but Battle Creek wouldn't keep me, because the team didn't want to be liable for the injury, because it was so recent.

Where did you go for spring training?

By then all the teams did their own training, and we trained in Battle Creek. They didn't want to be responsible, so they sent me home. Later in the season, when they had injures, the Belles called me up. I played in a few games, but it wasn't the same for me, as far as hanging on to the ball and trying to grip the bat. The league also had a "rookie rule," and they wanted me for a rookie in 1952.

I did return to the team in 1952, and again, with the damaged fingers, I wasn't really doing that well. I couldn't grip the bat real good. Late in the season, we were playing a game in Fort Wayne. I got a hit and slid into second, and I twisted my ankle. Jimmy Foxx and my manager, Joe Cooper, carried me off the field, and they thought it was broken. They called the hospital to have an ambulance there, but it turned out while the ankle wasn't broken, the ligaments and tendons had popped, so it was worse than a break. Of course, I didn't play anymore that year.

I got a contract with Battle Creek in 1953, but now I had another job, and I hadn't played that well in 1952 anyway, at least not as well as I knew I had done before. So I didn't go back, because I knew maybe I'd be keeping someone else from getting a chance, just because I was considered a "veteran." I didn't feel like I could do the game justice, and it kind of broke my heart, but I didn't go back.

To play amateur ball at that time, you had to sit out five years to get your amateur standing back to play fast-pitch softball. My manager for the Wyandotte Chemicals team went to bat for me, and they got my reinstatement in two years, because of my injury. I played underhand fast-pitch, because I could hang onto the ball better, because I could use all of my fingers. I played fast-pitch for years and years, until I got too old and slow. I switched to slow-pitch in 1976, and I played softball until 2010, the first year I didn't play ball. The Players Association was having our reunion in Detroit, and I was helping with that and too busy to play. My team didn't play that year, because they didn't have enough players, and I was their underhand pitcher. I still golf and bowl, and I'm active.

When did you get inducted into the Lincoln Park Sports Hall of Fame?

I was inducted as the first woman in the first class on April 19, 2001. I'm still the only woman in their Sports Hall of Fame, and they didn't have sports for girls in schools when I played.

Can you tell me about your part in filming the movie* A League of Their Own *in 1991?

They invited us to Skokie, Illinois, for tryouts around June of 1991. I think 65 former players that could still play ball went to the tryout, and I think 43 of us went on to Cooperstown that fall for the filming of the reunion game part of the movie.

In the movie, I was the one sliding into home, and Shirley Burkovich was trying to tag me out, and I was safe! *[She laughs.]*

That scene happened during our reunion game, and that game is seen when the credits are running near the end of the movie. Like I said, I slid into home. I was playing left field at one point, and I came running in to help with a rundown play between second and third base, and they didn't throw me the ball, but I was running back and forth. When they zoomed [the camera] in on the bench, I was the first one they zoomed in on, and they panned on down the bench.

We were in Cooperstown for eleven days for that five-minute part at the end. They put us up in a motel and paid us $50 a day as an extra. They wanted us to play the older roles, but we couldn't, unless we joined the Screen Actors Guild, and that was too expensive. So they got older actresses to play those parts, but they filmed the reunion game.

So they paid us $50 a day as extras and $40 a day for meal money, and they sat us half the time. We were there for twelve-hour days, and sometimes longer. Of course, you couldn't leave the set. It was a "hurry up and wait" situation. If they were ready, they didn't want to wait. We would just get someplace, and they wanted us back, but we did it.

I don't know how they put that stuff together, because hardly anything was filmed in sequence.

That's why Hollywood film editors win awards.

Boy, you got that right! And Penny Marshall wants everything perfect, which is good. But we'd get through shooting a scene, and she'd say, "That was good, that was good!" We'd think, "Oh, great!" But she'd say, "We're gonna do it again!" *[She laughs.]*

Everything was filmed four or five times, and sometimes twenty times. Penny Marshall didn't want just one good take. She wanted at least three good takes that she could pick from.

Helping film the movie was quite an experience. I wouldn't trade it for anything in the world, but I wouldn't want to do it again. They took Polaroid pictures when you went home at night, you know, if you had to be wearing certain things, or if you had to have your glove or anything in a certain spot on the field or on the bench. Pictures were taken of everything because it had to be exact later.

I know one time I slid into home, and I got dirt on my blue jeans. You couldn't wash your clothes. Two or three days later, I had to do something else. They put me back out on second base, and they said, "Where's the dirt?" I had to pick up dirt and rub it on the blue jeans so when I got into home again, there'd be enough dirt on the jeans. Some of it was comical, really, but it was quite an experience.

The last day, because the contracts with all the girls ran eleven days, we worked early in the morning, all night long, until six or seven o'clock the next morning to finish up at the Hall of Fame ballpark. There were people sleeping all over the place. It was harder on the crew, because they had to be there before us, and they were there after us. They were whacked out for the long hours they worked, but it was interesting to be part of a movie and see how things are filmed.

One time, right on Doubleday Field, Penny Marshall said she wanted to take some batting practice. So everything stopped, and Penny got up there, and she hit the ball pretty good. Penny was down-to-earth and really great. Matter of fact, Penny was at our reunion in San Diego last year. She's been to our reunions in California.

They show *A League of Their Own* on TV all the time, and we still get fan mail. It's just really nice. Lots of schools and libraries and senior citizens places call you to go out there and make speeches. It blows my mind that so many people are still interested in *A League of Their Own*.

Our AAGPBL Reunion is going to be in Syracuse, New York, in the fall of 2012. They are planning a trip back to Cooperstown for a day, and a number of events are planned, because this will be the twentieth anniversary of the debut of *A League of Their Own*.

MARY (FRONING) O'MEARA
South Bend, 1951–1954; Battle Creek, 1952
Interviewed on October 25, 2010.

Born: 1934
Height: 5'3"
Weight: 118
Positions: OF, RHP
Batted: R
Threw: R
Career Batting Average: .212 in three seasons
(no statistics available for 1951)

Mary Froning, along with Katie Horstman, was one of two players from tiny Minster, Ohio, to make the grade and earn a regular position on an All-American League team. Like Katie, Mary was beginning to excel at baseball when the circuit failed financially after the 1954 season. Froning was lively, outgoing, and attractive, and she enjoyed many of the pursuits of young people in the postwar era, notably playing games, riding bikes, swimming with friends, and softball. Typical of many teenagers, the blue-eyed blonde liked most sports. By the time she turned sixteen in 1950, she was already playing shortstop on Minster's Catholic Youth Organization team, displaying a strong arm, surprising speed, and a talent for the game. During one of the team's Sunday afternoon games in the spring of 1951, Mary was seen by a league scout. As a result, she was invited to a tryout in South Bend. Showing her stuff, including her speed, the 5'3" Minster schoolgirl, now a junior, competed with about one hundred others. Bright, talented, and self confident, she hoped to be chosen. "We had a week to try out and after several days, I knew I could beat out the other girls, because I could run faster, I could catch the ball, I could hit, and I could slide." Within a few days she received a contract. The offer was $50 a week plus expenses, and when Mary and her father looked at the offer, they realized it was for baseball, not softball.

The renamed American Girls Baseball League had eight teams in 1951, and a new rule required each team to start one rookie. South Bend already had recruits such as Janet "Pee Wee" Wiley and Audrey Bleiler, and Froning was used so little, mainly as a pinch-runner, that she is listed as having played less than 10 games. Returning in 1952, the year she graduated from Minster High, she was loaned for part of the season to Battle Creek, but Mary played only 13 games total, batting less than .100. Near the end of the regular season, South Bend was disrupted by a multi-player walkout, and manager Karl Winsch saw his team reduced to 12 players, counting Froning. Regardless, they won the Shaughnessy Championship over Rockford in five games, giving the Blue Sox a second straight playoff title. Froning returned in 1953, and when South Bend was unable to replace the departed veterans, she became the team's center fielder. Speedy in the outfield and on the bases, she liked the give-and-take of players kidding each other, enjoying the camaraderie while playing well. Teammates dubbed her "Fearless Froning," because she ran so hard after fly balls that she risked hitting the outfield fence.

The rise of Froning's career coincided with the decline of the league, and by mid-1954, circuit officials, now with five teams, hoped to reverse declining fan interest and speed up the game by introducing a regulation baseball and increasing the base paths from 75 to 85 feet. The number of home runs and extra-base hits increased around the circuit, and Froning also improved, boosting her average to .231 and hitting her three career home runs. Later, she liked to remember the daily routine of baseball, like getting up, going to practice each morning, taking batting practice in the afternoon, and listening to the manager's pregame talk. After the league folded, she became a stewardess for American Airlines, until she married Tom O'Meara in 1958. The couple raised four children, Kathleen, Susan, John, and Patricia. Looking back on the seemingly idyllic summers of the AAGPBL, Mary O'Meara deeply appreciates playing baseball in the nation's best women's league, living in South Bend, and getting to know so many great teammates.

Mary Froning, from Minster, Ohio, made South Bend's roster at age sixteen in 1951, and she was a regular in the outfield during the 1953 and 1954 seasons (courtesy Mary O'Meara).

JS: How did you first get involved in playing in the All-American League?

Froning: I was scouted where I grew up in Minster, Ohio. I was playing softball on a CYO team [Catholic Youth Organization] in Minster, and we usually played on Sunday afternoons against other small towns in the area. Minster only had about 1,500 people, so it was very small. A man who was on the board of directors of the South Bend Blue Sox was in town visiting his mother. He was out walking and saw me playing softball. This was in the early summer of 1951. He got my name and address, and I was sent a contract from South Bend.

What about the contract?

I believe his name was Schneider, and he owned a plumbing company in South Bend. I was sent a contract about a week later. I looked at it, and my dad looked at it, and he said, "This isn't softball. This is baseball." I said, "Baseball?" We came to find out that Fort Wayne had a team and they were located only about 70 miles away, but I had never heard about a women's league playing baseball or about the All-American League.

The contract asked me to come and try out for the Blue Sox team when I got out of high school. At that time, I was only 16 years old and finishing my junior year in high school. I talked the offer over with my parents, and they agreed to let me go to the tryouts. There were more than 50 girls that came to South Bend looking to fill four rookie positions for the manager, Karl Winsch. There was a new league rule that each team had to start the season with four rookies on the roster. We had a week to try out and after several days, I knew I could beat out the other girls, because I could run faster, I could catch the ball, I could hit, and I could slide. Because I could do all those things, I was one of the four rookies chosen by Karl Winsch, and that is how my baseball career got started.

I signed my first contract in 1951 with the Blue Sox, and my salary was $50 per week, plus expense money when the team traveled. When I was added to their roster, the Blue Sox already had an excellent team. They won both the league and the playoff championships that year. They had tremendous players. There were no positions open for a rookie, because they were all veteran players. They had four or five years of experience on me.

Early that first season, while I was sitting on the bench, the manager, Karl Winsch, asked me, "Are you willing to watch and learn from here?" I told him I was. The transition from softball to baseball was not the easiest, because the bases were farther apart, the pitching was overhand, and the ball was smaller. But I was on the team, so I watched a lot and contributed a little bit. I was used as a pinch-runner, and I batted a few times, and the team won the championship.

In 1952, I was one of the first ones that signed a contract to come back. I also graduated from Minster High School that year. I was on the Blue Sox roster again, but I still didn't play in very many games, because all the veterans came back. I was just happy, happy, happy to still be on the team and fill in whenever they needed me.

However, there was a problem late in the season between our manager, Karl Winsch, and one of our good players, Shorty Pryer. I was on the bench with Shorty, and she had taken her shoes off before the end of the game. Karl wanted her to go into the game, but because she had her shoes off, she wasn't ready to play. Words were exchanged, Karl got angry, and Shorty got suspended. Many of the veteran players got angry with Karl and talked about a strike. When the situation finally ended, Shorty Pryer left the team along with four or five other players, including Shirley Stovroff and Lib Mahon and Dottie Mueller.

When these players left the team, there were only 12 players left. We all got more playing time as a result. Because Stovroff, our catcher, quit, Wimp Baumgartner got a chance to catch, and I got a chance to play the outfield. We still had some really good pitchers, such as Jean Faut, Sue Kidd, Janet Rumsey, and Jette (Vincent) Mooney, and even Betty

Wagoner. We had a good team and we had good pitching. And we proved it. The Blue Sox won the playoff championship in 1952. That was an exciting experience.

In 1953, I signed another contract to play. Some players held off signing to try and get better pay. I never did that, because I just wanted to play baseball. I don't even remember what I was paid. In 1953, I played about every game and that was really nice for me. *[Editor's note: Froning played 111 games in 1953 and batted .208.]*

However, by 1953 the people coming out to watch games was decreasing, because the league was now competing with major league baseball, and they had TV coverage. Our league was in its eleventh year and was having financial problems. But I was still playing baseball, and I thoroughly enjoyed it. I also played with some of the greatest players in the league. Our pitcher, Jean Faut, for example, pitched two perfect games during her career.

In 1954, the league only had five teams and the South Bend team went through a number of changes. Jean Faut quit the league. We had a number of new players from other teams. Dolly Vanderlip and Lois Youngen and Wilma Briggs all came from Fort Wayne, and Betty Francis came from Kalamazoo. All of them were good players. By the middle of the 1954 season, the league wanted to speed up the game, and they went with the regulation nine-inch baseball. Dolly Vanderlip pitched our first game with the new ball.

Most of the players suspected that the 1954 season would be our last one. Some said, "I guess I'll go back to college and get some education," and a lot of them did. Others, like me, had to look for a job. When the season ended, we turned in our uniforms and hoped there would be a 1955 season, but it didn't turn out that way. However, I thoroughly enjoyed my baseball playing days.

When I began my search for a job after baseball, I went to Rockford, Illinois, the former home of the Rockford Peaches, because I had some friends there who told me that jobs were available. I also knew that I wanted to interview for a job as a flight attendant, and this would put me close to Chicago where interviews were held. I got a job with a large company in Rockford doing clerical work in their engineering department while I set up interview dates with several airlines in Chicago. It was during this time in Rockford that I met my future husband, Tom O'Meara. He had just been discharged from the U.S. Army and was starting a career in the health insurance field. My interviews in Chicago were successful, and I was hired as a stewardess with American Airlines. My final interview for the American Airlines job was with a man who was a big baseball fan, and he asked, "Did you play professional baseball?" Most of the questions in the interview after that were about my baseball experiences. It certainly helped me get the job.

I worked for American for about three years, flying out of Chicago. During that time, Tom and I became engaged, and we were married in 1958, after I left the airline. We settled in Madison, Wisconsin, where we still live. We have four children, Kathleen, Susan, John, and Patricia, who are all married, and we have eight grandchildren.

Do you have favorite memories from your baseball years?

Most of my memories are just of the routine baseball things — getting up and going to practice each morning and going back to the ballpark for batting practice in the afternoon. Then we would be in uniform in the locker room before the game, and our manager, Karl, would tell us different signs and what to expect from the different teams that we played. Then we'd go out on the field at Playland Park for the game with all the fans cheering. During the 1954 season, I hit three home runs, and one of them was an inside-the-park home run in South Bend — that was exciting!

I remember that my mother and father and my younger brother came up to watch me play games in Fort Wayne, which was only 70 miles away from my hometown of Minster. My family was very supportive of me during my baseball career. My twin sister, Martha, also played softball, and she tried out for the South Bend team, but she didn't like playing baseball. After high school graduation, she went to school and became a nurse.

Often as a promotion in Fort Wayne, each team would have three girls race from left field to home plate. Usually it would be Betty Wagoner, me, and another South Bend player against the three Weaver sisters from the Fort Wayne team — and I could usually win those races because, at age 18, I was a fast runner.

Most of the players shared rooms they rented in private homes near the ball park. I liked all of my roommates, but two of them, Dolly Vanderlip and Lois Younger, were special friends then and we are still good friends to this day. I had my first car in 1954, and the three of us would travel all around South Bend.

I have a lot of other memories, but the best memory is that I got to play baseball for four years and all the enjoyment I got from playing. I remember watching Jean Faut's perfect game in 1953 — that is quite a memory. She was a tremendous pitcher and a great third baseman. All of my memories about my days in South Bend are wonderful.

What do you remember about practicing and playing games?

It was according to whether we won or lost the game the previous day. If we won the game, we didn't have practice the next morning. If we lost, we had a morning practice. That was the baseball philosophy of our manager, Karl Winsch. And in practice, he would make us work hard on our strong points. My thing was to get on base as much as possible. If he batted me first, I would often bunt to get on base because of my speed. He felt that the hitters that followed had an advantage with runners on base. My batting average in 1954 was .231, which was a good improvement over 1953.

I enjoyed Karl as manager. Many of the other players didn't, but I enjoyed playing for him. A number of the players that I have talked with about their managers state that other managers, like Bill Allington of the Rockford Peaches, were big on teaching about the game, and often gave the players tests on the rules while traveling to the games. Karl taught us a lot about the game, but he was usually very easygoing, and I did enjoy him.

Do you have final thoughts about baseball and the league?

It's great that you are taking the time to interview players from the AAGPBL, but many of the great players have passed away. It's too bad that you couldn't talk to Gertie Dunn. Gertie was a very good player, an excellent shortstop, and she had great baseball sense. Betty Wagoner was an excellent player. She was a left-hander. Betty could play any position on the team. Her mother was the chaperone during that last year.

It's too bad the league had to end due to a lack of money. As for me, I didn't care if I was paid four cents a game. I was just so happy to be playing! Players knew that the pitchers usually made more than the outfielders. They knew that as you played more in the league, you could negotiate with the board of directors for more money. I never did. I was just so happy that I could be on the team, and I looked forward to playing baseball each year.

Janet "Pee Wee" (Wiley) Sears

Colleens on tour, 1950; South Bend, 1950–1952; Rockford, 1953

Interviewed on November 6, 2007, at Center for History in South Bend, Indiana.

Born: 1933
Deceased: 2010
Height: 5'4"
Weight: 110
Positions: 1B, Utility
Batted: R
Threw: R
Career Batting Average: .212 in four seasons

Janet Wiley, a sports-minded girl who was born in South Bend, was the fifth of six children of Adam and Lucy (Lawton) Wiley. Janet, or "Pee Wee," as friends called her, remembered playing the games kids could play in the street, but she was the only girl in the neighborhood good enough to compete with boys. Raised in a Catholic family, she attended St. Matthews Grade School and Riley High. When the All-American League came to town in 1943, the Blue Sox became her heroines. Following World War II, the league embraced community activities and encouraged cities to sponsor girls' leagues using AAGPBL rules, and South Bend's Recreation Department operated a 12-team Girls Baseball League for a few summers. Pee Wee practiced baseball with boys' teams, but she was not allowed to play in games. When the girls' league began, she joined a team that practiced and played at Lincoln School. Her father took her to see a few Blue Sox games at Bendix Field during the war years. When the Blue Sox moved to Playland Park in 1946, Pee Wee could walk one mile to see her favorites. She hung around the practices and sometimes played catch with the players. Starting

A South Bend native who first served as Blue Sox bat girl, Janet Wiley made the team in 1950. "Pee Wee," who finished her four-year career with Rockford in 1953, is pictured with South Bend in 1950 (courtesy Don Sears).

in 1947, manager Chet Grant made her the team's bat girl, and Marty McManus kept her on the job in 1948.

Wiley, who stood 5'4" and weighed just over 100 pounds while at Riley High, often rode to Blue Sox games on the handlebars of the bike pedaled by her future husband, Don Sears. Pee Wee's duties as bat girl included taking care of bats and balls before and after games, getting jugs of ice water or snacks from the concession stand, and doing favors for the players. In 1948 she was taken on South Bend's team bus for a trip to Rockford and on another journey to Kalamazoo. As she put it, "I got to ride on the bus with the stars!" In 1950, during the spring of her junior year, Pee Wee and 200 other teenaged girls attended a league tryout held at Playland, and she was one of the few who made it, thus launching her baseball dream. Positive, thoughtful, and spunky, she recalled receiving her contract and jumping around, almost like a scene from the movie *A League of Their Own*. The right-handed batter signed for $55 a week, but unlike most players, she lived at home. Pee Wee and Audrey Bleiler, another rookie, often got the bunt sign with other runners on base, but it didn't matter. They valued the opportunity to play professional baseball.

Wiley, a lifetime .220 hitter, experienced many ups-and-downs with the Blue Sox. She injured her right knee in a pick-up basketball game in 1950, and during her league years, she wrapped it for each game by using Benzoine and tape. In June 1952, after two seasons as a reserve first sacker, manager Karl Winsch, who believed her friends razzed him from the stands, suspended Wiley for speaking up to support a teammate who was benched for the nightcap of a doubleheader. Pee Wee was neither told why she was suspended nor invited back to the team. In 1953, the South Bend native played first base for Rockford. Within a month, she hurt her knee again. Following surgery for the third time, she gave up the game. Pee Wee and Don raised a family of six children, and she coached softball at the grade school level for ten years. Later, she enjoyed seeing segments of the filming of Penny Marshall's *A League of Their Own*, attending the reunions, and embracing the good times. Janet Sears likely spoke for every ballplayer in America, and certainly for girls, when she reminisced, "Every time they played the National Anthem, I thought, 'Where else in the world could I play professional baseball?' I felt blessed."

JS: *You're from South Bend?*
Sears: I was born and raised in South Bend.

When you were growing up, what sports did you play?
I played every game you could possibly play out in the street, in the back alley, on the basketball court. Whatever the season was, we played it. If it was football season, we played football. We used to play baseball and softball out in the street. I was usually the only girl playing — it was all boys. But I played tackle football on the field, too.

How many brothers and sisters did you have?
There's six of us altogether, and I was number five. My last brother is fourteen years younger.

Where did you go to school?
I went to St. Matthews' grade school and Riley High School, named after the poet, James Whitcomb Riley. I graduated from Riley in 1951. I played one summer of baseball in the league before I went back for my senior year.

How did you first find out about the Blue Sox?

They sponsored sandlot teams, and when I was twelve, the summer after the seventh grade, I pitched on the Lincoln School team in 1945, and we played the All-American League rules. Lincoln School was three blocks from my neighborhood, and the team sponsored by the Blue Sox played on their field. We played teams at the other parks around town. Before that, I practiced with boys' teams, but they couldn't put me in a regular game because I was a girl. Before 1945, there wasn't anything for girls to do in South Bend, except leather-braiding and wood-tapping and stuff like that. The Blue Sox had a "freebie" night one time in 1945 out at Bendix Field, and the first game I saw was on that night.

Do you know how many teams the Blue Sox sponsored?

I'm guessing there were at least ten or twelve teams playing All-American rules.

Can you describe Bendix Field?

All I can tell you about that is Bendix Field was clear across town. I grew up in the southeast part of South Bend, and the field was way over on the west side of town. My father took me to Bendix Field once or twice, and father of one of my friends took us one time. There was a bus that took people out there.

Do you remember anything about seeing that first Blue Sox game?

Connie Wisniewski was the pitcher for Grand Rapids, and I remember "Ziggy" Ziegler, and I remember seeing "Libby" Mahon for South Bend. I remember seeing Daisy Junor and Bonnie Baker and Marge Stefani for the Blue Sox. I fell in love with girls' baseball, even though it was still pretty much underhand. I would say there's all kinds of love. There's family love, love between guys and girls, and there's love of a certain sport, and that's what I had.

The next year, 1946, the Blue Sox moved to Playland Park, and that was only about a mile from where we lived. I managed to find out when the girls practiced in the morning, and I would go and stand around, and wait, and get closer to them, and I always had my glove with me. One of the younger players, Jenny Romatowski, started letting me play catch with her. She kind of took me under her wing, and in the winter, she was always sending me postcards from different places. In spring training, whenever they were, she encouraged me to keep trying.

The manager, Chet Grant, started letting me fill in at bat girl, and he asked me if I wanted to practice, when the veterans went up to take a shower and he wanted to work with the younger ones. He said, "I need a first baseman." Well, I didn't know anything about first base, but I could catch. So he came over and showed me the footwork, and I used to practice it, and that's how I became a first baseman.

But in the spring of 1947, I got a letter from the Blue Sox, and they asked me if I wanted to be bat girl. I wrote on the envelope, "My first contract." *[She laughs.]* So I was the Blue Sox bat girl in 1947 and 1948.

What all did the bat girl do?

I got ice water in jugs up at the concession stand on the hill behind the grandstand, and, of course, I was getting the bats and the baseballs. I would run to the concession stand to get a candy bar, if one of the girls wanted one, or get something from the clubhouse. I was a general "go-fer."

By that time, Don Sears [Don was present at the interview], who I later married, used to ride me to the ballpark on the handlebars of his bike. But we knew each other before that. I tackled him in football before I tackled him in marriage! *[She laughs.]*

Did you go on any road trips as a bat girl?

I got to go on a couple of trips, one to Rockford, and in 1948, one to Kalamazoo. It was really something. I got to ride on the bus with the stars! I was pretty well awe-struck. I would have kept on being the bat girl as long as they asked me.

When you were bat girl, who were some of the players you remember?

I remember Betsy Jochum, Libby Mahon, Shoo-Shoo Wirth, "Pinky" Pirok, Daisy Junor, Bonnie Baker, and Jean Faut. Jean had a heck of an arm — she could throw straight on a line from third base.

Tell me about the tryout the league held in 1950.

The league invited a couple of hundred girls to come to South Bend to try out. I was lucky, because I lived here and I didn't have to worry about living accommodations. The weather was so bad that most of the tryouts were held in a roller skating rink over at Playland. It was early spring, and we didn't get to go outside much, because the weather was really bad. I'm sure some players felt like they didn't get looked at much, because it wasn't outdoors. I remember Dave Bancroft was the manager.

I got a letter in the mail and they said I was chosen by South Bend. I was pretty excited. It was almost like the movie, *A League of Their Own*, except that I was jumping up and down at home! My mother must have been laughing up her sleeve, because she was in the kitchen cooking, and I sat down in my father's chair, and I said, "Oh, Mom, you might as well know now that I'm going to get paid, I smoke." She had to have known that, but I finally admitted it openly. I used to sneak cigarettes from my dad's bowl.

What did they pay you in 1950?

I got paid $50 a week. A couple of my friends, Audrey Bleiler, from Philadelphia, was one, that were my age and just starting in the league got $55. I always felt like they shorted me $5 or $10 a week because I lived at home, but I had to give my mom some money. They probably figured I lived at home for nothing, but I had to pay some, and I put gas in the car, too. I learned to drive that year, 1950, when I took Driver's Education in school.

What do you remember most about your first season in the league?

Gosh, the season went so fast! In the first part of June, Dave Bancroft sent me to what they called the "traveling teams," but I called it the "minor league." I played for the Colleens, and we played the Sallies, the other traveling team. We very seldom stayed in one city two nights in a row. I spent thirty days with the touring teams.

The Colleens got a notice to send me back. They sent me over to Macon, Georgia, and the Blue Sox flew me to Chicago. It was my first plane trip.

At that time, Dottie Mueller played first base. She was a veteran player, and she was a better hitter. If I got into a Blue Sox game, they would put me in during the later innings for defense. If I got in a game that Jeannie Faut pitched, I would be in there for defense.

What else do you remember about that first season?

I bunted a lot. The other players were very good about getting on base, and my friend Audrey Bleiler and I would usually get the bunt sign. I didn't mind at all. I did learn how to bunt that summer. Audrey and I were buddies.

So you're telling me you weren't a home run hitter?

I was lucky to get a single! *[She laughs.]* You remember the old saying, "Good field, no hit"? I have to laugh when I see a major league batting average at .220. I'd think, "I did that good!"

You probably felt pretty good at the time about what they were paying you.

I did feel good about the pay. I was able to save money. We were also getting $3 a day for meal money on the road. You even saved money out of that. I smoked, but cigarettes cost five cents a pack.

What was it like to travel?

I really didn't mind the traveling. Usually we'd get sing-alongs going on the bus.

So you played all of 1950 and 1951 and 1952 for South Bend, and you played for Rockford in 1953.

I played 1950 and 1951 for the Blue Sox, and part of 1952.

What happened in 1952?

In June 1952, "Shorty" Pryer was the second baseman, and Karl Winsch, the manager, benched her for the second game of a double-header. Shorty kept saying. "Why aren't I playing, Karl?" He just kept spitting his tobacco. So I said, "She's just asking a question, Karl." He said, "You go take a shower!" I said, "Roger, dodger!" It just came out.

So I went up, changed my clothes, and stood there until the game was over, still waiting for Karl to tell me where I stood. I don't know how he got out of there without me seeing him. I didn't know what to do, so I didn't go back. About a week later, Chet Grant came over. We went for a walk, and he said, "What do you want to do?" Chet Grant got me my unconditional release.

There's a record out at the Notre Dame Library [in the Dailey Notebooks] that doesn't speak well of me. Karl Winsch said that I got my friends to do "catcall" things down to the bench and everything during the rest of the games. After I was let go, I couldn't sit in the stands and watch. It was just too much.

He told some lies there. If you go to Notre Dame, it's in the minutes of the [South Bend] Board of Directors.

I don't talk about it very often, because I was a kid. I didn't know what I was supposed to do. When he avoided me, I figured, "Well, he doesn't want me."

Was that the only run-in you had with Karl Winsch?

Yes. I just figured he didn't like me and didn't want me around.

Was Karl a difficult manager to play for?

I don't think so. I didn't like him personally, but I could play for him. I didn't rebel at anything he said to do. In fact, if he'd said, "Jump ten feet," I would have jumped ten feet.

Karl did take four or five of us up to a Cubs game, and that was my first major league ball game. That's when I first became a Cubs fan. I wore a thin spring coat, and I about froze. That's when I found out how cold it can get at Wrigley Field. Karl had played minor league ball with Del Ennis, and he introduced us to him. The only thing I can remember is Ennis was taller, and he had the bluest eyes of any man I'd ever met up until that time.

So Chet Grant got you your unconditional release.

I still have the copy of my unconditional release. Chet Grant had set up a chance for me to go to Rockford and play for Rockford. I loaded up my car and I was going to meet the Rockford team in Kalamazoo, and I got almost all the way there, and I chickened out. I drove back home. I don't know if it was being homesick, or not knowing anybody, or what.

The next spring, 1953, Rockford called me and asked if I wanted to play for them. I said, "Yes, but I have to have two weeks off in the first of July. My boyfriend is in the Navy, and I've already made plans with my sister to drive down there and see him." They agreed.

A week before I was supposed to go on the trip, I was sliding into third base and jammed my right knee all the rest of the way. I already had a couple of surgeries on it, but this really did it. That was the end of my career.

You only played for Rockford a few months in 1953.
I played maybe a couple of months for Rockford, in May and June.

Do you remember some of the girls from Rockford?
I remember "Pickles," Delores Lee. She could throw two balls with one hand. She could throw it to home plate, or she could throw to first base to hold a runner.

What was the difference in playing for Rockford and South Bend?
I wish that I had gone to Rockford sooner, except that I couldn't have beaten out Dottie Kamenshek [at first base]. But I felt like I was just starting to learn how to play, to be relaxed at the plate. I felt like I would have hit better if I had been able to stay longer. I might not have, but I was starting to get more confident going to the plate.

I think a lot of it had to be the home people [in South Bend] expecting so much out of me. I was just more loose in Rockford.

So hurting your knee ruined playing baseball for you. Actually, the league only lasted one more year.
I had knee surgery there in Rockford. The doctor said, "What do you want to do with the rest of your life? Do you want to get married, or what?" He said, "Well, I suggest that's what you do. I wouldn't suggest playing ball." By the time I had that surgery, that was number three, and there's wasn't much left in the knee to hold it together. I've got an artificial knee now.

I originally hurt my knee playing pick-up basketball against some male teachers at high school on a Wednesday night. The first year I hurt my knee, in 1950, the doctor got me in touch with a Notre Dame trainer, and he taught me how to tape my knee.

So every night before a game, I put Benzoine, that yellow stuff, on the knee, and it would help the tape to stick. After the game, I'd have to peel it off. But I did it for every single game. It held my knee together.

You really wanted to play ball.
Oh, yeah!

What are some of your favorite memories about the league and the people you met?
I learned how different people are from different parts of the country, and yet how much alike we are. I loved meeting the different players from all over and seeing their values. I thought it was just really neat. The friendships that we formed to this day are very special.

When did you and Don get married?
We got married in 1955, after Don was in the Navy for a year. He had a 30-day leave, and we got married. We had six children, Allen, Donna, Nancy, Lucy, Bruce, and Tom. Bruce and Lucy are twins. We're both from South Bend and we've lived here all our lives.

What would you say about your experiences playing with the Blue Sox and the Peaches?
I'm very proud and very thankful for my experiences in the league. Every time they played the National Anthem, I thought, "Where else in the world could I play professional baseball?" I felt blessed.

Back then, we had our doings with Russia and other countries, and people were suppressed around the world. Here I was playing a game and getting paid for it. That's what I always thought about when they played the National Anthem.

I think my father was relieved once I signed to play, because he knew the league had rules about the players being young ladies. Up until that time, I was such a tomboy that I think he had his doubts. He figured now I might be on the right track.

So your family was in favor of you playing in the league?

They were in favor of me playing. In fact, I think my father was proud of me. He never showed emotions too much, but I think he was pretty happy.

The funny part is that all through the years, my direct family knew I had played professional ball. But it wasn't something you talked about with new friends or others — you just didn't talk about it. When Cooperstown came along [1988] and then they made the movie *A League of Their Own*, all of a sudden we're being asked for autographs. They've asked us to speak at schools and to groups. It's just been one thing and another in the last several years. We never would blow our own horns up until that time, so I really give Penny Marshall all the credit for bringing us back. I dare say if it wasn't for the movie, you wouldn't be doing this interview.

But the funny part about making that movie was that we were at some of the filming, and if you had a digital watch on and you were going to be in a scene, you had to take your digital watch off, and you had to take your reflector glasses off — they didn't have that stuff back then. I had a pastel-colored sweatshirt on, and I had to take that off. Anything that looked anywhere near modern, they couldn't do it.

If you look real close at the grandstand in several scenes, there's two men. One has a hat on and the other has a cap. But all they are is cardboard men to the waist, and they

Segments of *A League of Their Own* were filmed in Evansville, Indiana, in 1991. Pictured from left to right are Betsy Jochum, Janet (Wiley) Sears, and Lou Arnold, all former Blue Sox players, sitting in the stands with cardboard "fans" created to help fill the movie's cast of mid–1940s characters (courtesy Don Sears).

have them sitting in different spots. I have a picture of me with two of them. After we left, I said, "We should have gotten one." There were two different cardboard ones, but they're spaced all through the movie.

They were going to film one scene at second base, and I don't think it made it into the movie. The umpire and the girls were arguing, and in the stands, we had to pretend like we were discussing it. Here we were, flapping our lips, but we had to make it look like we were discussing the play.

They had a slingshot, the biggest one I've ever seen, and these two big guys would hold it, and another guy would pull it back, and they would shoot the ball to the outfield! *[She laughs.]* But in the movie, it looks good. They could get whatever hit they wanted out of that slingshot.

Playing in the league is something that I will never forget. Every reunion that I go to, I meet somebody that I knew by name, but I get to know them better than I ever did at the time.

Epilogue: From the 1954 Season to the Newsletter, the Reunions, A League of Their Own, *and Beyond*

After the league went out of business following the 1954 season, the players mainly returned to their families' homes or stayed in the league city where they played. For most, the choice was to begin a job or a career, get married and raise a family, or pursue advanced education — and many earned degrees, often starting with funds saved from playing baseball. For the most part, their All-American League experiences were left in scrapbooks, and their old equipment was stored in closets or attics. Most of the women played sports like softball, golf, basketball, volleyball, tennis, and others coached, or taught, or both. As former professional athletes, they enjoyed an active life. Still, their memories were usually stored away after answering a question or two, or several, and receiving the usual response, "You mean you played *softball*, not baseball?"

The league, however, indelibly impacted every player's life, because baseball was her game too. "Sports can help girls in many ways, and I became an advocate for girls in sports by the end of the 1940s," recalled Mary Pratt, who pitched for Rockford and Kenosha during the league's underhand and sidearm years. "The difference between girls playing sports today and those who played in the All-American League is that we had to dress, act, and look like ladies in addition to playing ball well. I believe our league elevated the level of competition in sports." Mary Lou (Studnicka) Caden, a right-handed pitcher for Grand Rapids for three seasons in the early 1950s, made a typical observation: "The league taught me how to be reliable, and it taught me how to get along with people. I made a lot of friends with the players, and I met a lot of the fans."

In 1973, Title IX, enacted as a provision of the Civil Rights Act of 1964, forbade discrimination based on sex at federally-financed schools and universities. A widespread result of this federal regulation was increased interest in women's sports in the 1970s. Reminiscing about raising three daughters with her husband Blaine, Jean (Geissinger) Harding, once the hard-hitting second sacker of the Fort Wayne Daisies, said her husband was a former pro catcher, and "our daughters got their athletic ability from their father as well as from their mother. All three daughters all got sports scholarships to go to college, and they all graduated. Their names are Ann, Karla, and Jana. The federal government started Title IX just about the time Ann was graduating from high school, so our daughters were able to use sports to get a college education, and that was great."

Around 1980, June Peppas spearheaded a movement to create a league newsletter, and the newsletter grew into the organization of a well-attended AAGPBL Reunion in Chicago in 1982. The interest in the newsletter and the first reunion mushroomed into several events, notably a second reunion in Fort Wayne in 1986, the formation of a Players Association in 1987, and a permanent display on Women in Baseball at the National Baseball Hall of Fame in 1988. Today the reunions are annual events. "We formed the nonprofit organization in South Bend, Indiana, at Fran Janssen's house," recalled Dottie (Wiltse) Collins, who became the moving force of the newsletter in the 1990s. "I started out as the treasurer, and things kept piling up, and I got involved with the newsletter."

These efforts also spurred the creation of two filmed documentaries about the AAGPBL. One documentary made in 1988 was called *A League of Their Own*, and it was produced by Kelly Candaele, the son of All-American star Helen (Callaghan) St. Aubin. The capstone of a decade of such events came in 1992 when Penny Marshall's acclaimed movie, also entitled *A League of Their Own*, hit the nation's silver screens.

Marshall produced a screen gem that has remained popular for twenty years, and given the quality and historical interest of the film, it will be seen by folks interested in the league for many more years. "The movie featured two sisters, but not any two particular sisters," explained Marge (Callaghan) Maxwell, who grew up playing ball with her sister Helen in Vancouver, British Columbia. "I've had people ask me, 'Who played your position?' I say, 'Nobody played my position. The movie was about the league.' And that's all I say. I think it was a good movie, and the people who acted in the show did a marvelous job."

Several former players participated in the filming of the "reunion game" shown at the film's end when the credits are running. Mary Moore, who started her three-year stint with the circuit on the 1950 developmental tour, recollected, "I know one time I slid into home, and I got dirt on my blue jeans. You couldn't wash your clothes. Two or three days later, I had to do something else. They put me back out on second base, and they said, 'Where's the dirt?' I had to pick up dirt and rub it on the blue jeans so when I got into home again, there'd be enough dirt on the jeans. Some of it was comical, really, but it was quite an experience." Shirley Burkovich, who began her three league years on the 1949 rookie tour, said, "The movie did make the AAGPBL famous, and we thank Penny Marshall every time we see her. If it had not been for Penny Marshall, we would still be obscure, unless you lived in one of those league cities at that time."

Fans of baseball, most of whom have played ball themselves as youths, go to ballparks to watch the game and to relive fun times from earlier years. Those who see *A League of Their Own*, whether they are male or female, younger or older, former star or clumsy amateur, also experience a reawakening of old memories such as when he or she was pulling on a uniform, or making a play in the field, or connecting for a clutch hit and hearing the crowd cheer, and enjoying the camaraderie of teammates. Indeed, the feeling that comes from making a really good play or contributing a big hit, no matter the level of the game, is stored forever in the recesses of the player's mind. And in the end, the game grips the athlete, and regardless of sex, baseball's hold on the mind and memory fades but doesn't die.

The All-American years, therefore, were usually the unique highlight in the lives for many players. As Marge Maxwell reminisced, "Playing in the league was what I call a tremendous time in my life." Wilma Briggs observed, "Those were good times, and good memories." Pat Scott explained, "I'm telling you right now, I owe a great deal to my time with baseball. I thoroughly enjoyed the girls that I played with, every one of them." Sophie Kurys concluded, "I don't where I would be if I hadn't played in the AAGPBL. It had a huge impact on my life, as I went into business in Racine. I loved Racine. It was a great little town, and the fans were terrific." June Peppas, doubtless reflecting the feelings of every woman who ever stepped on a league diamond, said, "We All-Americans are very proud of our accomplishments."

Index

Page numbers in **_bold italics_** indicate illustrations

AAGPBL Archives 49, 203; *see also* Center for History
AAGPBL Players Association 2, 7, 32, 37, 85, 93, 99, 102, 109, 125, 129, 147, 170, 181, 205, 208, 234, 260, 281, 297
AAGPBL Reunions *see* Reunions
Admiral Music Maids 59, 65, 103, 105, 107, 158, 159
Ahrndt, Ellen "Babe" ***98***, 99, 100; *see also* Proefrock, Ellen (Ahrndt)
Alabama College 245, 250; *see also* University of Montevallo
Alexandria, Virginia 184
All-American Girls Soft Ball League 21, 96
Allen, Betty 198; *see also* Mullins, Betty (Petryna)
Allen, Roger 198, 200, 201, 202
Allentown, Pennsylvania 170
Allington, Bill 11, 17, 31, 32, 33, 64, 73, 74, 83, 84, 139, 142, 153, 154, 173, 212, 229, 230, 232, 234, 236–237, 245, 260, 262, 264, 267–268, 270, 274, 275, 287
Allington's touring All-Americans (1955–1957) 196, 211, 212, 260, 263, 264, 269, 272, 273, 277
Alvarez, Isabel "Lefty" 15, ***116–123***, 270
Alverson, Noella (Leduc) *see* "Pinky" Leduc
Amateur Athletic Union 130, 133
Amateur Softball Hall of Fame 131
Amato, Angie ***149***
American Airlines 284, 286
American Girls Baseball League (AGBL) 185, 203, 220, 252, 284
American Institute of Business College 241
Angola, Indiana 139, 184
Applegren, Amy Irene "Lefty" 83, 85, 148, 194, 274
Arcadia, Wisconsin 227, 228, 229, 230, 231
Argentina 155
Arlington, Virginia 139
Army (U.S.) 27, 29, 56, 61, 71, 82, 83, 91, 131, 164, 168, 259, 260, 261, 263, 286
Arnold, Lenna "Sis" 124, 125
Arnold, Lou 50, 128, 167, ***171***, 193, 194, ***294***
Arnold, Norene 148
Atkinson, Barbara (Tetro) *see* Tetro, Barb
Austin, Texas 184

Baker, Mary "Bonnie" 11, 18, 56, ***75***, 95, 103, 105–106, 109, 174, 190, 193, 217, 242, 290, 291
Bancroft, Dave 125, 172, 190, 191, 291
Barney, Edith 186
Barr, Doris 42, ***63***, 95, 148
Barringer, Pat 187
Barrington College 136
Baseball Blue Book 37
Baseball Hall of Fame *see* National Baseball Hall of Fame
Bass, Dick 36, 56, 135, 137, 138, 206, 211
Batikis, Annastasia "Stash" 25–30, ***26***, 108, 111, 113
Batista, Fulgencio 117, 121, 122
Battle Creek, Michigan 216, 236, 256, 278, 281
Battle Creek Belles 59, 65, 76, 78, 117, 121, 130, 181, 184, 185, 189, 191, 204, 236, 256, 264, 278, 281, 284
Bauer, Arnold, and Nadine 47, 100
Baumgartner, Mary "Wimp" 17, 20, 123–129, ***124***, 143, ***149***, ***171***, 177, 189, 191, 192, 193, 194, 195, 196, 285
Beckett, Christine (Jewett) *see* Jewett, Christine
Belmont Hotel 48, 61, 62, 102, 105
Bendix Field (South Bend) 47, 48, 51, ***103***, 106, 288, 290
Bensenville, Illinois 97
Berg, Patty 262
Berger, Joan 268, ***271***; *see also* Knebl, Joan (Berger)
Berger, Margaret "Sunny" 87, 97
Bergmann, Erma 12, 129–134, ***131***, 224
Bernard, Joan 263, 266
Bernard, Tony 266
Berowski, Freddy 3
Beyer Stadium (Rockford) 19, 274; *see also* "Peach Orchard"
Bidwell, Charlie 105
Bigbee, Carson 133, 147, 148
Bigelow Field (Grand Rapids) 242, 255
Birmingham, Alabama 245, 250
Bittner, Jayne 142
Black, Don 65
Black, Heather ***63***
Blair, Maybelle ***149***
Blee, Robert, and Agnes and Nancy 117, 119, 120, 121, 123
Bleiler, Audrey 284, 289, 291
Bloomer Girls 105
Blue Island Park (Chicago) 254

Blue Island Stars 176, 177, 229, 230
Blue Sox *see* South Bend Blue Sox
Blue Sox Ushers Club 50
Blumetta, Kay 37, ***55***
Borchert Field (Milwaukee) 9
Boston, Massachusetts 92, 94, 96, 97, 240
Boston Garden 92, 93, 94, 96
Boston Globe 96
Boston University 92, 93, 95, 96
Boyle, Ralph "Buzz" 12, 130, 132, 133, 222
Braze, Adam 253, 255–256
Bretting, Betty (Fabac) *see* Fabac, Betty
Bridgeport, Connecticut 91, 93
Brief, Anthony "Bunny" 83, 84
Briggs, Rita 212, 262
Briggs, Wilma 22, 134–145, ***135***, ***149***, 185, ***207***, 209, 210, 211, 212, 261, 286, 298
Brodhead, Wisconsin 99, 100
Brokaw, Tom 50
Brooklyn, New York 163, 165
Brooklyn Dodgers 13, 105, 132, 163
Brown, Patricia L. 3*n*
Brown, Walter 92, 93, 96
Browne, Lois 21
Brumfield, Delores "Dolly" ***151***, 244, 245, ***264***; *see also* White, Delores (Brumfield)
Burkovich, Shirley 17, 145–150, ***146***, ***149***, 281, 298
Burlington, Kentucky 232, 234
Burnham City Hospital 269
Burns, Ken 7, 180
Bush, Guy "Mudcat" 65, 133, 185, 191, 256

Caden, Mary Lou (Studnicka/Braze) 252–259, 297; *see also* Studnicka, Mary Lou
Caden, Paul 253, 258
California 5, 10, 31, 32, 33, 36, 40, 41, 43, 97, 105, 111, 141, 149, 153, 154, 163, 165, 226, 240
Callaghan, Helen 36, 42, ***55***, 75, 76, 77, 79, 80, 81, 95, 135, 138, 143, 298; *see also* St. Aubin, Helen (Callaghan)
Callaghan, Marge 42, ***55***, 74, 95, 135, 138, 140, 143; *see also* Maxwell, Marge (Callaghan)
Callow, Eleanor ***207***, 274, 275
Cameron, Dorothy (Shinen) *see* Shinen, Dorothy

299

Campbell, Helen 147, 148; *see also* Hannah, Helen (Campbell)
Canada 5, 9, 97, 102, 108, 158, 162, 168, 200, 231, 246, 251, 270, 280
Canadian Baseball Hall of Fame 162
Canadian National Railway 197
Candaele, Bobby 36
Candaele, Casey 79
Candaele, Kelly 79, 298; *see also A League of Their Own* (documentary, 1986)
Cape Girardeau, Missouri 124, 125, 139, 190
Carcieri, Nick 136, 137
Carey, Mary 143, 144, 179, 193, 206
Carey, Max 11, 12, 13, 15, 16, 17, 19, 37, 56, 64, 117, 120, 132, 135, 136, 137, 138, 139, 140, 141, 143, 146, 147, 185, 186, 190, 211, 212, 234, 235, 236, 244, 246, 259, 260, 261, 262, 264, 267
Carey Cup Playoffs of 1949 16
Carnation, Washington 87, 91
Castillo, Ysora 118
Castro, Fidel 118
Catholic Youth Organization (CYO) 263, 266, 283, 284
Cato, Nancy (Mudge) *see* Mudge, Nancy
Center for History (formerly the Northern Indiana Center for History) 4, 49, 52, 101, 181, 203, 227, 288; *see also* AAGPBL Archives
Champaign, Illinois 269
chaperone(s) 6, 10, 15, 18, 28, 30, 50, 55, 66, 84, 88, 89, 94, 107, 132, 146, 147, 148, 161, 184, 186, 187, 195, 217, 226, 231, 242, 246, 247, 249, 255, 256, 260, 261, 267, 270, 287
Chapman, Dorothy (Maguire) *see* Maguire, Mickey
Charleston, West Virginia 184
Chattanooga, Tennessee 221, 227
Chester, Bea 105
Chester, Hilda 105
Chicago, Illinois 8, 9, 17, 29, 35, 44, 59, 61, 62, 85, 86, 87, 90, 92, 94, 96, 102, 104, 111, 124, 125, 138, 158, 164, 175, 177, 179, 181, 183, 186, 206, 218, 228, 229, 230, 233–234, 235, 240, 242, 246, 252, 253, 254, 258, 269, 273, 278, 280, 286, 291
Chicago Blue Birds 86, 90, 103, 105, 130, 134
Chicago Chicks 85, 103, 105
Chicago Colleens 14, 15, 16, 17, 118, 124, 125, 135, 146, 148, 176, 177, 181, 182, 184, 186, 187, 188, 199, 278, 280, 291
Chicago Cubs 8, 34, 47, 102, 111, 242, 292
Chicago League 65, 83, 89, 103, 104, 105, 106, 158, 159; *see also* National Girls Baseball League

Chicago Match Queens 130, 134
Chicago Police Department 253, 258
Chicks *see* Grand Rapids Chicks; Milwaukee Chicks (1944)
China 172
Chinese Communists 17
Choctaw, Arkansas 16, 188, 189, 190, 196
Cincinnati, Ohio 9, 44, 46, 72, 265, 266
Cincinnati Reds 270
Cione, Jean 248, 249
Civil Rights Act of 1964 297
Clark, Dan 49
Clarke, Gerry 180
Click Magazine 100, 101
Clinton, Arkansas 190, 194
Coast Guard 163, 165
Cobb, Ty 140
Coben, Muriel 94, 95, 97, 102, 104, 105
Coca-Cola (Coke) 112, 142, 192, 217, 270
Colacito, Lou 89
Colleens *see* Chicago Colleens
Collier's 15
Collins, Dottie (Wiltse) 2, 10, 16, 17, 28, 31–38, 51, 57, 76, 77, 78, 79, 80, 83, 85, 135, 138, 143, 205, 208, 226, 297–298; *see also* Wiltse, Dottie
Collins, Harvey 32, 33, 35, 36, 77, 95
"color" barrier 13
Comets *see* Kenosha Comets
Cook, Donna 194
Cooke, Penny (O'Brian) *see* O'Brian, Penny
Cooper, Joe 20
Cooperstown, New York 5, 34, 129, 149, 161, 282
Cordes, Gloria **207**
Costin, Jim 48, 81
Costin, Mina 48
Crawley, Pauline 191
Crews, Mary 10, 28, 80; *see also* Wisham, Mary (Nesbitt)
Cruthers, Charles "Press" 155
Cryan, Daniel 152, 156
Cryan, Marge (Villa) 150–156; *see also* Villa, Marge
Cuba 5, 51, 72, 112, 117, 118, 122, 183, 223, 249, 252, 254, 274

Daetweiler, Louella 95
Dailey, Dr. Harold 1, 12, 15, 47, 51, 167, 185, 292
Dailey, Mary 191
Daisies *see* Fort Wayne Daisies
Dancer, Faye 32, 33, **55**, **75**, 95, 112, 193
D'Angelo, Josephine "Jo" 106
Danhauser, Marnie **26**, 28, **63**, 206
Daniels, Audrey (Haine) 38–44, 77, 113, 159; *see also* Haine, Audrey
Daniels, Austin 40, 42, 44

Dannon Yogurt 266
Danville, Illinois 269
Dapkus, Eleanor "Ellie" **26**, 28, **63**
Darling, Frank 65
Davenport, Iowa 177, 240, 241
Davis, Geena 150, 209
Davis, Gladys "Terrie" 9, 95
Davis, Lavonne "Pepper" (Paire) *see* Paire, Lavonne "Pepper"
Dayle, Vince 178
Dayton, Ohio 270
Dearfield, Norma (Whitney) **149**
DeBeer Company 20, 172
DeCambra, Alice 217
Decker, Betty (Wanless) *see* Wanless, Betty
Deegan, Millie 37, 93, 96, 200
DeKalb, Illinois 200, 203
Dell Publishing 65; *see also Major League Baseball*
Delmonico, Lee (Surkowski) **149**; *see also* Surkowski, Lee
DeNoble, Jerre 112
DePaul University 265, 269
Derringer, Norman "Nummie" 98, 99, 102, 217
Des Moines Register 241
Deschaine, Alice (Pollitt) 274, 275, 276
DesCombes, Jeneane "Jeanie" 257
Detroit, Michigan 9, 10, 58, 76, 104, 173, 278, 279
Detroit Tigers 216, 277, 279
Deyotte, Anne (Surkowski) *see* Surkowski, Anne
Diane, Mary 273
Didrikson, Babe 262
DiMaggio, Joe 7, 280
Donahoe, Claire (Schillace) **149**; *see also* Schillace, Claire
Donahue, Terry 8, 156–163, **157**
Doubleday Field (Cooperstown) 282–283
Dowler, Jean (Lovell) *see* Lovell, Jean
Doyle, Dorothy (Harrell) "Snookie" 141, 150, 274; *see also* Harrell, Dorothy "Snookie"
Dries, Dolores (Lee) "Pickles" 274; *see also* Lee, Dolores "Pickles"
Dubuque, Iowa 177
Dunn, Gertie 19, 22, 124, 126, **171**, 172, 191, 193, 194, 287
"Dutiful Dozen" 126
The Dutiful Dozen (1997), by W.C. Madden 74

Earp, Millie 13, 243
East Greenville, Pennsylvania 169, 170, 173
East Greenville Cubs 169
East Greenwich, Rhode Island 22, 134, 136
Eastman, Charles 173
Edmonton, Alberta 80, 104
Eisen, Thelma "Tiby" 33, 95, 135, 138, 140, 141, 142, 186, 212, 261

Eisenberger, Joan 271; *see also* Berger, Joan
Eisenhower, Dwight 21
Elkhart, Indiana 128
Elkins, Lee 178
Elliott, Gloria (Cordes) *see* Cordes, Gloria
Emry, Betty *26*, 26, 28, 29, *63*
English, Madeline "Maddy" 28, 29, 62, *63*, 66, 95
English, Woody 23, *207*, 255, 256, 261
Ennis, Del 292
Erickson, Lou 228, *228*; *see also* Sauer, Lou (Erickson)
Erlanger, Kentucky 233, 235
Evansville, Indiana 50, 52

Fabac, Betty 95, 248
Faralla, Lillian "Lil" 127, 163–168, *164*, 195
Farrow, Elizabeth *55*, 87
Faut, Jean 1, 2, 12, 14, 17, 18, 19, 20, 51, 56, 73, 109, 114, 124, 126, 128, 141, 142, 143, 144, 145, 164, 167, 168–175, *165*, *171*, 191, 192, 193, 194, 195, 196, 220, 225, 242, 247, 285, 286, 287, 291
Fay, Bill 15
Ferguson, Dottie (Key) *149*, 159; *see also* Key, Dottie
Ferguson, Sarah Jane (Sands) *149*; *see also* Sands, Sarah "Salty"
Fernandez, Mirta (Marrero) *see* Marrero, Mirta
Fidler, Merrie 1–2, 4, 7, 13
Fidler, Walter "Wally" 142, 195, 196, 270
Field of Dreams (film, 1989) 233, 234
Fielder Field (Los Angeles) 165
Filarski, Helen 78, 126; *see also* Steffes, Helen (Filarski)
Fischer, Alva Jo "Tex" 148, 224, *225*, 226
Fisher, Lorraine 243
Flint, Michigan 2, 58, 59, 61, 65
Florreich, Lois 71, 106, 231, 232
Folder, Rose 85, *86*; *see also* Powell, Rose (Folder)
Ford, Whitey 280
Fort Sheridan, Illinois 29
Fort Wayne, Indiana 2, 11, 15, 35, 36, 56, 57, 64, 73, 76, 95, 116, 118, 123, 125, 135, 137, 143, 144, 145, 146, 147, 164, 166, 179, 180, 182, 197, 198, 203, 205, 208, 211, 230, 232, 245, 250, 260, 261, 262, 264, 266, 267, 270, 273, 281, 285, 287
Fort Wayne Daisies 9, 11, 17, 18, 19, 21, 22, 23, 40, 41, 54, 55, 57, 59, 75, 77, 78, 80, 106, 109, 112, 117, 118, 121, 122, 123, 125, 135, 137, 138, 142, 143, 150, 166, 178, 181, 182, 185, 190, 201, 202, 204, 206, 208, 210, 213, 220, 229, 234, 235, 236, 245, 247, 248, 253, 259, 260, 261, 262, 266, 270, 286, 297

Fort Wayne Yearbook (1947) 13
Foss, Betty (Weaver) 1, 22, 139, 140, 142, 208, 211, 212, 249, *265*, 287
Fox, Helen "Nicky" 62, 63, 95, 154, 249, 274; *see also* Nicol, Helen
Foxx, Jimmy 56, 139, 143, 172, 185, 212, 236, 245, 248, 249, 261, 263, 264, 265, 270
Francis, Betty 143, 144, 148, 175–180, *181*, 206, 286
Franciscan Sisters of the Sacred Heart 265, 269
Freeport, Illinois 19, 127
French Lick, Indiana 209
Frenchtown, Rhode Island 136
Fricker, Marian (Wohlwender) *see* Marian Wohlwender
Froning, Martha 287
Froning, Mary "Fearless" 128, *171*, 284, 286; *see also* O'Meara, Mary (Froning)

Gacioch, Rose 19, *49*, 64, 140, 171, *207*, 274
Gallego, Luisa 14, 118
Ganote, Gertrude 95
Garfield, New Jersey 271, 272
Gary, Indiana 201
Gascon, Eileen "Ginger" *149*
Gaston, Jimmy 70
Geissinger, Jean 22, 210, *259*, 264, 267; *see also* Harding, Jean (Geissinger)
Germany 131
Girls Baseball League (South Bend) 288, 290
Girls' Pro League (AAGPBL) 11
Gorman, Robert M. 1, 3, 4, 48; *see also The South Bend Blue Sox* (2012)
Gottselig, Johnny 61, 62, 63, 155, 166, 249, 255
Graham, Mary Lou *171*
Gran Stadium (Havana) *75*, *131*; *see also* Havana Stadium
Grand Rapids, Michigan 11, 111, 179, 197, 198, 200, 201, 202, 240, 241, 242–243, 255, 256, 258, 260, 272, 273, 276
Grand Rapids Chicks 11, 12, 16, 21, 22, 23, 40, 42, 65, 80, 106, 109, 111, 112, 121, 130, 132, 153, 181, 182, 185, 187, 189, 194, 198, 199, 200, 210, 219, 220, 222, 240, 243, 252, 254, 255, 261, 272, 276, 277, 297
Grant, Chet 50, 51, 155, 156, 169, 174, 242, 247, 248, 249, 289, 290, 292
Great Depression 21, 46, 59, 61, 66, 82, 92, 9, 108, 110, 122, 204, 205, 244, 279
Great Lakes Naval Station 29, 240, 242
Great War 66, 91, 93; *see also* World War I
The Greatest Generation (1998), by Tom Brokaw 50

Green, Dorothy "Dottie" 94, 96
Greenberg, Hank 277, 279
Greenbrier, Arkansas 189
Greenville, South Carolina 66, 67, 68, 69
Greenville Spinners 70
Gregorich, Barbara 15, 170
Greiner, Harold 56, 124, 125, 139, 201, 204, 205–206, 212
Griffin, Viola (Thompson) *see* Thompson, Viola
Griffith Stadium 184, 280
Groton, Connecticut 91, 93
Gutz, Julie 148, 248

Habben, Carol 272, 273, 275
Hageman, Jo 49, 95, 99, 100, 106, 249
Haine, Audrey 38, *39*, 40, *55*, 77; *see also* Daniels, Audrey (Haine)
Hall, Don 120
Hamilton, Mary Lou (Graham) *see* Graham, Mary Lou
Hanks, Tom 209
Hannah, Helen (Campbell) 226; *see also* Campbell, Helen
Harding, Blaine 260, 262, 297
Harding, Jean (Geissinger) 22, 38, *149*, 210, 213, 259–263, 297; *see also* Geissinger, Jean
Harmon, Annabelle (Lee) *see* Lee, Annabelle
Harnett, Ann 95
Harney, Elise "Lee" 56, 94, 97
Harrell, Dorothy "Snookie" 95, 165; *see also* Doyle, Dorothy (Harrell)
Haskins, Jimmy 32
Havana (Habana), Cuba 13, 18, 116, 117, 118, 154, 163, 164, 165–166, 223, 245, 246, 250
Havana Stadium 72; *see also* Gran Stadium
Heafner, Ruby 138, 211
Heber Springs, Arkansas 190
Heim, Kay 95
Helena Rubenstein Company 10, 86, 88, 94
Helsinki, Finland 84
Henderson State University 245
Heverly, Ruth (Williams) *see* Williams, Ruth
Hickson, Irene "Tuffy" *26*, 28, 29, *63*, 133
Hill, Betty (Luna) *see* Luna, Betty
Hill, Joyce 25, 26, 193; *see also* Westerman, Joyce (Hill)
Hillman, David 4, 5–7
Hillsdale, Michigan 209, 211
Hoffman, Barbara 114
Hoffman Hotel 50
Hohlmayer, Alice "Lefty" 248
Holgerson, Margie "Mobile" 246; *see also* Silvestri, Margaret (Holgerson)
Hollywood, California 270
Holmes, Agnes (Zurkowski) *see* Zurkowski, Agnes

Index

Horlick Field (Racine) 25, 27, 29, 59, 99
Hornsby, Rogers 252, 254
Horstman, Katie 22, 141, *149*, *210*, 213, 260, 261, 263–271, *264*, 283
Hotel Racine 48
Howe, Murray 186
Howe News Bureau 13
Hunter, Dorothy "Dottie" 38, 40, 95, 256, 257
Hunter's Point 241
Huntingdon, Pennsylvania 259, 260
Hutchison, Anna May 12, *26*, 28, *63*, 113, 115, 224

I Love Lucy 21
Illinois State University 47; *see also* Normal University
Indiana Central College 129; *see also* University of Indianapolis
Indiana University 47, 52
Indianapolis, Indiana 205
Indianapolis Speedway 178
Inglewood, California 31, 33, 35
International Business College 182
International Woodcarvers Conference 238
Irvington, New Jersey 273

Jackson, Lillian *55*
Jackson, Michigan 53, 54, 57
Jackson, Mississippi 125
Jacksonville, Florida 201
Jacobs, Jane *26*
James Madison University 187
Jameson, Shirley 28, *86*, 89, 95
Janssen, Frances "Fran" 2, 9, 37, 177, 180–187, 189, 195, 205, 297
Jasper, Texas 268
Jefferson City, Missouri 184, 186
Jenkins, Marilyn 22, 252, 256, 257, 261
Jewett, Christine 198, 199
Jinright, Mickey (Perez) 19, 274; *see also* Perez, Mickey
Jochum, Betsy 2, 9, 10, 12, 44–52, *49*, 73, 81, 95, 99, 100, 106, 242, 290, *294*
Jockey Underwear 248
Johnson, Arleene 77, 132, 140; *see also* Noga, Arlene (Johnson)
Johnson, Susan E. 17
Joliet, Illinois 269
Jones, Margaret (Russo) *see* Russo, Maggie
Jones, Marilyn 248
Jonnard, Bubber 41, *55*
Joplin, Missouri 184
Junor, Daisy 247, 290, 291
Jurasinski, Amy (Dunkleberger/Shuman) *see* Shuman, Amy

Kabick, Jo 10, 112, 280
Kalamazoo, Michigan 16, 179, 190, 197, 204, 214, 215, 217, 219, 221, 289, 290, 292

Kalamazoo Lassies 1, 16, 20, 21, 23, 117, 118, 121, 140, 167, 176, 178, 181, 185, 193, 204, 207, 208, 214, 217, 255, 286
Kaline, Al 2
Kamenshek, Dorothy "Dottie" 46, 47, 65, 83, 84, 86, 94, 95, 142, 150, 172, 207, 274, 293
Kansas City, Missouri 205
Keagle, Merle "Pat" 17, 95
Keating, Edie (Perlick) *see* Perlick, Edie
Kell, George 277, 279
Kellogg, Vivian "Viv" or "Kelly" 32, 43, 52–58, *54*, *55*, 79, 135, 138, 143, 212, 213
Kemmerer, Beatrice "Bea" *149*
Kenosha, Wisconsin 29, 62, 90, 93, 97, 99, 100, 108, 110, 111, 113, 152, 156, 160, 245
Kenosha Comets 9, 10, 19, 40, 43, 51, 62, 67, 71, 74, 76, 86, 88, 92, 95, 96, 106, 108, 111, 151–152, 153, 154, 198, 199, 245, 248, 249, 297
Kenosha Municipal Court 18
Key, Dottie 21, 95, 274; *see also* Ferguson, Dottie (Key)
Kidd, Sue 16, 17, 22, 119, 124, 125, 126, 127, 128, 143, 144, 145, *149*, *171*, 177–178, 181, 187–197, *188*, 285
Kinney, Ysora (Castillo) *see* Castillo, Ysora
Kissel, Audrey 41, *55*
Kline, Maxine 37, 141, 143, 145, *210*, 229, 232, 261; *see also* Randall, Maxine (Kline)
Kloza, Jack 82, 83, 84
Knebl, Andrew 272, 276
Knebl, Joan (Berger) 271–277; *see also* Berger, Joan
Knoxville, Tennessee 218, 219, 221
Koehn, Phyllis "Sugar" 14, 51, 71, 73, *86*, 162, 174, 247
Konwinski, Dolly (Niemiec) 256
Korean War 16–17, 21
Krick, Jaynie *149*, 218, 257
Kronk Gym (Detroit) 278, 280
Kruckel, Marie 174
Kunkel, Jack 209
Kunkel, Karen (Violetta) 209
Kurys, Sophie 9, 12, *26*, 28, 29, 58–66, *60*, *63*, 95, 106, 132, 133, 206, 231, 298

La Crosse State University 83, 84; *see also* University of Wisconsin at La Crosse
Lafser, Audrey (Kissel) *see* Kissel, Audrey
Lake, Eddie 277, 279
Lake Michigan 29, 43, 106, 152, 153, 155, 256
Lakefront Stadium (Kenosha) 43, 86, 88, 90, 152, 153, 248
Latin (South) American tour 152, 154–155
A League of My Own: Memoir of a Pitcher for the All-American Girls Professional Baseball League (2003), by Patricia L. Brown 3*n*
A League of Their Own (documentary, 1986) 79, 298; *see also* Candaele, Kelly
A League of Their Own (film, 1992) 3, 6, 12, 27, 29, 45, 50, 52, 54, 57, 61, 76, 83, 85, 90, 99, 100, 112, 134, 147, 158, 161, 172, 177, 178, 179, 187, 214, 218, 229, 230, 234, 241, 260, 279, 283, 289, 291, 294–295, 298
Leduc, Noella "Pinky" 22, 113
Lee, Annabelle "Lefty" *55*, 95
Lee, Dolores "Pickles" 293; *see also* Dries, Dolores (Lee)
Lenard, Jo 19, 148, *171*, 194, 223, *225*, 226
Leo, Fred 18
Leon, Rafael 117, 119
Lesko, Jeneane (DesCombes) *see* DesCombes, Jeanie
Lessing, Ruth "Tex" 32, *55*, 57, 240, 243
Liberty, Saskatchewan 199, 202
Liebrich, Barbara "Bobbie" 187, *207*
Life Magazine 11, 28, 185
Lincoln Park, Michigan 277, 278, 279
Lincoln Park Sports Hall of Fame 282
Little, Olive 94, 95, 97
Little Rock, Arkansas 125, 178, 188, 189, 190
Lloydminster, Alberta 9, 102, 104, 108
The Lone Ranger 21
Lonetto, Sarah 148
Long Beach, California 163, 165
Long Lake 216
Los Angeles, California 151, 163, 164, 165, 168
Los Angeles Examiner Championship 31, 33, 34
Los Angeles Times 16
Louise Pettus Archives and Special Collections at Winthrop University 4
Louisville Slugger bats 16
Lovell, Jean *207*, 217
Lucas, Iowa 240, 243
Luckey, Lillian 174
Luna, Betty 95, 124

MacLean, Lucella 49, *49*, 99, 100, 100, *103*; *see also* Ross, Lucella (MacLean)
Macon, Georgia 291
Macy, Sue 13, 182
Madden, Kristen 4
Madden, W.C. 74
Madison Square Garden 92, 93, 96
Madonna 161
Maguire, Dorothy "Mickey" 111, 132, 148
Mahon, Elizabeth "Lib" 1, 2, 17, 47, 51, 66–74, *67*, 95, 114, 126, 167, 174, 191, 242, 285, 290, 291

Mahoney, Marie "Red" 247
Major League Baseball 14, 65, 137; *see also* Dell Publishing Management Corporation of AAGPBL 11, 14, 16, 18
Mansfield, Marie 19, 141, 274, 275
Maquoketa, Iowa 175, 177, 180
Marion, Indiana 205
Markey, Morris 17
Marks, Gloria 95
Marlowe, Jack 180
Marquette Park 176, 177, 252, 253, 254
Marrero, Mirta 14, 15, 118, 120
Marsh Field (Muskegon) 20
Marshall, Penny 5, 50, 52, 79, 91, 149, 150, 209, 282, 283, 289, 298
Martin, Heinie 244
Maxwell, Marge (Callaghan) 74–81, 298; *see also* Callaghan, Marge
Maxwell, Mervin "Merv" 76, 80
Mays, Willie 64
McAdams, Mrs. Thomas 48
McAuley, Mildred (Warwick) *see* Warwick, Millie
McCall's 17
McCammon, Earl 19, 20, *171*
McComb, Joanne *149*
McCulloch, Colleen (Smith) 80
McCutchan, Alexandra "Lex" 89
McDaniel, Kay (Heim) *see* Heim, Kay
McFadden, Betty 105
McGann, Al 49
McManus, Marty 47, 50, 51, 67, 71, 73, 74, 86, 89, 90, 92, 94, 95, 97, 166, 289
Melaval, Saskatchewan 156, 158
Memorial Field (Fort Wayne) 36, 56, 125, 137, 141, 213, 249, 260, 262
Memphis, Tennessee 184, 187
Merrionette Park, Illinois 180
Meyer, Anna 71, 89
Meyerhoff, Arthur 11, 18, 170, 185
Miami, Florida 14, 72, 183, 186, 199, 246
Miami-Erie Canal 266
Michigan Bell 55, 278, 281
Michigan City, Indiana 216
Michigan State University 2
Middletown, New York 273
Midland Park, New Jersey 273
The Milton Berle Show 21
Milwaukee, Wisconsin 10, 25, 62, 82, 83, 84, 99, 100
Milwaukee Brewers 83, 179
Milwaukee Chicks 9, 10, 11, 100, 106, 140
Milwaukee Journal 100
Minneapolis Millerettes 9, 11, 14, 32, 33–34, 39–40, 41, 43, 47, 54, 55, 71, 75, 77, 106, 123, 181, 184
minor leagues 11, 14, 17, 20, 21, 34, 39, 94, 176, 177, 180, 184, 189, 234, 252, 254, 255, 291, 292

Minster, Ohio 263, 265, 266, 283, 284, 287
Mishawaka, Indiana 126
Missouri Sports Hall of Fame 131
Mobile, Alabama 244, 246, 251
Mokena, Illinois 269
Monmouth, Iowa 177
Montabello, California 151, 152, 154
Mooney, Jette (Vincent) 19, *171*, 193, 285; *see also* Vincent, Jette
Moore, Eleanor "Ellie" *207*, 261
Moore, Helen *49*, 50
Moore, Lucille 50, 242, 247
Moore, Mary 17, *149*, 277–283, *278*, 298
Moore, Roger 103, 104, 105
Moose Jaw, Saskatchewan 99, 104, 106, 157, 158, 198
Moroz, Evelyn (Wawryshyn) *see* Wawryshyn Evie
Morris, Carolyn 10, 64, 65, 78, 95, 97
Mudge, Nancy 206, *207*
Mueller, Dorothy "Dottie" 36, 112, 114, 115, 127, 158, 160, 217, 285, 291
Mullins, Betty (Petryna/Allen) 197–203; *see also* Petryna, Betty
Mullins, Don 198, 201, 203
Murphy, Leo 28, *63*, 64, 133, 193, 204, 206, 221, 229, 230, 231
Muskegon, Michigan 131, 132, 190, 221, 223, 226
Muskegon Belles 20–21
Muskegon Lassies 12, 13, 125, 130, 133, 146, 148, 150, 159, 176, 177, 189, 190, 198, 201, 219, 227
Myrtle Beach, South Carolina 70

Natick, Massachusetts 94
National Baseball Hall of Fame 2, 3, 5, 7, 30, 43, 52, 56, 64, 79, 93, 95–96, 105, 129, 131, 149, 161, 162, 187, 203, 227, 260, 294, 297
National Girls Baseball League 59, 65, 85, 86, 103, 130; *see also* Chicago League
The National Pastime (SABR, 2002) 208
National Youth Administration (NYA) 61
Naum, Dorothy "Dottie" 248
Navy (U.S.) 28, 29, 32, 77, 87, 90, 91, 174, 200, 201, 240, 241, 242, 293
Neal, Doris 277, 279
Nelson, Faye 279
Nesbitt, Mary *26*, 97; *see also* Wisham, Mary (Nesbitt)
New Orleans, Louisiana 190, 268
New York, New York 187, 271, 272, 280
New York Daily News 273
New York University 84
New York Yankees 200, 201, 270
Newark, New Jersey 187 271
Newhouser, Hal 277, 279

Newton, North Carolina 139, 191, 264, 267, 270
Nicol, Helen 10, 43, 59, 63, 94, 97; *see also* Fox, Nicky (Nicol)
Nicoli, Al 130, 132
Nicollet Park (Minneapolis) 9, 32, 34, 41, 45, 54
Niehoff, Bert 50, 99, 101, 107
Noga, Arleene (Johnson) 95; *see also* Johnson, Arleene
Normal University 87, 90; *see also* Illinois State University
North Adams, Michigan 209, 211
North Shore Elevated or El 29, 35, 62
Northside High School Field (Fort Wayne) 56
Novikoff, Lou 34–35

Oak Lawn, Illinois 252, 253
O'Brian, Penny 42, 77, 80
O'Donnell, Rosie 209
O'Dowd, Anna Mae *149*, 177
Official Girls' Baseball Rules of 1947 13
O'Hara, Janice "Jerry" 89, 90, 95
Oklahoma City, Oklahoma 184
Olinger, Marilyn "Corky" 243
Oliver Hotel 50
Omaha, Nebraska 268, 277
O'Meara, Mary (Froning) 22, 283–287, *283*; *see also* Froning, Mary
O'Meara, Tom 284, 286
Opa-Locka, Florida 14, 15, 132, 139, 164, 173, 181, 183, 185, 186, 198, 199, 204, 206, 214, 216
The Origins and History of the All-American Girls Professional Baseball League (2006), by Merrie Fidler 1, 4
"Orphans" 10, 77; *see also* Minneapolis Millerettes
Ozburn, Dolly (Vanderlip) *see* Vanderlip, Dolly

Paire, Lavonne "Pepper" 10, 28, 33, 35, 40, *55*, *63*, 95, 142, 198, 199, 243
Palos Park, Illinois 253
Parker, Dorothy (Naum) *see* Naum, Dottie
Pasadena, California 149
Pascagoula, Mississippi 12, 111, 130, 132, 151, 157, 158, 169, 170, 174, 219, 240, 244, 246
Pascale, Matt 268
Pat Scott Field (Walton, Kentucky) 234, 238–239
"Peach Orchard" 274; *see also* Beyer Stadium
Peaches *see* Rockford Peaches
Pearl Harbor, Hawaii 28, 32, 163
Pearson, "Dolly" 194
Pennsburg, Pennsylvania 169
Pensacola, Florida 186, 246
Peoria, Illinois 85, 87, 133, 160, 164, 217, 231, 273
Peoria Redwings 8, 12, 13, 16, 19,

36, 40, 42, 45, 47, 62, 78, 89, 109, 112, 113, 114, 115, 124, 125, 133, 157, 158, 159, 165–166, 181, 184, 189, 190, 193, 214, 216, 217
Peoria Stadium 160, 216
Peppas, June 23, 32, 37, 129, 179, 187, 203–209, *204*, *207*, 297, 298
Pepsi-Cola 218, 220
Perez, Migdalia "Mickey" 14, 118, 120; *see also* Jinright, Mickey (Perez)
Perlick, Edythe "Edie" 28, 29, *63*, 64, 113, 133
Perón, Juan 154
Peru, Illinois 33, 41, 88, 96; *see* Peru-LaSalle, Illinois
Peru-LaSalle, Illinois 39, 71, 75, 76, 86, 94, 98, 99; *see* Peru, Illinois
Peters, Marge 94
Peterson, Ruth *26*, 28
Petras, Ernestine "Teeny" *151*
Petrovic, Anna (Meyer) *see* Meyer, Anna
Petryna, Betty *197*, 198; *see also* Mullins, Betty (Petryna)
Philadelphia, Pennsylvania 267, 291
Philadelphia Phillies 172
Phoenix, Arizona 65
Pieper, Marge 236
Pirok, Pauline "Pinky" 51, 71, 95, 174, 248, 291
Piskula, Grace 81–85, *82*
pitching style: overhand 3, 13–14, 16, 18, 35, 37, 40, 42, 43, 45, 51, 64, 65, 78, 81, 89, 107, 112, 115, 130, 132, 135, 144, 158–159, 164, 166, 186, 194, 200, 204, 206, 211, 214, 223, 225, 243, 252, 254, 256, 285; sidearm 12–13, 14, 40, 42–43, 45, 51, 59, 64, 78, 81, 92, 95, 107, 112, 115, 127, 130, *131*, 132, 133, 152, 159, 164, 165, 166, 169, 174, 194, 195, 204, 206, 219, 222–223, 243, 254, 297; underhand 3, 10–12, 13, 14, 21, 35, 40, 42, 51, 59, 64–65, 78, 81, 84, 93, 115, 130, 159, 174, 214, 222, 242, 281, 290, 297
Pittsburgh, Pennsylvania 146, 147, 150
Playland Park (South Bend) 22, 50, 51, 81, 126, 144, 163, 168, 172, 173, 178, 188, 189, 191, 242, 247, 250, 286, 288, 289, 290, 291, 297
Pleasant Lake 50
Pokagon State Park 139, 184
Powell, Edward 87, 91
Powell, Rose (Folder) 10, 85–91, 93, 95; *see also* Folder, Rose
Pratt, Mary 86, 88, 89, 91–97, *92*, 297
Preserving Our Legacy: A Peach of a Game (2004), by Mary Pratt 93
Prichard, Alabama 244, 246
Proefrock, Ellen (Ahrndt) 97–102; *see also* Ahrndt, Ellen

Proefrock, William "Casey" 99, 100, 101
Providence, Rhode Island 135
Providence Journal-Bulletin 137
Pryer, Charlene "Shorty" 19, 68, 72, 114, 124, 126, 127, 148, 190, 191, 196, 223, 285, 292
Pung, Jackie 262

Quincy, Illinois 184
Quincy, Massachusetts 91

Racine, Wisconsin 25, 35, 62, 79, 84, 90, 97, 98, 99, 100, 102, 111, 112, 242
Racine Belles 9, 11, 12, 25, 59, 63, 66, 98, 106, 109, 112, 113, 115, 130, 133, 150, 204, 206, 219, 224, 229, 231, 281
Radatz, Ruth 108, 111
Randall, Bob 211, 213
Randall, Maxine (Kline) 209–214; *see also* Kline, Maxine
Rapp, Elizabeth (Farrow) *see* Farrow, Elizabeth
Rathbun, Iowa 239, 240
Rawlings, John 42, 78, 153, 243, 272, 273
RBI leagues 147, 150
Redden, Pete 50
Redman, Magdalen "Mamie" 252, 256, 257
Reds *see* Cincinnati Reds
Redwings *see* Peoria Redwings
Reed, Bob 22
Regina, Saskatchewan 104, 197, 198, 199, 200, 201, 202
Remington, Indiana 180, 182
Reunions: Chicago (1982) 32, 37, 52, 93, 97, 109, 115, 147, 158, 162, 205, 208, 297; Detroit (2010) 91, 278–279, 281; Fort Wayne (1986) 211, 213, 297; Grand Rapids (2001) 209; Houston (2006) 238; Milwaukee (2000) 99, 101, 115, 177, 179; Myrtle Beach (1997) 2, 37, 209, 226; San Diego (2011) 162, 231–232; South Bend (1993) 85; Syracuse, New York (2012) 283
Reynolds, Dick 137
Reynolds, Mary 193
Richard, Ruth 23, *207*, 274, 275
Richards, Lucille "Lou" (Stone) 26, 28; *see also* Stone, Lou
Ricketts, Joyce *207*
Rios, Georgiana 14
Risinger, Earlene "Beans" 220, 226, 243, 252, 256, 257, 261
Rizzuto, Phil 280
Roanoke, Virginia 2, 72, 186
Robinson, Jackie 7, 13
Rock Hill, South Carolina 67, 69, 173
Rockford, Illinois 85, 92, 173, 197, 217, 232, 273, 275, 276, 286, 289, 290, 293
Rockford Peaches 1, 9, 10, 11, 12, 16, 17, 18, 19, 21, 23, 32, 40, 42,
43, 54, 59, 64, 66, 73, 74, 78, 82, 84, 92, 94, 95, 96, 102, 104, 109, 124, 127, 128, 141, 147, 148, 153, 154, 164, 165, 171, 184, 185, 189, 192, 200, 229, 230, 231, 236, 246, 272, 273, 275, 276, 284, 286, 287, 289, 292–293, 297
Rogers, Bill 160
Rohrer, Kay 95
Romatowksi, Jenny 290
"rookie rule" 22, 262, 273, 281
Roosevelt, Franklin D. 2, 6, 61
"Rosie the Riveter" 13
Ross, Lucella (MacLean) 9, 10, 102–108; *see also* MacLean, Lucella
Ross, Mervyn 104, 108
Roth, Eilaine 206, 208, 214–218, *215*, 216
Roth, Elaine 204, 206, 208, 214, *215*, 216
Rountree, Mary 138, 160, 246, 257, 261, 262
Ruetz, Judge Edward J. 18
Ruiz, Gloria 14, 118
Rumsey, Janet 22, 124, 126, 127, 128, 145, *171*, 191, 193, 195, *207*, 285
Russell, Betty *63*
Russia *see* Union of Soviet Socialist Republics
Russo, Maggie 113, 193
Rusynyk, Betty (McFadden) *see* McFadden, Betty
Ruth, Babe 187
Ryan, Ada *55*

Sadorus, Illinois 265, 269
St. Aubin, Helen (Callaghan/Candaele) 298; *see also* Callaghan, Helen
St. Elizabeth Hospital 269
St. Louis, Missouri 130, 132, 133, 134
St. Louis Police Academy 130
St. Louis Sports Hall of Fame 131
Sallies *see* Springfield Sallies
Sams, Doris 20, 56, 132, 148, 170, 176, 178, 179, 185, 207, 218–227, *219*, *225*, 257
San Francisco, California 240, 241
San Pedro, California 163, 165
Sands, Sarah "Salty" *207*; *see also* Ferguson, Sarah (Sands)
Santa Barbara State College 165
Santa Monica, California 244
Sargent, Jim 1, 2, 7; *see also The South Bend Blue Sox* (2012)
Saskatchewan Baseball Hall of Fame 161
Saskatoon, Saskatchewan 102, 104, 105, 107
Satterfield, Doris "Sadie" 243, 252, 256
Sauer, Burton 229, 230
Sauer, Lou (Erickson) 227–232; *see also* Erickson, Lou
Savannah (Illinois) Ordnance 29

Savona, Freda 134
Schaeffer, Donna 123
Schelper, Oscar, and Mildred 17, 120
Schick, Yolande (Teillet) *see* Teillet, Yolande
Schillace, Claire 25, 28, 62, **63**; *see also* Donahoe, Claire (Schillace)
Scholarship Championship 59, 62, 86, 90
Schrall, Leo 217
Schriner, Dr. William 58
Schroeder, Dottie 11, 21, 49, **49**, 71, 95, 99, 100, **103**, 106, 135, 138, 139, 140, 141, 142, 143, 170, 173, 198, 201, 202, 206, **207**, 209, 210, 212, 213, 217, 240, 249, 250, 260, 261, 265, 269, 270
Scott, Pat 19, 232–238, **233**, 298
Screen Actors Guild 282
Sears, Don 289, 290, 293
Sears, Janet "Pee Wee" (Wiley) 288–295, **288**, **294**; *see also* Wiley, Janet "Pee Wee"
Sears, Roebuck 247
Seattle, Washington 91
Sells, Ken 93, 94, 95, 96
Seville-Biltmore Hotel 72
Seymour, Iowa 239, 240, 241, 243
Shaughnessy Playoffs 11, 12, 17, 18, 19, 23, 54, 59, 68, 124, 164, 170, 189, 204, 208, 211, 219, 220, 226, 229, 257, 260, 272, 275, 284, 286
Sheehan, Jack 44, 46
Shewbridge Field (Chicago) 228, 230
Shinen, Dorothy 95
Shinen, Kay 95
Shinners, Ralph 155
Shively, Twila "Twi" 159, 160
Shollenberger, Fern **151**, 206, **207**, 248
Shuman, Amy 172
Silvestri, Margaret "Mobile" (Holgerson) 257; *see also* Holgerson, Margie "Mobile"
Simmons Field (Kenosha) 248, 250
Skokie, Illinois 161, 282
Skupien, Mitch 252, 254, 255
Sloppy Joe's 112
Smith, Charlotte 62
Smith, Helen "Gig" 1
Smith, Jean **207**
Smith, Joyce 209
Smithsonian Institution 45, 52
Society for American Baseball Research (SABR) 2
Soldiers Walk (Arcadia, Wisconsin) 231
South Bend, Indiana 47, 52, 67, 73, 97, 99, 106, 107, 143, 145, 164, 172, 173, 178, 181, 182, 184, 193, 194, 201, 202, 241, 242, 250, 278, 284, 286, 288, 291, 293

South Bend Blue Sox 1, 3, 9, 12, 13, 15, 16, 18, 19, 20, 21, 22, 45, 59, 67, 68, 71, 74, 78, 81, 99, 100, 102, 103, 104, 105, 107, 109, 111, 113, 114, 115, 124, 125, 126, 128, 135, 136, 137, 139, 141, 142, 143, 144, 150, 164, 166, 169, 170, 171, 176, 178, 179, 180, 183, 186, 187, 189, 190, 191, 196, 198, 200, 236, 240, 242, 245, 247, 254, 272, 280, 284, 285, 287, 289, 290, 292
The South Bend Blue Sox: A History of the All-American Girls Professional Baseball League Team and Its Players (2012) 1, 3, 48, 52; *see also* Sargent, Jim, and Gorman, Robert M.
South Bend Community School Corporation 47
South Bend Tribune 48
South Bend Usherettes/Rockettes 129, 181, 189, 194, 195
South Carolina College for Women 70; *see also* Winthrop College
South High Field (Grand Rapids) 240, 242, 243, 255
South Orange, New Jersey 187
South Shore Elevated or El 48, 62
Spanish-American War 116
Sparta, Wisconsin 87, 90, 91
Spartanburg, South Carolina 70
"Sports, Breaking Records, Breaking Barriers" 45, 52; *see* Smithsonian Institution
Springfield, Illinois 85, 86, 87, 89, 130, 133, 148, 187, 234, 235
Springfield, Michigan 216
Springfield Sallies 14, 16, 17, 132, 135, 146, 177, 181, 184, 188, 189, 278, 280, 291
Stamford, Connecticut 271, 272
Stefani, Margaret "Marge" 95, 99, 100, 106, 174, 242, 247, 250, 290
Steffes, Helen (Filarski) **149**, 278, 280; *see also* Filarski, Helen
Stephens, Ruby **63**
Stevens, Lorraine (Fisher) **149**; *see* Fisher, Lorraine
Stls, Cliailes **26**, 28
Stoll, Jane "Jeep" 114, 126, 164, 167, **207**
Stolze, Dorothy "Dottie" 148
Stone, Lou **26**, 28, 29; *see also* Richards, Lou (Stone)
Stovroff, Shirley 114, 124, 126, 196, 285
Studebaker 49
Studnicka, Mary Lou "ML" **253**; *see also* Caden, Mary Lou (Studnicka)
Stumpf, Eddie 94
Suehsdorf, Adie 16
Surkowski, Anne 99, 106
Surkowski, Lee 49, 95, **98**, 99, 100, 106; *see also* Delmonico, Lee (Surkowski)
Swissvale, Pennsylvania 146, 147
Sycamore, Illinois 203

Tampa, Florida 247
Teillet, Yolande 77
television 16, 21, 64, 185, 187, 225
Tesseine, Marguerite (Pearson) *see* Pearson, Dolly
Tetro, Barb 200, 202
Tetzlaff, Doris 148, 260, 261
Thillen Stadium (Chicago) 255
Thompson, Viola "Tommy" 69, 70, 166, 173, 174
Title IX (1973) 175, 260, 263, 297
Toledo, Ohio 20, 266
Touching Bases 32, 181, 205
Trezza, Betty "Moe" 12, 28, **55**, 59, 63, **63**, 64, 174
Tronnier, Ellen 83, 85
Tucker, Betty 159

Union of Soviet Socialist Republics (USSR) 294
United Nations 16
University of Central Arkansas 189
University of Cincinnati 46
University of Hawaii 84
University of Indianapolis 129; *see also* Indiana Central College
University of Kentucky 234, 235, 237–238
University of Montevallo 250; *see also* Alabama College
University of Notre Dame 2, 49, 50, 51, 52, 107, 185, 292, 293
University of Southern Mississippi 245, 250
University of Wisconsin at La Crosse 26, 30; *see also* La Crosse State University

Van Orman, Harold 19, 21, 137, 237
Van Orman Hotel 137, 250
Vanalsburg, Diane **53**
Vancouver, British Columbia 74, 75, 80, 81, 298
Vanderlip, Dolly 22, 286, 287
Vialat, Zonia 14, 118
Villa, Marge 151, **151**, 248; *see also* Cryan, Marge (Villa)
Vincent, Jette 127, 191; *see also* Mooney, Jette (Vincent)
Virginia Western Community College 2, 4
Volkov, Kay (Shinen) *see* Shinen, Kay
Vonderau, Kate 261
Voyce, Inez "The Hook" 173, 174, 239–244, **239**, 252, 256

Waddell, Helen "Sis" 148
Wagner, Audrey 28, **86**, 89, 97, 225, 248
Wagoner, Betty 19, 22, 126, **171**, 181, 191, 192, 193, 194, 208, 285–286, 287
Walmsley, Thelma **63**
Walton, Kentucky 238
Wamby [Wambsganss], Bill 41, 56, 182, 222
Wanless, Betty "Duke" 143, 144

Ward, Norris "Gadget" 186, 187
Warner, Eleanor (Moore) *see* Moore, Eleanor
Warren, Nancy **131**, **207**, 222, 224
Warwick, "Millie" 95
Washington, DC 280
Waveland Park (Chicago) 27, 111
Wawryshyn, Evelyn "Evie" 138, 260, 261, 270
Weaver, Jean 139, 140, 208, 212, 261, 287
Weaver, Joanne "Jo" 22, 139, 140, 208, 212, 245, 249, 250, 261, 262, **264**, 287
Wegman, Marie "Blackie" 148
Weierman, Shirley **149**
Wellesley College 96
Wenzell, Marge **171**, 194, 280
West Allis, Wisconsin 50, 82, 83
West Baden, Indiana 146, 147
West Chester, Pennsylvania 260
Westerman, Joyce (Hill) 19, 108–115, **109**, **149**, 159, 160, **171**, 216, 231; *see also* Hill, Joyce
Westerman, Ray 109, **109**, 113, 114
Western Canadian Championship 157, 158
Western Michigan University 205, 208
Western Printing 65
When Women Played Hardball (1994), by Susan E. Johnson 3n, 17
Whillock, Jackie 194–195
White, Delores "Dolly" (Brumfield) 15, 244–251, **245**; *see also* Brumfield, Dolly
White, Joe 245
Whitehall, Wisconsin 229
Whiting, Betty 126
Whitmire, South Carolina 70

A Whole New Ball Game (1993), by Sue Macy 182
Wigiser, Margaret **55**
Wiley, Janet "Pee Wee" 50, 193, 284, 288, 289; *see also* Sears, Janet (Wiley)
Williams, Earl "Doc" 188, 189
Williams, Ruth 81
Williams, Ted 7, 76, 81, 113
Wilson, Mildred "Willie" 28, **63**, 231
Wilson, Woody 209, 211
Wiltse, Dan 31
Wiltse, Dottie 32, 34, 40, **55**, 95; *see also* Collins, Dottie (Wiltse)
"Wimpy," in *Popeye, the Sailor Man* 129
Winnipeg, Manitoba 38, 40, 41, 42, 43, 44
Winsch, Karl 19, 68, 72, 73, 74, 114, 124, 126, 127, 128, 143, 164, 166, 167, 170, **171**, 172, 176, 178, 189, 190, 191, 192, 193, 194, 196, 197, 284, 285, 286, 287, 289, 292
Winter, Joanne **26**, **63**, 64, 66, 95, 97
Winthrop College 67, 69, 70; *see also* South Carolina College for Women
Wirth, Shoo-Shoo 14, 126, 167, 174, 242, 247, 248, 291
Wisham, Mary (Nesbitt/Crews) 28, 95, 112; *see also* Nesbitt, Mary
Wisniewski, Connie 10, 13, 28, 51, 56, 65, 95, 106, 222, 243, 256, 290
Witzel, Norene (Arnold) *see* Arnold, Norene
Wohlwender, Marian 46, 47
Women at Play: The Story of Women in Baseball (1993), by Barbara Gregorich 15

Women in Baseball, exhibit at National Baseball Hall of Fame 297
Women's History Month 58
Women's Sports 182
World Championship [Softball] Tournament 76
World War I 94, 131; *see also* Great War
World War II 5, 8, 11, 29, 32, 44, 48, 49, 67, 75, 82, 83, 85, 90, 99, 102, 130, 133, 151, 152, 163, 165, 169, 170, 173, 180, 182, 240, 252, 279, 288
Wright, Mary "Mickey" 262
Wrigley, Philip K. 6, 8, 9, 11, 31, 44, 52, 57, 88, 92, 93, 94, 95, 96, 97, 254
Wrigley Building 231, 242
Wrigley Field 44, 48, 59, 61, 102, 292
Wyatt, Helen (Waddell) *see* Waddell, Helen "Sis"

Yankee Stadium 148, 195, 278, 280
Yankees *see* New York Yankees
Youngberg, Renae 208, 209
Youngen, Lois 192, 196, 236, 286, 287

Ziegler, Alma "Gabby" or "Ziggy" 21, 33, 56, 95, 185, 243, 244, 252, 255, 256, 257, 262, 276, 290
Zintak, Lenny 124, 125, 181, 184, 190, 195, 228–229, 230, 252, 254, 255
Zirkle, Fred 83
Zollner Pistons 37
Zoss, Barney 56
Zurkowski, Agnes **26**

www.ingramcontent.com/pod-product-compliance
Lightning Source LLC
Chambersburg PA
CBHW081540300426
44116CB00015B/2699